INFERENCE FR

Inference from Signs

Ancient Debates about the Nature of Evidence

JAMES ALLEN

CLARENDON PRESS · OXFORD

2001

OXFORD

UNIVERSITY PRESS

Great Clarendon Street, Oxford OX2 6DP

Oxford University Press is a department of the University of Oxford.
It furthers the University's objective of excellence in research, scholarship,
and education by publishing worldwide in

Oxford New York

Auckland Cape Town Dar es Salaam Hong Kong Karachi
Kuala Lumpur Madrid Melbourne Mexico City Nairobi
New Delhi Shanghai Taipei Toronto

With offices in

Argentina Austria Brazil Chile Czech Republic France Greece
Guatemala Hungary Italy Japan Poland Portugal Singapore
South Korea Switzerland Thailand Turkey Ukraine Vietnam

Oxford is a registered trade mark of Oxford University Press
in the UK and in certain other countries

Published in the United States
by Oxford University Press Inc., New York

First published 2001
First published in Paperback 2008

British Library Cataloguing in Publication Data

Data available

Library of Congress Cataloging in Publication Data

Data available

ISBN 978-0-19-825094-4 (Hbk.)
ISBN 978-0-19-955049-4 (Pbk.)

1 3 5 7 9 10 8 6 4 2

Typeset by John Waś, Oxford
Printed in Great Britain
on acid-free paper by
Biddles Ltd., Guildford and King's Lynn

FOR MY PARENTS

Acknowledgements

THIS book grew in fits and starts over a long period, and I have incurred debts to many people in many places while writing it. John Cooper and Robin Smith gave me valuable help as commentators on a paper that was an ancestor of part of Study I. Versions of that paper were also presented to the B Club at Cambridge and the Philosophisches Seminar of the Universität Hamburg, where audiences gave me much useful advice. Susanne Bobzien kindly sent me valuable comments on an earlier version of Study III. An anonymous referee for OUP made helpful suggestions. Colleagues and students at Pittsburgh have been exposed at one time or another to something from just about every part of the book, but especially Studies I and IV. I thank them for comments and encouragement. I am grateful to Peter Momtchiloff and Charlotte Jenkins at OUP and to John Waś for their help. I finished the draft submitted to the press at the beginning of my time in Hamburg as a Stipendiat of the Alexander von Humboldt-Stiftung, and I am grateful to the Stiftung for providing me with this opportunity and to the Philosophisches Seminar, especially Dorothea Frede, for making my time there so pleasant and rewarding. I have many times enjoyed the hospitality of Clare Hall and the Classics Faculty at Cambridge. I have profited from talking about some of the issues tackled in this book with Myles Burnyeat and Geoffrey Lloyd, and I owe a special debt to Michael Frede, under whose supervision I first began working on the part of this enquiry concerned with Sextus Empiricus, and Gisela Striker, to whom I am obliged not only for much illuminating conversation but also encouragement to persevere with the project. I hope my debt to other scholars living and dead will be clear in what follows. Readers who suspect that Robert Philippson and Friedrich Solmsen became heroes to me as I was working on different parts of this book will not be mistaken.

Some of the material has already appeared in print elsewhere. Study II is based on 'Pyrrhonism and Medical Empiricism: Sextus Empiricus on Evidence and Inference', in W. Haase (ed.), *Aufstieg und Niedergang der römischen Welt*, ii. 37. 1 (Berlin: De Gruyter, 1993). Study IV is based on 'Epicurean Inferences: The Evidence of Philodemus' De signis', in J. Gentzler (ed.), *Method in Ancient Philosophy* (Oxford: Oxford University Press, 1998). I should like to thank Walter De Gruyter and Oxford University Press for their kind permission to reprint this material.

J.A.

Contents

Abbreviations   xi

Introduction   1
1. The Scope of the Enquiry   1
2. Prospectus   7

Study I: Aristotle on Sign-inference and Related
            Forms of Argument   13

1. Rhetoric   15
2. Stages in Aristotle's Thinking about Argument   20
3. The *Analytics*-oriented Account of Rhetorical Argument   23
4. The Developmental Perspective   40
5. Sign vs. Demonstration in Aristotle   72
   Appendix A: The Text of *Rhetoric*, 2. 25, 1403ᵃ6–10   78
   Appendix B: Were There Other Developments in
   Aristotle's Rhetorical Theory?   79

Study II: Rationalism, Empiricism, and Scepticism:
            Sextus Empiricus' Treatment of Sign-
            inference   87

1. The Medical Background: Empiricism vs. Rationalism   89
2. Empiricism and Pyrrhonism   97
3. Two Kinds of Sign and Two Kinds of Argument against
   Signs   106
4. The Empirical Contribution   122
5. The Sceptical Credentials of Commemorative Signification   139

Study III: The Stoics on Sign-inference and Demon-
             stration   147

1. The Genus *Sign*   149
2. Stoic Signs and Stoic Logic   150

3. The Intended Application of the Stoic Theory   158
4. Stoic Divination   161
5. Sign-inference and Demonstration   170
6. The Purpose of the Stoic Theory   184
   Appendix: The Evidence for a Dialectical Origin of the
   Stoic Theory of Signs   188

Study IV: Epicurean Sign-inference in Philodemus   194

1. Epicurus   195
2. Philodemus and his Sources   205
3. Similarity vs. Elimination   208
4. Similarity as the Ultimate Basis of Signification   226
5. Epicurean Sign-inference   234

Conclusion   242

Bibliography   255

Index Locorum   265

General Index   276

Abbreviations

CAG	Commentaria in Aristotelem Graeca
CMG	Corpus Medicorum Graecorum
DG	*Doxographi Graeci*, ed. H. Diels
DK	*Die Fragmente der Vorsokratiker*, ed. H. Diels and W. Kranz
D.L.	Diogenes Laertius
K	*Galeni Opera Quae Exstant*, ed. K. G. Kühn (cited by volume, page, and line)
LSJ	H. G. Liddell and R. Scott, *A Greek–English Lexicon*, 9th edn., rev. Sir H. S. Jones, with the assistance of R. McKenzie (Oxford: Clarendon Press, 1940)
RE	*Real-encyclopädie der classischen Altertumswissenschaft*, ed. A. Fr. von Pauly, rev. G. Wissowa *et al.* (Stuttgart, 1894–1980)
S.E. *M.*	Sextus Empiricus, *Adversus mathematicos*
S.E. *PH*	Sextus Empiricus, Πυρρώνειοι ὑποτυπώσεις (*Outlines of Pyrrhonism*)
SM	Galen, *Scripta Minora*, ed. G. Helmreich, J. Marquardt, and I. v. Mueller (cited by volume, page, and line)
SVF	*Stoicorum Veterum Fragmenta*, ed. H. von Arnim

Introduction

1. The Scope of the Enquiry

EVIDENCE has been used to draw inferences for as long as there have been human beings. The aim of the present enquiry is to explore some of the more important attempts that were made to understand the nature of evidence after it became an object for theoretical reflection in the ancient Greek and Roman world. Although the word is an ancient one, the nature of evidence was not discussed under the head of 'evidence' in antiquity. Cicero introduced *evidentia* as a rendering of ἐνάργεια, the quality of being evident (*Luc.* 17). In this sense it entered European languages, including English, where, however, one tends to speak of 'self-evidence' because English uniquely recognizes the sense of 'evidence' at issue in this enquiry, viz. an item that is the basis of an inference or the ground for a conclusion. The relation between the two senses seems to be this: to serve as evidence for a conclusion, apart from supporting it, an item must be evident, or at least more evident than the conclusion. Only in this way can it permit us to infer a conclusion that we do not know from grounds that we do, thus adding to our stock of knowledge.

The term which was used most frequently in antiquity, and by which we shall for the most part be guided in this enquiry, was 'sign' (σημεῖον, *signum*), though in order to do justice to the extent of ancient interest in evidence and its uses we shall also have to attend to other expressions such as 'token' (τεκημήριον). The idea of inference from signs was well entrenched in the ancient Greek world, as we can see from remarks in early oratorical literature[1] and tragedy[2] to the effect that signs or tokens must be used to discover or make clear what is unknown. The extent to which tragedians themselves relied upon signs to produce the recognitions on which tragic plots rely is suggested by Aristotle's remark that the most

---

[1] See Hyperides fr. 195 Blass; Antiphon, fr. 72 Blass; Andocides 3. 2.

[2] See Sophocles, *OT* 916; Euripides, frr. 574, 811 Nauck. We owe these fragments and Hyperides fr. 195 to Clement of Alexandria's interest (*Stromata*, 6. 2).

common and least artful method of bringing about recognition is by signs; he gives as an example Odysseus' recognition by his nurse from a scar (*Po.* 16, 1454[b]20 ff.).[3] Historians concerned to put their conclusions on sound evidential foundations also employed the vocabulary of signs.[4] Herodotus notoriously argued that the length and path of the Nile correspond to those of the Danube, 'inferring by means of visible evidence the unknown' (2. 33).[5] Thucydides, having begun by reporting his inference (τεκμαιρόμενος) from the preparations he witnessed before it began that the war whose history he is about to relate would be the greatest in human history, proceeds, in the Archaeology, to support his contention by appeal to signs from which the smaller scale of earlier conflicts can be inferred (1. 20–1). He also famously remarked on the danger of mistaking for an exact sign (ἀκριβὲς σημεῖον) one that is not: consider, he suggests, the mistaken conclusions about the relative power of Athens and Sparta to which future observers would be led by the ruins they have left behind (1. 10).

And the basic idea of sign-inference can also be conveyed without any special reference to 'signs' or 'tokens'. Aristotle remarks that it is necessary to use visible things as witnesses for the invisible (*EN* 2. 2, 1104[a]13–14; cf. *EE* 1. 6, 1216[b]26–8). The authors of the Hippocratic corpus speak often of the need to learn or investigate what is hidden from or on the basis of what is manifest (*Vict.* 1. 11–12; cf. *VM* 22). But perhaps the most suggestive statement of the principle is Anaxagoras' dictum: 'the phenomena are the vision of the non-evident' (S.E. *M.* 7. 140 = B 21a DK).[6]

The use of signs as evidence for theories in natural philosophy, which Anaxagoras has in view here, was to prove especially important in stimulating reflection. For it is in this field that inference

---

[3] ἀναγνώρισις διὰ τῶν σημείων.

[4] Cf. H. Diller, '"Ὄψις ἀδήλων τὰ φαινόμενα', *Hermes*, 67 (1932), 14–42 at 21–2.

[5] συμβάλλομαι τοῖσι ἐμφανέσι τὰ μὴ γινωσκόμενα τεκμαιρόμενος. This is not what we should call history, but cf. 1. 57; 2. 43, 58, 104; 3. 38; 7. 238; 9. 100.

[6] ὄψις τῶν ἀδήλων τὰ φαινόμενα. According to Sextus, this dictum also met with the approval of Democritus. The practice of viewing the grasp of the non-evident won by inference as a kind of sight is also attested in the Hippocratic treatise *De arte*, ch. 11, where the vision of the eyes is contrasted to that of the mind (ὄψις τῆς γνώμης), and it lives on in the expression τὰ λόγῳ θεωρητά. On the meaning of the phrase itself in historical context see Diller, '"Ὄψις ἀδήλων'; G. E. R. Lloyd, *Polarity and Analogy: Two Types of Argumentation in Early Greek Thought* (Cambridge: Cambridge University Press, 1966), 338–41; and J. Barnes, *The Presocratic Philosophers*, 2nd edn. (London: Routledge, 1982), 538, 644 n. 5.

from signs promised the most by extending knowledge beyond what is directly given in experience to embrace both regions beyond the reach of observation and the hidden underlying nature of reality. Diogenes of Apollonia calls the facts to which he appeals in support of his contention that air is the first principle of all existing things 'mighty signs' (μεγάλα σημεῖα) (B 4 DK). In another early philosophical expression of the principle, Alcmaeon speaks of inference from tokens (B 1 DK). The Socrates of Aristophanes' satirical portrait in the *Clouds* infers a natural explanation for thunder from signs in the manner of Presocratic philosophy, instead of adhering to traditional explanations in terms of the agency of Zeus (*Nub.* 369). And it is to this practice that Gorgias alludes in his defence of Helen when he cites the ability of natural philosophers to convince us first of one opinion about non-evident matters and then another in support of his contentions about the persuasive power of logos (*Hel.* 13).

But the ancient term 'sign' was not confined to items that furnish evidence from which a conclusion is inferred any more than ours is. Signals of all sorts and words were also called signs. Augustine's celebrated discussion shows how wide was the range of things the ancients were willing to call signs. Writing in late antiquity, after the period with which we shall be concerned, he succeeded in producing an account that casts its net wide enough to capture pretty much everything that can be regarded as a sign (*De doctrina Christiana* 2. 1. 1):[7] 'A sign is a thing which brings it about by itself that something different apart from the impression it makes on the senses comes to mind.'[8] An item is a sign, then, through standing in a relation of a certain kind to a distinct item. This is the point of Augustine's contrast between signs and things. The distinction is between two aspects of the same item rather than between two exclusive kinds, for though not every thing need be a sign, every sign is, in addition to being a sign, also a thing. To regard a sign as a thing is to attend to features it possesses in abstraction from the use to which it is put as a sign, whereas to regard it as a sign is to view

---

[7] The emphasis Augustine lays on the perception of the sign excludes some relevant talk of signification, but it is not an essential part of his account. Cf. R. A. Markus, 'St. Augustine on Signs', in id. (ed.), *Augustine: A Collection of Critical Essays* (Garden City, NY: Doubleday, 1972), 61–91; and B. D. Jackson, 'The Theory of Signs in St. Augustine's *De Doctrina Christiana*', in Markus, *Augustine*, 92–147.

[8] Signum est enim res praeter speciem, quam ingerit sensibus, aliud aliquid ex se faciens in cogitationem venire.

it in the context of a relation that obtains between it and what it signifies (cf. Augustine, *De dialectica* 5). As Augustine's definition makes plain, whatever else we may wish to say about this relation, when grasped by the intellect, it supports a mental transition from sign to signified item.

These signifying relations are of many different kinds, however, some of which have nothing to do with inference. But the distinction Augustine immediately goes on to draw between natural and given signs brings us a step closer to the use of signs as evidence. Given signs crucially involve the intention to convey a meaning, an intention which must be grasped by the recipient of the sign if it is to succeed in discharging its communicative function.[9] Augustine introduces this distinction in order to prepare the way for his interpretation of Scripture as a system of divinely given signs, and therefore touches only very briefly on natural signs (2. 2. 3).[10] These he describes as those which signify in the absence of the intention essential to given signs (2. 1. 2). He presents a number of paradigmatic instances to illustrate natural signification—smoke as a sign of fire, a track as the sign of an animal's passage, and a facial expression as the sign of an affection of the soul—but says nothing about the relation or relations in virtue of which they signify the conclusions for which they furnish evidence.

But questions about the use of signs as evidence that were not at the centre of Augustine's concerns had been the object of much attention before his time. Before saying something about the different positions on offer in antiquity and their defenders, however, it will be useful to touch on some complicating factors that we have so far neglected. The distinction between natural and given signs has a great deal of intuitive plausibility to recommend it. But it is possible to imagine, and as we shall see, to find, conceptions of the signifying relation whose effect is to undermine this contrast in one way or another or to require that it be understood in a different way. Thus one position we shall consider, that of the Stoics, treats a large part of natural signs, or the signs we should be inclined to call natural, as

---

[9] If one were to pursue Augustine's distinction, the end result would be something like H. P. Grice's distinction between natural and non-natural meaning in 'Meaning', *Phil. Rev.* 67 (1957), 377–88, repr. in id., *Studies in the Ways of Words* (Cambridge, Mass.: Harvard University Press, 1989), 213–23; and Grice, 'Meaning Revisited', in N. V. Smith (ed.), *Mutual Knowledge* (London: Academic Press, 1982), 223–50, repr. in Grice, *Studies*, 283–303.

[10] Signa divinitus data, quae scripturis sanctis continentur.

a result of the providential order of nature, intended by God to serve humankind as signs. The effect of this view is to assimilate natural to given signs, though there is room for disagreement about whether such signs depend for their effect on the sign-giver's intention being grasped in the same way. Assimilation in the opposite direction is also possible, e.g. by treating a speaker's remarks as grounds or evidence that things are as the speaker says they are, evidence whose value depends on facts about the reliability of speakers in general or this speaker in particular, and the like.

The position of the medical Empiricists, which will occupy a large part of our attention, questions the framework we have so far relied upon at a still deeper level, however. Up to this point I have appealed freely to notions like evidence, inference, grounds for a conclusion, and the like to clarify the use of signs in which I am interested. But if to make an inference is to perform a mental act that crucially involves the grasp of the relation of justification holding between a conclusion and the grounds or evidence supporting it, a relation that can be formulated as an argument, which in turn invites evaluation as valid or invalid, then some participants in the debate will have denied that they were concerned with inferences at all. Nor will it help to distinguish between deductive and inductive forms of inference. Adherents of the Empirical view in question were thoroughgoing anti-rationalists who denied that the use of signs is a form of reasoning in which signs are taken as evidence furnishing a reason for a conclusion. In place of this narrowly inferential, or broadly rational, picture they seem to have put a roughly mnemonic conception of signification as a matter of being put in mind of the signified item by the sign. On their view, the ability to use signs is not a matter of reasoning, at least reasoning understood in a certain way, but depends rather upon dispositions to be reminded of associated items. And on this view too the difference between natural and given signs tends to recede. Something like Augustine's distinction can still be drawn, but the half corresponding to natural signs will have to be explained in different terms (cf. S.E. *M.* 8. 193, 200–1). To accommodate this view it will sometimes be necessary in what follows to construe talk of 'sign-inference' generously enough to cover ways of understanding the use of signs which would not, on a narrower or more familiar construction, count as inferring at all. To infer a conclusion from signs in this way is no longer a matter of grasping or appreciating

a relation between sign and signified that obtains independently
of the person drawing the inference. Rather, this kind of sign-
inference depends on a relation of association formed somehow in
the memory of the person drawing the inference.

Since the questions with which we shall be occupied were chiefly
discussed under the head of 'signs' and 'sign-inference', we should
also be alert to a widespread though not universal semantic tendency in the ancient use of these terms. Inferences and the grounds
on which they are based can be distinguished into kinds according
to several different principles. One can, for example, oppose inferences that serve the purpose of theory construction, e.g. in natural
philosophy, to those serving more quotidian ends, e.g. in the law
courts. It is also possible to distinguish inferences with conclusions
that cannot be confirmed by observation from those whose conclusions are about matters that are not in principle unobservable,
but which must be established by inference owing to contingent
circumstances that prevent direct observation. These two divisions
will tend to coincide. But inferences can also be divided into kinds
according to the nature of the warrant they furnish: for example,
is the principle on which the inference rests an empirically established correlation between sign and signified or a necessary relation
of consequence imposed by the nature of the matter at issue and
grasped by a special faculty of reason distinct from experience? We
shall find some ancient figures who suppose that this distinction
too coincides with the previous two. Lastly, it is possible to distinguish evidence which provides conclusive support for a conclusion
from evidence which merely serves to make a conclusion likely or
probable.

The tendency in question is to use the term 'sign' to designate
the inferior member of these contrasting pairs. Since what it is
to be inferior will vary depending on which contrast is in view,
what is imported by talk of 'signs' will differ accordingly. It can be
seen at its clearest if we also consider another term, in the use of
which the opposite tendency is to be observed, viz. 'demonstration'
($\mathrm{\mathring{a}}\pi\acute{o}\delta\epsilon\iota\xi\iota\varsigma$). To be sure, it would be a mistake to read too much of the
meaning acquired by the term 'demonstration' in Aristotelian and
Stoic logic into its use by other philosophers, or even to suppose
that its every occurrence in a Stoic or Aristotelian context need
refer to an inference satisfying the stringent standards imposed on

demonstration in their logical theories.[11] But 'demonstration' was
the term to which those concerned to mark out a distinction between
superior and inferior forms of inference often turned. Aristotle was
the first to exploit this potential systematically, but it is sometimes
apparent in the earlier uses of the term. Plato, for example, contrasts
merely plausible reasoning (εἰκός, πιθανολογία) unflatteringly with
demonstration in a number of passages (*Phd.* 92 C–D; *Tht.* 162 E;
Ti. 40 E).[12]

But as I noted above, the tendency is not universal. If we call
views of the kind we have been considering 'low' conceptions of
signification, taking care to acknowledge that what counts as low
for them need not be the same, it becomes clear that other schools
and figures held a 'high' conception of sign-inference, which did
not restrict the term 'sign' to inferior applications. We find this tendency in the Presocratic appeals to signs on which we have touched,
but this outlook reveals itself most clearly in a willingness to put
signs and demonstrations on a level with each other. So for instance,
in his methodological remarks near the beginning of the letter to
Herodotus, Epicurus speaks of signs and demonstrations without
implying that there is any difference between them (37–8). This
tendency was continued by Philodemus, the poet and Epicurean of
the first century BC, who is our principal source for Epicurean views
on these matters (*De signis*, IX. 4; XXXI. 6). It also determined the
form of the most extensive discussion of the subject to have come
down to us, that of Sextus Empiricus, the Pyrrhonian sceptic and
Empirical physician of the second century AD. He assigns the same
part in theory construction to demonstration and to sign-inference,
without recognizing a division of labour between them (*PH* 2. 96;
M. 7. 25, 394; *M.* 8. 140, 319).

2. Prospectus

The present enquiry has four parts, called 'studies' rather than
'chapters' to emphasize the extent to which the views and controversies under consideration, beyond differing from each other,

[11] The range in Aristotle's conception of demonstration is documented and described by G. E. R. Lloyd, 'The Theories and Practices of Demonstration in Aristotle', *Proceedings of the Boston Area Colloquium in Ancient Philosophy*, 6 (1990),
371–401, repr. in id., *Aristotelian Explorations* (Cambridge: Cambridge University
Press, 1996), 7–37.   [12] Cf. Lloyd, *Polarity and Analogy*, 423 with n. 3.

cannot be made to fit the pattern of a single continuous development in which positions are taken and defended with reference to a
framework common to all parties. Enough hints have already been
scattered to suggest how varied conceptions of sign-inference could
be, even at a quite fundamental level. Differences of outlook, but
also elements of continuity, will emerge as we proceed.

Study I is devoted to Aristotle, who, though obviously not the
first to use sign-inferences or speak of signs, was the first to cast a
theoretical eye on the subject. From the point of view of what was
to come later, his most important contribution may have been the
distinction between signs and demonstrations, which he may have
been the first to draw. In his hands, signs are assigned the inferior
part of mere evidence in a contrast with grounds that, beyond
justifying a conclusion, also serve to explain it. Despite the later
importance of other versions of the distinction between sign and
demonstration, it occupies Aristotle's attention only briefly and in
passing.

In the passages where Aristotle turns his attention explicitly to
inference from signs, in the *Prior Analytics* and *Rhetoric*, he has
in view the contrast between evidence which yields a conclusive
argument and evidence which only serves to make a conclusion
probable or likely. He calls the latter signs, the former tokens. This
was a path-breaking recognition that an argument may lack deductive validity without thereby relinquishing all claim to persuade
rational beings: in Aristotle's language, an argument may be *reputable* without being conclusive. Argument from signs, in the sense
specified by Aristotle here, is the weakest form of argument that
may still be reputable. After Aristotle this approach was largely
abandoned. None the less, in this study I shall follow Aristotle's
lead and concentrate on non-conclusive inference from signs and
the other forms of non-conclusive but reputable argument he discusses together with it. Only at the end of Study I will I touch on
his contrast between inference from signs and demonstration.

After Aristotle chronology can no longer serve us as an organiz-
ing principle. All the views to be examined are post-Aristotelian,
but our principal sources are no longer treatises whose authors expound their own views, but ancient secondary works, in which the
views of earlier, sometimes much earlier, figures are reported. This
is especially true of Sextus Empiricus, whose treatment of signs is
the subject of Study II. Sextus' method as a Pyrrhonian sceptic

is first to present the views of the so-called dogmatic schools—a procedure that is responsible for his immense value as a source—and then subject them to sceptical scrutiny. In his discussion of signs Sextus does something more. Although he rejects one of the forms of signification he distinguishes as dogmatic, he embraces the other form and insists that it is compatible with the sceptical way of life. These he calls indicative and commemorative signification respectively. The distinction between indicative and commemorative signs is another version of the contrast between high and low conceptions of signification. Indicative signification, which on Sextus' view promises lay bare the hidden underlying nature of reality, is the superior form and comes under sceptical attack. Commemorative signification, which does not stray beyond ordinary matters within the reach of observation, meets with Sextus' approval and is exempted from attack. Why it is so exempted is one of the questions we shall pursue.

But this is not the only issue raised by Sextus' discussion of signs. He treats the distinction as if it provided a neutral framework in terms of which the philosophical views that he examines can be classified without distortion. On closer examination this proves to be false, however. The terminology of commemoration and indication had its origin in the long-running debate between medical Empiricists and Rationalists. The medical origin of the terms need not by itself disqualify the distinction for the task Sextus assigns to it—the disagreement about the nature and origin of knowledge that divided medical Empiricists and Rationalists was entirely philosophical—but as we shall see, the distinction incorporates certain assumptions peculiar to that debate that make it unable to serve as the impartial framework that Sextus needs. For this reason, Study II has three tasks: first, to free the philosophical views that Sextus reports, especially the Stoic position, from the framework he used to classify them; second, to examine the debate about the nature of sign-inference between partisans of commemorative and indicative signification that was carried on in medicine; and last, to examine the sceptical credentials of the commemorative sign which Sextus embraces on behalf of Pyrrhonism.

Study III examines the Stoic theory of signs, now freed from the distorting influence of Sextus' framework. There I argue that, contrary to the expectations created by Sextus, it belongs among low views of signification and has more affinities with commemorative than indicative signification. But while the medical Empiricists distinguish a higher form of inference, indicative signification, only to repudiate it, the Stoics, like Aristotle, recognize superior forms of inference that they classify under the head of 'demonstration'. The Stoic distinction between signs and demonstrations takes a different form from Aristotle's, however, in a way that reflects some fundamental epistemological differences between Aristotle and the Stoa. And we shall see, as others have noticed before, that there was room within the Stoic position for disagreement and development: there were in fact a number of related Stoic positions, which seem to have differed mainly over whether and how demonstrations enter into scientific explanation.

Study IV examines the Epicurean views that are reported in the *De signis* of Philodemus. The work was composed several centuries before Sextus'. If the Epicurean authorities whose views Philodemus preserves were, as they would have us believe, nothing more than faithful exponents of Epicurus' own position, strict chronological order would suggest placing this study second after the examination of Aristotle. Even if, as is much more likely, the views we find in Philodemus are the product of a considerable amount of development after Epicurus' time, it is not clear that the period during which this development took place—the second and early first centuries BC—would justify placing this study after the others. I turn to Epicurean views last, however, not because they are the most recent, but because they are in some ways the strangest, and we shall be better able to appreciate the peculiar position they occupy after we have acquainted ourselves with the lines along which other ancient approaches to sign-inference developed.

The Epicurean approach to signification mixes primitive and sophisticated elements in a way that is unique in our sample of views, but perhaps characteristic of Epicureanism. The primitive element is the reliance on analogy, which is one of the most often noted and well-studied features of early Greek intellectual enquiry.[13] Empedocles famously appealed to the clepsydra to illustrate the process of respiration and to the lantern to illustrate the functioning of the eye (B 84, 100 DK). Anaxagoras and Democritus used a whirl or

---

[13] The magisterial studies by Diller, "Ὄψις ἀδήλων", and Lloyd, *Polarity and Analogy*, which I have already had occasion to cite, deserve special mention in this connection.

vortex as a model for the origin and present condition of the cosmos (Anaxagoras B 9, 12, 13 DK; Democritus B 167 DK). Herodotus' inference about the length of the Nile cited above furnishes an example from outside philosophy, and analogy was a favourite tool in Hippocratic medicine as well. It would be easy to add to these examples. Of course, analogy need not always function as a mode of inference; it can also suggest hypotheses which depend for their confirmation on evidence from another quarter. And it is not always clear to what extent the analogies so prominent in the thought of the period are viewed in one way or the other, or even to what extent the two uses of analogy are clearly distinguished. The pregnant formula of Anaxagoras cited above does not seem to discriminate. None the less, the fact that an evident item is of such-and-such a character or behaves in such-and-such a way is often presented in early Greek thought as cogent evidence that a non-evident item has a similar character or behaves in a similar way.

Apart from the Epicureans, none of the schools and figures whose views we shall be considering continues this tradition. This is not to say that analogical argument or the awareness of it disappears elsewhere. As we shall see, Aristotle discusses several forms of it under the head of paradigm or example. But Aristotle is at pains to distinguish it from deductive or syllogistic reasoning and is careful to note its deficiencies relative to deductive argument. The Epicureans, by contrast, remain committed to a full-blooded form of inference by analogy which does not yield an inch in cogency to other forms of argument. Indeed, we shall find some of them arguing that all sign-inference is at bottom dependent upon a method of similarity that licenses the projection of what is observed to obtain within experience onto what lies beyond the reach of experience.

In view of their debt to Presocratic natural philosophy, it is perhaps not surprising that Epicurus and his followers remained true to the analogical mode of inference. But they did more than simply follow tradition. Unlike their Presocratic predecessors, they squarely confront the questions that inference by analogy inevitably invites. Why should the fact that some items are observed to be of a certain character or behave in a certain way entitle us to conclude that items that we cannot observe are similar or behave in similar ways? And even if this hurdle can somehow be cleared, when and in what conditions are we justified in inferring what degree and kind of similarity? They tackled these questions at a time when a high

degree of logical sophistication about what is required for one thing
to follow from another had been achieved. The authorities whose
views are reported by Philodemus wrote to answer the charges of
certain unnamed opponents, usually and probably rightly supposed
to be Stoics. These opponents draw on the resources of a logical
theory, as we can see from the prominent part that is played in their
arguments by an appeal to the *conditional* (συνημμένον). Similarity
cannot, they maintain, supply the basis of true conditionals of the
kind required for the Epicureans' inferences to the non-evident.

But instead of dismissing this challenge, as Epicurus' notoriously
contemptuous attitude towards logic might have led us to expect,
the Epicureans accept it and attempt to show that similarity can
give rise to true conditionals of the required strictness. What is
more, they treat inference by analogy as one of two species of argument embraced by the method of similarity they defend. The other
is made up of what we should call inductive arguments or, if we
construe induction more broadly, an especially prominent special
case of inductive argument, viz. arguments from the observed behaviour of items of certain type to the conclusion that unobserved
items of the same type behave, have behaved, or will behave in
the same way. Though the Epicureans do not put it in quite this
way, their defence of the method of similarity can be viewed as a
quixotic attempt to show, in the face of determined opposition, that
similarity yields deductively valid arguments.

Aristotle on Sign-inference and Related Forms of Argument

THOUGH Aristotle was the first to make sign-inference the object of theoretical reflection, what he left us is less a theory proper than a sketch of one. Its fullest statement is found in *Prior Analytics* 2. 27, the last in a sequence of five chapters whose aim is to establish that:

> not only are dialectical and demonstrative syllogisms [συλλογισμοί] effected by means of the figures [of the categorical syllogism] but also rhetorical syllogisms and, quite generally, any attempt to produce conviction [πίστις] of whatever kind. (2. 23, 68ᵇ9–13)[1]

This account of sign-inference, then, is part of an effort to understand existing practices of argument in the light of the theory of the categorical syllogism, Aristotle's—and history's first—formal logic. It is presented again in two passages of the *Rhetoric*. As is made plain by its presence there and references to rhetoric in the above passage from *Prior Analytics* 2. 23 and to the enthymeme, the rhetorical counterpart of the syllogism, at 2. 27, 70ᵃ9–11, Aristotle had rhetorical argument principally in mind. But it is equally clear that he did not intend to confine the use of signs to rhetoric. *Prior Analytics* 2. 27 concludes with a discussion of sign-inference in another discipline, physiognomics, whose aim is to infer traits of character from perceptible physical features (70ᵇ7 ff.).

Nor should we expect otherwise. Talk of 'signs' and the notion of evidence to which it gives expression were no less a part of

---

[1] 'Of whatever kind' (καθ' ὁποιανοῦν μέθοδον) is taken by some interpreters to refer to the application of the categorical syllogistic to every discipline, by others to refer to its application to every type, method, or means of argumentation. Cf. M. F. Burnyeat, 'Enthymeme: Aristotle on the Logic of Persuasion', in D. J. Furley and A. Nehamas (eds.), *Aristotle's Rhetoric: Philosophical Essays* (Princeton: Princeton University Press, 1994), 3–55 at 31–2. The translation given here is indebted to Burnyeat, ibid., and W. D. Ross (ed.), *Aristotle's Prior and Posterior Analytics* (Oxford: Oxford University Press, 1949), 481.

ordinary language and thought in antiquity than they are in our own day. Signs were used in all the areas we touched on in the Introduction above, and appeals to signs are a notable feature of Aristotle's method of argument in just about every field he takes up.[2] It is also important to remember that, on Aristotle's view, rhetoric is not in the usual way a specialized discipline, but an art that brings system and method to ordinary, everyday practices of argument that are employed by everyone and in almost every sphere of life (*Rhet.* 1. 1, 1354ᵃ1–11). If argument by signs is especially prominent among the means of argument used by rhetoric, and rhetoric especially prominent among the areas in which argument by signs figures, this reflects the low or common character that Aristotle assigned to inference from signs. This is also why Aristotle tackles sign-inference in conjunction with argument by likelihood and argument by paradigm, the latter of which he treats as the rhetorical counterpart of induction, in both the *Prior Analytics* and the *Rhetoric*. They too are especially suitable to rhetoric precisely because of their inferiority relative to other, superior forms of argument, whose higher standards have no place there.

In this study I shall follow Aristotle both by paying particular attention to rhetoric and by investigating sign-inference in close connection with the other forms of argument that he considers especially characteristic of rhetoric. Too scrupulous an adherence to the boundaries Aristotle draws around sign-inference in his more theoretical moments, boundaries that neither he nor others always observe, would cut us off from much material relevant to our broader subject, the use of evidence. Aristotle's most notable achievement in this field was to have recognized explicitly for the first time that an argument that is invalid may nevertheless be reputable, i.e. furnish grounds for a conclusion by which rational human beings may legitimately be swayed. But Aristotle's path-breaking investigations in this area not only set him apart from his contemporaries and successors; there are also reasons to think his insights were isolated within his own work as well. For the receptive attitude towards invalid argument by signs, which accepts that they can afford reputable grounds for a conclusion, is clearly displayed only in the passages of the *Prior Analytics* mentioned above and in the pas-

---

[2] Cf. H. Bonitz, *Index Aristotelicus*, vol. v of *Aristotelis Opera*, ed. I. Bekker (Berlin: Reimer, 1870; repr. Darmstadt: Wissenschaftliche Buchgesellschaft, 1960), s.vv. σημεῖον, τεκμήριον, 677ᵇ9 ff., 750ᵇ6 ff.

sages of the *Rhetoric* that rely on them. Elsewhere we seem to find
a different and less receptive attitude. I shall explore the possibility
that this difference in attitude is due to a change in view related
to broader developments in Aristotle's thinking about argument,
paying particular attention to the influence of two factors: the sympathetic attention Aristotle brought to argument of the kind that is
most prominent in rhetoric and the application of formal logic to
the issue.

Unlike Aristotle's views about non-deductive but reputable inference, his contrast between signs and demonstrations inaugurated
a discussion that was taken up and carried on in post-Aristotelian
philosophy and recurs in one form or another there. It requires
no discussion in Aristotle's investigation of rhetorical argument,
where explanation of the kind demonstration aims to provide is not
at issue, but receives attention, if only in passing, in the *Posterior
Analytics*, which is concerned with scientific explanation. The issues raised by this contrast will occupy a large share of our attention
later, but I shall touch on it only in the last section of this study.

1. Rhetoric

Aristotle's *Rhetoric* begins with the bold declaration that 'rhetoric
is the counterpart of dialectic' (1. 1, 1354ª1 ff.). And Aristotle goes
on to use its affinity with dialectic both to defend rhetoric against
the charges brought by its enemies and to distinguish his own
conception of the discipline from that of its other defenders. The
most prominent of the complaints lodged against it in Plato's *Gorgias*, and repeated many times thereafter by other authors, is that
rhetoric cannot be an art because it lacks an object (458 E ff.). Aristotle's answer is that, properly speaking, rhetoric, like dialectic, is
not the science of a subject-matter, but a faculty for the discovery
of arguments (*Rhet.* 1. 2, 1355ᵇ26–35; 1356ª32–4; 1. 4, 1358ª22–6;
1359ᵇ12–16). Thus, though rhetoric and dialectic lack an object on
a level with the subject-matters which distinguish and define the
ordinary run of arts and sciences, they are arts none the less, because they dispose of a system or method oriented towards objects
of a different and rather special kind. Rhetoric is the faculty of dis-
cerning the potentially persuasive about each subject, dialectic that
of arguing from reputable premisses about any subject proposed

(*Rhet.* 1. 2, 1355ᵇ26; *Top.* 1. 1, 100ᵃ1 ff.; *SE* 2, 165ᵇ3–4). Their concerns are in some sense formal as opposed to substantive. In what sense is harder to say. As we proceed, it will emerge that there is more than one way to constitute a formal discipline of argument.

This broadly formal character is responsible for rhetoric's most alarming trait: the power, which it shares only with dialectic, of arguing with equal facility on either side of any question (1. 1, 1355ᵃ29–35). The two disciplines' argumentative and persuasive powers are not confined to a single object or tied to one set of conclusions, as is the more limited power to persuade and instruct about a single subject that belongs to the master of each of the ordinary arts and sciences (1355ᵇ28–32; cf. Plato, *Grg.* 453 D ff.). Aristotle does not pretend that this suspicion is groundless, but he maintains that there is a difference in the field of rhetoric corresponding to that between sophistic and dialectic, albeit one not marked in the same way by a terminological distinction, and he insists that dialectic and sophistic on the one hand, and their rhetorical counterparts on the other, differ from each other not as faculties (ἐν τῇ δυνάμει), but in purpose (ἐν τῇ προαιρέσει)(1. 1, 1355ᵇ17–21; cf. *Metaph. Γ* 2, 1004ᵇ22–5; *SE* 1, 165ᵃ31).[3]

It is essential to understand this remark in the light of the distinction Aristotle has just drawn in the immediately preceding passage of the *Rhetoric*, where he observes that it falls to rhetoric to discern the persuasive and the apparently persuasive, just as it belongs to dialectic to discern the syllogism and the apparent syllogism (1. 1, 1355ᵇ15–17).[4] His meaning is that it is possible to distinguish between the good and the bad in argument at a level lower than the moral purpose of the practitioner and the conclusions for which he or she argues: that is, practitioners will differ not only in the ends to which they apply their skills, but also in their choice of means. The dialectical and sophistical faculties and their counterparts in rhetoric are inseparable, not because there is no difference between sophistical and dialectical argument or between good and bad argument in rhetoric, but rather because to possess the understanding of argument that belongs to the dialectician one must at the same time share the sophist's grasp of trickery and deception, so too *mutatis mutandis* in the field of rhetoric. This impression is strengthened further by the distinction Aristotle draws between the

---

[3] On this use of προαίρεσις see Bonitz, *Index Aristotelicus*, 634ᵃ5–12.

[4] Cf. *SE* 1, 165ᵃ25; 9, 170ᵃ36–8, ᵇ8–11; 11, 172ᵇ5–8.

real and the apparent enthymeme corresponding to that between the real and apparent syllogism (*Rhet*. 1. 2, 1356ᵇ4; 2. 22, 1397ᵃ3–4; 2. 24, 1400ᵇ34–7, 1402ᵃ2–8). And if I may postpone for the moment the daunting question of what a topos is, his decision to organize his discussion of rhetorical argument around separate lists of topoi of the genuine and of the apparent enthymeme in *Rhetoric* 2. 23 and 24 respectively, just as he treats topoi of the genuine and the apparent syllogism in the *Topics* and *Sophistical Refutations*, points in this direction as well.

The fact that rhetoric is concerned in the first instance with genuine enthymemes is crucial to Aristotle's vindication of the rhetorical art. Although it is not the function of rhetoric to bring to light and secure the acceptance of correct conclusions, it makes an indispensable contribution to this end with its power to discover the persuasive on opposite sides of every question. For, Aristotle maintains, even though rhetoric is, like dialectic, a faculty of opposites, matters themselves are not like this: the true and the better are more readily argued and persuasive by nature (1. 1, 1355ᵃ36–8; cf. 20–2). We may compare his account of the value of rhetoric with the distinction he draws between the *function* of dialectic, which is to supply us with arguments for any proposed thesis, and its *uses*, among which is the assistance it affords us in our enquiries about the first principles of the sciences.⁵ It helps us to see what can be said on either side of a question, but it does not lay down rules that dictate our choice of the truth (cf. *Top*. 8. 14, 163ᵇ9–16). If rhetoric is to do the same in its own sphere, it must use arguments of genuine merit. Rhetoric's affinity with dialectic therefore requires that there be two parts to its ability to argue on both sides of the question. First, like the dialectician, the worthy orator knows how to argue by deceptive means for conclusions he knows to be false or on the side of a question he knows to be wrong; though he will not do this, the ability to do it is essential if he is to combat less principled opponents (*Rhet*. 1. 1, 1355ᵃ29–33; cf. *SE* 16, 175ᵃ17–19; *Top*. 1. 18, 108ᵃ26–37).⁶ But second, where the question is unclear, where there is much to be said on either side, the ability to argue on

---

⁵ πρὸς πόσα τε καὶ τίνα χρήσιμος ἡ πραγματεία . . . (*Top*. 1. 2, 101ᵃ25 ff.; cf. 8. 14, 163ᵇ9–16; *SE* 16, 175ᵃ5–16). χρήσιμος δὲ ἡ ῥητορική . . . (*Rhet*. 1. 1, 1355ᵃ20 ff.).

⁶ Perhaps Aristotle should have been more cautious here. The distinction does not decide the issue whether a reputable orator will always use only the most reputable forms of argument any more than the distinction between lying and telling the truth resolves the question whether a good human being will ever lie.

both sides of the question by reputable means can serve the cause of truth by bringing out the considerations that count in favour of opposed conclusions.

Rhetoric is not simply dialectic applied in rhetorical circumstances, however. The nature of the issues that it falls to rhetoric to discuss influences the character of its arguments even before the constraints imposed by the kind of audiences which it addresses and the occasions on which it is used are taken into account. These issues are, as Aristotle puts it, matters that permit of being otherwise and are not the object of an art or specialized expertise (1. 2, $1357^{a}1-7$, $13-15$, $^{b}23-7$; 1. 4, $1359^{a}30$ ff.; cf. *EN* 2. 2, $1104^{a}7-8$). Instead, there is an ineliminable roughness and inexactitude to them, which imposes correspondingly greater demands upon the faculty of deliberation. They differ from issues concerning individual moral agents by requiring a collective decision by a jury, assembly, or similar body, but are otherwise very much like them (cf. *Rhet.* 2. 21, $1394^{a}23-7$). Thus, much that Aristotle says elsewhere about practical reasoning can be said with equal justice of the arguments that orators must use and their auditors must evaluate. Indeed Aristotle appeals in a famous passage to the example of rhetoric to explain these features of practical reason (*EN* 1. 3, $1094^{b}12-27$; cf. 2. 2, $1104^{a}1$ ff.).

This is an important part of the reason why rhetoric comes by an indirect route to have, in a certain way, a subject-matter—not by being the science or art of it, but rather by finding a use in relation to it. Though in principle of universal scope, rhetoric finds its place in relation to the broadly political issues falling under the three genres of oratory: deliberative, epideictic, and forensic (1. 3, $1358^{a}36$ ff.). It is a hybrid discipline, an offshoot, as Aristotle notes, of both dialectic and politics (*Rhet.* 1. 2, $1356^{a}25-6$).[7] And this also accounts for its tendency to instability: the way it threatens to lose its distinctively rhetorical character and become a part of politics (1. 2, $1358^{a}23-6$; 1. 4, $1359^{b}12-16$).

For these reasons, Aristotle insists that mastery of the enthymeme requires, over and above the mastery of the syllogism furnished by dialectic, an understanding of what the matters with which en-

---

[7] But cf. J. Cooper, 'Ethical-political Theory in Aristotle's Rhetoric', in Furley and Nehamas (eds.), *Aristotle's Rhetoric*, 193–210 at 200, who notes how surprising it is that rhetoric's relation to politics is mentioned only in connection with the *pistis* of ethos here.

thymemes are concerned are like (ποῖα) and how this affects the character of enthymematic argument (1. 1, 1355ᵃ10–14).[8] The kinds of issues about which orators argue typically resist resolution by means of conclusive argument, and the fact that it is often possible only to offer considerations which, though of a certain weight, are not decisive requires a corresponding loosening or relaxation of the standards by which argument is to be judged in rhetoric (cf. 1. 1, 1355ᵃ10–14; 1. 2, 1357ᵃ13–15, ᵇ26).[9] It is this loosening or relaxation that is signalled by the terminology of the enthymeme and the paradigm, the rhetorical counterparts of the syllogism and the induction respectively. This is not to deny that it will often be advisable to present arguments in abridged form, so that good judgement in this area will be an essential part of the orator's equipment as a master of the enthymeme as well (cf. 1. 2, 1357ᵃ16; 2. 22, 1395ᵇ24–6). But, though I shall argue the point needs to be qualified, I take as read the case that the omission of premises is not

---

[8] οὗτος καὶ ἐνθημηματικὸς ἂν εἴη μάλιστα, προσλαβὼν περὶ ποῖά τε ἐστι τὸ ἐνθύμημα καὶ τίνας ἔχει διαφορὰς πρὸς τοὺς λογικοὺς συλλογισμούς. Note that Aristotle says περὶ ποῖα, not τίνα. I render ποῖα as 'what they are like' to emphasize that Aristotle is talking about the character of the matters with which the orator is concerned and its effects on the character of his arguments here and not the substantive factual knowledge that he elsewhere insists the orator will also need to have (cf. 1. 4, 1359ᵇ18–33). The word λογικός, as so often, signals a contrast between a way of proceeding by λόγος—words, statements, argument, or reasoning—considered, in one way or another and to one degree or another, apart or in abstraction from their content or subject-matter, and a way of proceeding which takes features of the subject-matter at issue into account. Here the effect is to oppose the rigour of the syllogisms employed in dialectic to the less rigorous character of the enthymeme. The former owe their greater stringency to dialectic's nature as a pure art of argument, unconcerned with the special features of concrete subject-matters. The reduced-stringency characteristic of enthymemes, on the other hand, is made necessary by the nature of the matters with which they deal. In the *Rhetoric* Aristotle often mentions the special features of these matters and their effect on the character of rhetorical argument (1. 2, 1357ᵃ14, ᵇ25–6; 4, 1359ᵃ30–9; 2. 21, 1394ᵃ24–7). Elsewhere, when Aristotle speaks of handling a subject λογικῶς, where this comes close to διαλεκτικῶς, he means to call attention to a style of enquiry that can—in a different way—be less rigorous than one that comes fully and properly to grips with the subject. The range of uses to which Aristotle puts λογικός is documented and discussed in illuminating detail by T. Waitz (ed.), *Aristotelis Organon Graece* (Leipzig: Hahn, 1844–6), ii. 353 ff. (ad *An. post.* 82ᵇ35), and A. Schwegler, *Die Metaphysik des Aristoteles* (Tübingen: Fues, 1847), iv. 48–51 (ad *Metaph. Z* 4, 1029ᵇ13).

[9] I borrow with gratitude talk of 'relaxation' from Burnyeat, 'Enthymeme'. The Aristotelian inspiration is furnished by a number of passages in which Aristotle speaks of arguing or demonstrating in more 'exact' and more 'relaxed' ways (*Rhet.* 2. 22, 1396ᵃ33–ᵇ1; *De gen. et corr.* 333ᵇ24; *Metaph. E* 1, 1025ᵇ13). On the broader significance of Aristotle's talk of relaxed and exact modes of argument see Lloyd, 'The Theories and Practices of Demonstration in Aristotle'.

a defining characteristic of enthymemes, but a frequent feature of
their presentation.[10] Arguments that do not qualify as syllogisms
in dialectic, even with all their premisses fully stated, will qualify
as enthymemes or rhetorical syllogisms, so too in the case of inductions and paradigms. Another way of putting the point is to say
that dialectic's concern with valid argument is replaced in rhetoric
by a concern with *reputable* (ἔνδοξος) argument. Although Aristotle
does not use the term in this way in the *Rhetoric*, as we shall see, he
does in the *Prior Analytics*.

The emphasis Aristotle places on rhetoric's affinity with dialectic in his opening remarks also serves to distinguish his approach
to the art from that of his contemporaries and predecessors in the
study of rhetoric. The rhetoric he defends is not theirs, which, he
complains, concerns itself almost entirely with appeals to the emotions and issues concerning the style and arrangement of speeches
at the expense of argument (1. 1, 1354ᵃ11 ff., ᵇ16 ff.). So harsh is
Aristotle's criticism that it comes as something of a surprise to find
Rhetoric 1. 2 treating appeals to emotion together with the presentation of the speaker's character and argument as the three varieties
of artistic proof or persuasion (πίστις) which it is the business of
the art of rhetoric to study (1355ᵇ35 ff.). This real or apparent
discrepancy has been the object of a considerable amount of attention.[11] But however it is to be viewed, there can be no doubt
that Aristotle meant to assign the central place in rhetoric to argument. My principal aim in what follows will be to enquire how
Aristotle's account of good and bad argument, and of good and bad
kinds of argument, in rhetoric differs from the account proper to
dialectic.

2. Stages in Aristotle's Thinking about Argument

This task is made more difficult, but also in some ways more in-

---

[10] Thus Ross, *Analytics*, 500: 'In modern logic books the enthymeme is usually
described as a syllogism with one premiss or the conclusion omitted . . . but this
forms no part of [Aristotle's] definition, being a purely superficial characteristic.'
For the argument in full and a history of the controversy cf. Burnyeat, 'Enthymeme'.
A. Kantelhardt also deserves a place among the many figures discussed by Burnyeat
for a brief but elegant statement of the essential insight, *De Aristotelis rhetoricis*
(Göttingen: Dieterich, 1911), 10; photographically reproduced in R. Stark (ed.),
Rhetorika: Schriften zur aristotelischen und hellenistischen Rhetorik (Hildesheim:
Olms, 1968).   [11] I shall touch on it in appendix B to this study.

teresting, by the fact that different parts of the *Rhetoric* rely on different stages in Aristotle's developing understanding of the syllogism, i.e. the object of study determined by the definition 'a *logos* in which, certain things being laid down, something different from them follows of necessity by their being so' (*Top.* 1. 1, 100^{a}25–7; *An. pr.* 1. 1, 24^{b}18–20). That every syllogism is, or is composed of parts that are, in one or the other of the valid moods of the three figures, i.e. that every syllogism is a *categorical* syllogism, is no part of the meaning specified by the definition. Rather, it is a conclusion for which Aristotle had to argue, and which he took himself to have established in the *Prior Analytics* (cf. 1. 23, 41^{b}1–3; 1. 28, 44^{b}7–8; 2. 23, 68^{b}9–13).[12] Indeed, we have excellent reasons for believing that the definition of the syllogism, and Aristotle's interest in the object it determines, antedated the categorical theory of the syllogism. The *Topics*, where the definition makes its first appearance, and its companion piece, the *Sophistical Refutations*, which closes with Aristotle's famous claim to have been the first to study the syllogism systematically, present the results of an enquiry pursued without the benefit of the categorical theory of the syllogism.[13] Their unfamiliarity with the categorical syllogism is in fact one of the principal grounds for the long-established view that the *Topics* and *Sophistical Refutations* are among the earliest of Aristotle's treatises.

Much the larger part of the *Rhetoric* looks to the *Topics* and *Sophistical Refutation* for its understanding of argument, while the categorical syllogistic is applied to the enthymeme in two short, self-contained passages, which appear to be later insertions, and chapter 27 of the second book of the *Prior Analytics*, to which they refer (*Rhet.* 1. 2, 1357^{a}22–58^{a}2; 2. 25, 1402^{b}13–1403^{a}16). This

---

[12] Cf. J. Barnes, 'Proof and the Syllogism', in E. Berti (ed.), *Aristotle on Science: The Posterior Analytics* (Padua: Antenore, 1981), 17–59 at 23–5, 44–6; F. Solmsen, *Die Entwicklung der aristotelischen Logik und Rhetorik* (Neue philologische Untersuchungen, 4; Berlin: Weidmann, 1929), 38 ff., esp. 41–2, 151; Kantelhardt, *De Aristotelis rhetoricis*, 49–50, 52–5; Burnyeat, 'Enthymeme', 9–10, 14–15; J. Brunschwig (ed.), *Aristote: Topiques I–IV* (Paris: Les Belles Lettres, 1967), pp. xxx ff.

[13] That Aristotle's claim to have been the first to study syllogizing refers to the project pursued in the *Topics* and *Sophistical Refutations* and not to the *Prior Analytics* was, I believe, first clearly stated and argued by C. Thurot, *Études sur Aristote: Politique, Dialectique, Rhétorique* (Paris: Durand, 1860), 195–7. For recent statements of the point see: J. Brunschwig, 'L'Organon: Tradition grecque', in R. Goulet (ed.), *Dictionnaire des philosophes antiques*, i (Paris: CNRS, 1989), 485–502 at 486–7; L.-A. Dorion (trans.), *Aristote: Les Réfutations sophistiques* (Paris: Vrin, 1995), 418 n. 479. Cf. Solmsen, *Entwicklung*, 41–2.

discovery is most closely associated with Friedrich Solmsen.[14] It is only one element in his account of the development of Aristotle's conception of rhetoric, which is itself part of a still more comprehensive theory of the development of Aristotle's logic. Though the whole of Solmsen's theory deserves the most serious attention, it is important to note that the parts of his argument do not all stand or fall together. Some of the developments he claims to find are more conjectural than others. I shall touch briefly on the most important of these later.[15] But the identification of *Topics*- and *Analytics*-oriented sections of the *Rhetoric* is among the least speculative. Although a formal logical theory need not affect a philosopher's unreflective style of argument, it is bound to leave its mark on his self-conscious treatments of the subject of argument once he has it, and be conspicuous by its absence before then.

---

[14] *Entwicklung*, 13 ff.; though there were some hints in earlier scholars, notably in Kantelhardt, *De Aristotelis rhetoricis*, 56, 59. Cf. Burnyeat, 'Enthymeme', 31 ff. with n. 76. Though it does not refer to the *Analytics*, *Rhet.* 1. 4, 1359ᵇ9 ff., seems to deserve a place among the later *Analytics*-oriented passages of the *Rhetoric*. Here we are told that 'what we said earlier is true, viz. that rhetoric is composed of the analytical science [ἀναλυτικὴ ἐπιστήμη—i.e. presumably the formal logic expounded in the *Prior Analytics*] and that concerned with characters [ἤθη]'. This is a very odd thing to say for a number of reasons, however. It refers to 1. 2, 1356ᵃ25–6, where Aristotle says that rhetoric is composed of *dialectic* and the study of character (cf. n. 7 above). διαλεκτική is found as a variant instead of ἀναλυτική at 1359ᵇ10 in some manuscripts, but editors have for good reasons regarded διαλεκτική as a late attempt at correction and preferred ἀναλυτική. Cf. R. Kassell, *Der Text der aristotelischen Rhetorik: Prolegomena zu einer kritischen Ausgabe* (Berlin: De Gruyter, 1971), 79–80. Solmsen, ibid. 225 n. 2, believes that this passage is a late addition by Aristotle himself, showing that he now believes διαλεκτική can be replaced by ἀναλυτική. Cf. also G. Striker, 'Aristotle on the Uses of Logic', in G. Gentzler (ed.), *Method in Ancient Philosophy* (Oxford: Oxford University Press, 1998), 206–26 at 221 n. 18. But the abrupt replacement of διαλεκτική by ἀναλυτική here is not the only peculiarity of 1359ᵇ9 ff. The immediate sequel proceeds as if we had been talking about διαλεκτική all along (1359ᵇ11–16). What is more, this is the only passage anywhere in Aristotle that speaks of ἀναλυτική, let alone ἀναλυτικὴ ἐπιστήμη. This reflects the fact that Aristotle seems not to have viewed formal logic as a substantive scientific discipline, but rather, as his successors were to insist, as an *organon*. On talk of ἐπιστήμη ἀποδεικτική at *An. pr.* 1. 1, 24ᵃ2, see J. Brunschwig, 'L'objet et la structure des Seconds Analytiques d'après Aristote', in Berti (ed.), *Aristotle on Science*, 61–90, according to whom Aristotle here means not the study of demonstration, but the knowledge it produces. In view of these considerations, I wonder if there is not more to be said for Thurot's spirited defence of διαλεκτική, *Études*, 248–54. 1. 3, 1359ᵃ6, may also be a stray *Analytics*-oriented passage (cf. n. 25 below).

[15] In appendix B to this study.

3. The *Analytics*-oriented
Account of Rhetorical Argument

(a) *Aristotle's exposition*

In the *Prior Analytics* and in the first of the *Analytics*-oriented passages in the *Rhetoric* (1. 2) Aristotle informs us that enthymemes are from likelihoods and signs (70ᵃ9–11; 1357ᵃ32–3). He returns to the subject in *Rhetoric* 2. 25, to ask whether and how each of these forms of argument is open to objection. A likelihood is, he says, 'something which comes to be for the most part' (*Rhet.* 1. 2, 1357ᵃ34), or with the subjective element on which depends its ability to support rhetorically effective arguments in view, as 'something people know comes to be or not for the most part' (*An. pr.* 2. 27, 70ᵃ4–5; cf. *Rhet.* 2. 25, 1402ᵇ15). An enthymeme from likelihoods is an argument bringing a particular case under an acknowledged general rule permitting exceptions (1357ᵃ34–ᵇ1). On the other hand, a sign is, according to *Prior Analytics* 2. 27, a premiss that is or is such as to be reputable (ἔνδοξος) (70ᵃ7).[16] In the same chapter likelihoods are also called reputable and the necessary character of the token is represented as a special case of the reputable: it is the *most* reputable of the sign-inferences (70ᵃ4; ᵇ4–5). These lines furnish the textual authority for the use of 'reputable' in relation to argument that I have already freely employed.

According to the pre-theoretical conception of the sign that furnishes Aristotle with his point of departure, a sign is 'something such that, when it exists, another thing exists, or, when it has happened, the other has happened before or after' (70ᵃ7–9).[17] In a sign argument, then, the sign—a particular fact or alleged fact—is put forward as a ground for the conclusion of which the orator wishes to convince his audience. When the argument based on it is reconstructed as a categorical syllogism, the sign is most often the

[16] 'That tends or is such as to be [βούλεται εἶναι] necessary or reputable'. Cf. Bonitz, *Index Aristotelicus*, s.v. βούλεσθαι, 140ᵇ41: 'saepe per βούλεται εἶναι significatur quo quid per naturam suam tendit, sive id assequitur quo tendit, sive non plene et perfecte assequitur'.

[17] The translation is that of Ross, *Analytics*, 498. The suggestion that this characterization be viewed as a pre-theoretical starting-point in this way is due to M. F. Burnyeat, 'The Origins of Non-deductive Inference', in J. Barnes *et al.* (eds.), *Science and Speculation* (Cambridge: Cambridge University Press, 1982), 193–238 at 197.

minor premiss predicating an attribute of a particular (as we shall see, the third-figure sign-inference requires a somewhat different treatment). So, for example, that this man has a fever is a sign that he is ill.

But although Aristotle plainly intends the division between likelihoods and signs to be exhaustive of the forms of rhetorical argument apart from paradigm (1357^a31-2), it is less clear that it is exclusive: may not one enthymeme satisfy both descriptions?[18] This question is worth pursuing a little further because its answer may help us understand Aristotle's analysis of rhetorical argument. For his principal aim is not to distinguish and define kinds of argument in purely formal terms, but to characterize formally kinds of argument already distinguished in the then current practice and—possibly—theory, such as it was, of rhetorical argument. And here the omission of premisses, which is a characteristic of the *presentation* of enthymemes, may throw light on the differences between types of arguments that Aristotle is trying to bring out by means of his distinction between enthymemes from signs and those from likelihoods, but which cannot be completely captured by analysis from the point of view of the categorical syllogistic.

It would be a mistake to picture the orator trimming premisses from full-blown categorical syllogisms that he has first framed before his mind's eye in order to present them in the form suitable to the rhetorical occasion. It is important to remember that Aristotle conceived the categorical syllogistic as, among other things, a way of bringing out and making explicit the often unstated premisses because of which the conclusion of a syllogism follows of necessity. This is the special task of analysis, from which the *Analytics* take their name. The analysis of arguments with the aid of the categorical syllogistic uncovers assumptions on which they depend that often go unnoticed and unsaid (cf. *An. pr.* 1. 32, 47^a13-18). And, I should like to suggest, whether an argument is to count as an enthymeme from likelihoods or signs depends in part on what, in the circumstances, can go unsaid. Very roughly, the two forms of enthymeme are distinguished by the element of the argument that, if you will, bears the greater weight in the context of argument. And this in turn will influence which premiss of the argument—

---

[18] The question is posed by J. Sprute, *Die Enthymemtheorie der aristotelischen Rhetorik* (Göttingen: Vandenhoeck and Ruprecht, 1982), 89–90.

when analysed as a categorical syllogism—is expressed, and which usually omitted.

In an enthymeme from likelihoods the crucial element on which the argument turns is the generalization under which the particular item in question is being brought. This must in all cases be stated, while the minor premiss, which states that the subject term of the major premiss belongs to the item under discussion, can and often will go without saying. And it is the generalization stated in the major premiss that is also the potential object of controversy. An orator who needs to oppose an argument from likelihood will try to show that his opponent's conclusion is not likely because it is based on a generalization that is false or in some way not appropriate to the case at hand—we shall have more to say about how this is to be done later. By contrast, he will treat the syllogistic structure of this argument and the truth of its minor premiss as unproblematic. This is what it is to treat an argument as an argument from likelihood, and to evaluate its merits and faults as such.

In the case of an argument from signs, on the other hand, the element on which the argument is seen to hinge will be the new piece of evidence to which the orator wishes to direct his auditors' attention and which counts as evidence against a background of uncontroversial assumptions. If we concentrate for the moment on the relatively simple case of the valid first-figure sign-inference, it is clear that the sign functions as a ground in this way in virtue of what we should call a covering generalization (cf. *An. pr.* 1. 32, 47^{a}16–17). And it is this covering generalization, e.g. that the feverish are ill, formulated in the major premiss, that is typically treated as part of the background of uncontentious assumptions in virtue of which the sign is able to serve as evidence for the conclusion at issue. For this reason, it can and typically will be omitted in the presentation of the sign-inference.

Note that I am not saying that a sign enthymeme must be presented with the major premiss omitted or that it ceases to be a sign enthymeme when this premiss is stated as well. Rather, I mean to be calling attention to the characteristics of arguments from signs and likelihoods that explain why they frequently omit premisses and why they omit the premisses they do. When an orator argues from signs he makes a fuss, as it were, about the sign, the minor premiss of his syllogism, and expects that if his opponent is going to make a fuss, it will be about the same premiss. The major premiss, whether expressed or not, on the other hand, he treats as uncontentious. As Aristotle notes when he considers objections to sign-arguments, an opponent's only hope against a first-figure sign-argument is to show that the premiss serving as a sign is false (*Rhet.* 2. 25, 1403ª13–16). In other words, Aristotle does not envisage someone objecting to the argument that an item is G because it is F that being F is not a sign of being G after all, but only that the item is not F in the first place. Of course, when the second- and third-figure sign-inferences are brought into the picture, their invalidity, which is revealed by their defective syllogistic structure, can be made the basis of an objection (1403ª2–5). Apparently the truth of the major premiss remains outside contention, however.

It seems, then, that whether an enthymeme should count as an argument from signs or likelihoods is not determined solely by facts about its premisses and structure that are independent of the way in which they are regarded by participants in a debate or the audience for an oration. On the contrary, it depends very much on the attitude of the participants. Indeed, it might be better to speak of an orator presenting or treating an argument as an enthymeme from signs or an enthymeme from likelihoods. Nothing prevents an opposing speaker from objecting, for example, that the covering generalization on which his opponent's argument from signs relies is subject to exceptions; but this would be to treat an argument put forward as an argument from signs as an argument from likelihood.

Let us now broaden the scope of our enquiry to include the second- and third-figure sign-inferences. Aristotle counts only arguments with affirmative and, if the subject term of the conclusion is not singular, universal conclusions as from signs, perhaps because of the pre-theoretical characterization of the sign which is his point of departure.[19] In any case, these restrictions ensure that of the three forms of sign-inference—one in each of the figures—only the first-figure sign-inference is valid.[20] Aristotle's offers the following as an example:

---

[19] How well does this reflect the theory or practice of contemporary rhetoric? Cf. [Arist.] *Rhet. ad Alex.* 1430ᵇ34–5, whose author appears to have a different view.

[20] A categorical syllogism in one of the three Aristotelian figures is an argument with two premisses in each of which two terms, a predicate and a subject, are related in one of four ways. These are: a=belongs to all; e=belongs to none; i=belongs to some; o=does not belong to some. For example, AaB means 'A belongs to all B'. Within the three figures, the major term is the predicate of the conclusion and the major premiss the premiss in which it is introduced. The minor term is the subject of the conclusion and the minor premiss the premiss in which it is introduced. The

P_1 All those with fever are ill.
P_2 This man has fever. (the sign)
C Therefore he is ill.

Recall that the mark of the second-figure syllogism is that its middle term is predicated of both the major and minor terms and that it can validly yield only negative conclusions.[21] Aristotle offers the following sign-inference as an example:

P_1 All those with fever breathe roughly.
P_2 This man breathes roughly. (the sign)
C Therefore he has a fever.

In the third figure major and minor terms are predicated of the middle term, and only particular conclusions can be validly inferred,[22] but the third-figure sign-inference invalidly deduces a universal conclusion. One of Aristotle's examples is:

P_1 Pittacus is wise.
P_2 Pittacus is good.
C Therefore the wise are good.

To mark the difference, Aristotle calls the minor premiss of the valid first-figure sign-argument a 'token' ($\tau\epsilon\kappa\mu\dot{\eta}\rho\iota\sigma\nu$).[23] Second- and

middle term occurs in both premisses but not in the conclusion. Thus the first mood in the first figure, *Barbara*, is represented as follows:

$$\frac{AaB \quad BaC}{AaC}$$

AaB is the major premiss, BaC the minor premiss, AaC the conclusion. A is the major term, B the middle, C the minor.

[21] Retaining A for the major term, B for the middle term, and C for the minor term, the first mood of the second figure, *Cesare*, is represented in this way:

$$\frac{BeA \quad BaC}{AeC}$$

[22] The first mood of the third figure, *Darapti*, with major, middle, and minor terms as before:

$$\frac{AaB \quad CaB}{AiC}$$

[23] Aristotle offers an etymological justification for his choice of terms, but Greek usage, including his own, offers little support for the distinction. Cf. L. Radermacher, *Artium Scriptores: Reste der voraristotelischen Rhetorik* (Sitzungsberichte der philosophisch-historischen Klasse der Österreichischen Akad. der Wiss. 227/3;

third-figure signs lack a name of their own (*Rhet.* 1. 2, 1357ᵇ4–5), but when he needs to contrast them with tokens, Aristotle calls them simply signs (ᵇ21–2; 1. 3, 1359ᵃ7–8; 2. 25, 1402ᵇ14).

How great an inferiority does Aristotle mean to attribute to the anonymous signs? The arguments to which they give rise are clearly not syllogisms, but are they enthymemes, legitimate albeit non-conclusive means of persuasion, as I have so far assumed without argument? Or is the status of an enthymeme to be withheld from them and reserved for enthymemes from tokens and likelihoods alone? The evidence regarding this point is conflicting. The latter is suggested by *Rhetoric* 2. 24, where the enthymeme from signs is treated as one of the topoi of merely apparent enthymeme (1401ᵇ9 ff.). The examples given there, though not analysed as categorical syllogisms, correspond to the second- and third-figure signs discussed in *Rhetoric* 1. 2 and *Prior Analytics* 2. 27. 'Lovers benefit their cities because Harmodius and Aristogeiton killed the tyrant Hipparchus', i.e. this pair (*a*) are lovers and (*b*) benefited their city (third figure). 'Dionysius is a thief, for he is wicked', i.e. thieves are wicked and Dionysius is wicked, therefore he is a thief (second figure). But here the fact that they are not valid (are ἀσυλλόγιστον) appears to be made a ground, as it did not seem to be in the *Analytics*-oriented passage, for their exclusion from the ranks of the genuine enthymeme (1401ᵇ9; cf. 1400ᵇ34; cf. also 2. 22, 1397ᵃ4). The same attitude is on display in the *Sophistical Refutations*, where argument from signs is presented as an instance of the fallacy of affirming the consequent and said to be especially common in rhetoric (5, 167ᵇ8–11).

It has been argued on the strength of this evidence that Aristotle meant to withhold the standing of a genuine enthymeme from the second- and third-figure sign-inferences, reserving it for the valid first-figure sign-inference alone.[24] But nothing in the official accounts of the sign in *Rhetoric* 1. 2 or *Prior Analytics* 2. 27 has prepared us for the exclusion of any of the forms of argument they analyse, and Aristotle includes the syllogistically invalid sign in the ranks of the enthymeme along with the token in *Rhetoric* 2. 25

1951), 214–15, the passages collected in which show small differences in the connotation of the two terms, and their use for purposes of elegant variation, rather than a substantive difference in meaning.

[24] Notably by Sprute, *Enthymemtheorie*, 88 ff.

$(1402^{b}13).^{25}$ What is more, in *Prior Analytics* 2. 27, as we have already noted, he maintains that the sign is a premiss that is, or is of a nature to be, necessary or reputable (ἔνδοξος) $(70^{a}6-7).^{26}$ The token is necessary; the remaining signs, it would then seem, must be reputable.

This apparent discrepancy has elicited different reactions. Solmsen made it part of his developmental account of Aristotle's rhetorical theory.[27] But the fact that expressions of a favourable attitude towards signs are confined to the later *Analytics*-oriented sections while an apparently less sympathetic attitude is adopted in the earlier *Topics*-oriented sections does not require that Aristotle changed his mind. There is another way to reconcile the different things Aristotle has to say about signs that is more promising than imputing to him either a consistently hostile or a consistently favourable attitude towards sign-inference. It has been rightly observed that the adversarial character of rhetoric makes it natural for him to mention what can be said against as well as in favour of each variety of argument.[28] All the same, I shall argue that it is not an accident that Aristotle's favourable remarks about signs are found in late *Analytics*-oriented, and his unfavourable remarks in early *Topics*-oriented, sections of the *Rhetoric*, but the result of a change in the direction of greater sympathy towards argument from signs, albeit a change of a rather complicated and elusive kind.

(b) The reputable character of invalid argument from signs

But any account of how Aristotle came to adopt a more favourable attitude towards invalid argument by signs must explain how he could at any time have regarded it as a reputable means of persua-

---

[25] He also does so at 1. 3, $1359^{a}6$. There are good reasons for suspecting this passage, however. Cf. Burnyeat, 'Enthymeme', 35 n. 90.

[26] In line with his view that within the broader class of sign-arguments only those from tokens qualify as enthymemes, Sprute argues that the reference at $70^{a}7$ to the sign as a reputable premiss ought to be deleted as an interpolation (*Enthymemtheorie*, 90 n. 114). The textual grounds for this step are slight; earlier, as Sprute himself notes, in effect the opposite conclusion, that it is the word 'necessary' which has been mistakenly interpolated, was reached by H. Maier, *Die Syllogistik des Aristoteles* (Tübingen: Laupp, 1896–1900), ii/1. 481 with n. 2. For the argument against cf. Burnyeat, 'Enthymeme', 33 with n. 83.

[27] Cf. *Entwicklung*, 22–3.

[28] S. Raphael, 'Rhetoric, Dialectic and Syllogistic Argument: Aristotle's Position in "Rhetoric" I–II', *Phronesis*, 19 (1974), 153–67.

sion. I shall take up this question first, before returning to consider
whether this view was the result of a change.

Although they are not characterized as reputable in the *Rhetoric*,
second- and third-figure signs are, to all appearances, treated as
sources of genuine enthymemes in the *Analytics*-oriented passages
and contrasted with tokens, which are once more distinguished by
their necessary character. Aristotle leaves us in no doubt what this
means. 'I call necessary the signs from which a syllogism arises, and
the token is a sign of this kind' (1357^a5-7). And he goes on to oppose
this necessity to the invalid, or non-syllogistic ($ἀσυλλόγιστον$), character of the second- and third-figure signs (1357^a27-32; $^b5$, 14, 22;
cf. 1403^a11). 'Necessary', then, means capable (when taken together
with an appropriate major premiss) of necessitating the conclusion
to which they are related in the corresponding enthymeme, i.e. the
necessitas consequentiae referred to in the definition of the syllogism.
This means that whether a premiss is to count as a sign or a token
depends not on its intrinsic character, but rather on the relations
obtaining between it, the second premiss, and the conclusion of the
argument constituted by all three. Being pale, for example, could
on different occasions be a (second-figure) sign of pregnancy, ill
health, or being afraid while serving as a token of whichever condition of the blood vessels—if there is just one—it is that makes one
go pale.

Difficulties arise, however, when we turn to the passage that introduces the discussion that we have been examining, where Aristotle contrasts the sign and its necessary character with the likelihood and its for-the-most-part character. This passage is concerned
to explain the distinctive characteristics of rhetorical argument as
consequences of its purpose, the conditions in which it is employed, and its subject-matter—issues on which Aristotle has already touched (cf. 1357^a1 ff.).[29] It marks the beginning of the first
Analytics-oriented insertion, and introduces the discussion of signs
and likelihoods (1357^a22-33):

Since there are few necessities from which rhetorical syllogisms arise [this
is justified by reference to the subject-matter of rhetoric already described]
and it is necessary to argue to conclusions that are for the most part and possible from starting-points of the same kind, and to necessary conclusions
from necessary starting-points (and this is clear to us from the *Analytics*),

[29] If, as it seems, 1357^a22 is the beginning of a later *Analytics*-oriented insertion,
the transition is a nicely managed one.

it is clear that some of the starting-points from which enthymemes are propounded will be necessary and some will be for the most part. But enthymemes are from likelihoods and signs, so that it is necessary for each of them to be the same as each.

The problem is that, while the necessary character of the token that is opposed to the invalidity of the anonymous sign enthymemes characterizes the relation between the premisses and conclusion of the argument, it appears that the for-the-most-part character of the likelihood belongs to a proposition in its own right, namely the proposition that serves as the major premiss of an enthymeme from likelihood. How, then, are we to understand the necessity of the token as it figures in both these contrasts?

In the *Prior Analytics* Aristotle maintains that syllogisms establishing *necessitas consequentis*, the unqualified or absolute necessity of the conclusion, must proceed from premisses which are also necessary in the same way (1. 8, 29^b29 ff.). Elsewhere he seems to commit himself to an analogue of the same principle applying to syllogisms with premisses qualified as for the most part true (*An. post.* 1. 30, 87^b22 ff.; cf. 2. 12, 96^a8-19, *An. pr.* 1. 27, 43^b33). The undeniably striking verbal similarities have led some to conclude that Aristotle is bringing together these two points here in the *Rhetoric*.[30] But as we have just seen, this is not how the necessity of the token is explained in the immediately following passage. And even if an occasional major premiss of a first-figure sign-syllogism were an apodeictic necessity, apart from leaving others which are not out of account, this is perfectly irrelevant to the use to which such a premiss is put in rhetorical argument, and no purpose would be served by calling attention to this fact here.

The solution, I believe, is to see that, at least in the limited case of the enthymeme from likelihood, where a for-the-most-part generalization is applied to a particular instance, Aristotle seems to have supposed that the effect of the for-the-most-part major premiss is to give rise to a for-the-most-part relation of consequence. The idea would have been that most of the enthymemes formed by applying a true for-the-most-part generalization to the individuals falling under its middle term will yield a true conclusion. Suppose, for example, that Bs are for the most part A. A will then belong to most of the individuals to which B belongs. Let $C_1 \ldots C_n$ be

---

[30] Cf. Sprute, *Enthymemtheorie*, 91–2 with n. 123, for references to proponents of this view and criticism.

the individuals that make up B.[31] Applied to each of $C_1 \ldots C_n$, the argument schema 'Bs are for the most part A, C_x is B, therefore C_x is A' will yield an argument with a true conclusion more often than not. If the premises represent the best state of our knowledge, then a particular instance of this argument form will furnish us with a reputable ground for taking its conclusion to be true.

What is more, the way for this conception of the enthymeme from likelihoods seems to have been prepared by the account of the enthymeme we find a few pages earlier in the *Rhetoric*, before the first *Analytics*-oriented passage (1356^b15-17):

> . . . when, certain things being [so], something different comes about besides them by their being [so], either universally or for the most part, this is called a syllogism there [i.e. in the *Topics* and in dialectic] and an enthymeme here [i.e. in rhetoric and the *Rhetoric*].[32]

Though this is not the only way of construing Aristotle's loosely formulated Greek, the most conspicuous departure from the definition of the syllogism in the *Topics* and *Prior Analytics* appears to be the replacement of the requirement that the conclusion follow of necessity by the requirement that it follow universally or for the most part, that is, it seems that 'universally or for the most part' is best understood here as a qualification applying to the relation between premises and conclusion rather than to either the premises or the conclusion.[33] Aristotle's point would then be that an argument can fail to be a syllogism but still qualify as an enthymeme, though its conclusion would still somehow have to follow for the most part. Understood in this way, the account of the enthymeme in this *Topics*-oriented and presumably earlier section of the *Rhetoric* prefigures and handily accommodates the enthymeme from likelihoods introduced in the later *Analytics*-oriented section, where it is conceived along the lines I have just suggested.

---

[31] Or a suitable finite initial sequence of the members of B, if B has infinitely many members.

[32] τὸ δὲ τινῶν ἔτερον τι [διὰ ταῦτα] συμβαίνειν παρὰ ταῦτα τῷ ταῦτα εἶναι ἢ καθόλου ἢ ὡς ἐπὶ τὸ πολύ. I follow Kassel in viewing διὰ ταῦτα as an interpolated gloss and have left it untranslated.

[33] So M. Wörner, *Das Ethische in der Rhetorik des Aristoteles* (Munich: Karl Alber, 1990), 352–3, and J. Barnes, 'Rhetoric and Poetics', in id. (ed.), *The Cambridge Companion to Aristotle* (Cambridge: Cambridge University Press, 1995), 295–85 at 271. A fuller discussion of the interpretative possibilities and the controversy concerning this passage can be found in Burnyeat, 'Enthymeme', 19–20 with n. 49, who also inclines to this view.

To be sure, this is not how Aristotle conceives syllogisms from for-the-most-part premisses outside the *Rhetoric*. As we noted above, he prefers to treat them along the same lines as demonstrative syllogisms from apodeictic premisses, i.e. as deductively valid syllogisms that necessitate their conclusions, which are, in addition, qualified by something like a modal operator transmitted to them from the premisses. But there are special features of the enthymeme and the rhetorical conditions in which it is used that may have recommended a different approach. Unlike the syllogisms with which Aristotle is concerned in the *Analytics*, an enthymeme from likelihood typically applies the for-the-most-part generalization expressed in its major premiss to a singular minor term and therefore draws a conclusion about a particular. This of course reflects rhetoric's concern with issues requiring decisions about particulars, e.g. whether this man is guilty of this crime, or this policy or plan of action should be put into effect, and the like. And it means that the conclusion of such an enthymeme cannot be qualified as for the most part, but as likely.

There is also a notorious problem with the view of syllogisms from for-the-most-part premisses that Aristotle appears to favour elsewhere, whether the character they transmit to their conclusions is belonging for the most part, as in the premisses, or being likely. Although the conclusion of a demonstrative syllogism with necessary premisses or, sometimes, a single necessary premiss will be necessary as well, the conclusions of an argument with the same syllogistic form from likelihoods will not be unqualifiedly likely in an analogous way. A conclusion validly deduced from true premisses according to the principle in question can be contradicted by a conclusion deduced from premisses no less true by arguments the principle is bound to regard as no less valid.[34] For the minor term can be the subject of different middle terms to which mutually exclusive characteristics belong for the most part. One may, for example, belong to a nation most of whose citizens are religious believers and to a profession most of whose members are unbelievers. But it cannot be likely without qualification both that one is a religious believer and that one is not.[35]

---

[34] For a discussion of this well-known problem in an Aristotelian context cf. Burnyeat, 'Enthymeme', 25–6.

[35] Now it must be conceded that these difficulties are less acute in the context of the *Posterior Analytics*. If the for-the-most-part premisses admitted there satisfy

Whatever other difficulties it may present, the solution that I have
suggested Aristotle does adopt in his account of the enthymeme
from likelihoods avoids, within its limited sphere, the problems
that confront the alternative account. At the same time, it explains
how such an argument can furnish reputable grounds for taking its
conclusion to be true. Of course it does not tell us how to judge
between the conflicting claims of enthymemes from likelihood to
opposed conclusions in the actual practice of rhetorical argumentation. It may, however, be a point in its favour that it does not treat
this as a problem to be solved by a theory of argument in advance of
the particular circumstances of an argument and the relations that
arise between the different likelihoods brought to bear in them.
This is a point to which we shall return.

For the present, we may also note that this account of enthymematic argument from likelihoods shows how it was possible for Aristotle to contrast the necessary character of the token with both the
argument from likelihoods and sign-arguments in the second and
third figures because a relation between premisses and conclusion
is ultimately at issue in both comparisons. The necessity of the
first-figure sign-inference, the enthymeme from tokens, is the necessity with which the conclusion follows the premisses of a valid
syllogism. The enthymeme from likelihoods, on the other hand,
can be viewed here as a curious hybrid: an argument in which the
relation between the premisses and the conclusion is affected by the
character of the premisses.

But the answer to the question how enthymemes from likelihood
can be reputable that is suggested by 1357^a22-33 makes it that
much harder to understand Aristotle's grounds for including the
anonymous signs in the ranks of the genuine enthymeme. The passage appears to conclude by equating the for-the-most-part with

other conditions imposed on demonstrative premisses, they will predicate attributes
per se of their subjects. In other words, they will state facts about the nature of their
subjects by attributing essential characteristics to them. If it belongs to the nature of
B to be A, even though A belongs to B in actual fact only for the most part, then A
may fail to belong to some individuals to which B belongs—let us designate them the
Cs. Tempting as it may be to think that the failure of A to belong to the Cs must be
due to a more specific nature of theirs which prevents them from being A, this is not
how Aristotle thinks of exceptions to this kind of for-the-most-part generalization;
indeed, the term C that I have contrived will have no standing in an Aristotelian
demonstration. But this solution is not available in rhetoric, where arguments, and
the descriptions under which items are considered, will rarely satisfy the conditions
that Aristotle imposes on demonstrative reasoning.

the likelihood and the necessary with the sign. Aristotle maintains that 'each is the same as each'. But even if this can be understood loosely enough to avoid an outright inconsistency, there is a deeper problem.[36] For in the train of thought that leads Aristotle to this conclusion, he appeals, as we have seen, to the fact that rhetoric is concerned with matters that permit of being otherwise to explain and justify the predominance of for-the-most-part arguments in rhetoric in a way which leaves the impression that the corresponding distinction he then draws between likelihoods and (necessary) signs exhausts the forms of legitimate rhetorical argument. It is hard to see where the invalid second- and third-figure signs are supposed to fit. So we are brought back to our original question about the source of the second- and third-figure signs' reputable character, which can be neither the necessity of the token nor the for-the-most-part character of the likelihood.

To this question Aristotle gives no direct answer, either here or elsewhere, and the rhetorical tradition, on which he exerted a significant influence, betrays some confusion on this point as well.[37]

---

[36] Cf. Burnyeat, 'Enthymeme', 37, who compares the present passage with 1356^b10, where 'each is the same as each', said of the enthymeme and the syllogism on the one hand and the paradigm and the induction on the other, is not a statement of identity.

[37] Distinctions between signs and tokens obviously indebted to Aristotle's are widespread. In a manner reminiscent of Aristotle, Quintilian calls tokens necessary and irrefutable signs (5. 9. 3), but he is also willing to call likelihoods non-necessary signs (5. 9. 8). This tendency to conflate signs and likelihoods is carried still further in a later rhetorical treatise, the anonymous Segueranius, whose author, reporting the views of the rhetorician Neocles (1st or 2nd cent. AD), contrasts tokens with signs, but takes the token to be an irrefutable likelihood and remarks that 'sign' is an expression typically used in place of 'likelihood', which he has earlier defined with reference to the for-the-most-part (*Rhet. Graec.* i. 379. 12–17 Spengel–Hammer). Eventually a distinction between tokens and signs based on a contrast between a relation between sign and signified which holds always and one which holds only for the most part or less often is attributed to Aristotle (*Rhet. Graec.* v. 407–8 Walz). How widespread this conception of Aristotle's views is hard to say (the text is a scholium of Planudes on Hermogenes' *Inventio*). But in a passage to which we shall turn again in Study III, Galen distinguishes two ways of contrasting signs with tokens, with the usage of rhetoricians in view (*In Hipp. prog.*, CMG v/9/2. 373. 1–14). The first, and to his way of thinking more correct, holds that tokens are necessary and always followed by that for which they are evidence, while signs are followed by that for which they are evidence only for the most part. It seems clear from the vocabulary Galen uses that he has an Aristotelian logic in mind. For he takes the necessity of the token to consist in the fact that one of the terms of which the premiss (πρότασις) is composed follows the other always, whereas in the case of the sign it follows only for the most part, presumably with the major premiss of a syllogism in Barbara in view. Elsewhere Galen describes the token as a syllogistic

Aristotle's silence on this point can and has been taken as evidence that he did not after all intend to count invalid sign-inferences as reputable enthymemes.[38] Those of us who believe that he did will see this as evidence of the lateness and incompleteness of his *Analytics*-based reflections on rhetorical argument. We can only speculate about the legitimate uses Aristotle may have envisaged for the invalid second- and third-figure sign-syllogisms; that they can be put to illegitimate use is clear enough. To conclude that a man is an adulterer on the basis of his taste for late-night walks would be reckless and unfair (cf. *SE* 5, 167^{b}8). But suppose that there are other signs of this kind, i.e. that this person has other features belonging to adulterers, e.g. a new interest in his personal appearance (cf. 167^{b}10–11; *Rhet.* 2. 24, 1401^{b}24): he will then belong to many such classes. The accumulation of signs, none of which is of much weight by itself, may in the end constitute a powerful though, as we should say, circumstantial case, and there is evidence that the rhetorical tradition took signs to be valuable in just this way (cf. [Cicero,] *Rhet. ad Heren.* 2. 11; Cicero, *Part. orat.* 39–40; Quintilian 5. 9. 9–10).[39]

Aristotle says nothing as explicit himself, but the resources of the categorical syllogistic, though not necessary, would have allowed him to explain how, by collecting signs in this way, an orator can make his case a stronger one in something like the following way. The fault of the second-figure sign is, in terms drawn from the categorical syllogistic, that its major premiss does not convert. The

---

sign, but says too little to make clear precisely how he intends the contrast between tokens and signs (*In Hipp. de acut. morb. vict.*, CMG v/9/1. 118. 1). The absence of any clear indications how signs might have made their conclusions reputable seems, then, to have made it all too easy to assimilate sign-arguments to for-the-most-part-arguments. Other references to a distinction between signs and tokens are collected by L. Spengel (ed.), *Aristotelis ars rhetorica* (Leipzig: Teubner, 1847), ii. 63 ff.

[38] Sprute, *Enthymemtheorie*, 99 with n. 166, cites 1357^{a}22–33 in support of his exclusion of the second- and third-figure sign-syllogisms from the ranks of the genuine enthymeme.

[39] Aristotle appears to say something similar himself when he notes that someone's accidentally and unintentionally beneficial acts can be cited in support of the conclusion that he has a good character: 'for when many similar actions of this kind are put forward in argument, it *seems* to be a sign of virtue and worthy purpose' (1. 9, 1367^{b}24–6). But since Aristotle is clearly thinking of a situation in which an orator cites acts which, to be sure, could have been the outcome of a virtuous person's good intentions, but were, as the orator well knows, unintentional, this passage does not tell us how he might have regarded an argument from an accumulation of signs that are not known to be immaterial in this way.

fact that the middle term, e.g. night-wandering, which belongs to the major term, adulterers, belongs to the accused party as well is taken as a ground for the conclusion that the accused is an adulterer, when that conclusion would follow of necessity only if the major term converts with the middle, so that the major term, adulterer, belongs to the whole of the middle term, night wanderer, making possible a valid first-figure syllogism in Barbara. But the effect of accumulating signs, of discovering that more and more of the terms that are predicated of the major term belong to the minor term as well, is to come closer and closer to a conjunctive middle term that is convertible with the major term, belonging not only to all but also to only the items to which the major term belongs. What is more, at some point in this progress the major term, though not convertible *in toto* with the conjunctive middle term formed in this way, will belong to it for the most part; that is, it will be a rare item that is subject to all these terms but not to the major.

Why, then, treat the second-figure signs separately rather than under the head of likelihoods and tokens? This would be to ignore the distinctive characteristics of *rhetorical* and kindred forms of argument which it is Aristotle's aim to capture. Typically neither the orator who aims to strengthen his case in this way nor his auditors will be in a position to determine the point at which the terms convert, so that he can predicate his major term always or for the most part of the conjunctive middle term to which his argument points. The analysis of second-figure signs just proposed shows how the successive presentation of such signs can make a case gradually stronger. And we should remember that sign-arguments will typically be put forward in the context of other arguments, which they may strengthen and be strengthened by in ways that are hard to specify.

How the third-figure sign can be the source of reputable argument is in some ways the hardest question of all. The premisses establish, if true, only that at least one item to which the minor term belongs is subject to the major term as well. If Socrates is wise and good, then we can safely say only that some of the wise are good. But the conclusion in support of which the sign is cited is that (all) the wise are good. Because neither Aristotle nor, so far as I am able to tell, the later rhetorical tradition says anything directly about the matter, any view about how third-figure signs give rise to reputable rhetorical argument must be still more speculative than the account of second-figure signs that has already been proposed. The clue that has the best chance of yielding results, I suggest, is afforded by the apparently inductive character of third-figure signs. We may be in a better position to see how Aristotle might have understood them if we can first see whether they had a part of their own to play in rhetorical argument different from that of the paradigm, the official counterpart of the induction in rhetoric. A closer look at Aristotle's account of argument by paradigm will also serve our broader aim of discovering how methods of argument that have their origin in dialectic were adapted to satisfy the requirements for reputable argument in rhetoric.

(c) *Comparison with induction*

Though so-called complete or perfect induction analysed by Aristotle in *Prior Analytics* 2. 23 is not representative of the arguments he elsewhere treats as instances of induction (ἐπαγωγή), the distinctive features of paradigms can be grasped most readily if we begin by contrasting them with complete induction as Aristotle himself does.[40] The aim of such an induction, according to *Prior Analytics* 2. 23, is to establish that a major term A holds of a middle term B by showing that it belongs to the minor terms $C_1 \ldots C_n$ which exhaust B, i.e. are, taken *in toto*, convertible with B. To forestall misunderstanding, it should be noted that Aristotle clearly does not envisage taking each of the potentially infinite individual particulars falling under B into account; rather, the Cs are the finite set of the species of B.

Paradigms, which are discussed in the next chapter, *Prior Analytics* 2. 24, do not at first seem very much like inductions, for while the characteristic direction of induction is from the particular or the more particular to the general, argument by paradigm is from particular to particular (cf. *Top.* 1. 12, 105ᵃ13–14; *An. post.* 1. 1, 71ᵃ8–9; *An. pr.* 1. 24, 69ᵃ14–15; *Rhet.* 1. 2, 1357ᵇ28). But Aristotle is able to treat paradigm as a form of induction because it combines two steps, the first of which is inductive in character.[41] The aim of an argument from paradigms is to show that a major term belongs to a particular through a middle term. In the example cited in the *Prior*

[40] Ross, *Analytics*, 47–8; K. von Fritz, *Die ἐπαγωγή bei Aristoteles* (Sitzungsberichte der bayerischen Akademie der Wissenchaften, phil.-hist. Klasse, 3; 1964); Lloyd, *Polarity and Analogy*, 405–8.

[41] Cf. Ross, *Analytics*, 488; Sprute, *Enthymemtheorie*, 83.

Analytics the conclusion to be proved is that a war between Athens and Thebes would be evil (69ᵃ1 ff.). This is to be accomplished through the middle term 'war against neighbours'; that is, it is supposed to be shown that a war between Athens and Thebes would be evil because it would be a war against neighbours (minor premiss), and wars against neighbours are evil (major premiss). The inductive step is to cite one or more examples in support of the major premiss that war against neighbours is evil—for example, as Aristotle suggests, that the war between Thebes and Phocis was evil. The result is an argument from a particular example (or examples) to a particular conclusion via a general principle exemplified by the first and applied to the second.

Viewed exclusively from the perspective of syllogistic validity, arguments from paradigm are of negligible value. The power of such arguments to make their conclusions probable will depend on more than can be captured by Aristotle's syllogistic analysis. He emphasizes this point himself by distinguishing between the taking or grasping ($\lambda \alpha \mu \beta \acute{\alpha} \nu \epsilon \iota \nu$) of the general principle expressed by the major premiss and the syllogizing or deducing of the conclusion in which it is applied to the particular instance in question (*Rhet*. 2. 25, 1402ᵇ17–18; *An. pr*. 2. 24, 69ᵃ15–16). But a well-chosen example, familiar to the audience, may help it to grasp more firmly and clearly a general principle of which it already has an inkling, and in this way to apply it more easily to the case at issue (*Rhet*. 1. 2, 1357ᵇ29; *An. pr*. 2. 24, 69ᵃ16). Note that past facts of the kind mentioned in the above example are only one species of paradigm. An orator may also manufacture examples for himself in the form of parables or fables (cf. *Rhet*. 2. 20, 1393ᵃ27 ff.). An example may, then, enable an audience to draw a true conclusion for good reasons, even though it is a wholly inadequate ground for that conclusion when viewed apart from the broader understanding that it is intended to assist.

This conclusion receives further support from the account of the refutation of arguments by paradigm that Aristotle offers in the *Analytics*-oriented section of *Rhetoric* 2. 25. There he tells us that the refutation of arguments from paradigm is the same as that of arguments from likelihood (1403ᵃ5). Unfortunately, the details of the comparison are obscured by a textual difficulty. We shall have to return to this problem later. For the moment, however, two things should be clear. The general principle exemplified by an example or examples and applied to a further particular instance claims nothing more for itself than the for-the-most-part character enjoyed by the likelihood, in this way reflecting the nature of the issues about which orators must argue that Aristotle has been at pains to accommodate in his account of the enthymeme (cf. *Rhet.* 1. 2, $1357^a13, {}^b26$). And, although a full defence will have to await a closer examination of the text, the comparison between the refutation of arguments from likelihood and that of arguments by paradigm shows that Aristotle does not envisage a special form of objection to arguments of the latter kind simply on the ground of its inductive weakness.

A paradigm that succeeds in being treated as such establishes a presumption in favour of the principle it illustrates. It is not to be dismissed because it rests on a tiny handful of instances, perhaps only one. The potential point of contention is not the first step from the paradigm to the principle it exemplifies; as we shall see, the burden is on the opponent to discover more evidence to the contrary or to find a special feature of the case in question that recommends treating it as an exception to the rule, just as in the case of a presumed likelihood. On the other hand, it is precisely the step from particular to universal that is potentially contentious in third-figure sign-argument. It is, of course, invalid, and its invalidity is a legitimate ground for objection (1403^a2-5). If the third-figure sign has a place of its own, it may be where this step needs more emphasis, whether because it is more contentious or because the general principle rather than its application is the focus of attention. In circumstances of these kinds, the orator must appeal to 'signs' rather than 'paradigms'.

4. The Developmental Perspective

Let us now return to the question we put aside earlier, viz. whether the receptive attitude towards non-conclusive argument by signs that is attested in the *Prior Analytics* and late *Analytics*-oriented sections of the *Rhetoric* represents a change from an earlier less receptive attitude and, if so, what that earlier attitude was and how Aristotle came to alter it. Such a change, if it did take place, is made harder to track by a number of factors. First of all, it did not occur against the background of a framework that it-self remained constant, as it would have if Aristotle had decided, say, that the topos of signs belongs among the topoi of the genuine enthymeme instead of, or perhaps as well as, among those of the apparent enthymeme. There are no topoi in the categorical syllogistic or the *Analytics*-inspired treatment of rhetorical argument. What became of the topoi after the introduction of the categorical syllogistic is a question shrouded in mystery, very probably because Aristotle never worked through the issue himself.[42]

What is more, whatever Aristotle may have intended by including a topos of signs among the topoi of the apparent enthymeme, he can never have meant to dismiss all the arguments that turn out to belong to the extension of the concept 'sign' as that concept is specified in the *Prior Analytics* and the *Analytics*-inspired passages of the *Rhetoric*. Some of the topoi of the genuine enthymeme in *Rhetoric* 2. 23 give rise to arguments that appear to belong to this extension.[43] An especially clear instance is furnished by the topos that recommends maintaining that the reason for which something might be done is the reason why it has been done (2. 23, 1399^{b}19–30). Thus, in the *Ajax* of Theodectes, Aristotle observes, it is argued that Diomedes chose Odysseus to accompany him not in order to honour him, but rather to shine by comparison with an inferior companion (cf. *Iliad* 10. 218–54). The reasoning depends on an invalid second-figure syllogism: inferior persons likely to make others shine by comparison are chosen; Odysseus was chosen by Diomedes; therefore he is an inferior person.[44]

To be sure, one could perhaps argue that Aristotle did not see this, or that these arguments had other features that made them superior to 'mere' signs in his view. But this will not take us very far, as Aristotle cannot *ever* have meant to reject as valueless everything that he was willing to designate explicitly as an argument from signs. This is shown not only by the appeals to signs—many of which are clearly not meant to be valid arguments—that Aristotle makes everywhere in his work, but also by the presence of such appeals in *Topics*-oriented sections of the *Rhetoric* itself, where

[42] Cf. Solmsen, *Entwicklung*, 26, 61–6. Such evidence as we have suggests that, after the elaboration of the categorical syllogistic, Aristotle and his successors viewed arguments formed in accordance with the topoi as syllogisms on the basis of a hypothesis.

[43] I am grateful to John Cooper for this point and the following example.

[44] Notice its resemblance to the argument from symptoms, where Aristotle does speak of signs, discussed in n. 39 above (1. 9, 1367^{b}24–6).

considerations designated as signs are put forward by Aristotle in support of various of his own views about the rhetorical art instead of being studied as one of its products (1. 3, 1358^{b}29; 2. 3, 1380^{a}15; 3. 2, 1404^{b}33).[45] Of course, it is one thing to use such arguments and another thing to accommodate them in a theory that explains how deductively invalid arguments can furnish reputable albeit inconclusive grounds for a conclusion. There seems, then, to be a tension between some of Aristotle's practices of argument, including practices of theoretical enquiry, and the attitude towards non-deductive argument by signs evinced by a theory of argument that attends to them only in connection with a topos of merely apparent enthymemes.

(a) Dialectic: the topoi

It remains, then, to consider whether a better understanding of the nature of the topoi, and the system they compose, has any light to throw on the problem. As has often been remarked, though Aristotle refers to and expounds an enormous number of topoi in the *Topics*, *Sophistical Refutations*, and *Rhetoric*, apart from a brief *obiter dictum* in the last of these, he has nothing to say about what a topos is. And what he says there, viz. that he calls a topos that into which many enthymemes fall, does not take us very far (2. 26, 1403^{a}18–19). Commentators have naturally turned for illumination to the *Topics*, which, true to its name, consists in large part of catalogues of topoi organized under the heads of the so-called predicables—accident, genus, property, and definition—the four ways in which a predicate can belong to a subject distinguished by Aristotle.[46]

The topoi we find in the *Topics* are, broadly speaking, heuristic devices by means of which a dialectician is able to find premises for

[45] A survey of the use of the term in the *Rhetoric* does not tell us very much. It is used most frequently in the discussion of the emotions, where Aristotle explains in response to what kinds of objects each of the emotions arises and often notes that we react with this emotion not only to these objects but also to signs of them. So, for example, we react with anger when we are slighted but also to signs of being slighted (2. 2, 1379^{b}16–19, 36; cf. 1381^{a}7, 1382^{a}30, 1383^{b}31–4, 1385^{b}7, 1386^{b}2). The closest we come to rhetorical argument by sign is, as already noted, in 1. 9, where Aristotle frequently mentions signs of character, thus implicitly referring to arguments in which orators invite audiences to infer conclusions about character from signs (cf. n. 39 above).

[46] Cf. J. Brunschwig, 'Sur le système des "prédicables" dans les Topiques d'Aristote', in *Energeia: Études aristotéliciennes offertes à Mgr. Antonio Jannone* (Paris: Vrin, 1986), 145–57.

an argument to the conclusion he is charged to advocate.[47] Another feature, belonging to most though not all of them, has attracted the most attention. These topoi are organized around something like a law of which relations of implication between the proposition in contention and other propositions are instances. In other words, they contain something like an argument formula or schema, and serve the dialectician by directing his attention to arguments that instantiate it. Setting out from the desired conclusion, the dialectician is able to discover the corresponding premiss that together with that conclusion instantiates the law. Thus if the question concerns whether a term A is predicated of a term B, propositions to which attention is directed in this way either imply that A belongs to B, so that they can be used to infer it, or are implied by it, so that their contradictories can be used to refute it, or are equivalent to it, so that they can be used either to refute or establish it. For example, to simplify somewhat, one topos recommends that we consider whether the opposite of A, namely C, is predicated of the opposite of B, namely D; if C belongs to D, infer that A belongs to B; if it does not, infer that A does not belong to B.[48] In order to illustrate the notion of a topos when it is introduced in the *Rhetoric*, Aristotle offers the topos of the more and the less. According to it, we are entitled to infer that the more likely of a pair of appropriately related propositions obtains if the less likely does or that the less likely does not obtain if the more likely does not (1. 2, 1358^a14 ff.). Thus, if a man beats his father, he should have no trouble beating his neighbours, while if the gods do not know everything, human beings certainly will not (cf. 2. 23, 1397^b12 ff.).

But to contain such a formula or schema is not part of what it is to be a topos—at least at the outset. To be sure, much of the *Topics* and *Sophistical Refutations* could reasonably be viewed as evidence that Aristotle was moving in the direction of a more regimented conception that would restrict the topoi to devices with the broadly formal character in question. Elsewhere, however, he speaks of topoi not only in relation to argument, but also in connection with the other two methods of persuasion studied by the

---

[47] Cf. Brunschwig (ed.), *Topiques*, p. xxxix.

[48] Cf. *Top.* 3. 6, 119^a38 ff., simplified along lines suggested by Theophrastus or Alexander; cf. A. Graeser (ed.), *Die logischen Fragmente des Theophrast* (De Gruyter: Berlin, 1973), fr. 39. Note that though topoi of this kind lend themselves to formulation with variable letters in this way, Aristotle did not do this before the *Prior Analytics*.

art of rhetoric, the presentation of the speaker's character and the
stirring of an audience's emotions (*Rhet.* 2. 22, 1396^{b}33–1397^{a}1;
3. 19, 1419^{b}27).[49] What all these items have in common, and what
does seem to belong to the original essence of a topos, is that each
is a way of handling a problem or, if you will, an angle of approach
to a task. Roughly speaking, a topos is something reflection upon
which can put an orator or a dialectician in mind of a measure that
will contribute to his end.[50] And as we shall see, not even all the
topoi of argument do this in a way corresponding to the standard
account.

It is these items which, when properly organized, make up or
constitute an art. And the basic idea of a component of an artistic
method or system is behind the surprisingly large number of expressions that Aristotle uses. Each of them succeeds in referring to
such components—and perhaps acquires a corresponding sense—
by focusing on a different aspect of theirs. A closer look at the
terminology and how Aristotle uses it will throw light on the nature of an Aristotelian topos and allow us to pose a question about
the relation between the topoi and the arguments whose topoi they
are that is important for our enquiry.

The idea behind the use of 'topos' at issue seems to be that of
a place whence an orator takes the idea for an argument, emotional appeal, or the like.[51] Aristotle's use of τρόπος for ways of
arguing requires no special explanation (cf. e.g. *SE* 4, 165^{b}23,
166^{a}23, 169^{a}18, 172^{b}5). It is a little more surprising to find στοιχεῖον
(element) used interchangeably with τόπος in the *Topics* and *Sophistical Refutations* and given by Aristotle as an alternative for τόπος in
the passage of the *Rhetoric* where he offers a brief explanation for
the notion of a topos (2. 26, 1403^{a}18–19; cf. 2. 22, 1396^{b}22).[52] We
are more accustomed to the meaning 'fundamental constituent, not
further divisible into more elementary constituents', the meaning

---

[49] Cf. Sprute, *Enthymemtheorie*, 168.

[50] Cf. ibid. 170–1.

[51] On the basis of *Top.* 8. 14, 163^{b}29, Solmsen suggested that this technical sense
was taken over from the art of memory (*Entwicklung*, 171 ff.). Cf. P. Slomkowski,
Aristotle's Topics (Leiden: Brill, 1997), 47 n. 22, who accepts Solmsen's proposal
but not the details of his interpretation of the passage. Evidence of this usage at the
right time is thin on the ground, and it may have originated within the discipline
of rhetoric itself. Cf. Sprute, *Enthymemtheorie*, 147–50, who cites Demosthenes 25.
76 (150).

[52] On this use of στοιχεῖον cf. Waitz, *Aristotelis Organon*, ii. 362.

exemplified by the letters of the alphabet and discussed by Aristotle in *Metaphysics Δ* (1014ᵃ26 ff.). But this is a derived meaning.[53]

The basic meaning of the verb στοιχέω is to put in a row or column. This idea is already brought into connection with the order into which the procedures of an art must be put in the *Prometheus Vinctus*, where Prometheus declares that he has ordered (ἐστοίχισα) the techniques (τρόποι) of divination, one of the arts he has bestowed on suffering humanity (484).[54] W. Burkert found traces of an early use of στοιχεῖον in pre-Euclidean geometry meaning something like presupposition or point of departure of use in a proof, without any reference to its simplicity or elemental character, and he argued that only later was it restricted to genuinely elementary propositions, presuppositions *par excellence*, the meaning familiar to us.[55] On his view, the row or column in question was the logical sequence of propositions in a proof; the στοιχεῖον completes the row, making of it a proof.[56] Whether our use of στοιχεῖον originated in this way in geometry and spread from there or was more broadly dispersed from the start is less important for our purposes than the kind of explanation for its meaning suggested by its early history. When, in the discussion of contentious argument in the *Sophistical Refutations*, Aristotle speaks of the elements of anger—the anger which makes one's opponent less effective in argument—he means ideas or devices for making people angry rather than fundamental constituents of anger (174ᵃ21). So too the elements of making one's arguments lengthy with a view to confusing an opponent, the elements of making one's opponent say paradoxical things, and the elements of enthymemes mentioned in the *Rhetoric* (*SE* 12, 172ᵇ31; 15, 174ᵃ18; *Rhet.* 2. 22, 1396ᵇ21–2).

Even more surprising than this use of στοιχεῖον, however, is the use of εἶδος in a few passages of the *Rhetoric* to mean a kind of point of departure for the discovery of enthymemes (1. 2, 1358ᵃ27, 31–3; 1400ᵇ15; 1403ᵇ13–15). Readers of Aristotle are more familiar with the sense of 'form' or 'species' or, more broadly 'kind', in which last sense it is also found in the *Rhetoric*, sometimes in uncomfortably close proximity to the novel sense at issue. There are, however, parallels in Isocrates—mostly using the synonym ἰδέα—that make it

[53] Cf. W. Burkert, 'Στοιχεῖον: Eine semasiologische Studie', *Philologus*, 103 (1959), 167–97. [54] Cf. ibid. 184.
[55] Cf. ibid. 189 ff. [56] Cf. ibid. 192 ff., 194 ff.

possible to see how the term was able to acquire this sense.[57] As we know, the term εἶδος seems first to have meant external form or visible characteristic, then feature or characteristic of the kind that is shared by many individuals. This was the point of departure for the developments that can be observed in Plato and also those reflected in Isocrates. In the usage of the latter, εἴδη are, in the first instance, features or characteristics of speeches or their parts—parts not only in the sense of sections, but also in the sense of style, argumentation, and the like. Such features can be at any level of generality. They can, for example, be kinds of speech: accusation, defence, recommendation of clients, and so on.[58] At a lower level they can be different varieties of argumentation, e.g. use of witnesses, use of enthymemes, and so on, or different manners or styles to which the orator turns again and again in the composition of speeches.[59] At a still lower level they can be particular stylistic devices or particular turns or devices of argument, which, following Aristotle, we should call topoi.[60]

The crucial step is to regard these features as objects of the rhetorical art, studied by it, imparted to its students, and consulted by its practitioners in the production of speeches. This can be observed in a number of passages where Isocrates reflects on the art

[57] Cf. H. Wersdörfer, *Die φιλοσοφία des Isokrates im Spiegel ihrer Terminologie: Untersuchungen zur frühattischen Rhetorik und Stillehre* (Kl.-Philol. Stud. 13; Leipzig, 1940), 43–54, 85–7, to whom I owe the following account. Although he prefers ἰδέα, Isocrates does sometimes use εἶδος, e.g., 13. 16 (cf. Wersdörfer, *Isokrates*, 87). Kantelhardt, *De Aristotelis rhetoricis*, 15–20, usefully collects a large number of passages from Aristotle and others which appear to exhibit affinities of one kind or another with the use in question, but without explaining how these different uses might be related.   [58] Cf. Wersdörfer, *Isokrates*, 44.

[59] In Isocrates 'enthymeme' does not yet have the technical sense of rhetorical syllogism that Aristotle will give it. Isocrates uses it, like διάνοια, to contrast the thought or content of a speech with its style, expression, or wording. Cf. Burnyeat, 'Enthymeme', 10–12, who suggests that 'consideration' best captures the meaning of the term in Isocrates and other pre-Aristotelian authors. Wersdörfer, *Isokrates*, 110, also identifies a sense of the word that comes into effect when the choice of artistic means in the production of speeches is at issue, viz. thoughts given a rhetorically effective turn ('rhetorisch wirksam zugespitzte Gedanken'). It is in this sense that the enthymeme qualifies as one of the ἰδέαι.

[60] Cf. Wersdörfer, *Isokrates*, 49–50. There are a few uses of ἰδέα and εἶδος in the *Poetics* that may betray an affinity with some of the senses identified by Wersdörfer. Thus in chapter 19, after directing his reader's attention to the *Rhetoric* for matters relating to thought (διάνοια), Aristotle remarks that it is necessary to work from the same ἰδέαι (sc. as in the *Rhetoric*) in order to argue, to inspire emotions, and the like (1456[b]2 ff., cf. 1450[b]34). These appear to be topoi, in the broadest least regimented sense. Cf. J. Vahlen, *Beiträge zu Aristoteles' Poetik* (Leipzig: Teubner, 1914), 280–1.

he promises to impart to his students: it consists of ἰδέαι from or by means of which speeches are composed and from which the orator must select with a view to his goal (10. 11; 13. 16; 15. 183; *Ep.* 6. 8). In these passages we come very close to Aristotle's use of εἶδος to mean something like point of departure for the discovery of enthymemes.[61] All that is required to explain the difference in emphasis in Aristotle is the central importance he assigns to argument in rhetoric.

There is one peculiarity in Aristotle's use of the term in the *Rhetoric*, however. In one early programmatic passage he reserves the term τόπος for points of departure for the discovery of arguments—as I have dubbed them—that are common, in the sense that they are not confined to any one discipline, but are able to give rise to arguments concerning any and every subject; and he tells us that those points of departure that are not common in this way, but consist of propositions belonging to certain subject-matters and give rise to arguments by furnishing themselves as premises, are called εἴδη (1. 2, 1358^{a}2–33).[62]

Elsewhere, however, Aristotle uses these terms and expressions almost interchangeably. This is especially true of the *Sophistical Refutations*, where the terms τρόποι, τόποι, and στοιχεῖα mingle very freely. Aristotle has no difficulty beginning a discussion with one, which he then carries on or concludes with one or more of the others. They can be interchanged so freely because they emphasize aspects of what are as a rule the same items. Features or characteristics of arguments are studied and codified for the sake of invention; once grasped, they are used to produce arguments to which they belong as features or characteristics. The term τρόπος may emphasize the side of artistic invention, while the term εἶδος emphasizes the features or characteristics of the product and the kinds of argument

[61] Cf. *Rhetoric* 2. 22, 1396^{b}28–1397^{a}1, where Aristotle speaks of the τόποι of the εἴδη. Here it seems the εἴδη are still conceived as certain features or characteristics of arguments while the topoi about them are the angles or points of view they afford for the discovery of those arguments.

[62] The fact that Aristotle seems to adhere to this distinction between εἴδη and τόποι in only one other passage (3. 1, 1403^{b}13–15), while ignoring it elsewhere (2. 22, 1396^{b}21, ^{b}28–1397^{a}1; 23, 1400^{b}15), is less important than has sometimes been supposed, e.g. by Kantelhardt, *De Aristotelis rhetoricis*, 20, 22. It is best viewed as a stipulation rather than a contribution to descriptive lexicography. It would not be the first time that Aristotle had legislated a terminological distinction that was not supported by his own earlier and, one suspects, later usage. I shall touch on some other consequences of this distinction in appendix B.

characterized by them.[63] One such interchange is of special interest
to us. In the first chapter of the *Sophistical Refutations* Aristotle
notes that it is possible for something to appear to be a syllogism or
a refutation without really being one (165ᵃ17–19). Such arguments
form a genus which the sophist, the man who would seem wise
without really being wise, must study. Aristotle then proposes to
explain how many εἴδη of sophistical argument there are (165ᵃ34–7).
'Forms' or 'kinds' recommend themselves here as the most natural
rendering. Aristotle returns to the forms of sophistical argument in
chapters 4 ff., where, he tells us, there are two ways (τρόποι) of refutation, (*a*) by expression and (*b*) apart from expression (165ᵇ23–4).
After treating fallacies of the first type, Aristotle turns to fallacies of the second type in the following words: 'refutations due
to expression are from these topoi, but of the fallacies apart from
expression there are seven εἴδη (4, 166ᵇ20–2). Here also 'forms' or
'kinds' appears to be the correct translation.

The same kind of interchange can be observed in the *Rhetoric* as
well. In the passage that has already come to our attention because
of the explanation it offers for the terms 'topos' and 'element',
Aristotle goes on to impose restrictions on what is to count as
a topos of enthymemes and a corresponding εἶδος (2. 26, 1403ᵃ17–
33). Though certain enthymemes are composed with certain ends in
view—Aristotle mentions amplification and depreciation, and the
refutation of an opponent—not every consideration that enters into
the invention of an enthymeme is a topos, nor is every corresponding
description under which a finished enthymeme falls a proper kind
of enthymeme. But genuine topoi do yield corresponding kinds of
argument, or so the easy transition from talk of τόποι to talk of εἴδη
suggests.[64]

The question to which the preceding discussion has been leading
is this: to what extent does Aristotle suppose, and is he justified
in supposing, that there is a correspondence between features or
characteristics—in the *Sophistical Refutations*, defects—of arguments, the devices for inventing or manufacturing arguments, and
types or kinds of arguments in a reasonably robust sense? For it is
not hard to see that Aristotle's system is prone to a great deal of

---

[63] Cf. e.g., 166ᵃ22–3, 33; ᵇ1, 10, 20, 22–3, 28, 37; 167ᵃ21, 36; ᵇ1, 21, 37.
[64] Nothing prevents Aristotle from calling magnification one of the forms (εἴδη)
common to all logoi (=speeches or kinds of speech) elsewhere, where forms of the
enthymeme are not at issue (1. 9, 1368ᵃ26 ff.).

overlap, and this of at least two kinds. On the one hand, it is possible to ask whether certain features or characteristics of arguments come to the same thing or whether some turn out to be versions or variants of one another. The same is true of corresponding devices for the invention of arguments with these features.[65] In one passage of the *Topics* Aristotle remarks that one topos effectively amounts to another (2. 2, 110ᵃ10–13). But features or characteristics and the corresponding devices for inventing arguments can be genuinely distinct without yielding mutually exclusive kinds of argument. Everything depends, of course, on the kind of features in question.[66] This will be even more true of topoi, devices for the discovery of argument, to the extent that they furnish angles or points of view for the invention of arguments that are not closely tied to particular features or characteristics of argument. The sophistical topos, as Aristotle calls it, of leading an opponent to a position against which one is well supplied with arguments furnishes an especially good instance (*SE* 12, 172ᵇ25). For this topos is a stratagem that can be put into effect by means of arguments of any and every kind, exhibiting the widest diversity of features.

Yet, as the evidence we have just been considering appears to show, Aristotle did want to divide arguments—at least roughly—into kinds with reference to the topos in which they originate. It seems that there was a certain amount of 'give' in the system, so to speak. On the one hand, the ideal of system and method that is part of the ancient conception of an art will have pushed in one direction, towards restrictions on what is to count as a τόπος or εἶδος of argument. Perhaps one version of this ideal would be best realized by a highly regimented system in which topoi correspond one by one to proper species of argument on whose essential distinguishing characteristics they are based. On the other hand, Aristotle's view of how an art develops or emerges over time as the result of deepening insight into, and gradual systematization of, measures

---

[65] Aristotle shows some interest in questions of this kind in the *Sophistical Refutations*, where he considers several proposals—mostly in order to reject them—for assimilating different fallacies or bringing them under a common head. Cf. Dorion, *Les Réfutations sophistiques*, 85–9.

[66] In this connection it is interesting to note Aristotle remarking, in the discussion of fallacious argument in the *Sophistical Refutations*, that nothing hinders one argument from suffering from more than one defect (24, 179ᵇ17 ff.). But in fact he does not go on to make the point I have just made. Instead he appears to think that fallacious arguments arise by and owe their fallacious character to a single central defect, which it is the task of solution (λύσις) to expose (cf. 20, 177ᵇ31).

found to be effective by experience leaves much room for departures from this and other ideals on grounds of proven worth and practical effectiveness.[67]

A glance at *Rhetoric* 2. 23, the chapter officially dedicated to topoi of the genuine enthymeme, is instructive in this regard. There we find signs of an impulse towards at least that imperfect level of regimentation characteristic of the *Topics* as well as traces of the opposite tendency. The expectations created by the standard analysis of the topos are fulfilled by the first few topoi catalogued. We have already touched on the first, from opposites ($1397^a7–19$), and the fourth, from the more and the less. The second, from inflections, licenses us to infer, for example, that just actions are good from the premiss that acting justly is acting well, and vice versa ($1397^a20–3$). The third, from relations to each other as Aristotle calls it, is based on the principle that if an agent acts in a certain way, e.g. justly, then the patient is affected in the same way, and conversely ($1397^a23–{}^b11$).

But the hope that the other topoi Aristotle will go on to describe are either based on or yield a classification of arguments, however crude and imperfectly systematic, distinguished with reference to laws of something like this kind, is quickly dashed. Some resemble substantive moral principles, thus possibly overlapping with the premisses and opinions proper to one field, to which Aristotle had earlier in the *Rhetoric* opposed the topoi common to all. Thus the fifth topos, from considerations of time, declares that what the beneficiaries of a good deed would have agreed to bestow on their benefactor as a fair recompense should not be withheld, once the benefit has been conferred, simply because the benefactor failed to extract a promise before acting ($1397^b27–1398^a3$).[68]

---

[67] In the *Topics* Aristotle warns against excessive and misleading systematization. After dividing the method into four parts corresponding to the four predicables, accident, proprium, genus, and definition, he notes that the issues treated under the first three all ultimately have to do with the last, for being an accident and a proprium are necessary conditions for being a definition, as is specifying the genus of the item defined ($1. 6, 102^b27–35$). (Matters are a little more complicated than this: cf. Brunschwig, 'Le système des "prédicables"'.) All the same, he maintains, it would be a mistake to seek for a single unified method, as, even if such a thing could be discovered, it would be altogether unclear and of no use to the business in hand (102^b35 ff.). This remark prepares the way for an overlap of a different kind: explanations of the topoi recur in the versions that apply to each of the four predicables.

[68] The topos that instructs us to consider inducements to and discouragements from an action is an example of an overlap with the εἴδη of a different kind

Many of them seem to be angles of approach or points of view which are not tied very closely to even broadly formal features of argument. And not a few of these are more rhetorical than those in the *Topics* in that they turn on features of rhetorical debate that have no place in dialectic. Thus the topos of turning against one's opponent what is said against oneself is illustrated by an example in which a defendant asks his accuser whether he would have committed the offence of which he—the defendant—is accused (1398^a3 ff.). Upon receiving the answer 'no', the defendant is to respond that in that case he himself would hardly have done so. As Aristotle notes, this will only work if the accuser's reputation is suspect. There is what we might call a topos of hypocrisy, which urges the speaker to contrast an opponent's avowed principles with his (probable) hidden motives (1399^a28 ff.), and what we might call a topos of consistency, which urges the speaker to contrast an opponent's earlier and later actions with a view to suggesting their inconsistency or in order to contrast them unfavourably with his own actions (1399^b13 ff.).

What we have looks rather like the results of a survey whose findings have not been integrated into a common framework, are ordered according to no discernible principle, and are described in ways that seem to reflect the terms in which they were conceived by their users or by auditors like Aristotle as they began to make out a topos common to many arguments. They are much more loosely formulated than the topoi of the *Topics*, and Aristotle relies to a much greater extent on illustrative examples. He tells us several times that the topos he is describing is the principal component of the art of a particular rhetorician.[69] He frequently cites examples from Isocrates in connection with topoi that appear to be generalizations of the examples; he draws in the same way on the speeches of Lysias, though without mentioning him by name, and also mines the tragedians for arguments.[70]

It is an interesting question how much of the disorder and lack

---

(1399^b30 ff.). For Aristotle's explanation differs hardly at all from the discussion of motives for action in the account of forensic oratory in book 1 (1372^a6 ff., 1372^a35). And neither appears to differ very much from the topos urging the orator to collect the good and bad consequences attendant upon actions so as to be able to advocate or oppose, accuse or defend, and praise or blame ($1399^a9–17$).

[69] Callippus 1399^a16; Callippus and Pamphilus 1400^a4; Theodorus 1400^b16; Corax 1402^a17 (in whose case the topos is of an apparent enthymeme).

[70] Cf. Kassel's Index Auctorum s.nn. Isocrates, Lysias, and the tragedians.

of system evident here reflects the incomplete state of Aristotle's researches, how much is due to the topical method itself, and how much to its application to the field of rhetoric. The *Topics* is to a certain extent better organized, but it too falls far short of yielding an exhaustive and exclusive system of kinds of argument. This failure need not be a problem by itself. From the point of view of a system of formal logic of the kind that Aristotle will go on to develop and expound in the *Prior Analytics*, these redundancies cannot fail to appear defective. But it is not necessarily a disadvantage for a method of invention, whose purpose is the discovery of arguments, if it allows arguments which from other points of view may count as the same to be discovered by different means.

But even so, we do seem to be faced with a problem when the topoi in question are themselves found on opposite sides of the divide separating topoi of real from those of apparent syllogisms or enthymemes. The most acute form of the problem arises when a topos specified in essentially the same terms is found on both sides. There is one apparently clear case in the *Topics*: a topos that recommends inferring that a predicate belongs to a subject without qualification from the fact that it belongs in a certain respect, somewhere, or at some time (2. 11, 115^{b}11 ff.), which resembles the fallacious topos of argument *secundum quid* discussed in the *Sophistical Refutations* (4, 166^{b}22–3; 5, 166^{b}37 ff.; 6, 168^{b}11 ff.; 25, 180^{a}23 ff.).[71] One may also wonder how great a difference there is between the apparently legitimate topos of names and the fallacious topos of homonyms in the *Rhetoric* (2. 23, 1400^{b}16; 24, 1401^{a}12). More common are cases in which arguments simultaneously satisfy descriptions corresponding to topoi on both sides of the divide and could be produced by either. We have already noted a few cases in which arguments satisfying descriptions corresponding to topoi of the genuine enthymeme in *Rhetoric* 2. 23 also satisfy the description that corresponds to the fallacious topos of signs. And it is telling to find Aristotle noting that it is possible to argue fallaciously in accordance with one of the topoi of genuine enthymemes, using the same term, 'paralogism', that he applies in connection with the topoi of apparent enthymemes (2. 23, 1397^{a}29; cf. 2. 24, 1401^{a}33, ^{b}8).[72]

---

[71] Alexander of Aphrodisias seems to have noticed this, as we can tell from his use of an example drawn from the *Sophistical Refutations* (*Top.* 214. 12 ff. Wallies); the reference is to *SE* 5, 167^{a}7 ff.

[72] He also describes one apparently legitimate topos as false (2. 23, 1400^{b}2).

Presumably there is a certain amount of give here as well. Producing arguments that are uniformly valid seems not to have been a necessary condition, in Aristotle's view, for inclusion in the ranks of topoi of genuine syllogisms. The point of the topoi seems to be more to set in train a process that results in the discovery of a valid syllogism than to provide a test or standard of validity itself. This seems to be the best way to understand the objections that are scattered liberally throughout the exposition of the topoi in the *Topics*.[73] For though Aristotle sometimes seems to raise an objection in order to correct the topos, so that the arguments to which it gives rise will now no longer be vulnerable to this objection, this is by no means always the case. Often enough it seems that the validity of the arguments in contention is to be decided by the two participants in the course of debate; it is not a question which the topoi answer themselves.

But even if originating in a legitimate topos is not sufficient to guarantee that a syllogism is valid, to the extent that topoi of genuine and apparent arguments are supposed to yield a corresponding classification, however rough, of arguments, it remains difficult to see how the pieces of Aristotle's system are to fit together. How, for example, is the practice of raising objections in the *Topics* related to the enquiry pursued in the *Sophistical Refutations* (1, 165ª17–18) into the causes because of which arguments are fallacious? Apart from the exception already mentioned, the topos of *secundum quid*, the topoi of fallacious argument appear to classify arguments along lines different from the topoi of the *Topics*. Are we to imagine that objectionable instances of the latter suffer from faults that can be analysed from the point of view of the former, while the unobjectionable ones do not? One example from the *Rhetoric* appears to satisfy this expectation nicely. It is the topos of relations to each other in accordance with which Aristotle says it is possible to argue fallaciously. As we saw, it depends on the principle that the action that corresponds to an instance of being acted upon that is, for example, just must itself be just, and vice versa. But Aristotle indicates that there are cases where, though it might be just for one person to undergo a certain punishment, it might not be just for certain persons to inflict it (1397ª23–ᵇ11). And something very much like

---

[73] I discuss this issue at greater length in 'The Development of Aristotle's Logic: Part of an Account in Outline', *Proceedings of the Boston Area Colloquium in Ancient Philosophy*, 11 (1995), 177–205.

this point is discussed in connection with the fallacious topos of division and combination in *Rhetoric* 2. 24 (1401^a24-^b3). Though it is just that the slayer of a spouse should die and that a son should avenge the murder of his father, put the two together and it becomes clear that it was not just for Orestes to slay Clytaemnestra. In this case, the two systems do complement each other. We can see how the topos of relations can give rise to a great many good arguments and some bad ones as well, whose defects are captured by a topos of the merely apparent enthymeme. This degree of co-ordination is exceptional, however, and Aristotle nowhere explicitly attends to our question.

Whatever other lessons we may wish to draw, then, it seems that the presence of a topos of signs among the topoi of apparent enthymemes does not by itself exclude the possibility that Aristotle early recognized a legitimate use for non-deductive arguments that he would later classify as second- and third-figure sign-inferences. The relation between topoi and the arguments whose topoi they are is loose enough for topoi of genuine syllogisms and genuine enthymemes to give rise to arguments that are neither, and perhaps for topoi of apparent syllogisms and apparent enthymemes to give rise to genuine syllogisms or enthymemes.[74] Yet to judge by the evidence that we have been examining, Aristotle never directly confronts the question whether deductively invalid argument by signs can be a legitimate or reputable means of persuasion in his *Topics*-oriented discussions.

Nor, apparently, does he confront it indirectly. The topoi of *Rhetoric* 2. 23 are, as we have seen, more rhetorical than those of the *Topics* in one sense; are they also more rhetorical in the sense that they reflect a more relaxed and tolerant attitude towards deductively invalid argument? Many of them are capable of giving rise to invalid arguments, as Aristotle acknowledges. Perhaps they tend to this rather more than the topoi of the *Topics*. But precisely the looseness of the relation between topoi and arguments on which we have dwelt means that this does not decide the issue. What is more, Aristotle makes a number of remarks in neighbouring chapters which strongly suggest that to fail to be a syllogism is thereby to fail to

---

[74] As it happens, an argument can be an instance of a fallacy, e.g. affirming the consequent, and be valid all the same. Cf. G. Massey, 'The Fallacy behind Fallacies', in P. E. French, T. E. Uehling, H. K. Wettstein (eds.), *The Foundations of Analytic Philosophy* (Midwest Studies in Philosophy, 6; Minneapolis: University of Minnesota Press, 1981), 489–500.

be an enthymeme as well (2. 22, 1397ᵃ3–4; 24, 1400ᵇ34–7, 1401ᵇ9).
Unless we suppose that he thinks that to unmask an argument as a
merely apparent enthymeme is not at the same time to put paid to
all of its legitimate persuasive powers, this is not very encouraging.
It remains the case that, outside *Analytics*-oriented passages, we do
not find a discussion of invalid sign-arguments from the perspective of an orator whose object is legitimate or reputable persuasion
by means of them.

(b) A developmental proposal

I suggest that attention to the different places occupied by signs
in the two accounts will furnish the clue we need. In the *Analytics*-inspired treatment signs occupy a place of central importance:
enthymemes are from likelihoods and signs; and once signs narrowly so called are distinguished from tokens, they are put beside
tokens, likelihoods, and paradigms as one of the four sources of
enthymemes (*An. pr.* 2. 27, 70ᵃ9–11; *Rhet.* 1. 2, 1357ᵃ32–33; 2. 25,
1402ᵇ12–14). By contrast, discussion of signs is confined to a rather
obscure corner of the earlier *Topics*-inspired system.[75] Unless we
suppose that a discussion of the legitimate use of signs has gone
missing, they receive explicit attention only as a source of apparent
enthymemes. At the very least, this is a striking change in emphasis.

For reasons that we have just been considering, we need not and
should not postulate anything as dramatic—or as easy to characterize—as a volte-face, a change from the simple rejection of a form of
argument as a legitimate means of persuasion to its wholehearted
acceptance. And, as we have noted, the fact that whatever change
may have taken place had to do so against the shifting background
of a change in framework complicates the question enormously.
Did Aristotle's change of attitude merely happen to coincide with
deeper systematic changes, so that one attitude revealed itself in the
context of the earlier system and the other in that of the later system?
Or was the change in attitude somehow more closely connected with
these systematic developments? We shall, for example, want to ask
whether one system accommodated or lent itself better to a proper
appreciation of invalid argument by signs. At the same time, we
must be wary of *post hoc* explanations here. It is tempting to see
in the *Analytics*-oriented account of the enthymeme the realization

---

[75] 'Das σημεῖον . . . begegnet in der Rhetorik noch einmal an völliger andersartiger
Stelle des Systems' (Solmsen, *Entwicklung*, 22).

of its superior potential in this regard. But Aristotle could have continued to view invalid argument from signs with suspicion after the introduction of the categorical syllogistic (as not a few commentators have supposed that he did). And the fact that we have an *Analytics*-based system that has been made to accommodate such arguments does not by itself mean that the *Topics*-oriented system could not have been made to do the same.

Nevertheless, it will help us to understand why Aristotle's attitude changed and what kind of change it underwent if we first consider how features of the *Topics*-oriented system and the presuppositions they reflect may have made it harder to accommodate the insights about the legitimate use of sign-inferences that are explicit in the *Analytics*-oriented account. For, I shall argue, a crucial part of the reason why Aristotle's views needed to change, i.e. why he was at first less receptive to argument from signs than he later became, was an uncritical, or insufficiently critical, application to rhetoric of the topical system worked out in the *Topics* and *Sophistical Refutations* with dialectic in view. This is of course compatible with different decisions about how to distribute responsibility between the system itself and various external factors which may have made it seem less than urgent to change or modify it. I shall touch on the complementary question whether the discovery of the categorical syllogistic and its application to rhetoric played a part other than that of a witness to the change in Aristotle's attitudes later.

The rules of dialectic restrict it to the use of syllogisms, i.e. arguments that necessitate their conclusions in the way specified by the definition of the syllogism (and, in an ancillary role, inductions).[76] Sophistry and eristic depart from dialectic most conspicuously by violating this rule. In order to achieve apparent victory in argument and to give the appearance of wisdom without its reality, they employ arguments that appear to be syllogisms without really being syllogisms. The *Sophistical Refutations* is in the first instance a guide to the invention of arguments by which to deceive (cf. 165ª28–37). The topoi catalogued in it prescribe how to induce mental slips and errors of reasoning and exploit them in order to produce the illusion that a conclusion has been validly deduced. Thus chapter 7 goes into a certain amount of psychological detail about the kind of mistakes people commonly make that are the basis of the deception

---

[76] On the ancillary role of induction in Aristotle's conception of dialectic see Brunschwig, *Topiques*, p. xxxii n. 2.

($\dot{a}\pi a\tau\dot{\eta}$) that sophistical argument aims to produce (169^a22, 37, $^b2$, 11; cf. 5, 167^b1, 8–12). The persuasive power of the arguments to which they give rise depends on this illusion and cannot survive without it.

The treatment of topoi of the apparent enthymeme in *Rhetoric* 2. 24 adheres closely to this model. The topos of signs follows on the heels of a topos which requires the speaker to use exaggerated and emotionally coloured language to induce the audience to reason invalidly ($\pi a\rho a\lambda o\gamma\acute{\iota}\zeta\epsilon\sigma\theta a\iota$) either that the accused is guilty, when the speaker is bringing an accusation, or that he is innocent, when the speaker is the accused (1401^b3–9). The discussion of signs, which includes the examples we have already noted, begins with the remark that this too is invalid ($\dot{a}\sigma\upsilon\lambda\lambda\acute{o}\gamma\iota\sigma\tau o\nu$). Under the head of the consequent, discussed in the immediate sequel, we find a number of other examples that could easily have been treated under the head of signs, as one of them is in the *Sophistical Refutations* (1401^b20 ff.; cf. *SE* 5, 167^b1 ff.). The fact that beggars sing and dance in temples, for example, can be cited in support of the conclusion that they are happy because this is the kind of thing happy people do (1401^b25–9). But as Aristotle notes, the way in which beggars and the happy do this is different, so that this topos comes under the head of omission or *ellipsis*. Plainly Aristotle is thinking of an orator who, though in full command of the facts that would set matters straight, chooses to manipulate the available evidence to his own deceptive ends by omission and selective presentation (cf. 1401^b2, 29, 34; 1402^a15).

We search in vain, however, for an acknowledgement that a sign-argument can be put forward in good faith, in circumstances that do not permit better arguments, and to auditors who do not mistake it for a valid syllogism, but take themselves to have been presented with considerations of a certain weight none the less. Like sophistry, rhetoric relaxes the requirements on the arguments it uses, but with this all-important difference. Yet, as we have noted, precisely the possibility of non-conclusive but reputable argument by signs that is unremarked in *Topics*-oriented parts of the *Rhetoric* is prominently advertised by the elevation of sign-arguments to the standing of genuine enthymemes in the *Analytics*-inspired passages. It seems, then, that Aristotle applied—at least at the level of systematic reflection—a conception of defective argument developed with dialectical debate in view to the field of rhetorical argument without taking its special characteristics sufficiently into account, while an

improved account that better accommodates those characteristics
is first offered in later *Analytics*-oriented passages.

(c) *Two approaches to argument from likelihood*

This suggestion receives additional support from the treatment of
apparent enthymemes based on likelihood in *Rhetoric* 2. 24, which
I promised to consider earlier. The case is in some respects different
from that of signs. Aristotle makes it plain in this chapter that he
also envisaged a legitimate use for likelihoods (1402ª16, 22–4). And
unlike a possible legitimate use for sign-arguments, argument from
likelihoods is discussed outside *Analytics*-oriented passages (*Rhet.*
2. 19, 1392ᵇ14–ª8). None the less, I shall argue, the application
of the topical framework, which was developed with dialectic and
sophistic in view, to rhetoric seems to have interfered with the
proper appreciation of argument from likelihood as well.

According to *Rhetoric* 2. 24, the apparent enthymeme from likelihoods is to be understood along the same lines as the fallacy of
secundum quid discussed in the *Sophistical Refutations*, where it is
characterized more fully as turning on a confusion of 'what is said
without qualification or simpliciter [ἁπλῶς] with that which is said
not without qualification, but in a certain way or place or time or
relation' (*Rhet.* 2. 24, 1402ª2–29; *SE* 4, 166ᵇ22–3; 5, 166ᵇ37–167ª20;
6, 168ᵇ1 ff.; 25, 180ª23 ff.). Aristotle's examples—that the unknown
is known because it can be known that it is unknown, or that what
is not is, because it *is* not a being—make it plain that he is thinking
of a technique for producing apparent contradictions.[77] Typically
one thesis is taken as obvious, while the other is demonstrated, or
apparently demonstrated, by means of the technique in question
(*SE* 5, 167ª7–14; cf. 166ᵇ34–6; 6, 168ᵇ14–16). The contradiction
is produced either by omitting the qualifications with which one
predication obtains and opposing it in this unqualified form to a
predication that does obtain without qualification, as in both of
the above examples, or performing the same operation on a pair of
predications both of which obtain with a qualification and opposing
the two unqualified predications obtained in this way to each other
(cf. 167ª7 ff.; 180ª28–9, ᵇ8 ff.).

---

[77] In the *Sophistical Refutations* we find 'what is not is because it *is* the object of
opinion' (5, 167ª1). In Greek the contradiction of the second example is sharper,
because we are obliged to accept 'I do not know *x*' and 'I do know *x* (that it is not
known)' when *x* is the unknown.

According to Aristotle, the same technique is applied in rhetoric when what is likely only in a certain way is taken for likely without qualification (*Rhet.* 2. 24, 1402ª7 ff.).[78] By means of it, one can argue, for example, that since unlikely events often do occur, the unlikely is likely after all. It is also on this topos, Aristotle maintains, that the infamous method of Corax and Tisias is based (1402ª17–23):[79]

If the accused is not open to the charge—for example, if a weakling is tried for violent assault—the defence is that he was not likely to do such a thing. But if he is open to the charge—that is, he is a strong man—the defence is still that he was not likely to do such a thing, since he could be sure that people would think he was likely to do it. So too in other cases, for the accused must either be open to the charge or not, but while both seem likely, one is likely, the other not without qualification but in the way described.

Aristotle's solution, based on his treatment of the fallacy of *secundum quid* in the *Sophistical Refutations*, draws on one of the most characteristic and distinctive parts of his philosophical method, namely the distinction between the central, unqualified application of a term and a range of related applications qualified in one respect or another. Failure to keep apart qualified and unqualified, or differently qualified, uses of a term is responsible both for deep philosophical perplexities and, not always unrelated, confusions deliberately induced by sophistry.

It is less clear to what extent the same solution can be applied to the technique of argument by likelihood, however. It is a conspicuous feature of the dialectical fallacies discussed by Aristotle that the contradiction the sophist aims to produce dissolves once clarity about the equivocation between qualified and unqualified, or differently qualified, uses of a term has been exposed. One then sees that it is not the same thing that is asserted and denied by the allegedly contradictory pair of propositions (*SE* 6, 168ᵇ11–12). To be sure, opposed arguments from likelihood can be reconciled by allowing, for example, that the suspect is likely to be guilty viewed in a certain way, as satisfying a certain description, and at the same time that he is likely to be innocent, regarded in another way, as satisfying another description. But what is required is a decision

---

[78] παρὰ τὸ μὴ ἁπλῶς εἰκός, ἀλλά τι εἰκός.

[79] Cf. Plato, *Phdr.* 267 A, 273 B–C. Material concerning Corax and Tisias is collected by Radermacher (ed.), *Artium Scriptores*, 28–35.

about whether, on balance, it is likely that the suspect is guilty or innocent.

I think that Aristotle did take himself to be offering a solution to this problem and, further, that it was at best a limited success. For he appears to have supposed not only that these arguments depend on a confusion of what is unqualifiedly likely with what is likely only with a certain qualification, but that one of the opposed likelihoods should prevail because, unlike the other, it really is likely without qualification. This seems to be the point he intends to make in connection with the first example he considers: the argument which appears to show that, because many unlikely events do occur, the unlikely will be likely. Aristotle replies (1402^a13–16): 'yet not without qualification, but just as the trick [συκοφαντία] is effected in eristic arguments by not adding the "according to what" or "in relation to what" or "how", here it is by the likelihood being not without qualification but in a certain respect likely.'

Now this case does seem to lend itself to a solution like that of the dialectical puzzles studied in the *Sophistical Refutations*. Once the equivocation on which it depends is exposed, it becomes clear that the conflict between the two likelihoods is only apparent, and there is no difficulty seeing which is relevant to the present question. A general, for example, could correctly judge that each of a series of engagements planned to begin simultaneously is likely to succeed, but, at the same time, regard it as unlikely that they will all succeed, and so plan accordingly. The fact that it is likely that some likely events will not occur does not imply that there are among these events some that are not likely. Notice, however, that it is not one and the same event that is likely and unlikely or two conflicting versions of one event which are each likely.

This solution already appears less satisfactory when applied to the style of argument made famous by Corax and Tisias (1402^a22–3). On those—surely more common—occasions on which the likely behaviour of the bigger man as such should prevail in argument, however, it is not clear that it owes its success in overriding or, so to speak, trumping the opposed likelihood to the fact that it is likely without qualification while the other is likely only with qualification. Certainly this likelihood could be trumped in its turn by others having to do with the temperament of either man, the state of his health, or any number of other factors.[80] And there is no reason to believe that the likelihood that should prevail, and that yields the conclusion which is on balance likely on a given occasion, does so because it is likely without qualification. Indeed, there may be no such thing as an unqualified likelihood or an unqualifiedly likely conclusion. In any case, it seems that the relations between likelihoods in virtue of which they override and are overridden by one another do not turn on a difference between being qualified and unqualified.

Aristotle's account appears to overlook this because it focuses on a small number of examples that share a curious reflexive character with some of the examples of the fallacy of *secundum quid* discussed in the *Sophistical Refutations*. In all of them, the second, apparently contradictory, proposition is produced by somehow taking the first into account. It is the non-being of what is not and the being unknown of what is unknown which are made the basis of the arguments that the one *is* and the other *is known* respectively.[81] It is the very likelihood that the stronger man attacked that is the basis for the argument that it is likely he did not and the fact that a number of events are (merely) likely that is the ground for the conclusion that it is likely that some of them will not occur. The way in which one likelihood is dependent or parasitic on the other may have made it easier to view it as somehow qualified by comparison with the other. It is also striking that, because of their reflexive character, all of these arguments are, if you will, *pure* fallacies. That is to say, what makes them disreputable arguments, so that anyone convinced by one of them has committed an error of reasoning, and anyone who puts them forward without having committed this error himself is guilty of deceit, is not sensitive to contingent and alterable facts concerning the evidence available in the circumstances of the argument. Within this limited sphere the model of the dialectical fallacy of *secundum quid* may throw some light on the misuse of likelihood. To see the likelihood that the stronger man did not attack in relation to the likelihood that he did, on which it depends entirely—assuming there are no other known

[80] Notice that in Plato's version of the infamous encounter between the weak man and the strong man, the first is also brave, the second also a coward (*Phdr.* 273 B–C).

[81] Cf. also the arguments discussed in *SE* 25, e.g. the person who, having promised to break an oath, fulfils an oath while breaking an oath, or the person who obeys an order to disobey an order (180^{a}34 ff.).

factors—is to know which is the real and which the merely apparent likelihood (cf. 1402ª26–7).

But there is ample scope for sharp practice and deceit outside such pure cases by the deliberate suppression and selective presentation of applicable likelihoods. In such cases the deceit consists in a deliberate failure to make the best use of the evidence available; though it uses arguments that would in other circumstances, where less or different information is available, rightly be judged good or reputable arguments, but here, in these circumstances, count as bad arguments because better ones can be made. But, as we have seen, this is not well described as a matter of deliberately confusing what is likely only with a certain qualification with what is likely without qualification. Nor does Aristotle's account show an awareness of the way in which argument from likelihood on both sides of a question can, by bringing to light the likelihoods that bear on the issue and the relations between them, help a deliberative body discover the conclusion that is on balance likely.

But, I should like to suggest, the *Analytics*-oriented section of *Rhetoric* 2. 25 (1402ᵇ12–1403ª16), which is devoted to the solution (λύσις) or refutation of rhetorical arguments, does a better job of accommodating these features of argument by likelihood and, therefore, does represent an advance over what we have found in the *Topics*-oriented account of 2. 24. This section begins abruptly after the *Topics*-oriented account of refutation that occupies the first half of the chapter, by observing that enthymemes arise from four sources: likelihood, paradigm, token, and sign.[82] It presupposes

---

[82] On the grounds for dividing the chapter into *Topics*- and *Analytics*-oriented sections in this way see Solmsen, *Entwicklung*, 27–31. Why not compare the *Analytics*-oriented account of refutation with the *Topics*-oriented account, which would seem to be the most natural way to contrast the two approaches to argument? Because the *Topics*-oriented account appears not to make contact with the same issues at all. It begins by noting that refutation (λύσις) is possible either by counter-syllogizing (ἀντισυλλογίζεσθαι) or by bringing an objection (ἔνστασις). There are, it continues, four ways of objecting, and it cites the *Topics*, presumably 8. 10, though the four kinds of objection there do not correspond to those mentioned here. The advice in the *Rhetoric* concerns ways of producing counter-examples to an opponent's contentions, but says nothing at all about how to challenge the cogency of his arguments, even though this is, according to the *Topics*, the only true λύσις (8. 10, 161ª1–2, 14). Thus it says nothing about the distinctive vulnerabilities of rhetorical argument and how to exploit them. What is more, it seems to be aware neither of the kinds of conclusions distinctive of rhetoric—for the opponent is pictured arguing for general principles—nor the fact, emphasized in the following *Analytics*-oriented section, that showing that the general principles that do figure in an opponent's argument are subject to exceptions is not sufficient (compare 1402ᵇ2–3

the *Analytics*-oriented account of rhetorical argument at *Rhetoric* 1. 2, 1357ᵃ22–1358ᵃ2, and, like it, refers to *Prior Analytics* 2. 27 (1403ᵃ5)—with the difference that paradigms are now treated as a kind of enthymeme rather than a species of argument co-ordinate with the enthymeme (cf. 1403ᵃ5–6). As we have already noted, the aim of the *Analytics*-oriented discussion of refutation of *Rhetoric* 2. 25 is to determine whether and how each of the forms of rhetorical argument distinguished by the *Analytics*-oriented account is open to objection, and we have already had occasion to consider what it says about arguments from signs. Aristotle begins his discussion of argument from likelihood by noting that such arguments are always open to a certain form of objection, since what is true only for the most part is subject to exceptions, but he insists that this objection is deceptive, producing an apparent and not a genuine refutation (1402ᵇ20–1403ᵃ3).[83] It establishes only that the opposed argument is not necessary, which is not sufficient ($\dot{\iota}\kappa\alpha\nu\acute{o}s$), as it is essential to show that it is not likely (1402ᵇ24–35); though judges are sometimes swayed by objections of this kind, he insists, they should not be (1402ᵇ30–4). His account of how to bring an adequate objection is less than ideally perspicuous, however (1402ᵇ35–1403ᵃ1):[84]

An objection shows an argument to be unlikely if it states what is more usually true [$\mu\hat{\alpha}\lambda\lambda o\nu$ $\dot{\omega}s$ $\dot{\epsilon}\pi\dot{\iota}$ $\tau\grave{o}$ $\pi o\lambda\acute{u}$]. This can be done either in respect of time or in respect of the matters at issue, though it will be most effective if in both ways, for if things are more often thus, this is more likely.

It is not easy to say what kind of procedure is envisaged here. One way of refuting an argument from likelihood is to show that the generalization on which it is based is not true for the most part. There are occasions for such an objection, but arguments from likelihood are vulnerable to another kind of objection as well. As we have already noted, two true for-the-most-part generalizations correctly applied to an instance falling under both of them can give rise to arguments to conflicting conclusions. Recall the example already mentioned which pits a likelihood based on a person's nationality

with ᵇ22–8). Has the *Analytics*-oriented section replaced part of its *Topics*-oriented predecessor? If so, no traces survive. The plan announced at the beginning of the chapter foresees neither the *Analytics*-oriented section nor anything not covered in the *Topics*-oriented section as we have it.

[83] It is a $\pi\alpha\rho\alpha\lambda o\gamma\iota\sigma\mu\acute{o}s$ (1402ᵇ26).

[84] A lightly modified version of the Oxford translation of Rhys Roberts, revised by J. Barnes.

against one based on his profession. Such arguments need not all
be on a level with each other. One likelihood may override or, as
I put it earlier, trump the other. In this case, for example, the fact
that most members of the profession to which the person in question belongs are unbelievers will, most likely, take precedence over
the fact that most of his fellow citizens are believers, though the
latter is no less true and could on another occasion be the basis of
an argument that won, and deserved to win, acceptance. Of course,
the same person may come under other generalizations in virtue of
satisfying other descriptions which may turn the tables yet again.

Now it seems likely that Aristotle has in mind here the first kind
of objection, which directly challenges the principle put forward
as a likelihood by the opponent.[85] But that he grasped and distinguished both kinds of objection is shown, I believe, by his account
of the refutation of enthymemes depending on paradigms, which,
he maintains, is the same as that of likelihoods (1403^a5–6). As we
have already noted, this is because an argument by paradigm claims
nothing more for the general principle which it supports with an example or examples before applying it to a further particular instance
than the for-the-most-part character enjoyed by the likelihood.

Unfortunately this does not emerge clearly from the text, where
something appears to have gone wrong. The solution favoured by
the most recent editor, R. Kassel, is a modified version of a suggestion proposed by Gomperz, whose point of departure was an
account of the passage's meaning advanced by Vahlen.[86] According to it, Aristotle describes two ways to oppose an argument by
example here. (1) One may grant that things are for the most part
as the opponent maintains, but show by means of one example that
they are not necessarily or always so. (2) Failing that, i.e. if one can
produce no counter-example and must therefore concede that the
opponent's generalization is true without exception, there remains
only the objection that it does not apply in the present case. This
emerges clearly from the text printed by Kassel (1403^a6–10):[87]

---

[85] Cf. Maier, *Syllogistik*, ii/1. 466 n. 1; Sprute, *Enthymemtheorie*, 118–19.

[86] Cf. Kassel, *Der Text der aristotelischen Rhetorik*, 143–4; T. Gomperz, 'Beiträge
zur Kritik und Erklärung griechischer Schriftsteller, III', *Sitzungsberichte Wien*, 83
(1876), 3–37 at 3–4, repr. in id., *Hellenika* (Leipzig: Veit, 1912), i. 236–74 at 236–8.
J. Vahlen, 'Zur Kritik aristotelischer Schriften (Poetik und Rhetorik)', *Sitzungsberichte der Wiener Akademie*, 38 (1861), 59–148 at 142–3, repr. in id., *Gesammelte
philologische Schriften* (Leipzig: Teubner, 1911), i. 13–105 at 99–100.

[87] πρὸς δὲ τὰ παραδειγματώδη ἡ αὐτὴ λύσις καὶ τὰ εἰκότα· ἐάν τε γὰρ ἔχωμεν ⟨ἕν⟩ τι

Enthymemes depending on examples may be refuted in the same way as likelihoods. If we have a single negative instance, the argument is refuted as a necessity, *even though* the positive examples are more and more frequent. Otherwise, we must contend that the present case is dissimilar, or that the conditions are dissimilar, or that it is different in some way or other.[88]

The problem is that, according to this view, Aristotle first recommends a type of objection that he has just dismissed as apparent rather than real when directed against an argument from likelihood. As we have seen, to succeed in bringing an objection of this kind is, so far, to have failed to produce a genuinely cogent objection.[89] Yet if we are to believe Vahlen *et al.*, Aristotle treats this as the best objection one can bring, and, rather than going on to describe a better objection as he did before, he proceeds to describe the objection which one is to fall back on in the event that one cannot even bring an objection of this first, but inadequate, kind. Having conceded that the opponent's generalization—*B*s are *A*—which he is now trying to apply to a further instance, say *C*, holds without exception, one can only argue that *C* is not a *B* after all. But if one is in a position to show that an opponent's argument is perfectly irrelevant, because the item at issue does not fall under the generalization exemplified by one's paradigm, in at least some favourable cases, this would be a vastly more cogent objection than one based on a single exception to the proposition that *B*s are (as a rule) *A*, and would seem to be better used as an objection of first rather than last resort. What is more, since the received text plainly goes on to describe an objection against an argument based on a principle that obtains only for the most part, Gomperz and Kassel are forced to delete part of it.[90]

It seems far more likely, then, that the received text, at least as it is usually understood, contains not more but less than Aristotle wrote: a crucial part of the objection, corresponding to the genuine objection to the argument from likelihood already discussed,

---

οὐχ οὕτω, λέλυται, ὅτι οὐκ ἀναγκαῖον, εἰ καὶ τὰ πλείω ἢ πλεονάκις [ἄλλως· ἐὰν δὲ καὶ τὰ πλείω καὶ τὰ πλεονάκις] οὕτω, ⟨ἐάν τε μή⟩, μαχετέον ἢ ὅτι τὸ παρὸν οὐχ ὅμοιον ἢ οὐχ ὁμοίως ἢ διαφοράν γέ τινα ἔχει.

[88] A modified version of J. Barnes's revision of Rhys Roberts's Oxford translation.
[89] In dialectic, where more is claimed for the principles established by induction, a single counter-instance is a sufficient objection (*Top.* 8. 2, 157^{a}34–7; 8. 8, 160^{b}1–5).
[90] '[These words: ἄλλως . . . οὕτω] die vom Zusammenhang geforderte ausnahmslose Geltung der vom Gegner behaupteten Erfahrungsregel nicht ausdrücken können' (Kassel, *Der Text*, 144; cf. Gomperz, 'Beiträge', in *Hellenika*, i. 237).

has gone missing or been misunderstood.[91] Taken in this way, the passage explains that the refutation of arguments from paradigm is like that of enthymemes from likelihood in that a single counter-instance establishes that it is not necessary, while it requires more and more frequent counter-instances to make a case that it is not likely. Only at this point does Aristotle go on to describe a further variety of objection, which we are to fall back on if we are unable to bring an objection of the second, but first adequate, type just mentioned: one should now attempt to show that the case at issue differs in some way or other.

His remarks here are, to be sure, little more than a hint. But since the concession that prepares the way for the last-mentioned objection grants only that the opponent's generalization does obtain for the most part, showing that the item in contention is somehow different need not involve showing that it does not, after all, fall under the subject term of the general principle illustrated by the paradigm. It can also be done by discovering a feature that shows that it is, or is likely to be, one of the exceptions. It is in this direction, I suggest, that Aristotle's injunction to 'contend that the present case is dissimilar, or that the conditions are dissimilar, or that it is different in some way or other' seems to point. One can, for example, grant that wars against neighbours are as a rule a bad idea, but argue that Athens should go to war with Thebes all the same because this war has another feature; for example, perhaps it would be a war against a power that is preparing aggression, which wars are as a rule better undertaken sooner rather than later. Unlike the alternative embodied in Kassel's text, this does do justice to the concessive structure of the argument.

If this is right, the *Analytics*-oriented account of objection in *Rhetoric* 2. 25 contains, as the *Topics*-oriented treatment of topoi of the apparent enthymeme in the preceding chapter did not, a clear recognition that it is possible to combat an opponent's argument from likelihood without impugning the likelihood on which it depends. It is puzzling why Aristotle mentions this kind of objection first in connection with argument by paradigm—assuming that the conjectural interpretation of $1402^b 35$–$1403^a 1$ above is correct—but it is plainly no less applicable to argument from likelihood. The objection described in the discussion of objection to likelihood and

---

[91] See appendix A to this study for suggestions about how the text is to be restored or understood to bring out the required meaning.

identified as the first legitimate objection in the account of enthymemes based on paradigm corresponds roughly to the picture
of defective argument by likelihood in *Rhetoric* 2. 24 by unmasking
a would-be likelihood as merely apparent, albeit in a very different
way. But the second accepts the likelihood on which the opponent's
argument depends and aims instead to show that, all the same,
the argument should not prevail in the present case. In this way,
it also does more justice to the deliberative character of rhetorical
argument by showing how the conclusion that is on balance most
reputable or is best supported by the evidence can emerge from debate in which opposed considerations are pitted against each other.

Note, however, that if the *Topics*-oriented treatment of likelihood
in *Rhetoric* 2. 24 is, like the treatment of signs in the same chapter,
a case of the topical framework somehow hindering or failing to accommodate a proper appreciation of rhetorical argument, the new
approach to likelihood in the *Analytics*-oriented section of 2. 25 is
not, like the new *Analytics*-oriented account of sign-argument, a
case of relaxing or loosening the standards of reputable argument.
For what we find is not the admission of a new class of reputable
arguments by likelihood, previously excluded or not explicitly acknowledged, but an improved understanding of the conditions that
determine the value of arguments that had been recognized as reputable enthymemes all along.

(d) The impact of the categorical syllogism

We have seen how the dialectical system expounded in the earlier
and more extensive *Topics*-oriented sections of the *Rhetoric* failed to
do justice to forms of argument prominent in rhetoric. And I have
argued that we find, albeit only in the form of a sketch, a better approach in the later *Analytics*-oriented insertions, which combines a
deeper understanding of argument by likelihood with a recognition
of the legitimacy of deductively invalid but reputable argument by
signs. On the basis of this, I suggested that Aristotle underwent a
change of attitude the result of which was less a reclassification of
argument types than a clearer recognition of the important legitimate uses of forms of argument that had previously received attention only as means of deception, and an improved understanding
of how their value is to be assessed. But so far we have used ori-
entation towards the *Prior Analytics* as a control, in order to ask
whether passages we know to be later because of their reliance on

the categorical syllogistic are different in other ways as well. The question I wish to pursue now is whether, apart from serving as a witness to developments in Aristotle's views about rhetorical argument, the discovery of the categorical syllogistic and its application to the field of rhetoric entered more directly into them.

All the cautions stated before remain in effect. The categorical syllogistic was neither a necessary nor a sufficient condition for the changes for which I have argued. Although Aristotle was not in a position, before the invention of the categorical syllogistic, to give the kind of answer to the question when and in virtue of what an argument is valid that a formal logical theory makes possible, he had a conception of deductive validity, revealed in the definition of the syllogism. He was therefore able to relax the requirement for deductive validity or not, as he saw fit. As we have already noted, there are some hints that he did so in the definition of the enthymeme at *Rhetoric* 1. 2, 1356^{b}15–17. And he could have continued to insist on deductive validity after the development of the categorical syllogistic. None the less, I should like to suggest that there is a set of closely related characteristics of the topical method that set it apart from the categorical syllogistic that *may* have made the latter better suited to accommodate non-deductive inferences by signs and thus *may*, in co-operation with other factors, have pointed the way to a better understanding of their power to play a reputable part in argument. At all events, they helped determine the form that this accommodation took, and consideration of them will help us better understand the development that Aristotle's thinking underwent for this reason at least.

The theory of the categorical syllogistic expounded in the *Prior Analytics* aims to give a precise formal account of valid argument—a task that had not been formulated, let alone attempted and accomplished, before. Every syllogistic mood has two premisses in each of which two terms, represented by variables, are related by one of four predicative relations, the logical constants of the system. The self-evident validity of the perfect moods is made the basis of rigorous proofs of the validity of the remaining moods, a process which Aristotle calls perfection. That the system of moods is adequate or complete is what Aristotle attempts to establish by means of the famous completeness proof of *Prior Analytics* 1. 23. There he argues that every syllogism, i.e. every argument satisfying the definition of the syllogism, is, or is composed of steps that are, in one of the moods, so that the validity of every syllogism is in effect secured by the perfect syllogisms of the first figure via the reduction of the imperfect moods to the perfect. On the strength of this result, Aristotle claims that every syllogism can be analysed into one of the moods of the figures, and explains how to do this in order to confirm, from another point of view, the completeness he claims for his system (*An. pr.* 1. 32, 47ª2 ff.). Because the categorical syllogistic provides an exclusive, and within its limits exhaustive, *system* of types or forms of valid argument, it makes possible a new kind of answer to the question when and in virtue of what an argument is valid. It is valid if and because it is formally valid, and it is formally valid if analysis reveals that it belongs to one of the moods of the categorical syllogistic. This was an extraordinarily impressive achievement, never mind that the categorical conception of logical form ensures that the limits within which Aristotle's results obtain are, as we can see but he did not, excessively narrow.

The method on offer in the *Topics* presents a very different picture. It is a system of invention, whose object in the first instance is to collect and arrange points of departure for the discovery of arguments. This is no less true of the *Sophistical Refutations*; it too is organized as a method of invention, though in this case of fallacious arguments. Yet, as we have seen, Aristotle seems to have supposed that, by and large, arguments can be roughly organized into kinds of valid and invalid argument under heads provided by the topoi, and this is as close as he comes to answering the question which arguments are valid and why. By comparison with the answer offered by the categorical syllogistic, it is extremely rough around the edges. As Aristotle acknowledges, not every argument to which a topos of genuine syllogisms or enthymemes gives rise is itself a genuine syllogism or enthymeme; nor, though he may not have noticed this, is every argument that satisfies the description corresponding to a topos of apparent syllogisms invalid. Which arguments are and why is not a question the topical system can answer; before the categorical syllogistic there is a sense in which Aristotle may not have had the conception of a systematic answer to this question.

Nevertheless, the features with reference to which the topical system distinguishes kinds of argument, rough as they may be, are, in a broad sense whose boundaries are hard to draw, formal. Like the moods of the categorical syllogism, many of the topoi can be applied repeatedly to new content to yield arguments which belong to the same kind in virtue of sharing the same form. Perhaps in the context of dialectic or would-be dialectic, where syllogisms are the only legitimate means of argument (apart from induction), there is a rough coincidence between the arguments produced in accordance with a topos of merely apparent syllogisms, the class of arguments characterized by the broadly formal defect described in that topos, and the intention to deceive by means of it. In this way an enquiry of the kind pursued in the *Sophistical Refutations*, into a method for the invention of deceptive arguments, can also serve the other purposes identified by Aristotle, which, though ultimately more important to him, are secondary from the point of view of the method's organization, i.e. to identify and expose the—usually deliberate—bad reasoning in the arguments of others and to help us guard against unintentional errors of reasoning in our own thinking (cf. *SE* 16, 175ª5 ff.).[92] But when conditions change, as we have seen they do in rhetoric, a system of kinds of this type will no longer serve even as a rough guide to good and bad argument. As we have seen, arguments suffering from the defects catalogued in the *Sophistical Refutations*, and known to do so both by their authors and those to whom they are offered, may be reputable none the less. And when they fail to be, it will be for reasons other than these defects.

It may be that the new level of precision and clarity that the categorical syllogistic brought to questions about which arguments are valid and why also helped bring the issue of the relation between an argument's validity and its legitimate claim to influence rational judgement into sharper focus, making it harder to avoid the question whether the latter extends further than the former.[93] According to this suggestion, the roughness and imprecision of the topical framework would have made it easier to imagine that the diminished rigour and stringency characteristic of rhetorical argument could somehow be accommodated by making a few adjustments to the topical framework taken over from dialectic without abandoning its division of arguments into good and bad kinds on broadly formal lines—perhaps by means of an increased reliance on the for-the-most-part.

---

[92] Knowledge of sophistical argument is an essential part of the dialectician's knowledge (*Rhet.* 1. 1, 1355ª29–33; *SE* 9, 170ª36–8, ᵇ8–11; 11, 172ᵇ5–8; 34, 183ᵇ1). Knowledge of how fallacies arise enables us to confront and solve them (*SE* 16, 175ª17–19; cf. *Top.* 1. 18, 108ª26–37).

[93] Cf. Burnyeat, 'Enthymeme', 38–9.

But whether or not the categorical syllogistic contributed to a change in the direction of greater receptivity towards invalid argument from signs by making this kind of illusion harder to sustain, it had the advantage of being unburdened by the assumptions characteristic of the topical method of invention which led Aristotle to attend to formally defective argument almost exclusively in contexts that presuppose an intention to deceive and to study them there only as means to this end. And Aristotle exploited its narrower focus on the formal conditions of validity to disentangle the question of an argument's validity from the intentions with which arguments of its form are used in the sphere of dialectical and sophistical argument. He used the theory of the categorical syllogism to help characterize the types of argument distinctive of rhetoric: the paradigm, two types of sign, the token, and the likelihood. It seems that his purpose was now not only to draw attention to the formal defects of some of them, but by so doing, to prepare the way for a better understanding of the considerations not captured by syllogistic analysis on which depends their power to afford nonconclusive but reputable considerations for a conclusion. Everything said in *Topics*-oriented passages about how these defects can be made to serve deceptive ends remains true, but the connection between these means and these ends that is presupposed in every *Topics*-oriented discussion of signs is explicitly severed. The effect of this approach, I suggest, is to direct attention away from the form of the argument, construed generously, and towards the broader context constituted by the argumentative circumstances in which it is used. Common to the *Analytics*-oriented discussions of likelihoods and signs is the recognition that the value of evidence advanced in reputable argument is not determined solely by the form of the argument and the truth of the premises. The power of invalid argument from signs to render a conclusion reputable depends on the other evidence that can be put forward in favour of the conclusion. The value of an argument from likelihood depends not only on the truth of its premises, e.g. that C is a B and that Bs are for the most part A, but also on other likelihoods that can be brought to bear on the case.

If the argument of this study is correct, while studying rhetorical argument on the basis of the loosely formal system of the *Topics* and *Sophistical Refutations*, Aristotle remained attached to the idea that there was a broadly formal answer to the question what makes

an argument a good one, but abandoned it when he had a rigorously
formal logic to work with. In striking contrast to the *Topics*-oriented
account of *Rhetoric* 2. 23–4, the *Analytics*-inspired system does
not distinguish *kinds* of genuine and merely apparent enthymemes
at all. Instead it describes only kinds of reputable or potentially
reputable argument.[94] The task of sorting the reputable from the
non- or disreputable members of these kinds no longer depends,
even roughly, on a formal feature they share as members of a kind.
But to the extent that this new approach better accommodates the
special features of reputable argument of the type employed by
rhetoric, it realizes an intention that Aristotle had had all along.

5. Sign vs. Demonstration in Aristotle

Although Aristotle developed the theory of the sign that is expounded in the *Prior Analytics* and the *Analytics*-inspired sections
of the *Rhetoric* with rhetorical argument primarily in view, as we
have already noted, argument from signs is not confined to rhetoric
(cf. *An. pr.* 2. 23, 68ᵇ9–14). Before leaving Aristotle behind, I want
to touch on a feature of his conception of signs that emerges from
this broader use that will be of considerable importance in the
studies to follow.

Within the class of signs—broadly so called—Aristotle distinguishes between those that furnish conclusive evidence, which he
calls 'tokens', and those which furnish only inconclusive evidence,
for which he reserves the term 'sign' in a narrower sense. But as we
have seen, the distinction between 'sign' and 'token' is not observed
in Aristotle's usage. It has already been put aside when he turns to
physiognomics in *Prior Analytics* 2. 27. For it is plain that the signs
with which physiognomics is concerned—and Aristotle speaks only
of 'signs' here—are meant to furnish conclusive evidence and give
rise to valid syllogisms in Barbara in the way characteristic of tokens (cf. 70ᵇ32 ff.). This is not an accident, however. The characteristic shared by both varieties of sign is more important to the
characterization of signs as they are used in physiognomics than
any differences between them. Signs furnish evidence. With their

---

[94] Perhaps the formulation of the definition of the sign in *An. pr.* 2. 27—the sign
is a premiss that tends or is such as to be (βούλεται εἶναι) necessary or reputable
(ἔνδοξος)—leaves room for the influence of these circumstances. See n. 16 above.

aid, we resolve questions of fact, whether the solution is conclusive or—in the old-fashioned sense of the term—probable. And it is the evidential function of signs that allows him to oppose argument from signs to demonstrations.

Demonstration (ἀπόδειξις) is the most estimable form of syllogism because of its distinctive epistemic function: a demonstration is a syllogism by grasping which one has knowledge (a συλλογισμὸς ἐπιστημονικός) (*An. post.* I. 2, 71ᵇ18). Knowledge, in turn, Aristotle describes as the condition produced by the grasp of a demonstration in this way (*EN* 6. 3, 1139ᵇ31–2). But by knowledge (ἐπιστήμη)—in this context at least—Aristotle has in mind something more than justified true belief. We know something without qualification, he explains, only when (1) we grasp the cause because of which it is as it is, and (2) it is not capable of being otherwise (*An. post.* I. 2, 71ᵇ9–16).

The effect of these restrictions is to place demonstration firmly on the theoretical or high side of the distinction I drew earlier. The second restricts the subject-matter of knowledge and its instrument, demonstration, to the necessary and unalterable nature of things, so that it has no application to contingent matters of fact. The first assigns to demonstration an explanatory task; if a demonstration is to produce knowledge satisfying this requirement, not only must it put the person who grasps it in a state of justified certitude, it must also give rise to understanding. This in turn requires that, beyond establishing its conclusion by means of a valid argument from true premisses, it must exhibit that conclusion as the consequence of appropriate first principles which are necessary and both self-explanatory and explanatory of the truth at issue. To this end, Aristotle requires that demonstration must be from premisses that are true, primary, immediate, better known than, prior to, and causes of the conclusion (I. 2, 71ᵇ20–2; cf. *Top.* I. I, 100ᵃ27–8). And it is principally by satisfying these restrictions on its premisses that a syllogism qualifies as a demonstration.

In the course of pursuing the implications of this account, Aristotle contrasts properly demonstrative syllogisms with those proceeding through signs on two occasions (I. 6, 75ᵃ33–4; 2. 17, 99ᵃ3). The context of the first is his claim that demonstrations must proceed from premisses (and reach conclusions) that are necessary and predicate attributes *per se* of their subjects (I. 6, 74ᵇ5–12; cf. I. 4,

73^{a}21–3).[95] Aristotle wants to connect this claim about the matter of demonstration, so to speak, with his requirement that it explain its conclusion by deducing it from the cause because of which it obtains. Very roughly, his point here is that demonstration can perform its explanatory function only if it is confined to necessary truths in the way he requires. On his view, one has knowledge in the richer sense that embraces the understanding of why a truth obtains when an attribute is grasped as belonging to the essential character of the subject or as a necessary consequence of that character (i.e. a *per se* accident, cf. 1. 7, 75^{b}1). This is not possible when one grasps merely that it follows validly, granted true but contingent premisses, but only if, in addition, one sees it as a consequence of necessities imposed by the nature of things. Thus, if one is to have knowledge of something, strictly speaking, one must grasp that it is so and why it could not be otherwise.

Notoriously, Aristotle relaxes this requirement by allowing demonstrations from premisses which state that an attribute which, though it belongs by nature, belongs for the most part only and not necessarily (cf. *An. pr.* 1. 13, 32^{b}5–22; *An. post.* 1. 30, 87^{b}19–27; 2. 12, 96^{a}8–19), but if the large issues raised by this variation in Aristotle's view are put to one side, it is clear that his point here is that arguments which rely at any stage on contingently true propositions—propositions which though true could be false—cannot produce knowledge of the right kind.[96] They may lead validly from true premisses to true conclusions, indeed they may even arrive at conclusions which are *necessarily* true, but the necessary truth of those conclusions will not be established by the argument; it will be established by the argument only if it proceeds from necessarily true premisses.

It is in support of this point that Aristotle refers to signs. We shall, he says, fail to grasp why the conclusion holds as a necessary truth (even when it is one) in arguments that rely on incidental

---

[95] Though Aristotle holds that these two features coincide, there are some difficulties about just how and why. Cf. J. Barnes (trans.), *Aristotle's* Posterior Analytics, 2nd edn. (Oxford: Oxford University Press, 1994), ad 74^{b}5–12, p. 126.

[96] On for-the-most-part premisses cf. Lloyd, 'Demonstration in Aristotle'; M. Mignucci, '"Ὡς ἐπὶ τὸ πολύ" et nécessaire dans la conception aristotélicienne de la science', in Berti (ed.), *Aristotle on Science*, 173–203; G. Striker, 'Notwendigkeit mit Lücken: Aristoteles über die Kontingenz der Naturvorgänge', *Neue Hefte für Philosophie*, 24–5 (1985), 146–64; L. Judson, 'Chance and "Always or for the Most Part" in Aristotle', in id. (ed.), *Aristotle's* Physics: *A Collection of Essays* (Oxford: Oxford University Press, 1991), 73–99.

truths just as we do with syllogisms through signs (75^a31-4).[97] Syllogisms through signs are offered as an instance of arguments that fail to qualify as demonstrations because, though valid, they rely on premisses which are only incidentally true. He does not mean that all such arguments are from signs nor even, though this is less obvious, that all arguments from signs are from contingently true premisses. Rather his point is that signs do not require necessarily true premisses to discharge their epistemic function of furnishing evidence from which a conclusion that resolves a question can be inferred.

Having necessarily true premisses is only a necessary condition for being a demonstration. This is clear from *Posterior Analytics* I. 13, where Aristotle discusses an argument that fails to be demonstrative despite satisfying many of the requirements and standing in a very close relation to an argument that is a demonstration. Aristotle does not himself apply the term 'sign' to this argument, instead describing it as an argument from what is more familiar (γνωριμώτερον) rather than from the cause (78^a27-9, $^b12$). But commentators have traditionally understood it as a sign-inference.[98]

Suppose the conclusion to be demonstrated is that the planets do not twinkle. If all that is near (in the appropriate sense) does not twinkle, and the planets are near, a syllogism in Barbara can be constructed deducing the required conclusion about the planets from their nearness. Let us call this argument 'Syllogism I'. Supposing all other requirements are satisfied, Syllogism I is a demonstration because its premisses explain its conclusion. Its middle term (nearness) is the cause because of which the major term (not-twinkling) belongs to the subject term of the conclusion (the planets) (cf. 2. 2, 90^a6-7; 16, 98^b19 ff.). It explains *why*, at the same time it shows *that*, the planets do not twinkle, for it is *because* they possess the first attribute that they possess the second. But suppose that the major premiss converts, i.e. not only does the predicate, not-twinkling,

---

[97] 'Incidental' does not always mean contingent, but it does here (cf. 75^a20-2).

[98] Cf. Themistius, *In an. post.* 28. 16–29. 3 Wallies (cf. 6. 25; 17. 22–7; 37. 8–11); Philoponus, *In an. post.* 97. 20 ff. Wallies (cf. 170. 27 ff.); implicitly in the *Suda*, s.v. ἀπόδειξις, i. 294. 18 ff. Adler; by the Oxford translator, G. R. G. Mure, in W. D. Ross (ed.), *The Works of Aristotle* (Oxford: Oxford University Press, 1928), i. 75^a33 n. 3, and Ross, *Aristotle*, 5th edn. (London: Methuen, 1949), 41; Barnes (trans.), *Posterior Analytics*, 254. For more information about the commentators from a different point of view, see now D. Morrison, 'Philoponus and Simplicius on Tekmeriodic Proof', in E. Kessler *et al.* (eds.), *Method and Order in Renaissance Philosophy of Nature: The Aristotle Commentary Tradition* (Aldershot: Ashgate, 1997), 1–22.

belong to all to which the subject term, being-near, belongs, but conversely, being-near belongs to all to which not-twinkling belongs. Then another valid syllogism in Barbara can be constructed by taking the converted major premiss and conclusion of Syllogism I as premisses and its minor premiss as conclusion (Syllogism II). Less formally, that the planets are near can be deduced from the more familiar fact that they do not twinkle (taken together with the fact that being near belongs to all to which not-twinkling belongs).[99] The middle term of Syllogism II, not-twinkling, is not the cause but the consequence of being near, however. Thus, Syllogism II reverses the order proper to demonstration and infers cause from effect. The result is a syllogism that does not qualify as a demonstration, in the strictest sense, because it merely establishes without explaining its conclusion. Syllogism II falls short by failing to proceed from premisses that are prior to, more knowable than, and causes of the conclusion ($1. 2, 71^b21-2$). In Aristotelian terms, it is a syllogism of *the that* ($\tau\grave{o}$ $\H{o}\tau\iota$), whereas a demonstration, in the strictest sense, is of *the because* as well ($\tau\grave{o}$ $\delta\iota\acute{o}\tau\iota$) ($78^a36-^b3$; cf. 2. 8, 93^a36-7; 16, 98^b19 ff.).[100]

The characteristic of signs that permits them to figure in a contrast with demonstrations, then, is that they furnish evidence in a syllogism to a conclusion that adds to our stock of knowledge *that*. To this end, a sign must be somehow clearer or more familiar than the conclusion of which it is a sign—this is what is meant by saying that it furnishes evidence for it—but it need not, and typically will not, explain the conclusion, though it may sometimes be explained by it.

Aristotle may have this point in mind when he adverts to signs

---

[99] The two syllogisms can be represented as follows:

C = planets; B = not-twinkling; A = being near

Syllogism I		Syllogism II	
BaA	AaC	AaB	BaC
BaC		AaC	

[100] The grammatical parallel between 'syllogisms of the that' and 'syllogisms of the because' in Aristotle's account of demonstration is misleading. The *that* is the conclusion of a syllogism, but the *because* is not the conclusion of an Aristotelian demonstration. A demonstration is a syllogism of the *because* as a whole, because it exhibits its conclusion as a necessary consequence of the causes *because* of which it obtains. Cf. G. Patzig, 'Erkenntnisgründe, Realgründe und Erklärungen (zu *Anal. Post.* A 13)', in Berti (ed.), *Aristotle on Science*, 141–56 at 143–4; repr. in G. Patzig, *Gesammelte Schriften* (3 vols.; Göttingen: Wallstein, 1993–6), iii. 125–40.

for the second time in *Posterior Analytics* at 2. 17. His point of departure here is the question whether it is possible to demonstrate that an attribute belongs to its subject by means of more than one middle term. Before going on to consider a number of complicating considerations, he answers that, if one demonstrates not by a sign or incidentally—i.e. demonstrates in the strictest sense—then it is not possible, but if one does, it is possible (99^a1-3). Since the question concerns alternative demonstrations of the same attribute, the argument by signs here cannot be the simple inversion of *explanans* and *explanandum* envisaged in 1. 13. But imagine a demonstration showing that A belongs to C via the middle term B, which is the cause because of which Cs are A. A could be the cause of a further attribute D, coextensive with it, or B could be the common cause of A and the coextensive D. It would then be possible to infer that A belongs to C via the middle term D as well as via B. This new syllogism via D, though no less valid than the other, would not be a demonstration in the strictest sense because D is not the cause because of which A belongs to C. But though not the cause of A, D could well be a sign of it.

This can be illustrated by an example used by Aristotle at *Post. an.* 2. 8, 93^a36 ff.[101] The interposition of the Earth (B) is the cause because of which the moon (C) is eclipsed (A). But it is also the case that, when the moon is in eclipse, it is unable to produce a shadow when it is full and there is nothing visible between us and it (D). That the moon is in eclipse can be inferred no better from the fact that it is undergoing interposition by the Earth (B) than from the fact that it casts no shadow (D). But whereas the latter, though well suited to serve as a sign of the eclipse by furnishing evidence for it, does not explain it, the former explains the eclipse, without being able to serve as a sign of it.[102]

Aristotle's contrast between demonstrations and inferences through signs depends on a distinctive conception of the highest purposes to which inference can be put that sets his position apart from others. An Aristotelian demonstration explains by embodying

[101] Cf. Ross (ed.), *Analytics*, 669.

[102] The contrast that concerns us is stated clearly and without the complications imposed by the syllogistic framework of the *Posterior Analytics* in *On Divination by Dreams*. Aristotle begins his enquiry by asking whether the dreams for which predictive power is claimed are signs or causes of the events they predict (or merely coincide with them irregularly) (462^b26 ff.). Cf. P. J. van der Eijk (trans.), *Aristoteles: De insomniis, De divinatione per somnum* (Berlin: Akademie-Verlag, 1994), 264–8.

or exhibiting an explanation. Other views that we shall examine continue to connect demonstration with explanation but assign demonstration the task of deducing an explanation or part of one from evidence.

APPENDIX A

The Text of *Rhetoric*, 2. 25, 1403ᵃ6–10

Below is the text as it appears in Kassel's edition of the *Rhetoric* and three proposals to restore or reinterpret the received text so that it yields the meaning which I argued it originally had. The restoration Solmsen proposes has the passage distinguish neatly between a first, inadequate form of objection like the merely apparent objection to an argument from likelihood based on an exception to the opponent's general principle, and two genuine forms of objection, one of which we are to fall back on if the first is not possible. Maier's understanding of the passage is the same, but he attempts to make it yield the desired meaning by ingenious if somewhat strained repunctuation. His solution has the disadvantage of only alluding to the second but first adequate objection in the sequence. By means of simpler and less strained repunctuation, Striker's solution, which was suggested to me in conversation, is able to read the passage so that it clearly mentions all three forms of objection, as in Solmsen's version, but without the need for a restoration. Other solutions may well be possible.

Kassel:

πρὸς δὲ τὰ παραδειγματώδη ἡ αὐτὴ λύσις καὶ τὰ εἰκότα· ἐάν τε γὰρ ἔχωμεν ⟨ἕν⟩ τι οὐχ οὕτω, λέλυται, ὅτι οὐκ ἀναγκαῖον, εἰ καὶ τὰ πλείω ἢ πλεονάκις [ἄλλως· ἐὰν δὲ καὶ τὰ πλείω καὶ τὰ πλεονάκις] οὕτω, ⟨ἐάν τε μή⟩, μαχετέον ἢ ὅτι τὸ παρὸν οὐχ ὅμοιον ἢ οὐχ ὁμοίως ἢ διαφοράν γέ τινα ἔχει.

Enthymemes depending on examples may be refuted in the same way as likelihoods. If we have a single negative instance, the argument is refuted as a necessity, *even though* the positive examples are more and more frequent. Otherwise, we must contend that the present case is dissimilar, or that the conditions are dissimilar, or that it is different in some way or other. (trans. Rhys Roberts, rev. J. Barnes, lightly modified)

Solmsen, *Entwicklung*, 29 n. 2:

πρὸς δὲ τὰ παραδειγματώδη ἡ αὐτὴ λύσις καὶ τὰ εἰκότα· ἐάν τε γὰρ ἔχωμεν ⟨ἕν⟩ τι οὐχ οὕτω, λέλυται, ὅτι οὐκ ἀναγκαῖον, ⟨ἱκανῶς δὲ λυθήσεται⟩, εἰ καὶ τὰ πλείω ἢ πλεονάκις ἄλλως· ἐὰν δὲ τὰ πλείω καὶ τὰ πλεονάκις οὕτω, μαχετέον ἢ ὅτι τὸ παρὸν οὐχ ὅμοιον ἢ οὐχ ὁμοίως ἢ διαφοράν γέ τινα ἔχει.

Enthymemes depending on examples may be refuted in the same way as likelihoods. If we have one thing that is not so, it is refuted as a necessity, but it will be refuted adequately if matters are more and more often the other way (i.e. not so). But if most things on most occasions are so, we must contend that the present case is dissimilar or that the conditions are dissimilar, or that it is different in some way or other.

Maier, *Syllogistik*, iia. 466 n. 1:

πρὸς δὲ τὰ παραδειγματώδη ἡ αὐτὴ λύσις καὶ τὰ εἰκότα· ἐάν τε γὰρ ἔχωμεν τι, οὐχ οὕτω λέλυται, ὅτι [=because] οὐκ ἀναγκαῖον, εἰ καὶ τὰ πλείω ἢ πλεονάκις ἄλλως· ἐὰν δὲ τὰ πλείω καὶ τὰ πλεονάκις οὕτω, μαχετέον ἢ ὅτι τὸ παρὸν οὐχ ὅμοιον ἢ οὐχ ὁμοίως ἢ διαφοράν γέ τινα ἔχει.

Roughly: Enthymemes depending on examples may be refuted in the same way as likelihoods. If we have a single objection against the paradigm-based enthymeme, it is not refuted in this way, viz. because it is not necessary even though the positive examples are more and more frequent. But if the positive examples are more and more frequent we must contend that the present case is dissimilar, or that the conditions are dissimilar, or that it is different in some way or other.

Striker:

πρὸς δὲ τὰ παραδειγματώδη ἡ αὐτὴ λύσις καὶ τὰ εἰκότα· ἐάν τε γὰρ ἔχωμεν ⟨ἕν⟩ τι οὐχ οὕτω, λέλυται, ὅτι οὐκ ἀναγκαῖον, ἐάν τε καὶ τὰ πλείω ἢ πλεονάκις, ἄλλως· ἐὰν δὲ τὰ πλείω καὶ τὰ πλεονάκις οὕτω, μαχετέον ἢ ὅτι τὸ παρὸν οὐχ ὅμοιον ἢ οὐχ ὁμοίως ἢ διαφοράν γέ τινα ἔχει.

Enthymemes depending on examples may be refuted in the same way as likelihoods. If we have one thing that is not so, it is refuted as a necessity, and if most things on more occasions are also not so, it is refuted in the other way. But if most things on most occasions are so, we must contend that the present case is dissimilar or that the conditions are dissimilar, or that it is different in some way or other.

APPENDIX B

Were There Other Developments in Aristotle's Rhetorical Theory?

As I noted earlier, the view that Aristotle's attitude towards invalid inference by signs changed is part of a more comprehensive developmental theory originally proposed by Friedrich Solmsen. In this appendix I wish briefly to consider how closely it may be related to other parts of Solmsen's theory. But first I should explain that my account does not emphasize the same factors that Solmsen did in the explanation of Aristotle's change of attitude towards sign-inference and other forms of argument. As a result, it reaches somewhat different conclusions about the kind of change that took place. Solmsen notes only that Aristotle is led by his logic to reject the invalid forms in his *Topics*-oriented phase, but later moved by a concern with the practical needs of the orator, so that he embraces two very different conceptions of the enthymeme at different times.[103] And he views the change from the one to the other as part of a gradual transition from a stricter, Platonic conception of argument to a more receptive attitude towards rhetoric as actually practised, which allowed Aristotle to incorporate elements from rhetoric and sophistic in a new synthesis whose last phase occurred at a time when the new forms of argument it recognizes could be analysed from the point of view of categorical syllogistic.[104]

But the practical needs of the orator to which Solmsen appeals could be of either or both of two kinds. An orator might persuade people more effectively by sacrificing standards of good argument. Though his motives for such a step might be unscrupulous, they need not be. He could still have the best interests of his auditors in mind, but judge that their intellectual deficiencies made it prudent to employ less rigorous arguments than he otherwise would have. But we can also imagine an orator or a rhetorical theorist who adopts more relaxed standards of argument because he believes that only in this way is rhetoric able to do justice to matters that do not lend themselves to resolution by means of conclusive argument, but require a decision based on the best and most reputable considerations available all the same. This would not be a matter of betraying or sacrificing intellectual standards, but of adapting them to suit the nature of the matters that rhetoric must tackle. Without denying that motives of the first kind figured in Aristotle's reflections—there are indications that they did (1355^a24; 1357^a3-4)—I have emphasized factors of the second kind, while, I suspect, Solmsen had considerations of the first kind in mind.

With this difference of emphasis noted, I think that there is much to be said for some of the other developments Solmsen believed he had found and, *mutatis mutandis*, the big picture to which they belong, roughly an intellectual development from youthful idealism untempered by experience to a more mature understanding of the ways of the world. In the most important of these, and the one that would have involved the most dramatic change, an early austere or puritanical conception of rhetoric, from which appeals to the emotions had been excluded, yielded to a more relaxed view that found a place for such appeals as well as argument. The

---

[103] *Entwicklung*, 22–3.   [104] Ibid. 26–7, 226–9.

evidence for this development is furnished by apparently contrasting attitudes towards appeals to emotion displayed in the first two chapters of the *Rhetoric* that we have already noticed: 1. 1 appears to condemn such appeals, while 1. 2 treats them along with argument and the presentation of the speaker's character as one of the three *pisteis*, or ways of imparting conviction, that constitute the art of rhetoric. But as we also noted earlier, it is harder to make a case for changes of this kind than for a change in Aristotle's views about argument, because we lose the control provided by the categorical syllogistic. If these other developments took place at all, they did so before its discovery and application to the field of rhetorical argument. The treatment of emotion and character is integrated in the earlier account of argument, which is based on the distinction between sources of argument that are common to all disciplines, the topoi, and those consisting of premises and opinions borrowed by rhetoric from more substantive disciplines, the εἴδη, for as we shall see, some of the premises and opinions used to invent arguments do double duty as bases for the presentation of the speaker's character.

What is more, critics of this part of Solmsen's position have plausibly explained how Aristotle could, without contradiction, have said harsh things about appeals to the emotions in *Rhetoric* 1. 1 and accepted such appeals along with the presentation of a speaker's character and argument as legitimate means of persuasion in 1. 2. According to this approach, the point of the polemic of 1. 1 is to criticize contemporary rhetoricians for devoting themselves entirely to the means of rousing emotions and issues of style and arrangement at the expense of argument. But once argument has been restored to the place of central importance, it was now possible for Aristotle to find a place for appeals to the emotions and the presentation of the speaker's character as well.[105]

But Solmsen's case depends not only on the contrasting attitudes displayed in the first two chapters of the *Rhetoric*, but also on apparent discrepancies in the terminology they use to express those attitudes. Aristotle's condemnation of his contemporaries for ignoring the enthymeme in favour of appeals to the emotions in *Rhetoric* 1. 1 is compatible with granting them a place, albeit a minor one, as appendages (προσθῆκαι) in rhetoric (1354ᵃ14). But it is harder to reconcile the way in which 1. 1 appears to confine the term πίστις to argument and to regard only πίστεις,

---

[105] Cf. Burnyeat, 'Enthymeme', 10 n. 26; Cooper, 'Ethical-political Theory', 194–5 with n. 3; Sprute, *Enthymemtheorie*, 37 ff., proposes to resolve the tension between the two chapters by viewing the first as Aristotle's sketch of an ideal rhetoric which could serve in a well-governed community, while in the second he goes on to take account of the less than ideal conditions in which rhetoric must actually be practised. Cf. J. Sprute, 'Aristotle and the Legitimacy of Rhetoric', in D. J. Furley and A. Nehamas (eds.), *Essays on Aristotle's* Rhetoric, 117–28. The tensions between the two chapters are strongly emphasized by Brunschwig, *Topiques*, pp. xcix ff.

so understood, as artistic (ἔντεχνοι) with the recognition of πίστεις of argument, affect, and emotion in 1. 2, all three of which are now called artistic because they are products of the orator's rhetorical method and opposed to the inartificial πίστεις, e.g. witnesses, contracts, testimony extracted by torture, that the orator finds rather than makes (1. 1, 1354ᵃ13–18, ᵇ16–22, 1355ᵃ3–14; 2, 1355ᵇ35 ff.).[106]

To be sure, *Rhetoric* 1. 1, 1355ᵃ3 ff., which begins with the remark that the artistic method (ἡ ἔντεχνος μέθοδος) is concerned with πίστεις, apparently pauses to observe that the enthymeme is only the chief or principal πίστις (ᵃ7–8).[107] But this observation clearly interrupts Aristotle's train of thought, whose point is plainly to equate the πίστεις studied by the rhetorical art with the enthymeme, characterized here as a rhetorical syllogism. Solmsen took the intrusive remark to be a later addition by Aristotle himself; Kassel prefers to view it as the work of an alien hand.[108]

Understood in this way as a clash in Aristotle's technical terminology, the problem was a cause for concern before the appearance of *Entwicklungsgeschichte*. F. Marx concluded that the remarks in the first chapter that presuppose πίστεις must be enthymemes could not be the work of Aristotle, but must instead be due to a peculiarly unintelligent editor.[109] Hints of a developmental explanation make their first appearance in enquiries whose primary focus is still on questions of composition. Thus A. Kantelhardt believed that both conceptions of the πίστεις are Aristotle's, but that they belong to two different versions of the *Rhetoric* clumsily joined by an unskilled editor, now playing a much-reduced but still pernicious part.[110] It was Kantelhardt who first noticed that the *Rhetoric* draws on two conceptions of the syllogism, one characteristic of the *Topics*, the other characteristic of the *Prior Analytics*, and that these belong to different periods in Aristotle's career. But he does not seem to have noticed that reliance on the categorical syllogistic is confined to a pair of brief passages, and he had little to say about what might be behind the difference in outlook regarding argument or the non-argumentative *pisteis* that he

---

[106] Cf. Solmsen, *Entwicklung*, 209; cf. 25 n. 2, 221 n. 4.

[107] 'Since it is clear that the artistic method concerns *pisteis*, and a *pistis* is a demonstration of a kind . . . and rhetorical demonstration is an enthymeme [and this is to speak without qualification the chief *pistis* [κυριώτατον τῶν πίστεων], and the enthymeme is a syllogism of a kind . . .'   [108] *Entwicklung*, 221 n. 4.

[109] 'Aristoteles' Rhetorik', *Berichte über die Verhandlungen der kgl. sächsischen Gesellschaft der Wissenschaften zu Leipzig*, phil.-hist. Classe, 52 (1900), 241–328 at 289; photographically reproduced in Stark (ed.), *Rhetorika*.

[110] Cf. Kantelhardt, *De Aristotelis rhetoricis*, 38–40; K. Barwick defends a similar view, according to which our *Rhetoric* is the result of joining two versions, but believes Aristotle was responsible. Cf. 'Die Gliederung der rhetorischen Τέχνη und die horazische Epistula ad Pisones', *Hermes*, 57 (1922), 1–62 at 16–17; 'Die "Rhetorik ad Alexandrum" und Anaximenes, Alkidamas, Isokrates, Aristoteles und die Theodekteia', *Philologus*, 110 (1966), 212–45 at 242–5.

detects, presumably because he was mainly concerned to enlist changes in Aristotle's views in support of his theory about the composition of the *Rhetoric*.

It must have seemed to Solmsen, then a student of Jaeger, that the *Rhetoric* cried out for study from a developmental perspective which would invert the relation that had hitherto prevailed between issues of intellectual development and questions about the composition of the work. But if we do decide to regard a change in attitude towards appeals to emotion of this kind as plausible, I suggest that it should be with a difference in emphasis analogous to the one that I proposed in connection with invalid argument by signs. For it is important to remember that, according to Aristotle, the effect of emotion is not only to interfere with or distort judgement; as we know from his ethical works, being properly affected can play an important part in making the right judgement or taking the right view of a situation.[111] Thus, if a rhetoric that makes a place for appeals to the emotions is more practically efficacious than one that does not, it need not be because it is less principled.

If Aristotle's attitude towards appeals to the emotions did change in this way, much of the case against Solmsen could be accepted by a defender of his theory. For accounts of how apparently discordant passages in the *Rhetoric* can be viewed as parts of a unified whole may perhaps also explain how, by viewing them in this way himself, Aristotle could have let these passages stand after the elaboration of his mature theory. For Aristotle's change in attitude would not have called for him to repudiate completely his earlier criticisms of other rhetorical theorists for their single-minded concentration on emotion at the expense of argument, though it would have required revisions that made it clear that, in their place, emotional appeals can be a legitimate part of rhetoric. If this is right, it is not necessary to view the remark about emotion in *Rhetoric* 1. 2, viz. that 'we say it is with emotion alone that contemporary rhetoricians have concerned themselves', either as perfectly consistent with all that has gone before in 1. 1 or the desperate effort of an editor to paper over a glaring contradiction.[112] It might instead be an indication how we are now to understand the criticisms of 1. 1. Of course, the discrepancy in the use of *pistis* and other discrepancies would have to have been eliminated if the *Rhetoric* had been reworked by Aristotle with a view to publication as his last word on the subject. But the *Rhetoric* does not satisfy this description any more than do the other works of Aristotle that have come down to us.[113]

[111] The kind of view I mean to reject is taken by Barwick when he speaks of Aristotle making concessions to vulgar rhetoric, 'Die "Rhetorik ad Alexandrum"', 23.   [112] So Kantelhardt, *De Aristotelis rhetoricis*, 40 with n. 1.
[113] What kind of book was able to tolerate so many discrepancies or even contradictions? Solmsen suggests that it may never have been Aristotle's intention to make of the *Rhetoric* a consistent intellectual whole; the practical usefulness of

None of this is to say that *Entwicklungsgeschichte* or Solmsen's version of it have all the answers. I have dwelt on the proposed change in Aristotle's attitude towards emotional appeals because, like the proposed change in attitude towards invalid inference by signs, it makes sense when viewed as the result of continued reflection on a set of problems which brought to light defects in earlier solutions and inspired new attempts to improve on them. This already sets these proposals apart from those contributions to *Entwicklungsgeschichte* in which the quasi-mechanical operation of an inner law of psychic development drives Aristotle's thought irresistibly forward by degrees from *Platonnähe* to *Platonferne*. And it has another important consequence. I have suggested that the two developments in question do lend support to each other by showing that Aristotle's thinking about rhetoric did evolve over time, by exhibiting certain suggestive similarities with each other, and by leaving traces in a work that was apparently updated from time to time without being completely reworked in the light of its author's latest discoveries. But they are independent of one another; each responds in its own way to separate problems, and could have taken place without the other.

I suspect that some of the characteristic faults of *Entwicklungsgeschichte* did prevent Solmsen from recognizing this as clearly as he should have. For along with a penchant for resorting to developmental explanations for features of the *Rhetoric* that can be explained as well or better in other ways, his theory exhibits a tendency to exaggerate the relation between developments in different areas. Thus Solmsen supposes not only that Aristotle held at different times the different views about non-argumentative means of persuasion described above and that there were *Topics-* and *Analytics*-oriented phases in his conception of rhetorical argument, but that there was a third intermediate phase in his thought about argument simultaneous with the second, more receptive, view of non-argumentative means of persuasion. At this stage a purely dialectical conception that draws only on the (common) topoi yields to the hybrid conception of rhetorical argument that draws on both the topoi and the premises and opinions borrowed from substantive disciplines and designated εἴδη.

Solmsen's reason is the admittedly peculiar way in which the discussion of the three *pisteis* is structured. The εἴδη turn out to be widely acknowledged truths about the good and the bad, the noble and the ignoble, and the

---

the parts meant more to him than thoroughgoing scientific precision (*Entwicklung*, 225; cf. Sprute, *Enthymemtheorie*, 146, 190). Barwick suggests that it was a lecture manuscript to which Aristotle made additions over time ('Die "Rhetorik ad Alexandrum"', 245). But it is not necessary to take as definite a view as Barwick about the type of book the *Rhetoric* was in order to view it as an unpublished manuscript that grew and was altered over time, not a definitive version meant for the public. And this clears the way for viewing *some* of the difficulties it presents as due to changes in Aristotle's views.

just and the unjust, which are the defining concerns of the three genres of oratory Aristotle distinguishes: deliberative, epideictic, and forensic (1. 3, 1358ᵇ20 ff.). And the treatment of the three genres which occupies most of what is left of book 1 is roughly organized into sets of εἴδη, now called premises and opinions (2. 1, 1377ᵇ18; 2. 18, 1391ᵇ23–6), belonging to each genre (deliberative: 1. 5–8; epideictic: 1. 9; forensic: 1. 10–14). Aristotle appends his treatments of the two non-argumentative *pisteis*, ethos and pathos, here.

Since received views about virtue and vice, the noble and the base exploited as premises by orators charged to praise or blame are part of the knowledge on which they draw, in a different way, in the presentation of character as well, part of the second *pistis*, ethos, can also be brought within this frame: the same items serve as topoi of very different kinds of artistic effect (1. 9, 1366ᵃ23–8; cf. 2. 1, 1378ᵃ16). The third *pistis*, concerning emotion, cannot be made to fit quite so easily, and the chapters dedicated to it are sandwiched uncomfortably between a brief cross-reference to the discussion of virtues and vices (1378ᵃ16) and the fuller discussion of different types of character from another point of view to which *Rhetoric* 2. 12–17 are devoted. The discussion of argument resumes in 2. 18, and only in 2. 23 does Aristotle take up the (common) topoi, fulfilling the plan implied by the distinction between the topoi and the εἴδη in *Rhetoric* 1. 2.

If the *pisteis* apart from argument are a later addition to the dialectically oriented rhetoric announced in *Rhetoric* 1. 1, so it seems are the opinions and premises of the three oratorical genres with which they are connected and the hybrid conception of rhetoric to which the three genres belong.[114] But though this may be right, the evidence—a number of not very deeply embedded cross- and back-references—will also support an alternative explanation, according to which the hybrid conception was Aristotle's original view and the new material concerning the non-argumentative *pisteis* was inserted in its present place in the *Rhetoric* because of the dual use of some of the opinions and premises.[115] My aim here, however, is not to attempt a complete reassessment of Solmsen's theory, but rather, by indicating where its strengths and weaknesses lie, to suggest that the development in Aristotle's conception of rhetorical argument which has been the principal object of our concern does fit well with other plausible developments in Aristotle's thinking about rhetoric, while at the same time reaffirming that it is ultimately independent of them. Whatever other merits or faults may belong to his theory, Solmsen deserves high praise for directing attention to the hard evidence

[114] *Entwicklung*, 222–5.
[115] Cf. Barwick, 'Die Gliederung', 16–18; 'Die "Rhetorik ad Alexandrum"', 239–42.

for change furnished by the appearance on the scene of Aristotle's formal logical theory and making it the point of departure for his further
enquiries.[116]

[116] Cf. O. Primavesi, *Die aristotelische Topik: Ein Interpretationsmodell und seine
Erprobung am Beispeil von Topik B* (Munich: Beck, 1996), 60.

Rationalism, Empiricism, and Scepticism: Sextus Empiricus' Treatment of Sign-inference

THE most extensive and wide-ranging discussion of signs to have come down to us, and at the same time the discussion that gives the most prominence to signification, is found in Sextus Empiricus (*PH* 2. 97–133; *M*. 8. 141–299). This faithfully reflects the prominence accorded to signs in the framework Sextus adopts in order to classify and expound dogmatic positions in epistemology before subjecting them to sceptical scrutiny. Potential objects of knowledge are divided into two classes by this framework. The first comprises phenomena or evident matters (φαινόμενα, πρόδηλα, ἐναργῆ), i.e. truths that can be known immediately without being inferred from other truths, typically because they are accessible to direct perceptual observation, but perhaps in other ways as well. To the second belong non-evident matters (ἄδηλα), which lie beyond the reach of direct apprehension. Knowledge of these, when possible at all, must rest on grounds or evidence afforded by other truths. These in turn must be grasped immediately as evident truths or inferred from other truths themselves, with the result that everything we know is known either because grasped immediately as an evident truth or ultimately on the strength of truths apprehended in this way. According to Sextus, knowledge of evident matters is treated by the philosophers in their theories of the criterion, while the transition (μετάβασις) from the evident by means of which non-evident matters are apprehended is discussed under the head of signs and demonstrations (σημεῖα, ἀποδείξεις) (*M*. 7. 24–6; cf. 396; 8. 140, 319; *PH* 2. 96).

The question naturally arises whether Sextus is right to treat this division of epistemic labour as undisputed common ground

between the contending schools of dogmatic philosophy, and therefore right to use it as a framework with which to classify their positions. It does appear to suit the Hellenistic schools of philosophy
rather better than some of the earlier figures to whom Sextus as-
cribes theories of the criterion in *M*. 7. Indeed, as we shall see,
in some respects it seems to suit Epicurean views rather well. Yet
apart from a passing mention of Epicurus, Sextus seems to have
nothing to say about distinctively Epicurean contributions to the
study of sign-inference. Instead he assigns pride of place to a Stoic
definition of the sign, which he subjects to lengthy and intensive
scrutiny. But though we have a fair amount of evidence about Epicurean views, traces of a Stoic theory of signification are remarkably thin on the ground outside Sextus. And Sextus' own polemical
treatment of the Stoics' definition leaves obscure the use the Stoics
had in mind for it and, therefore, the significance it may have had
for them.[1]

But the most puzzling questions raised by Sextus' discussion
arise in connection with the distinction he draws between commemorative and indicative signs. The relation between the distinction and the Stoic theory has given rise to a considerable amount
of controversy. And Sextus' surprising and unexpected announce-
ment that the Pyrrhonist objects only to indicative signs, but is
happy to make use of commemorative signification, has always presented a challenge to students of ancient scepticism, who have naturally wondered whether, as sceptics, the Pyrrhonists are entitled
to a form of signification, depending, as it seems it must, on notions
of evidence, inferential soundness, and the like, which seem to have
no place in scepticism.

In this study I shall argue—in agreement with a view first advanced by Robert Philippson—that the distinction between commemorative and indicative signs had its origin in a dispute between the ancient medical school of self-styled Empiricists and the
more heterogeneous group of medical theorists they polemically
designated as Rationalists; in particular, that the commemorative

---

[1] The paucity of testimony outside Pyrrhonism has led scholars to wonder whether the amount of attention the Pyrrhonists pay to the subject is not out of proportion to its actual importance for their opponents. And the discrepancy between the
subject's importance for the Pyrrhonists and for other philosophers seems already
to have been apparent in late antiquity. The *Suda* defines the sign oddly as 'the item
through which non-evident matters are apprehended among the sceptics which they
abolish by means of argument' (iv. 351 Adler).

conception of signification is a contribution of medical Empiricism.[2] This will require that the question raised by Sextus' endorsement of the commemorative sign be tackled as part of the broader problem presented by the relation between Pyrrhonian scepticism and Empirical medicine, not least in the person of Sextus himself, who, as his name indicates, was an Empiricist as well as a Pyrrhonist. Although the pursuit of the medical connection will take us beyond the strict confines of the philosophical schools, the issue in contention will remain philosophical: the nature and scope of the inferences that it is possible to make from directly given evidence. None the less, the effect of this study's enquiries will be to undermine the close connection between Stoic philosophy and the distinction between commemorative and indicative signification presupposed by Sextus. Though Sextus represents the distinction as an exhaustive and exclusive classification of kinds of sign-inference, on closer inspection it will emerge that the distinction incorporates assumptions peculiar to the medical debate in which it originated, with the result that it cannot be applied more broadly without substantial qualifications. I shall take up questions about the character and purpose of the Stoic theory and its relations to Sextus' framework in the next study.

1. The Medical Background: Empiricism vs. Rationalism

One of the more intriguing facts in the history of ancient Greek medicine and philosophy concerns the close relation between the Empirical school and Pyrrhonian scepticism. According to the list preserved by Diogenes Laertius, apart from Sextus Empiricus himself, at least three of the eight heads of the Pyrrhonian school after Aenesidemus, its probable founder, were also Empirical physicians (D.L. 9. 115).[3] This overlap in membership was neither a coincidence nor an unexpected correlation of the kind that turns out to have a surprising and originally unsuspected explanation. Rather, it reflects a high degree of freely acknowledged philosophical affinity between the two schools.

But strong as it was, this affinity did not amount to a complete

---

[2] R. Philippson, *De Philodemi libro, qui est Περὶ σημείων καὶ σημειώσεων et Epicureorum doctrina logica* (Berlin: Berliner Buchdruckerei Actien-Gesellschaft, 1881).

[3] Cf. K. Deichgräber, *Die griechische Empirikerschule: Sammlung der Fragmente und Darstellung der Lehre*, 2nd edn. (Berlin: Weidmann, 1965), 19.

identity in outlook. Medical Empiricism was not simply an application of Pyrrhonism to the field of medicine. Indeed, it predates
Aenesidemus' defection from the Academy in the first century BC,
which was almost certainly the real origin of Pyrrhonism.[4] Thus
chronology would seem to suggest that influence was exerted in the
opposite direction.[5] And though it is not clear how strong his claims
to be a Pyrrhonist were, Aenesidemus' predecessor in Diogenes'
catalogue, Heraclides, was very likely Heraclides of Tarentum, the
most renowned Empirical physician of antiquity; and his predecessor according to the same list, Ptolemy of Cyrene, was probably an
Empiricist as well.[6] But Pyrrhonism was not a generalization of the
conclusions first reached about medicine by the Empiricists either;
for it is clear that Pyrrhonism received its main impetus from another source, the long tradition of scepticism in Greek philosophical
thought, particularly that of the New Academy.

In any event, the temptation to identify Pyrrhonism and Empiricism too closely is checked by Sextus' own explicit remarks on the
subject. For when he turns to the question whether Pyrrhonism
is not in fact equivalent to medical Empiricism, Sextus returns a
surprisingly firm negative answer (*PH* 1. 236–41). Not only is he
severely critical of the unsceptical firmness with which Empiricists
maintain that knowledge of non-evident matters is impossible, he
even goes so far as to suggest that Pyrrhonists interested in a medical
career would be better advised to practise as members of the competing school of Methodist physicians. This has sometimes been
taken to imply that Pyrrhonism developed close ties with Methodism at the expense of its earlier connections with Empiricism, but
on closer inspection, Sextus' remarks seem to be a strongly worded

[4] This is the standard view. For a recent defence see J. Mansfeld, 'Aenesidemus
and the Academics', in L. Ayres (ed.), *The Passionate Intellect: Essays on the Transformation of Classical Traditions Presented to Professor I. G. Kidd* (New Brunswick,
NJ: Transaction Publishers, 1995), 235–48, who is responding to a challenging alternative account proposed by F. Decleva Caizzi, 'Aenesidemus and the Academy',
Classical Quarterly, NS 42 (1992), 176–89.

[5] On the origins, development, and basic character of medical Empiricism see
Deichgräber, *Empirikerschule*, 251–95; M. Frede, 'The Ancient Empiricists', in id.,
Essays in Ancient Philosophy (Oxford: Oxford University Press, 1987), 234–60; H.
von Staden, 'Experiment and Experience in Hellenistic Medicine', *Bulletin of the
Institute of Classical Studies*, 22 (1975), 178–99. English translations of three crucial
texts by Galen with the editor's discussion of the principal issues are to be found
in: M. Frede (ed. and trans.) and R. Walzer (trans.), *Galen: Three Treatises on the
Nature of Science* (Indianapolis: Hackett, 1985).

[6] Cf. Deichgräber, *Empirikerschule*, 19.

warning against a dogmatic tendency in Empiricism rather than a complete renunciation of it. Nevertheless, Sextus' rebuke should remind us of the real tension existing between the two schools despite their affinities.

If we are to understand the complex relations between the two schools—both the features that recommended them to each other and the differences over which they were actually or potentially divided—we must first form a clearer picture of the character of Empiricism; and we shall be able to do this most easily if we remind ourselves of how the Empirical position arose in the first place as a reaction to the situation medicine found itself in at the time of the school's origin in the third century BC. Roughly speaking, the first Empiricists claimed to be able to detect a common approach behind the strikingly diverse positions actually taken by the medical theorists whom they classified, for this very reason, as Rationalists; and they blamed this approach for the impasse at which, as it seemed to them, medicine had arrived.[7] Again to speak very roughly, Rationalist physicians held that, if medicine is to achieve its aim of curing the sick and safeguarding the good condition of the healthy, it must grasp the basic underlying nature of both the human body and the unhealthy affections to which it is prone. This knowledge, they supposed, would enable the physician to decide on the therapies best adapted by nature to counteract the forces producing the diseased condition and the regimens best suited to fortify a healthy body against illness (cf. Galen, *De sect. ingred.* iii. 7. 1 ff. *SM*; *De caus. continent.* 141. 1–3 Deichgräber). Hence Rationalist medicine devoted a large part of its energies to theory, the physiology and pathology in which, it held, therapy and hygiene must be grounded. The discovery of theory was the task of reason, and the Rationalists were so called because of their conviction that reason enables us to grasp the matters knowledge of which is essential to medicine.

The conception of reason appealed to by the Rationalists, and challenged by the Empiricists, was not inalterable; its boundaries could shift considerably, and in the hands of different participants in the debate they did. Thus Asclepiades of Bithynia, the medical theorist who seems to have made the strongest claims for reason

---

[7] On what membership in a medical school involved see H. von Staden, 'Hairesis and Heresy: The Case of the Haireseis Iatrikai', in B. F. Meyers and E. Sanders (eds.), *Jewish and Christian Self Definition*, iii (London: SCM Press, 1982), 76–100.

and against experience, argued that unaided experience has no contribution to make to the composition of the arts at all, for reason
must be involved at every stage from the very beginning. On his
view, because the finite number of heads under which the infinite
variety of distinct experiences is organized are not themselves given
in experience, but discovered by reason, the Empiricists' claim to
base medical knowledge on the observation of what occurs many
times in the same way is untenable from the start (cf. Galen, *De sect.
ingred*. iii. 9. 9–13 *SM*; *Subfig. emp*. 88. 25 Deichgräber; *On Medical Experience*, 85 ff. Walzer). And he cited the identification of the
twenty-four letters of the Greek alphabet, by means of which verbal sounds can be grasped and understood in their infinite variety,
as an example (*On Medical Experience*, 88 Walzer). But according
to Galen, who had no patience with this line of argument, most
Rationalists adopt a more responsible position which, while conceding that experience makes a valuable contribution to medicine,
insists that reason has a significant further contribution to make
which experience cannot supply (cf. Galen, *De sect. ingred*. iii. 9.
13–19 *SM*; *Subfig. emp*. 43. 11–14 Deichgräber; *On Medical Experience*, 98 Walzer). For his part, Galen seems to have subscribed to
the most generous version of this more tolerant Rationalist view.
He tells us that he wrote his *Subfiguratio empirica* to show that the
physician who makes no use of reason, though unable to master the
whole of the art, will be able to arrive at a limited but adequate
version by means of experience alone (88. 19–24 Deichgräber).

  Thus the view Empiricists opposed to Rationalism was not
merely the contradictory of Asclepiades' complete disparagement
of experience, but a stronger contrary one. For their basic position was that experience based on a physician's own observation
(αὐτοψία), and drawing on the previous observations of earlier practitioners (ἱστορία), was fully sufficient for artistic knowledge. They
are often found arguing that the use of reason the Rationalists
claimed to make was not possible and that the faculty of reason,
at least as understood by Rationalism, was a chimera (cf. Galen,
Subfig. emp. 87. 7 Deichgräber), but this was not their last line of
defence. For they sometimes conceded the powers claimed for reason by the Rationalists in order to argue that, even so, reason had
nothing to offer which could not already by achieved by unaided
experience (cf. *De sect. ingred*. iii. 10 *SM*; *On Medical Experience*,
153–4 Walzer).

Nevertheless, if we put aside this last, concessive argument of the Empiricists and return to their first charges, we can make out a Rationalist conception of reason that remained fairly constant through the debate. The Rationalists' emphasis on theory reflected a view of artistic or technical knowledge that had received strong support from the philosophers. Real artistic knowledge, on this view, must go beyond the experience that, for example, certain measures are effective, even when that experience is very extensive; it must embrace an understanding of why they have the effects they do. This requirement that a genuine art must be able to give a rational account of the nature of its subject-matter, one enabling its practitioner to specify the underlying causes in the light of which he chooses certain measures in a given situation, was given its most influential formulation by Plato (*Grg.* 465 A, 501 A; *Phdr.* 270 B). To be sure, the Rationalists seem to have made stronger claims about the practical indispensability of theory than some of the philosophers; but even on this issue they were drawing quite reasonable implications from the philosophers' conception of artistic knowledge, according to which artistic knowledge, properly so called, is systematic and complete.

The point is well made by Aristotle, who requires that the true artist have at his disposal all the possible means of securing the end at which his art aims, so that he need never omit any available measure that may contribute to success (*Rhet.* 1355^{b}10–12; *Top.* 101^{b}5–10).[8] In this way, the artist's specialized knowledge should enable him to succeed as often as the nature of the matters with which he is concerned permits. But this in turn may well require a theory by which the means at the disposal of the artist are systematically related to the nature of the matters with which he must deal. Without it, according to the Rationalists, the Empiricist will be at a loss when confronted with new conditions not previously attested in his experience or that of his authorities (cf. Galen, *De loc. aff.* viii. 14. 7 ff. K = fr. 85 Deichgräber; *De sanitate tuenda*, iv/2. 161 CMG = 161. 26 ff. Deichgräber). At the same time, because he understands the nature of the body and can infer from the symptoms it exhibits what the nature of its affliction must be, the Rationalist will be able to decide on the measures best suited to counteract the unhealthy affection at work, even when the affection and the symptoms to which it gives rise are new to him.

[8] Cf. Brunschwig (ed.), *Topiques*, 117 n. 3.

Thus, according to the Rationalists, it was only by means of their kind of rational theory that the medical art was possible; unassisted experience is inevitably incomplete and unsystematic (cf. *De sect. ingred.* iii. 9. 4–6, 21–2 *SM*).

The theories developed by the Rationalists all have one thing in common that is especially important for our purposes, however: they go beyond what is accessible to observation in order to embrace the hidden, unobservable nature of things. Precisely what this means is rather harder to say. For views about what is given in experience as opposed to what is grasped with the aid of reason are themselves subject to disagreement. Thus, for Aristotle the grasp of a thing's nature requires a rational understanding distinct from, though dependent on, experience, even the kind of experience that embraces reliable generalizations on which effective practice can be based (cf. *Metaph. A* 1, 981^a5–12; *EN* 10. 9, 1180^b16–23). Akin to this way of conceiving of the issue is a view which allows that there are evident causes, i.e. directly observable items which are causes but are not revealed as causes by experience; to grasp them as causes we must understand the natures in virtue of which they bring about their effects; and these are not given to observation, but grasped by rational understanding.

With all of this the Rationalists agreed, but with a special emphasis. Rationalist theories typically explain observable outcomes by reference to the action of unobservable, subsensible entities and processes. Frequently these are what they mean when they speak of non-evident items ($\tau\grave{\alpha}$ $\check{\alpha}\delta\eta\lambda\alpha$); for it is often only at the subsensible level that the real nature of things comes into play, and hence at which the necessary connections enforced by a thing's nature become apparent to reason. An especially clear example is furnished by the view of Asclepiades of Bithynia, according to which most diseases are the result of the excessive or deficient flow of imperceptible bodies through invisible channels in the body.[9] Of course, not all theories fall quite so clearly into this class. Humoral theories, which were very prevalent, appeal to items that, with the notorious exception of black bile, are observable when they emerge from the body; but the natures in virtue of which they determine the internal condition of the body are not open to inspection in the same way. In any event, the point should be clear enough: any theory

---

[9] Cf. J. T. Vallance, *The Lost Theory of Asclepiades of Bithynia* (Oxford: Oxford University Press, 1990).

that stands a chance of furnishing the kind of understanding the Rationalists seek must go beyond experience, even when a fairly generous conception of experience is in force.

Reason, then, reveals the non-evident causes behind what is evident. True, reason is not responsible only for the transition from the evident to the non-evident; the grasp of the underlying nature of the patient's condition it affords points to or, as the Rationalists say, indicates the appropriate treatment. But this too is a matter of revealing underlying natural connection hidden from observation. Thus it is not hard to understand why the discovery of the non-evident should figure so prominently in transmitted accounts of Rationalist positions, for the claim that reason makes accessible an underlying reality beyond the reach of experience, and the use made of what is discovered in this way, are the most conspicuous and distinctive features of this kind of position. Certainly these are the components of reason as conceived by Rationalism by which the Empiricists are most struck, and they often identify reason with the transition to the non-evident.[10]

Reason can support inferences to the non-evident, according to the Rationalists, because it affords us a grasp of the nature of things. Given one truth about items with natures of a certain kind, certain further truths must obtain in consequence while others are excluded. Reason, conceived in this way, is the faculty by which these relations of consequence and exclusion (ἀκολουθία and μάχη) are disclosed (cf. Galen, *Subfig. emp.* 87. 7; 89. 12–15 Deichgräber).[11] With its aid, observed conditions can be made the basis for inferences to the unobserved, for there are non-evident conditions which cannot fail to obtain when certain observable states of affairs do. In an example frequently cited by Sextus, the sweat observed on the skin allows us to infer that there must be invisible pores through which it passes, called intelligible pores (νοητοὶ πόροι) because, though invisible, they can be grasped by the mind (S.E. *PH* 2. 98, 140, 142; *M.* 8. 146, 306, 309).

All this the Empiricists denied in the first pre-concessive phase

---

[10] Cf. Galen, *Subfig. emp.* 62. 24–31 Deichgräber; *De sect. ingred.* iii. 11. 16–19 *SM*; *On Medical Experience*, 100, 102, 103, 104–5, 107, 111, 132–3, 135, 136, 137, 139, 141, 153 Walzer.

[11] Talk of a natural ability to detect relations of consequence and exclusion is very widespread in our sources from the post-Hellenistic period, but the idea seems to go back to the Stoa. Cf. Galen, *In Hippocr. de med. officina*, xviiiB. 649 K = *SVF* ii. 135; Cicero, *De legibus*, 1. 45; *Luc.* 22; S.E. *M.* 8. 275.

of their dispute with Rationalism. Their main reason for denying that we have a faculty of this sort, and the ground they cite most frequently in their arguments, was the Rationalists' manifest inability to agree on a single, tolerably consistent, account of the matters at issue, or even the broad outlines of one. Instead, it seemed that the Rationalists had produced a various and ever growing assortment of conflicting theories, for each of which the authority of reason was claimed with apparently equal justice so far as an outside observer could determine (cf. Celsus, *Proem.* 28; Galen, *De sect. ingred.* iii. 11 *SM*; *On Medical Experience*, 103, 133–5 Walzer). It appeared that reason did not speak with one voice as the Rationalists had promised it would; and the Empiricists were inclined to suppose that their opponents were guided less by the irresistible force of rational argument than by their own speculative fancies. To their way of thinking, the rational compulsion their opponents' arguments appear to exert is nothing more than the kind of superficial plausibility that an orator can lend to almost any thesis if he speaks artfully enough (cf. Celsus, *Proem.* 39; Galen, *De sect. ingred.* iii. 9. 6–7, 10. 9 *SM*; *Subfig. emp.* 64. 31 Deichgräber).

To be sure, the Empiricists were not the first physicians to have raised doubts about the effectiveness of rational methods in medicine. Criticisms had been voiced before the emergence in the third century BC of a distinct school of Empirical medicine. The famous attack on hypotheses with which the Hippocratic treatise *De vetere medicina* opens is a conspicuous early example. Later Diocles of Carystus reproached his colleagues for the unsound and highly speculative postulation of causes when their ends would have been better served by careful attention to what can be discovered by experience (Galen, *De aliment. facult.* vi. 455. 5 ff. K = fr. 112 Wellman).[12] And Herophilus, whose student Philinus of Cos is sometimes credited with founding the Empirical school,[13] posed

---

[12] Cf. W. Jaeger, *Diokles von Karystos: Die griechische Medizin und die Schule des Aristoteles* (Berlin: Weidmann, 1938), 25 ff., and the important reassessment of Diocles' date and intellectual affinities by H. von Staden, 'Jaeger's "Skandalon der historischen Vernunft": Diocles, Aristotle and Theophrastus', in W. M. Calder (ed.), *Werner Jaeger Reconsidered* (Athens, Ga.: Scholars Press, 1992), 227–65. Questions about how much broader methodological significance the passage has have been raised by P. J. van der Eijk, 'Diocles and the Hippocratic Writings on the Method of Diaetetics and the Limits of Causal Explanation', in R. Wittern and P. Pellegrin (eds.), *Hippokratische Medizin und antike Philosophie* (Hildesheim: Olms, 1996), 229–57.

[13] Cf. [Galen], *Introductio seu Medicus*, xiv. 683. 11 ff. K = fr. 6 Deichgräber.

some questions about the status of medical theory and the causal claims it appears to license.[14] Yet it appears that none of these figures intended to deny the possibility that reason may in fact be able to make the kind of discoveries that the Rationalists maintained it could. An Empiricist would certainly sympathize with the author of *De vetere medicina*'s remarks about the speculative character of his opponents' theories (*VM* 1. 3).

But *De vetere medicina* goes on to offer an account of health and disease that makes free use of natures, powers, and causes in a way that the Empiricists would not have permitted. And it is clear that its author does not suppose, as the Empiricists do, that any account framed in terms of these notions is *eo ipso* beyond the power of ordinary methods of observation to discover and confirm. Nor did the caution Diocles and Herophilus urged on their fellow medical practitioners prevent them from theorizing about health and disease. Rather, it appears their aim was to alert the medical profession to the danger of rash speculation, and perhaps to urge a measure of tentativeness about even the results of well and carefully conducted enquiry. It remained for the Empiricists to construct a full-blown epistemological position denying that reason furnishes us with the means to infer conclusions about non-evident matters. The moral they were inclined to draw from the conflict between their opponents' different theories was not that the Rationalist programme needed to be pursued with greater caution than hitherto, but that it was doomed to failure from the start. Knowledge of the non-evident, they argued, was in principle unobtainable.

2. Empiricism and Pyrrhonism

It was this stand, when militantly asserted, that prompted Sextus' criticism of the Empirical school (*PH* 1. 236).[15] But this is not the Pyrrhonists' only complaint. For the vigour with which (at least some) Empiricists repudiated knowledge of the non-evident was matched by their quite unsceptical complacency about matters they

[14] See the material on 'Theory of Method and Cause' collected and discussed by H. von Staden, *Herophilus: The Art of Medicine in Early Alexandria* (Cambridge: Cambridge University Press, 1989), 115 ff. Cf. F. Kudlien, 'Herophilos und der Beginn des medizinischen Skepsis', *Gesnerus*, 21 (1964), 1–13.

[15] The Methodists levelled the same criticism against Empiricism (cf. Galen, *De sect. ingred.* iii. 14 *SM*).

take to be evident (cf. Galen, *De sect. ingred.* iii. 11. 22 *SM*; *Subfig. emp.* 68. 5 Deichgräber). Thus they often appear willing to take the agreement we apparently can and typically do reach about evident matters as a positive reflection on their secure evidential status. And they believe that an explanation for the agreement obtainable about evident matters is ready to hand: the direct access to the evident world given us by our senses ensures that, when conditions permit the proper exercise of our perceptual faculties, we shall agree on the truth of the matter at issue (cf. Galen, *On Medical Experience*, 133–5 Walzer). On the other hand, they continue to find claims about non-evident matters suspicious even when they are supported by widespread agreement (cf. Galen, *Subfig. emp.* 67. 32–5 Deichgräber).

The Pyrrhonists were more even-handed. The arguments they brought against dogmatic claims to non-evident knowledge, many of which they shared with the Empiricists, had to be weighed in the balance against the opposing case. As far as the Pyrrhonist can see, he is not in a position to resolve the resulting disagreement and put behind him the dilemma posed by the stand-off to which his enquiries have led. Thus he is left with little alternative but to suspend judgement about whether knowledge of non-evident matters is possible. He is certainly in no position to rule it out, and for all he knows his opponents may one day be able to demonstrate its possibility convincingly. But if they are less firmly convinced of the impossibility of non-evident knowledge than the Empiricists, the Pyrrhonists are equally unsure of whether our grasp of evident matters is more secure. Thus the comparative ease with which agreement is reached about evident matters, which the Empiricists take as evidence for the essential soundness of our perceptual powers, is not granted immunity from sceptical criticism by the Pyrrhonists. They question whether we are right to give preference to what majorities agree on by disqualifying dissenting voices, even when they are in a very small minority (cf. *PH* 2. 43–4; *M.* 7. 327 ff.; 8. 53–4). They challenge the assumption that anything at all is evident by arguing that the senses do not give us direct access to any part of the world (cf. *M.* 7. 364–8; 8. 357–60, 364–6, 396). And of course, they bring forward every kind of argument that might tend to cast doubt on the veracity of the senses. Hence they are led to suspend judgement about evident no less than non-evident matters.

To be sure, at times they argue in a way that depends on a strong contrast between the secure standing of evident and observable matters with the unsettled condition of conclusions about the non-evident (cf. *M.* 8. 322–5). But when Sextus is being careful, he indicates clearly that his apparent endorsement of empirical knowledge is merely a provisional concession, necessary before arguments against the dogmatists' claim to be able to draw secure inferences from the observed to the unobserved can be made, and not an expression of genuine conviction (cf. *PH* 2. 95–6; *M.* 8. 141–2, 396).

Thus Empiricism, at any rate in its dogmatic form, seems to have differed from Pyrrhonism in something like the following ways:

(1) While he allows that knowledge of evident matters is possible, the Empiricist firmly believes that non-evident matters are unknowable (ἀκατάληπτα); and while he permits himself no beliefs about the latter, he is firmly attached to some of his beliefs about the former.

(2) As a sceptic, the Pyrrhonist suspends judgement on all matters alike (ἐποχὴ περὶ πάντων), whether classified as evident or non-evident; and he makes no exception for the question whether non-evident matters are knowable.

Put so bluntly, the differences between the two schools make it hard to see how there could have been any affinity between them at all. Yet their overlapping membership suggests that their teachings cannot have been as obviously incompatible as the picture just sketched might suggest. To see our way clear of this difficulty, we must add more detail to the picture, so that we shall be able to make out what difference the qualification 'dogmatic' makes, i.e. what the non-dogmatic form of Empiricism acceptable to Pyrrhonism was like. The best way to do this, however, is to approach the issue from the other side by asking how a Pyrrhonist, committed as we have seen to universal suspension of judgement, could also have been an Empiricist, or indeed anything other than a sceptic, i.e. a practitioner of universal suspension of judgement.

Although a proper answer to the question would require more time than we can spare, the rough outline of one is not hard to make out. For a closer inspection reveals that, in a rather special and highly qualified way, the Pyrrhonist will have beliefs or δόγματα (*PH* 1. 13). What is more, he will form his beliefs under

the guidance of a criterion, τὸ φαινόμενον (*PH* 1. 21–2). Thus the
subject of his beliefs will be the phenomena, or what is apparent
to him. But this seems rather odd, for the term φαινόμενα is often
used, like ἐναργῆ or πρόδηλα, to designate evident matters, which are
directly given to observation, in contrast to non-evident matters,
which are accessible, if at all, only indirectly by means of inference
from the evident (cf. *PH* 1. 9; *M.* 7. 358; 8. 362). Hence it appears
we have escaped from one difficulty only to find ourselves in another. For apart perhaps from the excessive fervour with which the
Empiricists deny that non-evident matters are knowable, there now
seems to be very little in Empiricism to which the Pyrrhonists could
object. Indeed, Pyrrhonism begins to appear suspiciously like Empiricism, and this suspicion is not diminished when we learn that
the Pyrrhonists claimed to raise questions and suspend judgement
only about non-evident matters (*PH* 1. 13, 193, 198; D.L. 9. 103,
105). If it is no longer so hard to understand how an Empiricist
could at the same time be a Pyrrhonist, it may be because it is so
difficult to see how a Pyrrhonist could really be a sceptic.

But this appearance is deceptive. Although the two positions can
be stated in identical terms—viz. suspend judgement about the
non-evident and adhere to the phenomena alone—Pyrrhonism and
Empiricism put the contrast between evident and non-evident to
very different uses. We know what the Empiricists intended by it.
They shared an epistemological framework with their Rationalist
opponents, according to which possible objects of knowledge come
in two clearly distinguished kinds: the first made up of evident
matters directly accessible to observation, the second of items inaccessible to direct observation but sometimes accessible through
inference from evidence furnished by items of the first sort. The
Empiricists accept the distinction, only denying that reason furnishes us with the means of making inferences from the evident
to the non-evident. Hence they deny that non-evident matters are
knowable. The Pyrrhonists do not adopt this framework in quite the
same way, however. And what they intend by their talk of φαινόμενα
and ἄδηλα is correspondingly different. As they see it, every possible object of knowledge, no matter how classified, is potentially
non-evident and unknowable when viewed in a certain way. Hence
they can fairly claim to suspend judgement on all matters, viewed
in this way, while suspending judgement only about non-evident
matters.

The next two questions are obvious: Viewed in what way are all matters non-evident and unknowable? And what, then, supposing an answer of some kind can be given to the first question, does the Pyrrhonist adherence to the phenomena come to? Again, we lack the time to give the issues that have been raised the attention they deserve, but it may be possible to sketch an answer in rough outline.

A good point of departure is furnished by traces of what is not so much another view of non-evidence as a different angle of approach to it. To this way of thinking, a matter is non-evident to the extent that it is unclear, in doubt, or disputed.[16] Of these matters, those that are subject to resolution are fit subjects for enquiry (*quaestio*, ζήτησις), through which doubts are put to rest, controversies resolved, and enquiry brought to an end (cf. Cicero, *Luc.* 26). Given certain assumptions, the distance between this way of conceiving matters and the division between evident and non-evident matters with which we are already familiar is not very great. For as we have already seen, according to both Rationalists and Empiricists, matters accessible to direct observation do not set in train protracted disputes; there is a simple method of getting clear about them, namely direct inspection. At the same time, the matters that the two schools agree in classifying as non-evident cannot be cleared up so easily. They stand in need of resolution, or perhaps we should say resolution of a special sort, namely an inference which draws on a stock of already acquired apprehensions.

If the inferences from the evident to the non-evident so highly valued by dogmatic philosophers and Rationalist physicians are to lead to secure conclusions, they must be furnished with starting-points by evident matters directly given to observation and not requiring the support of further evidence themselves. And though he does not propose to draw any inferences, at least not any of the objectionable Rationalist variety, the dogmatic Empiricist too must have a stock of secure apprehensions acquired by means of direct observation. Thus there must be more to an evident impression than being somehow directly given and non-inferential. It has to be self-evident; part of what is given must be an unshakeable assurance of its own veracity.

Dogmatic philosophers of the Hellenistic period, particularly the Stoics, devoted much energy and ingenuity to the case for the

---

[16] πᾶν τὸν διάφωνον ἄδηλόν ἐστι (*M.* 8. 178; cf. *PH* 3. 6); τὸ ζητούμενόν ἐστιν ἄδηλον (*M.* 8. 336).

existence of self-evident impressions of the type required. But that
case was challenged, no less persistently and ingeniously, first by the
sceptical Academy and later by the Pyrrhonists. Their arguments
appeared to show that questions can always be raised about suppos-
edly self-evident impressions. The best known was the Academy's
argument that every true impression can be matched with a false
impression indistinguishable from it (cf. *M.* 7. 402 ff.; Cicero, *Luc.*
41–53, 83–6). This argument implies that none of our impressions
has an intrinsic character of the kind that it could have only if it
arose in conditions that make it true. Since, in the last analysis, we
have nothing to go on apart from our impressions, we can never
eliminate the possibility of mistaking a false for a true impression;
no impression provides the kind of assurance or guarantee required
of a self-evident impression. And there are further arguments with
the same implications, familiar to us from Sextus' writings. Thus,
for instance, though it does not loom as large as it was to in modern
philosophy, there are traces of an argument systematically ques-
tioning whether our impressions really resemble the objects they
purport to be like (cf. *M.* 7. 357). And the Pyrrhonists were also
happy to exploit Democritean arguments for what may appear to
be an even more damaging conclusion: the world our senses seem to
put us in touch with, the world of secondary properties, has no real
existence, while the atoms which do really exist are devoid of sensible properties like colour (*M.* 7. 135; 8. 6, 184, 354–5). And they
observe that, though the phenomenal world is made up of objects
which appear to move and undergo change, the arguments of the
Eleatics have called the reality of change and motion into question
as well (cf. *PH* 3. 65).

Of course, the Pyrrhonian sceptic does not believe that he has
firmly established these conclusions, but he does seem to have
uncovered problems which, if unresolved, must be regarded by
the dogmatists, applying their own conception of non-evidence,
as rendering everything non-evident. His experience is that every
question, when made an object of philosophical enquiry, appears
to be unresolved, and in this way non-evident. To see where this
leaves the Pyrrhonian sceptic, we must turn to the idealized historical sketch Sextus provides to explain the origin of scepticism
(*PH* 1. 12, cf. 28–9). The sceptic begins, according to this story,
just as the dogmatist had, by undertaking a search for philosophical
understanding; he takes very seriously the idea that he can put an

end to the disagreement and confusion to which ordinary experience gives rise by using reason to come to a deeper understanding.
Thus, far from repudiating the rationality by which his dogmatic
opponents set so much store, he sees himself as making fuller and
more conscientious use of it than they do. His opponents appear
to him to have brought their search to a premature conclusion by
opting arbitrarily for one of a number of conflicting possibilities
without giving the others their just due. As he sees it, philosophical
enquiry has not converged on a clear and consistent resolution of
the problems with which it is faced; instead, it has multiplied disputes and discovered new difficulties at every turn, in the process
opening up a bewildering variety of alternative answers to every
question to which it is applied, apparently without being able to
resolve the ensuing conflict. He has little alternative but to suspend
judgement.

From the point of view of dogmatic philosophy, his life should
be an utter disaster, if not actually impossible, in consequence. For
questions on whose resolution it crucially depends remain completely open. Hence the Stoics, who are representative of dogmatic
philosophy on this point, accused the Academics, who argued much
as the Pyrrhonists were later to do, of trying to render everything
non-evident and thus overthrow life (cf. Cicero, *Luc.* 32, 105, 110).
The Academics, and later the Pyrrhonists, responded by turning
this charge against their accusers. Since it is by failing to satisfy
requirements imposed by the dogmatists that everything threatens
to become absolutely and wholly non-evident, perhaps, then, it is
those requirements which should be held responsible for rendering
everything non-evident and unknowable (cf. *M.* 8. 396; 11. 165).
The Pyrrhonists underscore this point by saying that all things
are non-evident with the qualification 'as far as it is a matter of
philosophical reason' (ὅσον ἐπὶ τῷ λόγῳ).[17]

---

[17] This understanding of this and similar formulae and the account of Pyrrhonian
belief to which it belongs are indebted to M. Frede, 'Des Skeptikers Meinungen',
Neue Hefte für Philosophie, 15–16 (1979), 102–29, repr. and trans. in id., *Essays in Ancient Philosophy*, 179–200; an alternative deflationary reading has been defended by
J. Brunschwig, 'La formule ὅσον ἐπὶ τῷ λόγῳ chez Sextus Empiricus', in A.-J. Voelke
(ed.), *Le Scepticisme antique* (Cahiers de la *Revue de théologie et de philosophie*, 15;
Geneva, 1990), 107–21, repr. in *Études sur les philosophies hellénistiques: Épicurisme,
stoïcisme, scepticisme* (Paris: Presses Universitaires de France, 1995), 321–42, trans.
in id., *Papers in Hellenistic Philosophy* (Cambridge: Cambridge University Press,
1994), 244–58. Some reasons for continuing to prefer a more philosophically suggestive interpretation are suggested in my review of Brunschwig, *Études*, in *Review of*

And this fact must be considered in connection with the sceptic's discovery that he seems to get on quite well without resolving
the philosophical difficulties his enquiries have brought to light.
For it is the Pyrrhonian sceptic's surprising experience that the
impasse to which his continuing engagement with philosophical
enquiry leads does not leave him without impressions on a great
many topics, or the means of adding to them; this despite the fact
that his investigations have suggested countless ways in which his
impressions may be deceptive. And it would be hard to be more
acutely conscious than he is of how little the fact that things appear
in a certain way may imply about how they really are. Nevertheless,
things do appear to him in a certain way.

One possibility that he cannot avoid considering is that the apparent failure of philosophical enquiry to afford us insights into the
underlying nature of things, on the basis of which we could criticize
and correct appearances, reflects at least as badly on philosophical
enquiry as it does on the appearances. In such a situation, the assumption that mere reliance on the phenomena, and on ordinary
ways of resolving the disagreements they present, is inadequate and
in need of philosophical revision cannot itself go unquestioned. The
Pyrrhonist's experience is that reason's inability to return philosophically satisfying answers does not mean that he cannot arrive
at any answers at all. By following the appearances and ordinary
everyday ways of thinking about them, he can. And Sextus can
sometimes sound like a defender of robust common sense against
pernicious philosophical subtleties (cf. *PH* 2. 102; *M*. 8. 156). But
the Pyrrhonist does not dismiss the challenge philosophy poses.
His impressions remain highly suspect from the vantage-point of
philosophical enquiry, which he is no less capable of occupying
than his dogmatic opponent. Thus he suspends judgement with
the qualification 'as far as it is a matter of reason', and he finds
all claims and their denials equal in point of plausibility with the
same qualification (*PH* 1. 227). Yet he finds that the impressions
and ordinary habits of thought he falls back on provide him with

Metaphysics, 52 (1998), 132–4. How to understand Sextus' claim that the Pyrrhonists allow themselves beliefs at *PH* 1. 13, indeed, whether the *dogma* he speaks of
there qualifies as belief, is the subject of lively debate. The paper of Frede, with
whose view I am most in sympathy, is reprinted along with crucial contributions
to the debate defending alternative views by M. F. Burnyeat and J. Barnes in M.
Burnyeat and M. Frede (eds.), *The Original Sceptics: A Controversy* (Indianapolis:
Hackett, 1997), 1–24.

the guidance he needs to decide and to act. This is the Pyrrhonian sceptic's situation in rough outline. If it has about it an air of incompleteness, this is because the question how much or how little the qualifications 'as far as it is a matter of reason' and 'as far as it is a matter of appearance' add or detract is itself one of the issues raised but left unresolved by philosophical reflection.

Obviously much more would have to be said before we could begin to do justice to the Pyrrhonian outlook, but perhaps this is enough to give us a sense of just how different this rather curious and complicated point of view is from that of the dogmatic Empiricist. But if it is the dogmatic character of the Empiricists' views, rather than their content, to which he objects, the next issue to be addressed is how a Pyrrhonist, occupying the vantage-point just described, could also somehow have held a recognizably Empiricist position. We have seen what kind of character the contrast between φαινόμενα and ἄδηλα takes on in Pyrrhonism: everything becomes non-evident when viewed in connection with dogmatic standards of evidence. The result is that the matters the Empiricist identifies as phenomena have no epistemological advantage in the eyes of the Pyrrhonist, for they are subject to unresolved philosophical questions no less than the Empiricist's non-evident matters. Nevertheless, as we have seen, the Pyrrhonist will have views of a certain kind, namely views about what appears to him to be the case, the phenomena.

Thus it seems the Pyrrhonist, having put everything on the same level and suspended judgement on every matter regarded as an object of philosophical enquiry, will feel free to hold views on any topic whatsoever, as long as these views are held in a properly sceptical, circumspect, non-committal spirit, in full consciousness of just how little the fact that things appear in such a way to the believer may matter when, so to speak, the stakes are raised. Why, then, did the Pyrrhonists so often find themselves left with Empirical views, even though it is possible to dogmatize about the phenomena identified by the Empiricists no less than about the obscure and esoteric matters so prominent in Rationalist theory? The answer cannot be that the Pyrrhonist takes up Empiricism in acknowledgement, however hesitant, of the evidential superiority of the phenomena and the ordinary, everyday kind of experience which furnish the Empiricists with the basis for their art; for as we know, he recognizes no such superiority. It must rather be that, as it happens, he finds himself left with views which largely correspond to the ordinary, everyday views of common experience; these are the appearances he follows for lack of anything better, while remaining acutely conscious of the questions that can be raised about them. And in view of this affinity between Pyrrhonism and ordinary experience, the attraction Empiricism holds for the Pyrrhonist is not surprising; for according to the Empirical conception, technical, artistic knowledge is just a more complicated and comprehensive version of ordinary experience, more systematic and extensive than the layman's, but not radically different in character (cf. *M.* 8. 291). Hence there is a large measure of rough agreement between Pyrrhonists and Empiricists about the content of the phenomena, and the former will typically find themselves without an impression of any kind about the matters classified as non-evident by the Empiricists.[18] Thus, though it was in principle open to the Pyrrhonist to hold views on just about any subject-matter sceptically, it seems that as a matter of fact it was Empiricism which found the most favour with Pyrrhonists.

This, then, is the situation of the Pyrrhonian Empiricist. It is by no means unproblematic. The two views are in tension, and their combination is potentially unstable. As far as the Pyrrhonist is concerned, the Empirically identified phenomena enjoy no epistemic advantages over matters about which things do not seem one way or the other to him. In choosing to adhere to them, he is not yielding, even implicitly, to their superior force as evidence, but going along with or falling back on all he is left with despite the stand-off at which he has arrived through his enquiries. And on the other hand, it is not hard to see that the Empiricist was faced with a standing temptation to allow his doubts about the power of reason to disclose the non-evident, and his reliance on the phenomena, to harden into dogmatic certainties.

3. Two Kinds of Sign and Two Kinds of Argument against Signs

Let us now turn to the issue which is our principal object of interest and in which the tension between Pyrrhonism and Empiricism comes into especially sharp focus: Sextus Empiricus' handling of

[18] On the Academics cf. Cicero, *Luc.* 110, 122.

sign-inference. The subject arises quite naturally in the course of Sextus' exposition and critique of dogmatic epistemology. For the purpose of his examination, as we have seen, he adopts a dogmatic distinction between evident and non-evident matters, according to which knowledge of the first is acquired by direct inspection, while conclusions about the second must be inferred through sign-inferences and demonstrations from the evidence furnished in this way (*PH* 2. 13; *M*. 7. 22). Evident matters are the province of the criterion, and Sextus goes on to challenge the dogmatists' claim that it is possible to infer conclusions from evident matters, i.e. use them as signs, only after a sustained sceptical examination of their accounts of the criterion. Since such inferences will be possible only if directly given evidence furnishes us with secure starting-points, Sextus concedes the case against the criterion for the sake of argument (cf. *PH* 2. 95–6; *M*. 8. 140). But as we would expect, and he strongly emphasizes himself, this is a provisional concession only, not a retreat from the questions the sceptic has raised about evident knowledge.

Sextus' treatment of signs is of particular importance for our purposes because the crucial distinction in terms of which he frames the issues—between commemorative and indicative signs—is a medical one, used by Empiricists and Rationalists to state an important part of their disagreement. The Empiricists claimed to rely on commemorative signification while denying the possibility of indicative signification, which was in turn vigorously defended by the Rationalists. This historical claim is nowhere endorsed by the explicit testimony of Sextus, who mentions only dogmatic philosophers and Rationalist physicians (*M*. 8. 156).[19] Nevertheless, as we proceed

---

[19] As we have already noted, the view that commemorative and indicative signification were of respectively Empirical and Rationalist origin was first advanced by R. Philippson, *De Philodemi libro*, 65 ff., who collected much of the relevant evidence. A fuller discussion of his views is to be found below. The view has since met with a measure of favour. Cf. V. Brochard, *Les Sceptiques grecs*, 2nd edn. (Paris: Vrin, 1887), 270 with n. 3; D. Glidden, 'Skeptic Semiotics', *Phronesis*, 28 (1983), 213–55; M. R. Stopper, 'Schizzi pirroniani', *Phronesis*, 28 (1983), 265–97 at 295 n. 76; K. Hülser, *Die Fragmente zur Dialektik der Stoiker* (4 vols.; Stuttgart: Frommann-Holzboog, 1987–8), iii. 1328–9 ad fr. 1026; P. Natorp, *Forschungen zur Geschichte des Erkenntnisproblems im Altertum* (Berlin: Wilhelm Hertz, 1884), 146 ff.; Burnyeat, 'The Origins of Non-deductive Inference', 212; D. Sedley, 'On Signs', in Barnes *et al.* (eds.), *Science and Speculation*, 239–72 at 241 n. 8. The other main tendency has been to attribute the distinction to the Stoics: cf. Glidden, 247 n. 39, for references to authorities holding this view. Ebert believes that it belongs to a theory of signs first developed by the Dialectical school and then taken over by the Stoics: T.

enough evidence should accumulate to leave little doubt that we are dealing with a medical distinction which, though not unrelated to important strands of thought in the professional philosophy of the time, is strongly coloured by the approach taken to these issues by the leading schools of medicine; so much so that it cannot be applied to the philosophers' positions without seriously confusing matters, although this is what Sextus and his Pyrrhonian precursors, in common with the doxographical tradition, seem to have done (cf. [Galen], *Historia philosopha*, 605. 9–18 *DG*). But if this is right, by vehemently endorsing commemorative signification and opposing its indicative counterpart, Sextus embraces the Empirical position in a way he does nowhere else; indeed, it looks as if he has let his guard down and failed to observe his own strictures against the uncritical acceptance of Empiricism. At the same time, a large part of the argument Sextus brings to bear on the topic of signs cannot easily be made to serve his announced purpose, to overthrow the indicative sign while leaving the commemorative signification which aligns him with Empiricism in place. What seems to have happened is that two different controversies have been conflated: the Empiricists' battle with Rationalism and the Pyrrhonists' battle with dogmatic philosophy. There is some question, then, whether the Empiricists' position on sign-inference is any less vulnerable to the sceptics' anti-semiotic arguments than the other positions available. Thus we are brought back to the question of whether there is a place for the Empiricists' positive teachings in Pyrrhonism.

Sextus takes up the topic of signs twice, at *PH* 2. 97–133 and at *M*. 8. 141–299. There is an important difference between the two passages that will furnish us with the clue we need to clear up one of the main difficulties his account presents. But both treatments are introduced in the same way, with a distinction between commemorative and indicative signification, and assigned the same purpose of abolishing the latter. And we would do best to begin with this distinction ourselves. Since the first of the problems we must face can be stated most easily in connection with the discussion in *PH* 2, let us begin there. Sextus prepares the way for the distinction with a division of the types of non-evident matters to be revealed by the different varieties of sign (*PH* 2. 97–8; *M*. 8. 145–8). Absolutely non-evident matters (καθάπαξ ἄδηλα) are forever beyond the reach

Ebert, *Dialektiker und frühe Stoiker: Untersuchungen zur Entstehung der Aussagenlogik* (Göttingen: Vandenhoeck and Ruprecht, 1991), 45 ff.

of human apprehension; whether the number of stars is odd or even is an example. Naturally non-evident matters (ἄδηλα φύσει), like the invisible pores in the body, are only incapable of coming under direct observation, though they can be grasped by means of inference. Finally, temporarily non-evident matters (πρὸς καιρὸν ἄδηλα) have an evident nature, but are rendered non-evident by external circumstances. So for instance, the city of Athens is non-evident to someone at a sufficiently great distance from it. The commemorative sign reveals temporarily non-evident matters, the indicative sign naturally non-evident matters (*PH* 2. 99; *M.* 8. 151, 156).

The division is an awkward one. If human powers of apprehension are held fixed, being non-evident is reducible to something like an intrinsic feature of the item's nature which prevents it from being apprehended, whether directly or by any means at all. Evident matters are likewise such by nature that they can fall under evident apprehension. In this sense, temporarily non-evident matters are evident, though not directly apprehended owing to contingent, extrinsic circumstances (cf. *PH* 2. 98; *M.* 8. 145). Thus the division uneasily joins two kinds of non-evident item with a condition of evident items. And there is some evidence to suggest that the Empiricists supplemented an existing distinction in order to explain in what sense they allow that there are signs by means of which conclusions about non-evident matters can be drawn, while in another sense crucial to their Rationalist opponents they continue to deny the possibility of access to the non-evident through signs (cf. Galen, *De sect. ingred.* iii. 11. 10–12 *SM*; [Galen], *Def. med.* xix. 394. 8–12 K).

Sextus, however, attributes this distinction simply to the dogmatists before proceeding to attribute the following pair of definitions to them (*PH* 2. 100–1; cf. *M.* 8. 152–4): 'They call the commemorative sign [ὑπομνηστικὸν σημεῖον] that which having been evidently co-observed with the signified, together with its occurrence when the signified matter is non-evident, leads us into a recollection [ὑπόμνησις] of what was co-observed with it but is now not manifest.' While the indicative sign (ἐνδεικτικὸν σημεῖον) is 'as they say, that which has not been evidently co-observed with the signified, but from its own nature and constitution [ἐκ τῆς ἰδίας φύσεως καὶ κατασκευῆς] signifies that of which it is a sign.' At *M.* 8. 154 he expands on this definition of the indicative sign with the colourful remark that 'it is said to all but break into speech signifying that of which it is a sign'.

Before continuing we should pause to note a feature of commemorative signification that it appears to owe to the Empiricists' distinctive anti-rationalism. Because this feature reflects a peculiar set of Empirical assumptions which were not widely shared, the division between commemorative and indicative signs could not have been applied without modification to a wider range of views on the subject. This implies that the distinction is medical not only in its origin and terminology, but in a stronger sense that prevented it from mapping easily onto related distinctions as they might have been drawn by contemporary philosophers. At first glance, commemorative signification would appear to be a kind of inference or reasoning based on generalizations grounded in long observation of empirical regularities, a familiar enough idea. But this is not quite right. Notice that the feature called attention to by its name is not the co-observation ($\sigma\upsilon\mu\pi\alpha\rho\alpha\tau\acute{\eta}\rho\eta\sigma\iota\varsigma$) on which it depends, but commemoration ($\acute{\upsilon}\pi\acute{o}\mu\nu\eta\sigma\iota\varsigma$). And this stress on commemoration is a consequence of the very strong line the early Empiricists took against reason.[20] For odd as it may sound, early Empiricists tried to explain in terms of memory what others had attributed to reason. So strong was the view taken by these Empiricists that, for example, they refused to grant reason a role in the discovery of composite drugs made up of a mixture of ingredients which had proved effective when applied singly against the same ailment in different cases. Instead, they preferred to say that these were discovered by chance or suggested by dreams, even though it was fairly obvious that some elementary reasoning had made it seem likely that mixing the different ingredients would produce a remedy that was effective in a larger number of cases (cf. Galen, *De meth. med.* x. 163. 14 ff. K = fr. 105 Deichgräber).

Their opposition to reason extended to reasoning from evidence to a conclusion or, properly speaking, to making inferences at all. Thus our first description of signs as a matter of inference needs

---

[20] For a fuller and more detailed treatment of the Empiricists' attitude towards reason, and developments in that attitude, see M. Frede, 'An Empiricist View of Knowledge: Memorism', in S. Everson (ed.), *Epistemology* (Cambridge: Cambridge University Press, 1990), 225–50, and id., 'The Empiricist Attitude towards Reason and Theory', in R. J. Hankinson (ed.), *Method, Metaphysics and Medicine: Studies in the Philosophy of Ancient Science* (Edmonton: Academic Printing and Publishing, 1988), 79–97.

to be qualified. For although the mental transition they make from sign to signified may look like a rational inference, involving a grasp of the relation of evidential support between ground and conclusion, the Empiricists chose to understand it differently. Reaching a signified conclusion on the basis of an evident sign was not, according to their alternative account, a matter of being compelled by the evidence, of seeing the force of the grounds which support the conclusion; and it was certainly not a matter of grasping the natural necessities by means of which certain observable states of affairs require or exclude other, unobservable ones. Rather, it was a matter of being put in mind of or reminded of what has been observed and committed to memory. Thus apparent instances of inference in medicine, e.g. transitions from symptoms to a suggested therapy, are treated by the Empiricists as cases of being induced to recollect, and they regarded artistic expertise as largely a matter of acquiring dispositions to be reminded of certain things by certain observations.

This emphasis on memory helps to explain a part of the Empiricist account of signification which would otherwise be difficult to understand: their insistence that commemorative signification is not a method of discovery, that it does not reveal anything new about the world. This feature of the commemorative sign is strongly emphasized by the definition in the pseudo-Galenic *Definitiones medicae* (xix. 396. 12–14 K): 'The commemorative sign is, as the Empiricists say, a matter apparent and known from pre-observation, useful for the recollection [ὑπόμνησις] of some known matter.' And Galen too stresses that the Empiricists' opposition to inference leads them to declare that 'nothing is able to be known from another thing, but all things have need of knowledge from themselves' (*De sect. ingred.* iii. 10. 23–4 *SM*).

This appeal to memory may well strike us as rather suspect, for it seems to run the risk of obscuring a crucial difference between being reminded and coming to know. Though the memory of previous observations may play an important part when we see smoke and conclude there is a fire over the hill, the smoke does not remind us of something we did not know—nothing can do that—rather, it seems that we have been given the evidence we need to infer a conclusion that is a new piece of knowledge. Commemoration does not appear to be a very plausible substitute for reasoning, then. But if we leave matters here, we shall not have done the

Empirical position justice. The Rationalist conception of reasoning and inference, which requires a grasp of the underlying nature of things and the relations of consequence and exclusion that obtain between states of affairs as a result, cannot easily be made to fit the kind of transitions of which the Empiricists made use. And we are all familiar with conceptions of rational grounds, evidence, and inference according to which the kind of empirically grounded inferences on which the Empiricists relied—and without which we can hardly do ourselves—turn out to be groundless. If reasoning is what the Rationalists claim it is, then what the Empiricists were doing was not reasoning. In such a situation the Empiricists' appeal to a richer conception of memory and of what it is to be reminded may not have been so unsatisfactory after all.

None the less, later Empiricists did make a place for reasoning of a kind, which they called *epilogismos* to distinguish it from the sort of reasoning advocated by the Rationalists, which they called *analogismos*. Presumably they were moved by something like the above considerations. We can see the difference between the old and the new Empirical views very clearly when Galen passes, in the space of a few lines, from the claim we have already met, that nothing can be known from another thing, to an account of epilogism stressing its use in the *discovery* of temporarily non-evident matters (*De sect. ingred.* iii. 10. 23–4; 11. 9–10 *SM*). This remark also makes it clear that epilogistic inference came to cover the ground previously covered by the commemorative sign. Its two distinguishing features were that it involved nothing more than the kind of perfectly ordinary reasoning common to all human beings and that it was concerned exclusively with the phenomena.[21] But this means that epilogism was not reasoning as the Rationalists understood it. It neither furnished nor depended on the special insights beyond ordinary experience that were at the heart of the Rationalist conception of reason; nor did it derive its force from a grasp of the relations of consequence and exclusion enforced by the nature of things as analogism was supposed to do.

That epilogism is not reasoning as the Rationalists would have recognized it is made particularly clear by the Empiricists' expla-

---

[21] On the first see Galen, *De comp. medic. sec. gen.* xiii. 366. 5 ff. K = 150. 13–15 Deichgräber; *On Medical Experience*, 133, 140 Walzer. On the second see *De sect. ingred.* iii. 11. 8 *SM*; *On Medical Experience*, 133–5 Walzer; *Subfig. emp.* 62. 24–31 Deichgräber.

nation of why they put their faith in the agreement among the different witnesses preserved in medical history. They were at pains to emphasize that their motivation was not the kind of rational justification which might be offered, and to which some unwary members of the school inclined. For as they point out, one could say that agreement is a sign of truth, and go on to explain why the nature of the matters at issue makes agreement a reliable indicator of truth (cf. *Subfig. emp.* 68. 25 ff. Deichgräber). But this would be an analogistic and dogmatic approach. An Empiricist will give an epilogistic account, saying that it is just a matter of experience that agreement and truth go together in this way. The same is true of the Empiricists' account of the transition to the similar, their method of producing suggestions about measures they might try when confronted with cases of a kind not previously met with by relating them in one way or another to cases about which the collective experience of the medical art does have something to say. Menodotus, in particular, took special care to distinguish the Empiricists' real motives for relying on the practice from a possible rational account in terms of the underlying nature of the items revealed by similarity or something along those lines. It is not, he says, using the Empiricists' favourite term of abuse for Rationalist inference, because the transition to the similar is *plausible*, but because it has been effective in experience, that they make use of it (*Subfig. emp.* 70. 14 ff. Deichgräber).

It is surprising to find Sextus taking no notice of this development in the Empiricists' attitude towards reason and inference. It should have been well enough entrenched by his time. For Heraclides of Tarentum seems to have been the first Empiricist clearly to acknowledge a role for reason (*Subfig. emp.* 87. 12 ff. Deichgräber). And Sextus' precursors, Menodotus and Theodas, who were both Pyrrhonists and Empiricists, clearly endorsed epilogism (50. 3; 87. 25 ff.). Perhaps some light was thrown on this topic in Sextus' medical writings, and their loss is especially to be regretted for this reason.

Yet we should not make too much of this omission. For it is not so much that the Empiricists decided to use reason as they had not before, but rather that they decided to describe what they had been doing all along as reasoning. But it still counted as reasoning only in the ordinary, non-technical acceptance of the term, and not, as we have seen, as it figured in the Empiricists' debate with the Rationalists. Thus we may well doubt whether the radical anti-rationalism of the early Empiricists was uppermost in Sextus' mind when he cited the distinction between commemorative and indicative signs. Rather, Sextus and the tradition on which he relies seem to have been interested mainly in the features of the commemorative sign that Sextus chooses to emphasize in his account: its exclusive application to evident matters and its basis in the observation of co-occurrent and sequential events. Indeed, it was only by ignoring the anti-rational, non-inferential component of the commemorative sign as originally conceived that Sextus and his predecessors were able to represent the division as part of an uncontroversial, generally accepted framework. Hence it is probably not necessary to attribute to the Pyrrhonists with whom Sextus aligns himself by endorsing commemorative signification a primitive Empirical view that may have fallen out of favour among the Empiricists themselves.

But this is not to say that the Pyrrhonian endorsement of commemorative signification reported by Sextus is without difficulties. For on this reading of the situation, the Pyrrhonists accepted a kind of inference based on co-observation of evident matters while rejecting indicative inferences to the non-evident. But we have just seen that it is dogmatic Empiricists, and not Pyrrhonists, who grant favoured epistemic standing to evident matters. If Pyrrhonists tend largely to follow the phenomena identified by Empiricism, it is only in a complicated and highly qualified way. Unlike the less sceptical of the Empiricists, the Pyrrhonists do not maintain that knowledge of evident matters is on a more secure footing than the Rationalists' alleged knowledge of non-evident matters. And Sextus is at pains to emphasize that he concedes such a standing to evident matters only provisionally (*PH* 2. 95–6; *M.* 8. 141–2). Indeed, the assumption allowed to enter the argument in this way, that there are matters which are evident by nature (cf. *PH* 2. 98; *M.* 7. 145), probably attracted more sceptical attention than any other single tenet of the dogmatists. Yet the distinction between evident matters and the different varieties of non-evident matters, in terms of which Sextus characterizes commemorative and indicative signs, builds on just this assumption. It is, as he notes himself, one of the dogmatists' distinctions, as is the distinction between the two types of sign (cf. *PH* 2. 97). Thus Sextus' endorsement of commemorative signification occurs within a framework he claims to have adopted only as a concession for the sake of argument, and the account of commemorative signs is framed in terms of assumptions from which he has carefully distanced himself by marking them as dialectical concessions. Suspicion of the commemorative sign's sceptical credentials is not altogether unwarranted, then.

But let us postpone consideration of the commemorative sign's sceptical credentials for the present. Another problem must be confronted first; for not only does Sextus endorse the commemorative sign, when it has been characterized in a conspicuously dogmatic manner (as we shall see, this need not pose an insuperable obstacle to its acceptance by the Pyrrhonists), but much of the argument he actually furnishes is at cross purposes with his avowed intention to direct his whole case against the indicative sign while sparing the commemorative sign (cf. *PH* 2. 102; *M.* 8. 156). Many of Sextus' arguments pay no heed to the distinction between commemorative and indicative signs, but are directed against a Stoic account of signs whose connections with the indicative/commemorative framework are rather more complicated than Sextus' aims require. It is almost certainly not an account of indicative signification, for it seems to cover the kind of cases meant to be captured by the commemorative no less than the indicative sign (though the Stoics, of course, will have no truck with the peculiarly Empirical anti-inferential component of the commemorative sign). And what is more, though the argument for this conclusion will have to wait until the next chapter, the Stoics may well have intended their account to apply more to the former than the latter.

Indeed, so great is the gap between the arguments Sextus brings against this Stoic account and the preceding characterization of indicative signification that we are hard pressed in the *PH* 2 passage to find even a trace of the promised anti-indicative argument, and it is only with difficulty that arguments answering to this purpose can be recovered from the longer treatment of signs in *M.* 8. My suggestion is that the opposition between commemorative and indicative signs was equated, almost unconsciously, with the opposition between sceptical and dogmatic approaches to signification, the Stoic account having been taken as a representative example of the latter (cf. *PH* 2. 104). Once this error was firmly in place, arguments against the sign as conceived by the Stoics were simply assumed to answer the need for arguments against indicative signification.

This suggestion is faced with some formidable obstacles, however. Indeed, the claim just advanced is explicitly contradicted by the text, which goes on, immediately after the definition of the indicative sign cited above, to equate it with the sign as defined by the Stoa (*PH* 2. 101): 'whence they also define the last-mentioned sign in this manner: "an indicative sign is an antecedent proposition in a sound conditional revelatory of the consequent"'.

A good way of approaching this passage and the issues it raises is to consider the arguments of Robert Philippson, who was the first to call attention to the problem posed by this occurrence of the Stoic definition and, generally speaking, the difficulty of reconciling Sextus' stated aims with the arguments he actually proceeds to make.[22] He observed that the definition here assigned to the indicative sign recurs only a few paragraphs later at *PH* 2. 104, and again at *M*. 8. 245, as the Stoics' definition of the sign without any qualification. What is more, several examples used by Sextus to illustrate features of the commemorative sign recur in the account of Stoic signification, which suggests that the scope of the sign defined by the Stoics was intended to embrace signification grounded in co-observation. The examples—that a scar is the sign of a preceding wound and a wound in the heart of imminent death—are first employed to illustrate the nature of co-observation, by making it clear that it does not cover only items occurring at the same time, but sequential conjunctions of sign and signified as well (*M*. 8. 157). Later the same examples, now in appropriately propositional form, reappear to illustrate a special feature of the Stoic sign: though it supports present/past and present/future as well as present/present inferences, the conditional and its antecedent are presently true, differences in time being captured by tense (*M*. 8. 254–5).

To be sure, the Stoics may have held that their inferences, even those to evident matters, were grounded in more than observed co-occurrence, in something like a natural connection of the kind exploited by the indicative sign. But this seems unlikely. The only epistemological requirement imposed by the definition, and the only part of it that might appear to be related to the characterization of indicative signification, is that it be revelatory (ἐκκαλυπτικόν); but on closer inspection, this turns out only to exclude conditionals in which the antecedent cannot be evident without the consequent being equally evident. Thus, 'If it is day, it is light' is a true conditional, but the consequent is not revealed by the antecedent because

---

[22] Philippson, *De Philodemi libro*, 59–60.

it cannot fail to be manifestly self-evident when the antecedent is true (*M*. 8. 251). And as we have already noted, the evidence we have attests to a strong Stoic interest in empirically based inference. Thus although there are some obvious problems with it as well, the account in the pseudo-Galenic *Historia philosopha* seems to be closer to the truth when it treats essentially the same definition as a generic characterization of the sign with commemorative and indicative subspecies (*DG* 605. 10–19).

When we turn to Sextus' case against the sign, we find that the arguments from *PH* 2. 104 ff. make no reference to indication, nor do they come to grips with the epistemological issue over which the partisans of commemorative and indicative signification disagreed, namely whether directly given, observable evidence will support inferences to the non-evident. Instead, until *PH* 2. 118 they all hinge very closely on details of Stoic logical theory. The fact that, on the Stoic view, the sign turns out to be a proposition, and hence an immaterial *lekton*, is turned to account first. As Sextus observes, it is not evident whether there are such things as *lekta*. Being non-evident, that there are requires confirmation through a proof. But since proofs are systems of *lekta*, on the Stoic view at issue, we cannot rely on a proof as long as the existence of the *lekta* remains in doubt (*PH* 2. 109). The reference to the sound conditional in the definition is then made the basis of arguments turning on the famous dispute about the truth conditions of the conditional (*PH* 2. 110–12; cf. *M*. 8. 265). The Pyrrhonists appear, then, to have used the Stoic definition as a pretext to introduce a stock set of arguments focused on the tenets of Stoic logic, thereby shifting the focus of the argument away from the epistemological issues which we expected to be at the centre of the dispute to questions about the constitution and logical character of the sign. And the brief selection of arguments that turn on more widely held assumptions with which Sextus supplements the anti-Stoic section brings us no closer to the main epistemological issue (*PH* 2. 118 ff.).

Again it was Philippson who first observed that these arguments were no less effective against the commemorative (or co-observational) than the indicative sign. In order to explain both this inconsistency and the mistaken equation of indicative and Stoic signs at *PH* 2. 101, he advanced a chronological hypothesis.[23] Aenesidemus, as reported by Photius, and Diogenes Laertius

---

[23] Ibid. 61.

represent the Pyrrhonists' arguments as directed against the sign quite generally (D.L. 9. 96; *Bibliotheca* 212, 170ᵃ12 ff.), and Sextus too often writes as though this were the point of his arguments. Hence, according to Philippson, opposition to signs of all types without exception was the older and more genuinely sceptical Pyrrhonian stance. On the other hand, as we have seen, much convincing evidence suggests that the doctrine of the commemorative sign originated in the Empirical school of medicine. On Philippson's view, Sextus, or one of his more recent sceptical predecessors, adopted the commemorative sign under the influence of Empiricism. At some point thereafter, a futile effort was made to reconcile the commemorative sign with the inherited arguments. This doomed enterprise produced the treatment of signs in *M.* 8, which was rendered self-contradictory by the irreconcilable conflict between the opposition to signs of every kind and the positive commitment to the commemorative sign.

Philippson believed the passage in *PH* 2 was the later of the two, composed after Sextus had realized how untenable the position of the longer work was.[24] In consequence of this realization, and in order to eliminate the conflict between advocacy of the commemorative sign and the anti-Stoic arguments by restricting their apparently general scope, Sextus equated the Stoic sign with the indicative sign at *PH* 2. 101. Philippson concludes that commemorative signification is (*a*) essentially alien to the negative thrust of scepticism and (*b*) a late addition to Pyrrhonism. And these conclusions were in keeping with his larger view that the only point of contact between the two schools was in the area of negative anti-dogmatic argument; no place could be found for the Empiricists' positive teachings in Pyrrhonian scepticism without rendering the resulting position internally inconsistent.[25]

This position quickly found a persuasive opponent in Natorp, whose criticisms will furnish us with another crucial component of the solution to the problem we are considering. In opposition to Philippson, he maintained that commemorative signification was philosophically compatible with Pyrrhonism and had been a part of its teaching since the time of Aenesidemus.[26] To be sure, he agreed with Philippson about the comprehensive character of the Stoic definition, and he too believed that Sextus' anti-Stoic arguments are

[24] Ibid. 63.   [25] Ibid. 52.
[26] Natorp, *Forschungen zur Geschichte des Erkenntnisproblems im Altertum*, ch. III.

directed against a conception which embraces the commemorative sign.[27] But he went on to observe that these arguments abolish the sign only as conceived by the Stoics and not otherwise, so that there would be a conflict between Sextus' endorsement of the commemorative sign and the anti-Stoic arguments he employs only if he were committed to the Stoic definition of the sign. Finally, Natorp observed that the fact that the sceptic's case is sometimes represented by Sextus and other authors as directed against the sign quite generally is in keeping with a well-attested sceptical practice. The cases against the criterion, against dogma, and against assent do not prevent Sextus from conceding a version of each of these to the sceptic.[28]

The disagreement between *PH* 2. 101 and the rest of Sextus' treatment of sign-inference is the main textual difficulty for this view. The claim that there is no inconsistency in Sextus' position that needs to be removed or hidden makes it a puzzle why such an effort was apparently made in this passage. Natorp's solution is to identify the Stoic definition at *PH* 2. 101 as an interpolation.[29] This seems to me to be the correct solution, and not only for the reasons adduced by Natorp. Philippson observed that the restriction 'All Stoic signs are indicative' was inconsistent with what he took to be the earlier treatment of Stoic semiotics in *M*. 8 as well as the apparently unrestricted scope of the definition when it appears two paragraphs later at *PH* 2. 104. And he concluded that the equation of the indicative sign with the sign as defined by the Stoa at *PH* 2. 101 was a correction which freed Sextus from the contradiction which had vitiated the earlier account. But this interpretation appears to achieve consistency by fiat; if the Stoic account does apply to both kinds of signs, as it apparently does, saying it applies only to the indicative sign will not make it so. The arguments directed against the Stoic account will still be equally damaging to both kinds of sign, just as Sextus is supposed to have feared, according to Philippson.

But there are further difficulties with his proposal. Not only must we find Sextus guilty of being either deceitful or oblivious: *PH* 2. 101 is sharply at odds with the whole thrust of Sextus' treatment of signification. The way in which the Stoic definition is introduced

---

[27] Ibid. 138.
[28] These are my examples. Natorp mentions good, evil, and the telos as well (100 ff.). [29] Ibid. 142 ff.

at *PH* 2. 101 implies that it is an alternative characterization of
the indicative sign, acceptable to the very same dogmatists whose
first definition it follows. Reasons have already been given showing
that the Stoic account applies to more than indicative signs; but
it is also not true, even if this is overlooked, that all those who
subscribe to a theory of indicative signification accepted the Stoic
account, and Sextus could not have meant to suggest this. For as we
shall see in more detail soon, in *M*. 8 he distinguishes two general
accounts of the indicative sign, one treating it as an intelligible
item, as the Stoics do, and one treating it as a sensible item, as
e.g. the Epicureans do. What is more, when the Stoic definition is
reintroduced at *PH* 2. 104, it is clearly represented as an instance of
the kind of theory under investigation. For Sextus gives its apparent
exactness as his reason for concentrating on the Stoic account (cf.
M. 8. 396).

Thus Natorp's suggestion that we are faced with an interpolation
at *PH* 2. 101 seems to be correct, and it has received a large measure of support from other investigators.[30] Moreover, Sextus can be

---

[30] Cf. W. Heintz, *Studien zu Sextus Empiricus* (Halle: Niemeyer, 1932), 50; J.
Mau, the text's most recent editor, also accepts the bulk of Natorp's arguments
(216 n. ad *PH* 2. 101). Cf. A. Goedeckemeyer, *Die Geschichte des griechischen Skeptizismus* (Leipzig: Dieterich, 1905; repr. Aalen: Scientia Verlag, 1968), 304 n. 1; O.
Rieth, *Grundbegriffe der stoischen Ethik* (Berlin: Weidmann, 1933), 183 ff., and A.
Schmekel, *Die positive Philosophie* (Berlin: Weidmann, 1938), i. 356 n. 1, who have
come down on Philippson's side. Brochard, *Les Sceptiques grecs*, 269 with n. 1, 343
with n. 3, believes that the text is sound and its meaning partly so. On his view, the
Stoic definition was intended to apply to all signs, regardless of whether the matters
they signified were non-evident by nature or non-evident only for the time being;
but the relation of signification depended in all cases on a necessary connection
between sign and signified. Brochard follows Philippson in supposing that the distinction between commemorative and indicative signification was a later innovation
of the medical Empiricists. As a result the relation between the Stoic definition and
the indicative sign is imperfect, and the identity asserted at *PH* 2. 104 incorrect. For
the Stoics do not, on his view, confine rationally graspable necessary connections
to relations of signification whose second member—the signified item—is naturally
non-evident, as the distinction between commemorative and indicative signs does.
But once the assumption that necessary connections are to be found only in relations
of this kind is in effect, the signs captured by the Stoic definition will be coextensive
with indicative signs, and Sextus' conflation of the former with the latter becomes
understandable. In his review of Heintz, *Studien*, Philippson grants that the first appearance of the Stoic definition at *PH* 2. 101 is extremely awkward, but he suggests
that it may have been a later addition by Sextus meant, as he argued in his dissertation, to eliminate the contradiction between his arguments and his advocacy of the
commemorative sign (*Berliner philologische Wochenschrift*, 53 (3 July 1933), 594–8).
Although I agree with Natorp that we are probably dealing with an interpolation by
another hand, the conclusion that the identification of Stoic with indicative signs is

effectively defended from Philippson's charge of self-contradiction along the lines Natorp suggests. For an attack on the sign as conceived by Stoic logical theory poses a problem for Sextus only if he accepts the Stoic position under attack. Yet some of the difficulties Philippson has brought to light cannot be disposed of so easily. If Natorp was right to observe that it is only the commemorative sign as conceived of by the Stoics which is affected by Sextus' arguments, this is no less true of the indicative sign. And if Philippson's original charge, that Sextus' arguments are too strong for his purposes because they endanger the kind of sign he wants to endorse, has missed the mark, it may be because something like the opposite charge, that they are too weak, is correct. For Sextus' arguments are misdirected. As things stand, their target is a theory which cuts across the commemorative (or co-observational)/indicative distinction so that they pose as much of a threat to one as they do to the other. When the argument is concluded, the prospects of one sign should be no brighter or dimmer than those of the other. Yet though we have been left in exactly the same position with respect to each kind of sign, we are supposed to adopt one while renouncing the other.

Thus though the evidence Philippson has collected will not support the strong charges he brought, they will support the lesser charge of breach of promise; for Sextus has failed to deliver the promised argument against the indicative sign. And we are now in a position to see just what was the cause of Philippson's suspicions. The task Sextus set for himself at the beginning of each passage was the abolition of the indicative sign, defined with reference to its epistemological function, inference to the non-evident. This fact and the provisional concession that knowledge of evident matters is possible lead us to expect that the dogmatic claim that evident knowledge underwrites inferences to the non-evident and unobservable will be contested. Yet nowhere in the *PH* 2 passage is battle joined over this, the central epistemological issue. Instead, it is the constitution of the sign and its logical structure which are the focus of argument, precisely the kind of issue which we would have expected Sextus to set aside or bracket, just as he had set aside questions about knowledge of evident matters, in order to grapple directly with the epistemological issues.

a mistake, on which Philippson agrees with Natorp and Heintz, is more important for present purposes than a decision about whose mistake it was.

But if Sextus' arguments do not further his stated intention to oppose indicative signification only, it is not because they do not serve
a sceptical purpose. *PH* 2–3 are only an outline of the Pyrrhonist's case against dogmatism, and it is for the sake of concision that
Sextus often concentrates his attention on the Stoic view of the
matter at issue. The Stoic theory of signification and the sceptical
argument brought to bear against it are intended to exemplify dogmatic theories in general and the kinds of arguments which can be
directed against them, respectively (cf. *PH* 2. 104; *M.* 8. 396). And
the style of argument Sextus employs against the Stoic position,
intended as it is to show that the sign is inconceivable as far as the
things said about it by the dogmatists are concerned (*PH* 2. 104,
118), helps advance another important sceptical purpose. Because
they turn so closely on assumptions which are clearly peculiar to
the Stoic position, there is less danger that they will be mistaken
for attempts to enforce negative sceptical conclusions dogmatically.
Instead, this approach reminds us of the moral the Pyrrhonist is
left with by his practice of argument; since the unwelcome sceptical conclusion is arrived at in the context of dogmatic philosophical
theory, that theory is called into question at least as much as the
matter it promises to explain. And it is not just the conclusions of
the sceptic's arguments which are restricted or qualified in this way,
but the attitude to which he is led thereby. As we have seen, the
sceptic suspends judgement on every issue so far as it is a matter of
philosophical reason. The problem, then, is not that the arguments
do not advance the Pyrrhonists' sceptical aims, but that they do not
promote the end Sextus says they do. If anything, the question is
whether that end is properly sceptical.

4. The Empirical Contribution

Our examination thus far has reached some rather surprising conclusions. We have had to postulate missing arguments answering
to Sextus' avowed aims, and an unstated purpose served by the
arguments he does make. How these confusions were possible will
become clearer if we turn to the discussion of signs in *M.* 8. There
we finally do find the epistemologically oriented, anti-indicative
arguments for which we have so far searched in vain. Unlike the arguments presupposing the Stoic theory which predominate in the

PH 2 passage, these arguments do respond to the account of indicative signification with which Sextus begins and are compatible with advocacy of the commemorative sign. Indeed, closer examination reveals that they were almost certainly framed by the first partisans of commemorative signification, the medical Empiricists. For they can be fully understood only against the background furnished by the continuing debate between Empiricists and Rationalists about the nature of artistic inference, and of artistic expertise quite generally.

The discussion of signs in *M.* 8 is not organized along the same lines as the treatment of the same topic in *PH* 2. The bulk of the arguments are divided into two groups corresponding to the two possible dogmatic views of the sign distinguished by Sextus: that it is a sensible ($a\dot{\iota}\sigma\theta\eta\tau\acute{o}\nu$), or that it is an intelligible ($\nu o\eta\tau\acute{o}\nu$). This distinction is employed frequently in Sextus' writings. But though it makes for a certain neatness in presentation, as we shall see, it can do more to obscure than to illuminate the matter at issue. Roughly speaking, it is used to draw two quite different contrasts. First, there is the epistemological distinction we have already encountered between items which are directly given to observation and those which must be grasped by inference from the sensibles. Invisible pores and atoms are intelligible in this sense. Second, there is a way of using the contrast to draw an ontological distinction between two radically different kinds of entity with reference to our means of epistemic access to them. According to a certain kind of Platonism, for example, the senses put us in touch with the material world, for what it is worth, while the intellect enables us to come into contact with a realm of immaterial, intelligible items. The view is nicely captured in the *Sophist* by a remark of the Eleatic Stranger comparing the debate over immaterial entities to a battle between gods and giants in which the gods hold that only certain *intelligible* and *immaterial* forms truly exist (246 B).

When the two types of distinction are not carefully kept apart, however, there is some danger of confusion. This is especially clear in a passage where Sextus lumps Plato and Democritus together as adherents of the view that only intelligibles are true (*M.* 8. 4). What Democritus means is that no statement framed in terms of sensible properties stands a chance of being true, since the world of secondary properties with which the senses appear to put us in touch has no real existence, while the atoms, which do really exist, must be discovered by the intellect because they cannot be seen or touched. But though they are too small to be perceived, the atoms are no less material for all that; and this Democritean conception of the intelligible is obviously very different from the Platonic, in which intelligibility and immateriality go hand in hand.

A confusion like this one, albeit of a rather more complicated and elusive kind, seems to have affected Sextus' discussion of signs in *M*. 8. The view considered in the section devoted to the intelligible sign is, once again, the Stoic theory. The same kind of arguments hinging on unresolved questions about the existence of the *lekta* and the definition of the true conditional are brought against it once again (*M*. 8. 257 ff.). As we have seen, those arguments concern the sign's constitution and logical structure, not its epistemological function. And as we would expect in the light of this fact, it is not in an epistemological sense that the sign as conceived by the Stoa is classified as an intelligible. Rather, it is because the Stoics make the sign a propositional *lekton*, and thus an immaterial object of thought. Presumably, from the epistemological point of view, the Stoics would have agreed that signs are sensibles. And that they allowed for this possibility is clear from another passage, where Sextus classifies the Stoics among the philosophers who hold that some sensibles and some intelligibles are true. But as he notes, these sensibles are not true straight away, but only with reference to the corresponding intelligibles (*M*. 8. 10). The point is that, according to Stoic logical theory, only propositions, immaterial objects of thought, can be true. Nothing in the physical world, with which we are acquainted through the senses, is properly speaking true; but that does not prevent propositions about physical features of the world, including the propositional content of our perceptual impressions, from being true.

The difficulty, as I shall argue, is that the preceding selection of arguments is not directed, or not wholly directed, against a parallel conception of sensible, material constitution of the sign. Rather, it is chiefly concerned with the epistemological question whether directly given, perceptual knowledge can underwrite inferences to the unobservable, i.e. whether indicative signification is possible. This is at first hard to see because the arguments are framed in terms of a highly reductive causal theory of perception, which made it easier to view them as a counterpart of the anti-Stoic arguments by which they are followed.

If true, this reading makes it possible to see how the difficulties with which we were confronted by the discussion in *PH* 2 could have arisen. Suppose for a moment that we have found a set of arguments whose point of departure is the provisional concession with which Sextus begins, that knowledge of evident matters is possible, and which do serve his avowed purpose by contesting the possibility of inference to the non-evident in a way that leaves the commemorative sign unaffected. We have found them joined uncomfortably to another set of arguments of which they are not a proper counterpart by means of a doxographical dichotomy of dubious relevance. My suggestion is that the dichotomy between sensibles and intelligibles was used to press the anti-Stoic arguments, which were conceived with a quite different purpose in mind, into the service of the anti-indicative cause by joining them to a body of argument that does advance that purpose. Once all the arguments classified in this way were thought to aim at indicative signification, when the time came to produce a shorter outline of the sceptics' case, the Stoic position could be taken out of the context created by the sensible/intelligible dichotomy and treated as an example of an indicative-sign theory.

The suggestion is unaffected by the order in which *PH* 2 and *M*. 8 were composed. Even if *M*. 8 is the later work, it may well reflect the contents and arrangement of the sources behind both accounts better; what is crucial is that these sources used the sensible/intelligible dichotomy as a means of fitting the anti-Stoic arguments into the anti-indicative polemic. The fact that the very brief treatment of the sign in Diogenes Laertius' account of Pyrrhonism is organized around the same dichotomy lends some support to this assumption (9. 96).

To be sure, even if the expectation that we shall be examining two approaches to the sign distinguished along epistemological lines is not fulfilled in the case of the Stoic theory, it might still be possible, contrary to my earlier claim, that we are dealing with two properly paired, genuinely alternative, positions. To constitute a genuine counterpart to the anti-Stoic arguments, the arguments against the sign as sensible would have to be directed against an alternative conception of the sign's constitution. And some of them clearly are. Thus, for example, the argument that signs cannot be sensibles because they are said to be true or false clearly depends on the Stoic view that only immaterial, intelligible propositions are bearers of

truth (*M.* 8. 207). The very first line of argument which Sextus takes
up, hinging on the philosophers' dispute over whether sensibles are
true, furnishes another example (*M.* 8. 183 ff.). For at issue in this
dispute is whether the world is made up of the kind of sensible
properties with which the senses seem to put us in touch or we
are only brought up against our own empty affections in sense
experience (cf. *M.* 7. 241; *M.* 8. 4 ff.).

Both arguments fail to connect with the concession with which
the discussion of signs began: that a grasp of evident matters of
sense is possible. But after it has been conceded again, distinctively
anti-semiotic argument does become possible (*M.* 8. 187 ff.). The
first argument after this concession, which in one form or another
will dominate the rest of the discussion until the Stoic theory is
taken up at *M.* 8. 244 ff., is set out as follows (*M.* 8. 187–8):

(*a*) Every sensible occurs naturally to everyone similarly disposed and is
grasped to an equal extent by all such people.

(*b*) For example, it is not that Greeks take hold of white colour in one way
while barbarians do so in another . . . the same is true of skilled artists
and laymen . . . all take hold of it in the same way, as long as their
senses are unobstructed.

(*c*) But the sign as sign does not seem to move everyone similarly disposed
in the same way, but to some there is not in general a sign of anything
at all, even if it [*i.e. the sensible*] is manifestly occurring to them, while
to others it is a sign, but not of the same thing to all of them.

(*d*) The same phenomena, e.g. in medicine, are signs of one thing to Erasistratus, of another to Herophilus, and of still something else to Asclepiades.

The argument is then summarized as follows:

(*e*) If the sensible moves all similarly, but the sign does not, the sign will
not be a sensible.

This is illustrated by a comparison with fire and other sensible
substances (*M.* 8. 189):

(*f*) Again, if the sign is sensible, it is necessary that, just as fire, which is a
sensible, burns everything capable of being burnt and snow, which is
constitutionally a sensible [χιὼν αἰσθητὴ καθεστηκυῖα], chills everyone
able to be chilled, the sign ought to lead everyone to the same signified
matter, if it is to be numbered among the sensibles.

The assumption that the occurrence (ὑποπίπτειν) of sensibles to someone, his grasping of them (λαμβάνειν), his taking hold of them (ἀντιλαμβάνεσθαι), and their moving him (κινεῖν) all come to the same thing helps make the argument appear a natural continuation of the preceding constitutionally oriented arguments. The expression 'sensible', it seems, is being used to pick out sensible substances, items which can be perceptually detected, as the examples in (*f*) make clear. And the first difficulty for the claim that we are dealing here with an epistemologically oriented argument against indicative signification is the way it appears to concern itself with the causal powers of these sensible stuffs rather than the central epistemological issues. But this is not the only difficulty, for even if we put it aside and assume that we are faced with an epistemological argument from disagreement over the semiotic implications of agreed-upon sensibles, the argument will still pose a problem. The view that signs are sensibles, and that everyone perceives sensibles alike, should not mean that everyone must draw the same conclusion about non-evident matters from them. The argument makes sense only if it is assumed that the whole semiotic import of a sign must be sensibly given; so that if sensibles impart information about the sensible world by acting on the sense organs in a certain way, information about what is signified must be imparted by the same means in the same way. But it is hard to see why indicative-sign theorists would want to make such an assumption. Rather, we would expect them to insist that in using a sensible as a sign we take an inferential step beyond the perceptually given content of the sign, so that, if you will, being moved by the sensible *qua* sensible is not the same as being moved by the sensible *qua* sign.

Consider the evidence cited in section (*b*). Why is attention called to the differences between Greeks and barbarians, artists and laymen? Apparently to focus attention on a characteristic each of the paired groups shares across their differences, the ability to grasp sensibles. But the examples seem better suited to explain just why there is a difference in the semiotic conclusions reached by different people on the basis of the same evidence. Elsewhere Sextus cites the difference between Greeks and barbarians to help illustrate the Stoic view that grasping what is said or signified (τὸ σημαινόμενον) when articulate speech takes place is different from merely hearing the sounds; Greeks and barbarians may hear the same sounds when Greek is spoken, but only the former understand what is said (*M*.

8. 12).[31] But why, we may well ask, is the layman not in exactly the same position with respect to the sign as the barbarian is regarding spoken Greek? The skilled artist and the Greek speaker are in a position to make something of the sounds and appearances which their opposite numbers are not. Why the evidence presented should count against the (indicative) sign, then, is something of a mystery, for it seems a defender should be only too happy to respond using the points made in Sextus' argument in his positive account of the sign. Moreover, if this is a fault, surely the commemorative sign is just as guilty, as some partisans of indicative signification are said to have maintained (*M*. 8. 193).

The lack of agreement among accomplished physicians cited in section (*d*) might be a little more unsettling to the defender of signs, however. If the method of inference to which medical artists lay claim is a sound one, and their common point of departure is an agreed piece of observable evidence, it would not be unreasonable to expect their initial agreement to carry over to their conclusions. Thus the persistent, unresolved disagreement about the signification of signs, which prevails even among the most highly qualified physicians, will tend to call both the conflicting theoretical conclusions and the method through which they were reached into question. And as we have seen, arguments from disagreement of this kind played an important role in the medical Empiricists' polemic against their Rationalist opponents.

But the argument Sextus offers us is a long way from this argument, which, though more modestly tentative, is much more compelling. For Sextus seems to insist that any disagreement at all, between any parties no matter what their qualifications, falsifies the identification of the sign as a sensible. Hence there are two questions that need to be answered if we are to make sense of this argument and connect it with the more straightforward Empirical argument from disagreement with which it has just been contrasted:

(1) How did what ought to be an epistemological argument take on the character of an argument about the causal powers of sensible substances?

(2) What enables Sextus to restrict his opponent to the sensible *qua* sensible, in epistemological terms to the proposed sign's phenomenally given epistemic content, i.e. why is the appeal

[31] Cf. Porphyry, *De abstinentia*, 3. 3.

to anything that might account for the fact that different
people draw different semiotic conclusions from the same
agreed phenomenal evidence ruled out of bounds, with the
result that any such disagreement disqualifies the claim of
the phenomena to be signs?

We can turn for help to a similar, and presumably earlier,
argument taken by Sextus from book 4 of Aenesidemus' Πυρρώνειοι
λόγοι (*M*. 8. 215 ff.):

(A) If (i) signs are phenomena and
    (ii) the phenomena appear similarly to everyone similarly
    disposed,
    then (iii) signs appear similarly to everyone similarly dis-
    posed.
(B) Not (iii).
(C) But (ii).
Therefore not (i).

In contrast to what has gone before, Aenesidemus' argument is
framed in more clearly epistemological terms; it speaks of phenomena and the appearance they present, rather than sensibles and
the way they act on the sense organs. But this does not make all
that much difference in the final evaluation of the two arguments.
For despite its straightforward epistemological character, and the
meticulous formal analysis to which it is subjected (*M*. 8. 215–38),
Aenesidemus' argument seems to depend on the same implausible
assumption which threatened to vitiate Sextus' earlier argument.
As we have already observed, there is no reason why differences of
opinion cannot arise over the semiotic implications of signs whose
manifest, phenomenal content is undisputed. Signs, the phenomena
which furnish the advocates of sign-inference with their point of
departure, do appear similarly to all those similarly disposed, as
phenomena; but this is in no way inconsistent with their failure to
occur as signs of the same things to the same persons. Aenesidemus'
argument depends, then, on an extremely implausible assumption,
just as the earlier argument had. In this case it is that, if signs are
phenomena, their semiotic content must be part of their phenomenal content, which is accessible to everyone whose senses are in
good order. But on the face of it, this is no more plausible than
the claim that, if spoken utterances are meaningful sentences, their

meaning must be part of what can be heard by anyone whose audi-
tory equipment is in working order; so that, if someone who meets
this last condition fails to understand an utterance which others
claim to understand, it cannot really be a meaningful sentence.[32]

Before taking up the problem presented by this assumption and
its counterpart in Sextus' earlier argument, we can turn for help
with our first question to Sextus' summary of Aenesidemus' argument (*M*. 8. 240–1): 'If the phenomena are equally apparent to
all, and they have a power indicative of the non-evident [ἐνδεικ-
τικὴ δύναμις], non-evident matters ought to occur equally to all,
since the same causes are at work and a similar underlying matter is present.' Here, if anywhere, we can see the transition from
Aenesidemus' epistemological argument to the puzzling causally
oriented argument found earlier. Instead of arguing, as we would
have preferred, that if indicative signification is a real possibility,
the warrant provided by the agreed phenomena ought to furnish
just about everyone with the evidence needed to draw the same conclusion, Sextus proceeds as if the causal account of the formation
of sense impressions were equally central to the account of impressions arrived at through indicative sign-inference. These derived
impressions are supposed to be produced by, and in the course of,
the same process in which external objects act on the underlying
matter of the sense organs to produce sense impressions. If semiotic content is contained in the sign's phenomenal content, and this
phenomenal content is explained by a causal theory of perception,
then the same account must hold good of its semiotic content.

Thus, once the assumption making semiotic content part of the
phenomenally given epistemic content of the sign is in place, the
shift to a causally oriented type of argument can be explained (question 1). But we have still to explain how this assumption could
have been allowed in the first place (question 2). Some help is afforded by another argument preserved by Sextus, which seems to
be halfway between the Empirical argument from disagreement
and the arguments incorporating this problematic assumption (*M*.
8. 274):

This also must be said, whatever the sign should turn out to be, either
it has a *nature* suited to indicating and disclosing the non-evident or we
remember what is co-revealed with it. But it does not have a nature indica-

---

[32] Cf. Plato, *Tht*. 163 B–C, where Socrates presents Theaetetus with a related
difficulty by which he is not even momentarily troubled.

tive of non-evident matters, since it ought then to indicate the non-evident equally to all.

This argument works by exploiting the claim that the phenomena have a natural power for indicating the non-evident which was part of the initial characterization of the indicative sign. To be sure, that claim need imply no more than that there are underlying connections between evident and hidden matters entailed by the rationally graspable natures of the matters at issue. The task of making out these connections could be quite difficult, perhaps so difficult that it was possible only for those with a thorough grounding in natural philosophy. But a stronger reading is required if Sextus' argument is to have any force; a natural power of indication must be grasped by means only of the perceptual and cognitive equipment with which we are furnished by nature without theoretical instruction or specialized artistic expertise. In other words, the strong interpretation of nature in this argument depends on a contrast between art and nature, between abilities which are given to everyone by nature, barring unusual circumstances, and the kind of expertise that belongs only to a few because it must be acquired by specialized study. And this reading receives support from the characterization of the indicative sign according to which it signifies straight away, all but breaking into speech (*M.* 8. 154; *PH* 2. 101).[33]

This argument, then, is potentially much stronger than the simple argument from disagreement. For according to the argument now being considered, disagreement is more than an epistemological liability: it is strictly incompatible with the existence of a natural power of indicative signification, understood in a certain way. Nevertheless, it is not yet the same as Aenesidemus' argument, for it takes the claim that the phenomena have a natural indicative power to imply that signified matters must be agreed on by nearly everyone just as the phenomena are, without assuming that agreement about the former is somehow already part of the agreement about the latter. What we still need to explain, then, is the transition

---

[33] With this conception of natural signification we might compare a similar view of demonstration to which Galen strongly objects (*De ord. lib. prop.* ii. 82. 3–10 *SM*): 'Observe well how many physicians and philosophers turn in opposite directions when they are shown up because they have never studied demonstrative method, some of them asserting that there is no such thing, while some of them not only declare that demonstration exists, but that it is grasped naturally [φύσει] by everyone, as though there were no need for learning and practice at all.'

from treating agreement about what is signified as a distinct consequence of the natural indicative power of the phenomena to the
claim that such agreement is part of the natural agreement about
what is phenomenally presented. This assumption must have some
hold on Sextus' opponents if the argument is to have any force for
them at all.

We may be able to see how it did if we bring the arguments in
which it figures into closer connection with the controversy between
medical Empiricists and Rationalists. As we have seen, the Empiricists claimed to be able to do without theory and the knowledge of
non-evident matters it was supposed to make possible; instead, they
maintained that artistic expertise need involve nothing more than
knowledge of the phenomena. As a result, they appeared to be vulnerable to a certain kind of Rationalist challenge. Knowledge of the
phenomena, as is generally agreed, is available to everyone whose
senses are not impaired because it requires nothing more than the
abilities with which we are furnished by nature. But artistic knowledge is different from lay knowledge: it is difficult of attainment
and available only to those who have undergone specialized training. As the Rationalists observe, the knowledge that distinguishes
the artist from the layman is of the hidden or non-evident; this is
an essential part of what makes it artistic, not natural, knowledge.
But according to the Rationalists, the Empirical account fails to do
justice to the specialized and, if you will, non-natural character of
artistic expertise.

A specimen of this form of argument is preserved by Sextus in the
section dedicated to his opponents' defence of the sign (*M*. 8. 280):

If there is no theorem peculiar [ἴδιον] to an art, the art will not differ from
non-art [οὐ διοίσει τῆς ἀτεχνίας ἡ τέχνη]. If, however, there is a theorem
peculiar to an art, it will either be a phenomenon or something non-evident.
But it will not be a phenomenon because the phenomena are similarly
apparent to all without instruction [ἀδιδάκτως]. Yet if it is non-evident, it
will be discerned through a sign, and if anything is discerned through a
sign, there will be a sign.

This argument has the appearance of a cogent demonstration that,
as long as they wish to lay claim to an art at all, the Empiricists are
committed to knowledge of the non-evident and the semiotic means
of achieving it. And if this is right, their own purely phenomenal
account of artistic expertise must be inadequate.

There is, however, an answer, a version of which is also preserved by Sextus (*M.* 8. 291):

There is no theorem of any speculative or theoretical art at all ... but there is a theorem that belongs exclusively to the art which is occupied with the phenomena. For frequent observation and historical research give rise to theorems [διὰ γὰρ τῶν πολλάκις τετηρημένων ἢ ἱστορημένων ποιεῖται τὰς τῶν θεωρημάτων συστάσεις], and things frequently observed and studied by history are the special property of those who have made the most frequent observations, not common to all.

And Galen reports a similar response to the same challenge by the Empiricists, who point to the examples furnished by seamen, mushroom-fanciers, bakers, and the like. So, for example, without any knowledge of the nature of seeds, the baker will know which flour to select to make the best bread. Observation and history, they point out, have led them to knowledge which is not given to everyone, although it is not of objects, qualities, or processes which lie beyond the reach of the ordinary power of evident apprehension that is given to all.[34]

The arguments of Aenesidemus and Sextus which have so puzzled us acquire a point when viewed as an attempt on the part of the Empiricists to bring the same kind of argument against the Rationalists. For satisfied with their own account of the difference between artistic expertise and lay knowledge in terms of observation, history, and memory, the Empiricists were now in a position to argue that the Rationalists are guilty of precisely the charge that they had brought against Empiricism. Rationalism fails to do justice to the special character of artistic knowledge, according to their argument, because it grants the phenomena a natural power of indication, thus making their semiotic implications accessible to the layman. The result is that an art involves knowledge available to the layman no less than to the artist. This explains why the arguments brought by Sextus and Aenesidemus rule out appeals to anything beyond the sensibles or phenomena as such that might account for disagreement about their semiotic implications. And it also explains why these arguments do not affect the commemorative sign; for the Empirical conception of expertise as a complicated set of dispositions based on specialized observation and history, which

[34] 'For we find that of the bulk of mankind each individual making use of frequent observations gains knowledge not attained by another' (*On Medical Experience*, 98–9 Walzer; cf. *De meth. med.* x. 126. 10 ff. K = fr. 45 Deichgräber).

they sometimes called memory, accounts for the ability of experts to make something of the evidence that laymen cannot. Hence the argument that signification is a matter either of nature or memory, but not of the former because the result would be to erase the difference between artist and layman (cf. *M.* 8. 274, 291).

But how the complete identification of sign and phenomenon or sensible could have emerged from these arguments is still to be explained. Some insights which will help us to see how the Empiricists' argument could have taken this form are furnished by the pseudo-Galenic *De optima secta*, in which examples of the type of Rationalist argument on which it seems to be modelled are preserved (i. 106–223 K).[35] Early in the work, while discussing the requirement that the theorems of an art be useful, the author remarks (110. 14–16): 'It is essential that the apprehension of the theorem not be common to laymen [ἰδιῶται], but peculiar [ἴδιος] to artistic experts [τεχνῖται].' It seems that some people have erred, he proceeds, by taking the phenomena to be the principle or ἀρχή of the arts, a mistake for two reasons, only the second of which need concern us here: if one makes the phenomena the principle of an art, one will be unable to distinguish art from non-art. The problem is the one which we have already seen cited by the proponents of indicative signification in Sextus (cf. *M.* 8. 280). The phenomena are no less apprehensible by the layman than by the expert. According to the account in question, then, the artist will have nothing more than the layman, but this flies in the face of the obvious fact that artists must have something more in the way of knowledge.

Whose error is at issue is not said, but in the next section a very similar argument is directed explicitly against the Empiricists. Its point is to show that the Empiricists' own system of medicine requires knowledge of non-evident matters, which implies that the Empiricists, despite their protestations to the contrary, are committed to the use of reason (122. 11–124. 8, *passim*). The argument is fairly straightforward in outline: observation of all the phenomena is not possible, hence there must be something more (πλέον τι) to those phenomena it is necessary to observe. We are then confronted

---

[35] The question of authorship was investigated by Iwan von Müller, who concluded that the book is composed of three separate works, none of whose possibly different but like-minded authors is Galen. See his 'Über die dem Galen zugeschriebene Abhandlung Περὶ τῆς ἀρίστης αἱρέσεως', *Sitzungsberichte der philosophisch-philologischen Klasse der K. Bayer. Akademie der Wissenschaften* (1898), 53–162.

with a dilemma: either the phenomena as phenomena, *qua* phenomena, or in and of themselves (ὅσον ἐφ' ἑαυτοῖς)—a number of Greek
expressions are used—are useful for the discovery of remedies or
they are not. The phenomena as such do not differ from each other,
however, hence they should all be equally useful: for example, it
should be just as profitable to observe a patient's blanket and the
bed on which he lies as anything else. But this cannot be so, hence
it is not the phenomena as such which are useful (cf. Galen, *On
Medical Experience*, 91–2 Walzer).

This conclusion is backed up by further argument: the phenomena in so far as they are phenomena (φαινόμενα καθόσον φαίνεται)
are equally apparent to all, so that the layman is as knowledgeable
about them as anyone else (123. 17–18). Thus, if on the basis of
the phenomena alone it were possible to grasp which of them need
to be observed, there would be no difference between the experience of the Empiricist and the inexperience of the layman (124.
1–2). Since it is not clear to everyone, but only to experts, which
phenomena ought to be observed, what ought to be observed is
not itself apparent. Like the defence of signification preserved by
Sextus, which insists that signification must be possible if there are
to be theorems belonging exclusively to experts, the present argument challenges the Empiricist to point to something extra, over
and above the phenomena in and of themselves that will explain
how his expert knowledge differs from the untrained practice of
the layman (cf. *M*. 8. 280).

This extra item, the Rationalists assume, can be discovered only
by reason. This is made especially clear by another argument, the
point of which is once again to compel the Empiricist to identify the characteristic that marks off or indicates the evident items
(symptoms in this case) which he chooses to observe (133. 16).
Such a characteristic must be either phenomenal or non-evident;
it cannot be the former, but the latter can be apprehended only by
reason (133. 19–134. 8). Hence the observation which is supposed
to give rise to Empirical knowledge is impossible without reason
(134. 10–11).

Thus these arguments, like the defence of signification transmitted by Sextus, put pressure on the Empiricists to acknowledge the
inadequacy of a purely phenomenal account of artistic expertise
and concede a role to reason in the composition of the medical
art. Most important for our purposes, however, is how similar the

Rationalists' positive account of the extra something grasped by
reason in the *De optima secta* is to the account of signification to
which Sextus believes his opponents cannot appeal without contradicting their claim that the phenomena have a natural power
of indicating the non-evident. We shall be able to see why a little
more clearly if we examine some further details of the Rationalist
position as they are reported in the *De optima secta*. The Rationalists granted a crucial role to the indication of beneficial remedies
by hidden causes (119. 12 ff.). The phenomena, on the other hand,
lead the way to the apprehension of the hidden items which indicate
the appropriate therapies (120. 3–5; 159. 1–2; 162. 12–13). Thus
there are two stages of inference in Rational medicine: the first from
apparent items to the hidden, underlying cause of the affliction, the
second from the cause revealed in this way to the indicated therapy.
The second stage, the indication of the therapy, is a rational inference from the nature of the affliction requiring treatment. Naturally
questions about the first stage of inference will arise, to which the
theory of indicative signification furnishes one answer by making
the transition from the phenomenal symptoms to the underlying
pathology a rationally compelling inference, just like the indication
of the cure.

There is, however, a problem here. The Rationalists of the *De
optima secta* hold, as we would expect, that indication is from hidden
causes (119. 17 ff.). But the reason why causes are hidden is not,
or not only, because they exist or take place at the subsensible
level. Rather, it is because the cause *qua* cause is not apparent
but hidden (120. 2–121. 9). And this is because a cause may be
essentially a relational item like a father, a slave, or a brother; though
each member of the pair is an evident item, the relation by which
they are related is not itself evident (121. 16–18). Thus grasping
something as a cause involves grasping it as related to the item of
which it is the cause, and this is beyond the power of unassisted
perception. The same is also true of the items whose relation is
revealed by indicative inferences, including that from an outcome
to its necessary antecedent causal conditions. And later in the work,
a procedure corresponding to indicative signification is explained in
this way by means of an example. Spontaneous episodes of lassitude
point to plethora. While laymen recognize lassitude when they see
it, they are ignorant of the fact that plethora is revealed (δηλοῦται)
thereby. On the other hand, the medical artist knows the theorem

revealing the relation between the two (187. 17; 188. 7–8; 189. 7). According to the Rationalists, then, a grasp of the theorems of an art is the extra something necessary to distinguish the expert from the layman which the Empiricists are unable to supply. Indeed, it is in the interest of the Rationalist position to insist as strongly as possible on the gap separating the layman from the artist.

The point is not, or not quite, that truths about the sensible world are perfectly discrete, brute facts without any implications beyond themselves. They may well have such implications. It is, rather, that what is sensibly or phenomenally given, taken by itself, has no such implications. There may be all the difference in the world between what is implied by the nature of a thing capable of giving rise to phenomenally presented properties of a certain sort and what is implied by those properties themselves. Even to grasp that they can be supported only by a thing with a nature of this kind may require a grasp of more than is given to perception, construed narrowly in this way. Thus certain relations in which the phenomena stand to other items are not given phenomenally, but require a grasp of something additional, namely a theoretical understanding of the natures of the matters revealed to the senses which is not itself so revealed.

But this picture of the phenomena can also be used against the defender of the indicative sign, as the following argument preserved by Sextus shows (*M.* 8. 206): 'The sensible *qua* sensible is conceived absolutely, e.g. the white, the dark, the sweet, the bitter, and everything of that sort. But the sign *qua* sign is constitutionally a relative; for it is conceived in accordance with its relation to the signified.' Such a defender will be vulnerable if he combines this conception of the phenomena with a form of foundationalism that makes them the sole basis of theoretical knowledge. Asked to justify his theory, he may be forced back to a position where, in order to avoid appealing to disputed matters, he claims that his views follow naturally from what is indisputably evident. His position will then be prone to a certain kind of difficulty. If the basis on which the theory is to be erected is too severely restricted, nothing, or nothing as interesting as what is sought, seems to follow from it. Yet the starting-points cannot be too greatly augmented without introducing controversial assumptions that seem to require support no less than the theories. Thus proposed examples of indicative signification will often look very plausible when viewed in connection with the appropriate theory, yet seem rather less plausible when taken on their own. But the theorems that might lend them plausibility are just the sort of thing that stand in need of the support sign-inferences are supposed to afford.

The claim that the phenomena indicate by their own nature and constitution is now understood to mean not simply that their implications must be open to all, but that they indicate by their own nature as phenomena; indeed, it is for this reason that their implications are open to all. And what is it for a phenomenon to impart information by its own nature as a phenomenon, if not to impart it phenomenally, i.e. as part of its perceptually given content, hence clearly, directly, and indisputably? The nature of the phenomena is to be discrete and perspicuous; they have no hidden depths from which latent information might be extracted. Any information allegedly imparted by the phenomena in virtue of their own nature as phenomena is subject to evaluation in the light of the same necessary conditions, i.e. being subject to all but universal agreement. This last step is licensed when the commitment to indicative signification is combined with a very restrictive view of the content of the phenomena of the kind detailed in the *De optima secta*. This, then, is the train of thought behind Sextus' first major argument and the argument of Aenesidemus which it closely resembles.

The Rationalist will be vulnerable to these arguments if, having made the phenomena epistemologically discrete, he renounces, for foundational reasons, all appeals to anything beyond the phenomena which might explain how they can provide evidence for conclusions of the kind that are drawn in indicative inference. But if inference from signs was envisaged as the means by which the theorems were to be deduced from the phenomena, the Rationalist is in difficulties; the basis for his inferences, by his own account, may be too restricted. The main difference between this Rationalist and his counterpart in the *De optima secta* is that the latter has a well-developed view about the information available to the expert over and above what is available phenomenally to everyone alike, while the former is faced with the task of getting everything going from the ground up, so to speak, relying only on what is given to the layman. That this puts him in a nearly impossible bind is made only too clear by the Rationalist position described in the *De optima secta*, which, without worrying about how it is to be acquired, emphasizes the role of the extra, non-phenomenal knowledge of rational connections in nature which distinguishes the artistic expert, while at the same time restricting the information to be gleaned from the phenomena with the utmost stringency.

5. The Sceptical Credentials of Commemorative Signification

Thus we have at last come upon a set of arguments that advance Sextus' declared aim: to oppose the indicative sign while upholding the commemorative sign. The arguments directed against the Stoic theory were unsuited to this task because they are equally effective against both varieties of sign as long as that theory is in effect, equally beside the point when it is set aside. But the considerations advanced by the arguments we have just been considering cannot be set aside in the same way; they must be confronted squarely by an advocate of indicative signification.

As we have seen, these arguments can be traced back to the Empiricists, who, as inventors of the commemorative sign and opponents of indicative inference, will have shared Sextus' stated goals. But as we have also discovered, some of these arguments, and the Empirical influence they appear to reflect, are to be found already in the work of Aenesidemus. Thus, though right to detect a gap between the sceptical purposes advanced by the anti-Stoic argument and the end Sextus intended them to serve, Philippson was probably wrong to conclude that the Pyrrhonists' adoption of this end was the result of relatively late and superficial Empirical influence. To be sure, the fact that the position taken by Sextus, in whole or in part, was familiar to and may have belonged to Pyrrhonism from early on does not have to imply that it should have. But this brings us back to our original question: can the commemorative sign, and the medical Empiricism whence it sprang, find a place in Pyrrhonian scepticism?

Because of Pyrrhonism's distinctive peculiarities as a philosophical view, it is not possible to return a straightforward and unqualified answer to this question. As long as the acceptance of a belief is understood in a certain way, as it is by other schools, it is not open to the Pyrrhonist to have any beliefs. But though he will suspend judgement on all matters and have no beliefs in this way, nothing prevents the Pyrrhonist from non-dogmatically holding views from the dogmatic acceptance of which he refrains. As we have seen, to speak very roughly, it will be their character and not their content which distinguishes his beliefs from dogmatic beliefs. At the same time, the Pyrrhonist will not accept, even non-dogmatically, all the views about which he suspends judgement when they are construed as dogmatic positions. He discriminates. And he will be guided in his discrimination by the Pyrrhonists' criterion, the φαινόμενον, how things seem to him (*PH* 1. 21). As it turns out, how things appear to the Pyrrhonist by and large corresponds to how they appear in ordinary life; and it also appears to him that the way to go about acquiring and revising impressions is to follow pretty much the practices favoured in ordinary life. Medical Empiricism appealed to the Pyrrhonists because it appears to be little more than a more specialized and complicated version of ordinary experience, what one is left with if one cultivates experience of certain matters with enough diligence and concentration. And, as Sextus tells us, commemorative signification recommends itself for the same kind of reason, because it belongs to the ordinary, everyday practice of life (*PH* 2. 102; *M*. 8. 158).

But as we have also seen, it is not because ordinary beliefs and practices come furnished with superior epistemic credentials that the Pyrrhonist relies on them; all the questions opened up in the course of his enquiries remain open for him. Rather, the appearances he goes along with, which largely correspond to those of the ordinary man and the Empiricist, are what he is left with, what he falls back on. Hence they are endorsed by him in a highly qualified and circumspect manner compatible with suspension of judgement on all matters as far as philosophical reason is concerned; the Pyrrhonist tends to accept what the ordinary man and the Empiricist accept, as we might say, but not as they accept it. But at the same time, medical Empiricism, for all its sceptical appeal, is in danger of hardening into dogmatism, even if the result is a form of dogmatism distinguished by its vigorous repudiation of the tenets cherished by more easily recognized dogmatists. And on closer inspection, the component of Empirical medicine with which we are presently concerned, the commemorative sign, is not entirely free of traces of this Empirical dogmatism. Given the care he devoted to distinguishing Pyrrhonism from Empiricism, it is surprising and troubling that Sextus, or the Pyrrhonian tradition on which he relied, took so little notice of this danger; it may be that he is at least partially guilty of the lapse against which he was at such pains to warn his fellow Pyrrhonists.

We have already noted in passing the most glaring, though perhaps in the last analysis most superficial, sign of such a lapse: the commemorative sign, as introduced by Sextus, is not appreciably freer of dogmatic entanglements than its indicative counterpart. The evident matters which are said to furnish both kinds of signification with starting-points can be affirmed only by a dogmatist; they have a place in Pyrrhonian argument solely as a dialectical concession. And although the Pyrrhonist may tend to find the matters identified as evident by Empirical physicians and dogmatic philosophers apparent, to allow that things appear to him in a certain way is not to accept their contention that they are evident, if by this it is meant that there are secure directly given matters of fact. But it is not hard to see what Sextus should have said or what the Pyrrhonist who wishes to continue relying on the commemorative sign will say at this point: the items from and to which commemorative signification proceeds need not be anything more than Pyrrhonian phenomena. Being reminded of one thing by another on the basis of past experience will, then, just be a matter of following the appearances.

More troubling, perhaps, are the traces of the Empiricists' crude anti-rationalism that the commemorative sign seems still to bear. Later Empiricists, as we have already noted, relaxed their strictures against reason. To be sure, epilogism, the kind of reason which they approved, did not amount to reason as dogmatic philosophers or Rationalist physicians understood it. Rather, it is just reasoning of an ordinary everyday variety, on behalf of which few claims can be made—just the kind of development with which we might have expected the Pyrrhonists to sympathize. The suspicion that they did is strengthened by the prominent part played in this innovation taken by Empiricists, like Menodotus and Theodas, who were also Pyrrhonists.

To these indirect grounds for suspicion of the commemorative sign may be added Sextus' own testimony that, unlike the Rationalist and the Empiricist, the Pyrrhonist is not inseparably attached to the opposition between commemoration and indication. From Sextus' cautiously approving discussion of Methodist medicine we learn that one of the characteristics it shares with Pyrrhonism is its undogmatic and indifferent use of terms (*PH* 1. 239). As the

Pyrrhonist makes his sceptical declarations, e.g. 'I determine nothing', so the Methodist makes use of terms including 'indication'.
Indication was of course anathema to the Empiricists. But as made
use of by the Methodists, according to Sextus, indication does not
involve a grasp of the hidden, underlying nature of things; it is a
matter, rather, of attending in a quite ordinary and commonsensical
way to appearances. Sextus compares it to the compulsion exerted
by the affections by which everyone, the Pyrrhonist included, is
led, for example, to drink by thirst, to nourishment by hunger
(*PH* 1. 238). In general, he says, things naturally alien to us compel us to free ourselves from them. Thus even a dog pricked by
a thorn will try to remove it. And the guidance furnished by the
affections contrary to nature towards the items which seem to be
remedies is called 'indication' undogmatically by the Methodists
(*PH* 1. 240). Note also how freely they speak of what is natural
here. If this is reason—as it is by the Empiricists' strict standards—
it is obviously of a kind which falls far short of what is demanded
by Rationalist physicians and dogmatic philosophers. And it is not
difficult to imagine that a Pyrrhonist, induced by his enquiries to
suspend judgement on all matters as far as philosophical reason is
concerned, might find himself falling back on reason of this kind.
For, unlike the Empiricist, he lacks a special, if you will dogmatic,
motive for implausibly construing cases that look like reasoning of
an ordinary and unexceptionable sort as instances of remembering
or lucky guesswork.

   The problem, however, is not so much the absence of a place
in Pyrrhonism for commemorative signification as Sextus' failure
to appreciate the need for the same kind of careful explanation he
devotes to Methodist indication to bridge the gap between Pyrrhonism and the Empirical assumptions with which the commemorative
sign is bound up. For as we have just seen, the Pyrrhonist, unlike
the Empiricist, is not inalterably opposed to indication, as long as it
is understood in something like the way the Methodists understand
it, as part of the common, ordinary way of following, or if you will
reasoning about, the phenomena. Presumably, if the Pyrrhonist en-
dorses commemorative signification, it will be in a non-dogmatic
manner which is not incompatible with such allowances. The distinction between reason and memory so vital to the early Empiricists will not have the same kind of grip on him. But Sextus seems
to have forgotten that there are more ways of dogmatizing than by

laying claim to knowledge of non-evident matters. It is possible to dogmatize by vehemently rejecting the possibility of such knowledge and by adopting a certain attitude to so-called evident matters as well.

We are also indebted to Sextus' favourable treatment of Methodism for forcefully reminding us of this last point. One of that school's most striking features is that conditions which other physicians treat as non-evident are apparently treated by it as observable. Indeed, the Methodist position, with its talk of dilation and constriction, is a direct descendant of Asclepiades' corpuscular theory, a paradigm of the kind of Rationalism which depends on a special power of reason to grasp the hidden reality behind the appearances. But the Methodists were not claiming a mysterious power to perceive what others held must be inferred by the use of reason. Rather, they seem to have supposed that there were observable conditions of constriction and dilation, which might or might not correspond to hidden underlying conditions of the kind postulated by Asclepiades. Though it would not do to push the comparison too hard, we may note that it is not necessary to be convinced of a humoral theory, or even to understand it, to be able to identify bilious or phlegmatic persons.

How the developments which gave rise to the Methodist position came about is beyond the scope of the present enquiry;[36] for our purposes, it is the insight it affords into what the Pyrrhonists mean by adherence to the phenomena that is important. The Pyrrhonist is not a dogmatic phenomenalist, someone in the grip of a theory about what is directly given to observation, faced with the difficulty of explaining how other things he knows are somehow based on knowledge that is acquired in this way. When he claims to rely on the phenomena, he does not limit himself to the phenomena sanctioned by such a theory. Much of what he considers as apparent will be accounted phenomenal by such theories, but not all of it.

---

[36] Cf. L. Edelstein, 'Methodiker', in *RE* suppl. vi (1935), 358–73, trans. in id., *Ancient Medicine*, ed. O. and C. Temkin (Baltimore: Johns Hopkins, 1967), 173–91; M. Frede, 'The Method of the So-called Methodical School of Medicine', in Barnes *et al.* (eds.), *Science and Speculation*, 1–23, repr. in id., *Essays in Ancient Philosophy*, 261–78; G. E. R. Lloyd, *Science, Folklore and Ideology: Studies in the Life Sciences in Ancient Greece* (Cambridge: Cambridge University Press, 1983), 182–95. Our understanding of the Methodists will be enhanced by the publication of M. Tecuşan (ed.), *The Fragments of the Methodists* (2 vols.; Studies in Ancient Medicine, 24; Leiden: Brill, forthcoming).

This is made especially clear when, immediately after introducing the phenomenon as the Pyrrhonists' criterion, Sextus goes on to explain that this implies living undogmatically in accordance with the observance of ordinary life (βιωτικὴ τήρησις), which in turn divides into four departments: the guidance of nature, the compulsion of the passions, the tradition of laws and customs, and the teaching of the arts (PH 1. 21–4; cf. 237). Obviously, much of what falls under these heads is not going to count as an appearance in any strict, technical sense. Such is also the case, it seems, with number, a topic on which Sextus briefly touches in his discussion of time (PH 3. 151 ff.). He makes no explicit reference to the phenomena here, only to the customary practice adhered to by the Pyrrhonist, but his reliance on the guidance it affords is clearly intended to count as an instance of what is meant by adherence to the phenomena, though the grasp of number was notoriously not thought to be a part of the phenomena in the strict, technical sense of what is given to direct observation (cf. Plato, Tht. 185 B).

But the narrower, more dogmatic conception of the phenomena is one by which the Empiricists were tempted. This is especially clear if we contrast the anti-indicative arguments due to them with Sextus' anti-Stoic arguments. The latter hinge on theoretical claims peculiar to that position, and they present difficulties to its adherents, as is emphasized by Sextus' declaration that his goal is to make a case for the inconceivability of the sign as far as what is said about it by the dogmatists (PH 2. 104). The situation is not so clear when we turn to the anti-indicative case made in M. 8, however. To be sure, the assumption that there are evident matters, which must be granted so that the question whether they are also capable of indicating the non-evident can also be posed, is clearly marked as a dialectical concession. And I have attempted to show that some of the other assumptions exploited by the argument have the right kind of dialectically essential hold on the Empiricists' Rationalist opponents. But precisely these assumptions, if uncritically and unqualifiedly accepted, would support a dogmatic Empiricist position. For the narrow conception of the phenomena, of what is given to observation, exploited by the arguments against the indicative sign implies that the phenomena, because they are epistemically discrete, are by nature incapable of supporting inferences to the non-evident. And this in turn suggests that nothing remains but to record the patterns of co-occurrence and sequence as the Empiricists do.

Of course, nothing prevents the Pyrrhonist from making use of these arguments. He is free to take arguments from any source he likes, for his use of an argument does not imply a commitment to the assumptions on which it rests. The same is true of the Pyrrhonian Empiricist. But there is evidence that at least some Empiricists were concerned to isolate something like the phenomenally given and reject as unwarranted anything that goes beyond it. In his discussion of different views about the pulse, Galen reports an Empirical objection to the view that the physician detects a dilatation of the artery when he takes the pulse (*De dign. puls.* viii. 780. 14 ff. K = 133. 1 ff. Deichgräber). According to the Empiricists, this is an unwarranted speculative assumption; what is detected is only rhythmical pressure against the thumb. Now it is especially interesting that Galen attempts to answer their objection by appealing to a recognizably Pyrrhonian conception of the phenomena. For he cannot understand why the Empiricists do not allow that they seem to detect a dilatation of the artery, while remaining in doubt about whether, in the nature of things, it really dilates. Though he ultimately does not think much of this practice, Galen thinks that consistency with it should require the Empiricist to grant that it seems to him that the artery dilates when he takes a patient's pulse in just the way that he grants that he is awake and that there seems to be a sun, a moon, and an earth, about the reality of none of which he is willing to commit himself. Galen may well be right on this point; this is what a Pyrrhonian Empiricist probably should say.

But the Empiricists about whom Galen complains are surely representatives of the dogmatic tendency in Empiricism identified and criticized by Sextus. They embraced the assumptions of the anti-indicative case preserved by Sextus as more than useful bases of sceptical argument. This is a danger against which the Pyrrhonist must arm himself, and against which Sextus should have warned him in the same energetic terms he employed earlier in his strictures against dogmatic Empiricism. From the Pyrrhonian point of view, Empiricism has much to recommend it, but so too does Methodism. The Pyrrhonist is free to take from these schools what is of use to him, but his interests are not identical with theirs. In particular, the Pyrrhonist's stand on inference will not be identical to the Empiricist's, for his attitude is not structured in terms of the same contrast between evident and non-evident. The Empiricist's dogmatism on this issue is something from which he will keep his distance. It is a sign of how close the relations between the two schools must have been that Sextus can, despite his own warning, take over a significant component of Empirical teaching uncritically and confuse the sceptical case represented by the anti-Stoic arguments, aimed at calling attention to the confusion that results when inference, regardless of subject-matter, is made the object of dogmatic philosophical attention, with the case of an interested party against inference to the non-evident.

STUDY III

The Stoics on Sign-inference and Demonstration

In the previous study I argued that the close relation between the Stoic theory of signs and the framework of commemorative and indicative signs presupposed by Sextus Empiricus does not survive examination. In particular, the assumption that the Stoics were to be identified with the partisans of indicative signification is mistaken. If the argument I presented is right, the opposition between commemorative and indicative signification belongs to a debate between medical Rationalists and Empiricists, and Sextus' discussion of signs was shaped by the concern, shared at that point by Empiricists and Pyrrhonists, to abolish the indicative sign while upholding the commemorative sign. The Stoic theory of signification owes its prominence in Sextus to the conflation by Sextus, or the tradition on which he relies, of this medical debate with another debate between the Stoics and opponents who may well have been Pyrrhonists but were now contesting a different issue. But if the terminology of 'commemoration' and 'indication' and some of the assumptions incorporated in the corresponding conceptions of signification were alien to the Stoa, it remains to be asked whether the Stoic theory can be put into some kind of relation with the framework defined by commemorative and indicative signification: was it meant to apply, *mutatis mutandis*, to analogues of the indicative sign, the commemorative sign, or both, or even to varieties of sign not captured by this apparently exhaustive division?

That this question can be raised at all shows just how little we know about the Stoic theory. In particular, the Stoics' reasons for propounding a theory of signs in the first place are unclear. As we have seen, Sextus treats sign-inference and demonstration as if they had essentially the same purpose: to extend the reach of human knowledge through inferences building on directly evident starting-points secured by the criterion (cf. *M.* 7. 25; cf. *PH* 2. 96; *M.* 7. 394–6; *M.* 8. 140, 319). For the purpose of expounding dogmatic epistemology, he adopts what I earlier called a high conception of signs. Though there is abundant testimony that the Epicureans and some medical theorists conceived of sign-inference in something like this way, such evidence as we have suggests that the Stoics treated inferences of this kind under the head of demonstrations (cf. D.L. 7. 45; Cicero *Luc.* 26; *Div.* 2. 103). Apart from Sextus, our sources are remarkably silent about a Stoic theory of signification. Sextus himself devotes no small amount of attention to the Stoic theory of demonstration, with the result that, as things stand, his separate full-length treatments of sign-inference *and* demonstration almost seem to be redundant (*PH* 2. 134 ff.; *M.* 8. 300 ff.). We may be in a better position to understand the Stoic theory of signs, then, if we can discover a division of labour between signs and demonstrations.

I propose to do this by distinguishing different areas of application for semiotic and apodeictic reasoning in Stoic epistemology. The case for the correctness of this account is based on three claims:

(1) There was a widespread and persistent tradition in the ancient world of calling pieces of evidence that stand in weaker relations to the conclusions they support 'signs'. The contrast between weaker and stronger came in a variety of forms, and the tradition embraced contrasts between signs and causes, signs and conclusive evidence, and signs and demonstrations.

(2) The Stoics distinguished very carefully between strong and weak relations of evidential support, and they regarded reasoning on the basis of both as indispensable; neither sages nor fools are, on their view, able to rely solely on a grasp of the former. Thus the Stoics needed a distinction between weaker and stronger kinds of reasoning from evidence of the kind traditionally made in terms of 'signs'.

(3) The Stoic theory preserved by Sextus is suited to meet this need. What is more, the details of its construction suggest that it was introduced with this end in view.

Let us first turn to Sextus Empiricus' exposition of the Stoic theory to prepare the way for the development of claims (2) and (3), before returning to point (1) and the place of the Stoics' contribution in the broader context of the ancient discussion of sign-inference.

1. The Genus *Sign*

One conclusion about the relation between sign-inference and demonstration according to the Stoics can be drawn right away. Sextus Empiricus makes frequent reference to the dogmatic view that demonstration is of the genus sign (*PH* 2. 131, 134; *M.* 8. 140, 180, 277, 289, 299). Though Sextus does not name the Stoics, the justification he offers for this view draws on the language and content of Stoic accounts of the sign and demonstration.[1] According to a principle accepted by the Stoics, an argument is valid if and only if the conditional formed by taking the conjunction of the premises as an antecedent and the conclusion as a consequent is true (cf. S.E. *PH* 2. 135 ff.; *M.* 8. 415 ff.).[2] And the requirement that the premises of a demonstration must be true and revelatory of the consequent ensures that their conjunction will qualify as a sign according to the Stoic definition of the sign as 'an antecedent in a sound conditional revelatory of the consequent' (cf. *M.* 8. 277). Loosely speaking, then, demonstrations are signs.

The generic status of the sign furnishes a clue about what the contrast between signs and demonstrations might have been. If demonstration is a species of the genus sign, though all demonstrations will be signs—more precisely, sign-inferences—there will be signs that are not demonstrations. The Stoics were accustomed to refer to the species of a genus whose members meet only the requirements for inclusion in the genus, but not the more restrictive conditions for membership in one of its other species defined by further differentia, as homonymously so called with the genus (cf. D.L. 7. 78; *SVF* iii. 170). If this is true of the genus sign, the expression 'sign' will be especially suitable for pieces of evidence satisfying the generic requirements of the sign, but not the more restrictive requirements that must be satisfied by (conjunctions of) demonstrative premises. To be sure, the latter are also entitled to be called signs, but there is a more informative designation available for them as well. If this is the right approach, the generic notion of the sign serves to capture a minimal notion of being evidence for a

---

[1] Cf. Burnyeat, 'The Origins of Non-deductive Inference', 212–13.
[2] Cf. B. Mates, *Stoic Logic* (Berkeley: University of California Press, 1953), 74 ff.; M. Frede, *Die stoische Logik* (Göttingen: Vandenhoeck and Ruprecht, 1974), 105–6.

conclusion: being the antecedent of a conditional when the further condition that the consequent is revealed by the sign is met.

What further differentia might have separated demonstrations from signs so called homonymously with the genus? Chrysippus famously held that there are no single-premissed arguments (μονολήμματοι λόγοι), a view from which his student Antipater dissented (cf. *PH* 2. 167; *M*. 8. 443; Alexander, *In an. pr.* 21. 25 Wallies; *In top.* 8. 16 Wallies). On this view, an atomic proposition cannot be the only premiss of a demonstration because demonstrations are arguments. There are true atomic propositions that are antecedents in conditionals and revelatory of their consequents which cannot, therefore, be the premisses of demonstrations by themselves. This feature could have been used to determine membership in a class of 'homonymous' signs so that it would correspond to a subclass of premisses of single-premissed demonstrative arguments not allowed by Chrysippus. If further restrictions are imposed on demonstration, however, homonymous signs will be distinguished by other characteristics as well. The restriction I have in mind is on the kind of relation between the propositional components of a demonstration's hypothetical premisses. Atomic propositions that stand in the appropriate, stronger relation to what they signify will qualify as homonymous signs by the first criterion. But if a sign of this kind is taken together with the appropriate conditional, and the signified consequent deduced as a conclusion, the result will be a demonstrative inference. On the view under consideration, however, other atomic propositional signs standing in a weaker relation to what they signify can be turned into arguments in this way, but not into demonstrations. The full two-premissed argument will still be only a sign-inference.

2. Stoic Signs and Stoic Logic

As we have seen, the Stoics define the sign as 'a proposition antecedent in a sound conditional and revelatory of the consequent' (*PH* 2. 104; *M*. 8. 245). There are small differences between the versions of *PH* 2 and *M*. 8, but the most important part of the definition, the appeal to the conditional relating sign and signified, is the same in both.[3] The conditional was the subject of a

---

[3] In the *PH* 2 version the sign is said to be a προκαθηγούμενον, in the *M*. 8 version,

famous controversy in antiquity,[4] which provided the Pyrrhonists, always eager to exploit disagreements within and between dogmatic schools of philosophy, with scope for sceptical argument. As we saw in the previous study, the dispute is duly pressed into service in this way by Sextus in the sceptical examination of the Stoic account of signs (*PH* 2. 110–12; *M*. 8. 245, 265). But the controversy is of concern to this enquiry for another reason as well. On its resolution by the Stoics themselves depends the answer to the question about the kind of relation between sign and signified that the Stoic theory is intended to capture.

Somewhat surprisingly, the most detailed treatment of the different criteria (κρίσεις) of the conditional to survive from antiquity is in Sextus' just-mentioned examination of the Stoic theory of signs (*PH* 2. 110–12). In this passage rival accounts of the true conditional are organized in a sequence: each imposes a new, more restrictive, set of necessary and sufficient conditions so that those specified previously are now necessary only. And each new account is illustrated with an example carefully chosen to focus attention on the special features of the criterion under consideration. This example counts as true in accordance with it, but not by the next more restrictive criterion, and by being counter-intuitive, each example also furnishes a motive for the move to a stricter account meant to exclude would-be conditionals like itself. Thus Philo's truth-functional account is illustrated by the conditional 'If it is day, I am talking'. The second account is that of Diodorus, according to

a καθηγούμενον; at *PH* 2. 106 Sextus defines the προκαθηγούμενον as a true antecedent (ἡγούμενον) in a sound conditional, whereas the requirement that the antecedent be true is introduced differently at *M*. 8. 249, apparently as a further requirement imposed on the sign. The manuscript reading in the parallel passage of the *Historia philosopha* is ἡγούμενον, which Diels replaces with προκαθηγούμενον (*DG* 605. 11). These variations seem to reflect some uncertainty about whether, in calling one proposition, *P*, a sign of another, *Q*, one is saying only that *were P* true it *would* be evidence that *Q* is as well, a relation which is captured by the conditional 'If *P*, then *Q*', or asserting that *P is* evidence for the conclusion *Q*, which one now infers, in which case one is stating something stronger than a conditional, namely something like what the Stoics called a paraconditional, 'Since *P*, then *Q*', which is equivalent to the conditional together with the assertion of the antecedent (cf. D.L. 7. 71, 74). On these variations see Burnyeat, 'The Origins of Non-deductive Inference', 224, who, however, sees a deeper and more serious problem here than I do.

[4] Cf. S.E. *M*. 1. 309–10; 8. 112, 428; Cicero, *Luc*. 143; The controversy is discussed by Frede, *Die stoische Logik*, 81; W. Kneale and M. Kneale, *The Development of Logic* (Oxford: Oxford University Press, 1962), 128 ff.; Mates, *Stoic Logic*, 42 ff.

whom the true conditional 'neither permitted nor permits beginning with a truth and concluding with a falsehood'. At first glance,
this account seems to mark the transition to a non-truth-functional
account of implication with its talk of 'permission' (ἐνδέχεται), but
when Diodorus' non-modal account of possibility, according to
which a proposition is possible ('is permitted') if it either is or will
be true, is taken into account, his criterion requires that a true
conditional be true by the Philonian criterion at all times, and it is
equivalent to an uncredited account mentioned by Sextus produced
by adding one word to the Philonian account so that it requires only
that the conditional *never* begin with a truth and conclude with a
falsehood (*M.* 8. 416).[5] Like the Philonian account, it approaches
the truth of the conditional through an independent assessment of
the truth of its component propositions. Sextus' example—'if it is
not the case that the elements of things are without parts, the element of things are without parts'—makes it clear why this account
did not satisfy everyone. The conditional was supposed to capture
the relation of consequence in virtue of which one proposition is
said to follow another, and dissatisfaction with an account which
allows a proposition to follow its contradictory is not surprising.
This in turn explains the demand for a stricter form of implication.
And this need is apparently supplied by Sextus' third account in
terms of συνάρτησις, which means 'connection'.[6] According to it, a
true conditional is one in which the contradictory of the consequent
is incompatible or in conflict (μάχεται) with the antecedent (D.L. 7.
73; S.E. *PH* 2. 111).

The connective account is attributed to the Stoics by Diogenes
Laertius (7. 73), and on the basis of a somewhat complicated argument, it seems to be the account advocated, and perhaps introduced,
by Chrysippus.[7] According to Cicero, Chrysippus objected to the
formulation of astrological theorems as conditional schemas such
as 'If someone was born at the rising of the dog star, he will not die
at sea' (*Fat.* 12 ff.). If they are formulated in this way, Chrysippus
maintained, we shall hold conditionals such as 'If Fabius was born
at the rising of the dog star, he will not die at sea' to be true. But

---

[5] Cf. Mates, *Stoic Logic*, 37.   [6] Cf. Frede, *Die stoische Logik*, 84 ff.
[7] Cf. ibid. 86 ff.; I. Mueller, 'Introduction to Stoic Logic', in J. M. Rist (ed.), *The
Stoics* (Berkeley: University of California Press, 1978), 1–26 at 18 ff.; and now S.
Bobzien, *Determinism and Freedom in Stoic Philosophy* (Oxford: Oxford University
Press, 1998), 156 ff.

if this conditional is true, the contradictory of the consequent will be in conflict with the antecedent. Clearly the connective account is presupposed here. But according to Chrysippus, when the antecedent is true, it will be necessary, because of another view of his, since it is a truth about the past. This in turn will make the consequent a necessary proposition as well, which Chrysippus wants to avoid because he holds that what will not happen, e.g. Fabius' death at sea, is nevertheless often possible. Chrysippus proposes to solve this problem by formulating astrological laws of this type as negated conjunctions, e.g. 'It is not the case that anyone was born at the rising of the dog star and he will die at sea', that appear to capture the same truth-functional relation as the Philonian conditional.

More is at stake in the choice between Philonian and connective accounts of consequence than the particular problem that Cicero mentions, however. Very roughly speaking, the Philonian conditional makes the minimum commitment sufficient to support hypothetical reasoning. When it is in force, 'If P, then Q' *entitles* us to draw the conclusion Q when P is true, but the issue in dispute in the controversy about the true conditional concerns what it is for one proposition to *follow* from another, and if more is expected of 'following', viz. that P logically excludes the contradictory of Q, i.e. that the conjunction of P and the contradictory of Q is necessarily false, the Philonian account does not require that Q *follow* from P. It may be that no human being born at the rising of the dog star ever dies at sea even though being born at the rising of the dog star does not by itself exclude the *possibility* of death by drowning; nevertheless, if this theorem of astrology is true, and Fabius was born at the rising of the dog star, one is entitled to draw the conclusion that he will not die at sea. But that Fabius will not die at sea follows on this stronger understanding of 'follows', if it does follow, from another proposition or propositions with which its contradictory is not compatible. Thus Chrysippus' reasons for withholding the standing of a conditional from astrological laws, and the way he contrasts conditionals and negated conjunctions, also suggest that the incompatibility, unspecified in the definition of connection, is logical.

The difference between this kind of entitlement and the stricter relation of consequence that the connective account is intended to capture has two epistemologically significant consequences. First, a relation of consequence between the component propositions imposed by the concepts expressed in them can in principle be apprehended independently of a grasp of the truth of the antecedent and consequent; thus conditionals stating relations of consequence of this kind can be used to infer truths to which no independent epistemic access is possible. Secondly, such a relation can be explanatory in a way that Philonian conditionals are not. The grasp of a Philonian conditional entitles us, in the appropriate conditions, to draw the conclusion *that* the consequent is true, and it has a place in an account of how we are justified in accepting the conclusion; but it leaves the truth of the consequent unexplained, for the antecedent may, by itself, be compatible with the contradictory of the consequent. To say *why* things are as the consequent represents them it is minimally necessary, on the view at issue, to specify the conditions which made it impossible for them not to be so. But a proposition stating such conditions will be the antecedent of a connective conditional with this proposition as a consequent.

As we have seen, a contrast resembling this one was also important to the medical Rationalists. They contrasted the relation of consequence exploited by their inferences with the relations of observed consequence, precedence, and succession relied upon by their Empiricist opponents. Consequence, as they understand it, is authorized by the nature of the matter itself apart from experience and is called indication (Galen, *De meth. med.* x. 126. 10 ff. K = fr. 45 Deichgräber; *Institutio logica*, 24. 14–16 Kalbfleisch). As we have noted, the question arises: assuming that commemorative and indicative signification have been correctly traced back to the epistemology of the medical schools, and that the terminology associated with them was not used by the Stoa, might it not still be true that the sign as conceived by the Stoa is related to one or the other or both of them? The burden of the argument of the last study was that the sign defined by the Stoics is not to be identified with the indicative sign. And I have promised to argue in this study that the intended scope of the Stoic theory was, in a sense still to be explained, weaker inferential relations, more suited to the matters with which the commemorative sign is concerned. But as we have seen, the medical Rationalists seem to have drawn on the Stoics when developing their own views. Some spoke of 'connection' ([Galen], *De opt. sect.* i. 116–17 K). Galen speaks of 'emphasis' (*De meth. med.* x. 126. 10 ff. K = fr. 45 Deichgräber), the last of the accounts of the criterion catalogued at *PH* 2. 110–12, which may be another version of the connective conditional it follows.[8] And at one point Sextus contrasts the Empirical conception of consequence directly with Stoic views (*M.* 8. 288). These affinities between medical Rationalism and Stoicism need to be examined before we proceed.

The rationalism of the medical Rationalists involves two closely related ideas:

(1) Events, processes, and objects, some of them observable, oc- cur, take place, and exist as they do because of the unobserv- able, underlying nature of the items that make up the physical world.

(2) Knowledge of these natures and the necessary relations of consequence and exclusion they impose can in many in- stances be grasped by the exercise of reason.

Very roughly speaking, then, the Rationalists believe in a fit be- tween mind and nature. The conceptually authorized relations that obtain between propositions and are grasped by reason capture nat- ural necessities imposed by the nature of things. In this regard it is significant that Galen can speak both of rational consequence and a natural-relation consequence in affairs (*Subfig. emp.* 44. 10; 63. 20–6; 64. 7 Deichgräber), and of relations of consequence and exclusion between propositions (*logoi*) and affairs (*pragmata*) (*In- stitutio logica*, 33. 7, 20 ff. Kalbfleisch). Stoic dialectic is well suited to capture such an outlook, but how closely do Stoic views square with the Rationalists' assumptions? This is, roughly speaking, a question about the kind of interpretation the Stoics envisaged for the relations of consequence and exclusion discussed in their logical theory.

The Stoics were in broad agreement with (1). The form taken by this agreement reflected the unprecedented rigour and complexity they brought to the study of causality, however. And this in turn af- fected their attitude towards (2). Although, as we have already seen, the idea of a natural grasp of consequence and conflict seems to go back to the Stoa, I shall argue that the Stoics were in general far more circumspect than many medical Rationalists about the claims they were willing to make on behalf of the capacity for rational

[8] Cf. Frede, *Die stoische Logik*, 90–3.

insight into the nature of things.[9] The Stoic discussion of causality is an extremely complex subject, not made easier to understand by the state of the evidence available to us. It deserves far more detailed consideration than is possible here; in the brief and over-simplified summary that follows I touch on only a few points essential to the present enquiry.[10]

Notoriously, the Stoics were committed determinists. They were nevertheless concerned to show that human beings' actions are in their own power and thus to leave a place for individual moral responsibility. Chrysippus seems to have contributed the most to the causal theory they developed to this end. He held that everything comes about in accordance with fate, but that the actions performed by human agents are in their own power and not necessitated by causes external to the agent. Although ancient commentators already seem to have been unsure about how the many different distinctions of causes into kinds drawn by the Stoics were intended to fit together, it seems that the crucial part in the causation of an outcome was assigned to the so-called containing cause (αἴτιον συνεκτικόν).[11] The containing cause apparently owes its name to the Stoic view that objects are held together by a fine mixture of fire and air, which in animate beings is the soul (cf. Alexander, *De anima*, 115. 6 ff. Bruns). Thus the containing cause plays a part akin to that of the nature or Aristotelian form of an object. Its character and the range of states of which it is capable bring about and explain what the object does. Without antecedent causes, the containing cause

---

[9] Cf. Galen, *In Hippocr. de med. officina*, xviiiʙ. 649 K = *SVF* ii. 135; Cicero, *De legibus*, 1. 45; *Luc.* 22; S.E. *M.* 8. 275.

[10] Cf. M. Frede, 'The Original Notion of Cause', in M. Schofield, M. Burnyeat, and J. Barnes (eds.), *Doubt and Dogmatism: Studies in Hellenistic Epistemology* (Oxford: Oxford University Press, 1980), 217–49; S. Bobzien, 'Chrysippus' Theory of Causes', in K. Ierodiakonou (ed.), *Topics in Stoic Philosophy* (Oxford: Oxford University Press, 1998), 196–242. On the broader issues of determinism, freedom, and moral responsibility in Stoic philosophy see Bobzien, *Determinism and Freedom*. I have also profited from an unpublished paper by D. Frede, 'The Stoic Notion of Causality', delivered at the Colloquium in Classical Philosophy, Princeton University, Dec. 1975.

[11] How, for example, are containing causes and the antecedent causes with which they are contrasted related to the distinction between perfect and principal causes and auxiliary and proximate causes that Cicero reports (*Fat.* 41)? Are containing causes perfect and principal causes or is the concept of a perfect and principal cause that of a kind of antecedent cause which lacks and must lack an extension, the point of its introduction having been to stress that causation requires the co-operation of several factors, external antecedent factors and an internal containing cause (as is argued by Bobzien, 'Chrysippus' Theory')?

will not enter the various states which explain and bring about the behaviour of the object, but antecedent causes do not explain or necessitate the effects of which they are antecedent causes. Chrysippus' example is the rolling of a cylinder. The cylinder is set going by a push from without, but it is its own fitness for rolling that keeps it going once it has started. The fitness plays the part of the containing cause, the push that of the antecedent cause (Cicero, *Fat.* 43–4). Since fate is the eternal sequence of antecedent causes, though all things come about in accordance with fate and nothing occurs without being fated, none of them is made necessary simply by fate (Cicero, *Top.* 59; *Fat.* 41, 44; Plutarch, *De Stoic. repugn.* 1056 B). In particular, people do what they do because of their own natures, not because they are compelled by external and antecedent causes.

There are obvious difficulties with the view, as ancient opponents of the Stoa were not slow to point out, and it is not clear that they will disappear entirely from a fuller, more careful account than that given here. None the less, it should now be possible to say a little more about the Stoics' affinity with the Rationalist temper. The crucial idea is that explanation and necessity enter the picture together with the full causal explanation made possible by the containing cause. Only explanation of this kind will account for the necessitation of the effect, hence only this relation of cause to effect is formulable as a connective conditional.[12] And it would seem that once we had specified the nature of something, the containing cause of all its behaviour, we could apply our natural grasp of consequence and conflict and arrive at connective conditionals linking that nature in its different states with the different behaviours of which it is capable. A similar procedure would make possible the formulation of connective conditionals capturing the relation between outcomes and their causally necessary conditions, a more common subject for

---

[12] Among the jumble of types of propositions in Stoic logic in the report of Diocles Magnes that is preserved by Diogenes Laertius is a causal proposition (αἰτιῶδες ἀξίωμα) formed by means of the conjunction 'because' (διότι), e.g. 'Because it is day, it is light' (D.L. 7. 72). The causal proposition 'Because *P*, *Q*' is true when 'If *P*, then *Q*' is true, *P* is true, and 'If *Q*, then *P*' is not true (D.L. 7. 74). It is hard to know what purpose this type of proposition was meant to serve. It cannot have been to regulate all talk of causes, as the Stoics will not have wanted to restrict the expression 'cause' to items that are sufficient for their effects. Note also that, according to this account, it would be improper to say, for example, 'Because heavenly body *X* is near, it does not twinkle' if it is true that 'If heavenly body *X* does not twinkle, then it is near'.

signification. Thus the Stoics have at their disposal all the material necessary for an analogue of the indicative sign. But as this rough account shows, the Stoics' position recognized other possibilities as well. Though the statement of a given outcome will form the consequent of a connective conditional whose antecedent specifies the causally sufficient conditions for that outcome, it can also be combined with a different antecedent to form a conditional satisfying only Philonian requirements, or equivalently, be the contradictory of the second conjunct of a negated conjunction whose first member is the antecedent of the corresponding Philonian conditional. These Philonian conditionals or negated conjunctions may relate the outcome to antecedent causes or even to items that do not bear any causal relation to, but are somehow correlated with, the outcome.

3. The Intended Application of the Stoic Theory

Had we been able to assume that the reference to the true conditional in the Stoic definition of the sign was to the connective conditional, the relation between the Stoic theory and the framework of commemorative and indicative signs would have been much clearer. The Stoic sign would, then, have been an analogue of the indicative sign in something like the way just described. But in the exposition of the Stoic theory at *PH* 2. 104 ff. Sextus unhesitatingly identifies the kind of conditional at issue as Philonian: 'The true conditional is the one which does not begin with a truth and conclude with a falsehood.'[13] The possibility of a disagreement over which type of conditional is to be applied in the case of the sign is closed here; it emerges first in the sceptical examination of the Stoic definition (110–12). This apparently unequivocal pronouncement in favour of the Philonian criterion does not recur in *M*. 8, but even there it is granted a certain prominence. In the first exposition of the Stoic theory, Sextus remarks: 'They assert that, though there are also many other criteria [κρίσεις], one among them is this, which will be set out, though it too is not agreed upon' (245). There follows a brief exposition of the Philonian account. Though it is far from clear what this means, it may reflect a view which, like *PH* 2. 104 ff., identifies the Philonian as the correct account, while anticipating

---

[13] Cf. A. A. Long and D. Sedley, *The Hellenistic Philosophers* (2 vols.; Cambridge: Cambridge University Press, 1987) i. 210, 264.

the argument that will exploit the disagreement about the truth conditions of the conditional.

Arguments presupposing a commitment to the Philonian under-standing lend further support to this interpretation (*PH* 2. 116; *M*. 8. 266–8, cf. 451). They work by presenting the Stoics with a dilemma. The signified matter is either pre-evident or non-evident. If the former, it is not signified by the sign because evident in its own right. But if it is non-evident, we shall not know whether it is true or false, and hence whether the conditional at issue begins with a truth and ends with a falsehood.[14] The force of this argu-ment depends on the supposition that the Philonian conditional is at issue, as the problem it presents is of just the kind that resort to the connective conditional should solve.[15] And the impression that the Philonian account was correctly cited at *PH* 2. 104–5 is also strengthened by the paradigmatically co-observational examples cited in the exposition of the Stoic theory (*M*. 8. 254–5). A wound in the heart fits into that account as an antecedent cause which does not by itself necessitate, or explain, death. And the full causal account, of which the infliction of a wound and the subsequent ap-pearance of a scar are only parts, would need to be specified before we were able to see how the alteration of the epidermis necessary for the production of the scar itself relates to the antecedent causal agency of the wounding.

But there is more than one way to interpret the choice of the Philonian account at *PH* 2. 104. We have already seen what form an analogue of the indicative sign would take in the context of the Stoic theory and how that theory is applied to paradigmatic cases of co-observational signification. Though the observation of correlations among events cannot support connective conditionals, it may give us a reason to accept Philonian conditionals in which the correlated events are related. It is possible, then, that the weakest and most inclusive account of the conditional was specified to capture sign-conditionals grounded in observed conjunctions and sequences as well as those satisfying stricter connective standards. The Stoics would then have recognized two classes of signs very much like

[14] Of course, this evidence could point in the opposite direction. Preference could have been granted to the Philonian account in order to prepare the way for this line of argument. This view is entertained but not adopted by Frede, *Die stoische Logik*, 79.

[15] Sextus claims that it applies no matter what the choice of conditional, however (*M*. 8. 266).

commemorative and indicative signs, even if they did not refer to them by their medical names.[16]

Though there is much about this view that is right, I shall defend a position differing from it on two points. First, though it is right to connect the choice of the Philonian account of the conditional with observation-based signs, there are relations between signs and what they signify other than the co-observational that can be formulated only as Philonian conditionals. And the Stoics recognized some of these non-co-observational grounds for conditionals and used the expression 'sign' in connection with them. Hence the distinction between commemorative and indicative signs is not exhaustive of the range of materials to which the Stoics' semiotic theory was applied, and the adoption of the Philonian account was a way of extending the theory to cover more than commemorative or co-observational signs. Second, as I have already mentioned, I wish to argue that the notion of the sign was not so much extended to cover cases that permit the formulation only of non-connective conditionals as it was developed with them in view. Of course, conditionals that satisfy the stronger, connective account will also satisfy the weaker Philonian criterion, and, as long as they satisfy the other conditions, qualify as sign-conditionals. But it will be possible to say something stronger and more informative about them, namely that they qualify as demonstrative premisses according to a strict account of demonstration. Hence, though true, it would be misleading to call them sign-conditionals.

If this is right, the Stoics intended their theory primarily to cover types of inference that depend on hypothetical premisses satisfying only the minimal standards imposed by the Philonian conditional. Chrysippus' criticism of Chaldean astrologers and other diviners is evidence of a strong interest in weaker hypothetical connections, but he insisted on formulating them as negated conjunctions. Thus we can conclude that the theory must be pre-, or as I shall argue, post-Chrysippean, because Chrysippus insisted on stronger than truth-functional truth conditions for the conditional.[17] The best way to support the interpretation I have just sketched, and fill it out with more detail, is to take the hint dropped by Chrysippus and turn

---

[16] Cf. Burnyeat, 'The Origins of Non-deductive Inference', 222.

[17] Hülser (ed.), *Die Fragmente zur Dialektik der Stoiker*, iii. 1326–7, cites this as a reason for taking the theory to be late. The opposite conclusion is reached by Ebert, *Dialektiker*, 36–7. On Ebert's views see n. 51 below and the appendix to this study.

to the Stoics' views of inference and reasoning in divination. Stoic views on this subject are worthy of special attention because they promise to throw light on Stoic conceptions of sign-inference quite generally and because an unusually large amount of information about them is preserved in Cicero's *De divinatione*.

4. Stoic Divination

Divination was of interest to the Stoics because they held that it supported certain of their most cherished tenets, the existence of providence and the occurrence of all things in accordance with fate. But there may have been another reason for the attention they paid to the subject. Chrysippus directed the remarks preserved in Cicero's *De fato* against Chaldean astrology, according to which the configuration of stars at a man's birth exerted a causal influence on his fortune (15–16). Though they typically attached great importance to time-hallowed and widely dispersed customs like the practice of divination, the Stoics felt duty-bound to scrutinize them and to reformulate them in the light of their own canons of sound method. And their account of divination was in large part an attempt to free it from aetiological pretensions by bringing it into line with the more modest strictures of other less ambitious but more securely grounded arts. This they did principally by reinterpreting it along empirical lines.[18]

Thus part of the Stoics' interest in divination may have been due to their view that it stands in need of reform to a greater extent than other arts. This is important for our purposes because we can form a picture of the Stoics' understanding of reasoning and inference in the arts quite generally on the basis of what they say about divination. And the fact that they defined divination as 'the power of recognizing and understanding the signs sent by God to human beings' promises to tell us something about the practical point of the very formal account of the sign preserved by Sextus (cf. Cicero,

---

[18] This more empirical reconstruction of divination, especially astrology, was very influential. Causal and empirical accounts are opposed to each other not only by Sextus (*M.* 5. 1 ff.), but by Plotinus (2. 3. 1; 3. 1. 5) and Augustine, who, though generally hostile to astrology, finds the non-causal account which explains the predictive power of signs in terms of observed correlations less objectionable than the causal account (*De civitate Dei*, 5. 1): 'Quod si dicuntur stellae significare potius ista quam facere, ut quasi locutio quaedam sit illa positio praedicans futura, non agens (non enim mediocriter doctorum hominum fuit ista sententia) . . .'

Div. 2. 130; S.E. *M.* 9. 132; Stobaeus, *Ecl.* ii. 170 Wachsmuth). For it may well have been the appeal to signs in contexts like that of divination that prompted the technical exactitude of the definition which Sextus cites as the justification for his concentration on the Stoic account (*PH* 2. 104).

In the first book of the *De divinatione* Cicero's brother, Quintus, expounds and defends the art of divination. In the second Cicero criticizes his brother's position from the point of view of Academic scepticism. The Stoic character of the position defended by Quintus is vouched for by Cicero's remark that his brother has defended the views of the Stoics in the Stoic manner (*Div.* 2. 8; cf. 1. 11, 82, 118; 2. 100). According to Quintus, divination comes in two forms: artificial and natural (1. 12, 34, 72; cf. 2. 26–7; cf. [Plutarch], *Vit. Hom.* 212). We have already met with this contrast. 'Artificial' means technical or artistic; it refers to the kind of expertise which is acquired by instruction and training in contrast with lay abilities which are exercised in the course of ordinary life by means of ordinary natural capacities and without specialized study. Natural divination, on the other hand, depends on capacities which, if not quite ordinary, are natural because they owe nothing to specialized training and instruction. The relatively straightforward messages sent by the gods to human beings in the form of dreams and during bouts of prophetic madness are examples. Establishing the claim that the distinction between commemorative and indicative signification is not exhaustive will require an investigation of the application of the notion of the sign to the varieties of evidence with which both artificial and natural divination are concerned. But because co-observational evidence appears to be the most important component of artificial divination, let us consider it first before turning to those varieties of evidence that do not belong to the co-observational paradigm.

Quintus first introduces co-observation as if it were the only concern of artificial divination (*Div.* 1. 12): 'There is a certain nature or power which sometimes through significations observed over a long time and sometimes through a certain excitement and divine inspiration announces what will come to be.' This method is referred to here as long observation, *diuturna observatio* or *diuturnus usus* (cf. *ND.* 2. 166–7). And the prominence it is accorded is evidence of the affinity between the Stoic position and empirical accounts of artistic method. As we should expect, the knowledge gained by long observation is carefully distinguished from the knowledge of underlying causal mechanisms. It is knowledge of outcomes, *eventa*, knowledge *that* things come about as they do, not of the reasons *why* or the cause. Quintus' exposition draws on the kind of examples from agriculture, navigation, and medicine familiar to us from the medical Empiricists' defence of their position (*Div.* 1. 16):

I do not enquire why this tree alone blooms three times, why it obligingly provides the fruits of its mature bloom as a sign that it is time to plough. I am content with this: even if I do not understand why each thing comes about, I know that it does.

What root of scammony is able to accomplish by way of purgation, what aristolochia is able to do against snakebites . . . I see; why they are able to act as they do I know not.

What the reason or explanation [*ratio*] for signs of wind and rain is I do not clearly know, but I know and approve their powers and their outcomes. Similarly in the case of a fissure or a cleft in the entrails, I know what power they have [i.e. what they signify], but what their cause is I do not know.

And use is made of the contrast between knowledge of the reason *why* and knowledge of the fact *that* throughout the first book of the *De divinatione* (12, 16, 29, 35, 86, 109, 127). This is of course at the heart of the empirical understanding of the arts, according to which a grasp of the recurring patterns of sequence and co-occurence among the matters with which an art is concerned, if detailed and extensive enough, is a sufficient basis for artistic expertise, even though these observable regularities may be, and most likely are, superficial consequences of the underlying causal processes in the knowledge of which necessitation and explanation would coincide. Medical Empiricism was only the most articulate and self-conscious form taken by a broadly empirical tradition in antiquity. And the Stoics' affinity with this tradition embraces counterparts of the standard features of empiricism familiar to us from medical Empiricism. The same appeal is made to long observation on the part of the artist to explain his expertise in areas of which the layman is ignorant even though the episodes observation of which is the source of his specialized knowledge are no less accessible to the layperson than to the artist: 'In all things great length of time spent in long observation brings about an incredible body of knowledge [*scientia*] even without any stimulus or impulse from the gods [i.e. revelation through natural divination] when what results from what and what signifies each thing has been observed with continuous attention' (*Div.* 1. 109). And the Stoic account makes a distinction between the artist's own experience and the experience of others collected in and preserved by history corresponding to the medical Empiricists' distinction between autopsy and history: '[Those who have mastered artificial divination], even if they do not discern the causes, nevertheless see the signs and marks [*signa et nota*] of the causes, as a result of applied diligence and memory, to which along with the records of the ancients the kind of divination called artificial owes its origin' (*Div.* 1. 127; cf. 1. 12, 72).[19]

There are, then, good reasons for connecting the Stoics' account of artificial divination with the account of co-observational signification expounded by Sextus and due originally to medical Empiricism, without the Empiricists' distinctive anti-rationalism. Indeed, their account of divination seems to represent an application of the empirical outlook to divination, and it acquires a polemical edge from being consciously opposed to a quasi-rationalist, causal account. This impression of an affinity between Stoicism and empiricism is strengthened by the Stoics' well-known hesitancy concerning aetiology. The reaction of some of them to Posidonius attests to the strength of this tendency. Strabo remarks that 'There is much aetiologizing and Aristotelizing in [Posidonius], which our people [the Stoics] shun because of the hiddenness [ἐπίκρυψις] of the causes' (2. 3. 8).

We can see what the dominant Stoic attitude was towards at least a large part of aetiology from Galen's account of Chrysippus' views about the location of the ruling part of the soul. According to Galen, Chrysippus believed:

The answer to this question escapes us because there is neither manifest perception [of the matter], as there is in other cases, nor are there any sure tokens [τεκμήρια] by means of which one may syllogize a conclusion. The disagreement [ἀντιλογία] among philosophers and physicians would not otherwise have grown to such proportions. (*De plac. Hipp. et Plat.* 152. 23–7; cf. 170. 23–7; 220. 5–9 De Lacy)

Deprived of direct evidence or conclusive inferences, Galen reports, Chrysippus fell back on a battery of plausible but non-conclusive arguments based on etymology, mythology, and other considera-

---

[19] Divination seems to have an advantage over other empirical arts because of the enormous length of time during which records have been kept. The Babylonian astrologers are said to have records going back 470,000 years (*Div.* 1. 36).

tions. Galen complains that he behaves more like an orator than a philosopher (192. 3–7), and that he jumbles together scientific and merely rhetorical or dialectical premises (110. 20–112. 2). Though Galen's relation to medical Rationalism is a complicated one, the rationalist strand in his thinking stands out clearly here. He thinks that a great deal more is within reach of demonstrative methods than Chrysippus is willing to allow. And his view that the effort lavished by Chrysippus and other Stoics on the rigorous formulation of syllogistic theory was wasted, because the resulting system was not put to use establishing truths about matters such as these, reveals much about his own views of demonstration and logic quite generally (114. 1 ff.).

In addition to representing an affinity with empiricism in its own right, the Stoics' hesitant attitude towards aetiology supplied them with another motive for relying on experience-based inferences of the kind conspicuous in their account of divination. And Chrysippus seems to have been perfectly conscious of this, for he was quite willing to adopt some of the traditional terminology of the empirical arts. According to Plutarch, he urges us to remain silent about matters that stand in need of *experience* and *history* if we do not have anything stronger or clearer to say, so as to avoid errors such as Plato's about the absorption of liquid nourishment by the lungs (*De Stoic. repugnan.* 1047 C).[20]

There is one respect in which Stoic empiricism had an advantage over its artistic counterparts, however. The Stoics believed that the world is governed by divine reason, by which it is providentially ordered for the benefit of mankind. Thus they had an answer to the challenge: how does the undoubted existence of past regularities, however well attested, justify the conclusion that they will continue to obtain? Since the universe is ordered and governed by reason, it is not surprising that it exhibits order and regularity. And since human beings have a share of reason, it is only natural that they should grasp part of this order. What is more, since it is part of the aim of divine reason to enable human beings to fulfil their part in the life of the cosmos (*Div.* 1. 82; 2. 130), the Stoics maintained that 'The world was so created at the beginning that certain signs run ahead of certain things' (*Div.* 1. 118, cf. 35). Human beings, then, are entitled to rely on the pre-established patterns of correlation on which sign-inference builds.

[20] The reference is to *Ti.* 70 C–D, 91 A.

But these affinities between the Stoic and empirical perspectives need to be set beside no less significant differences between the two outlooks. These emerge very clearly from Chrysippus' arguments for locating the ruling part of the soul in the chest as opposed to the head. It will be recalled that Galen, from a rationalist perspective, complained that Chrysippus did not go far enough in his use of demonstrative method, in effect that his approach was not sufficiently rational. But from the medical Empiricists' point of view, his willingness to resort to imperfectly conclusive but nevertheless plausible ($\pi\iota\theta\alpha\nu\acute{o}\nu$)[21] or reasonable ($\epsilon\check{v}\lambda o\gamma o\nu$)[22] arguments for his position makes him open to the opposite charge of being too much of a rationalist. According to them, rational arguments never achieve anything more than plausibility ($\pi\iota\theta\alpha\nu\acute{o}\tau\eta s$) or likelihood ($\epsilon\grave{\iota}\kappa\acute{o}s$) (Galen, De sect. ingred. iii. 10. 8–9 SM). And as we have seen, they regarded this plausibility as epistemologically valueless. On their view, it was not that the evidence provided a degree of support, respectable but short of conclusive; rather, they took plausibility to be a purely subjective feature of an argument, a matter of striking someone as convincing, usually someone already made receptive by too much speculative rationalist theorizing. This was clear, the Empiricists claimed, because conflicting theories of all kinds could and had been made plausible by different sects of dogmatists, a fact which attests to the rhetorical power of their advocates more than their medical insight (cf. Celsus, Proem. 27–9).[23]

Thus the most rigorous members of the ancient empirical tradition ruled out of bounds a type of speculative conjectural argument that was acceptable to the Stoics. The Stoics' favourable attitude towards merely reasonable or plausible argument is relevant to this enquiry because it was not only in the area of theoretical speculation that they allowed arguments of this kind. The initial impression created by Div. 1. 12, that artificial divination is based solely on signs grounded in long observation of constant conjunctions, is dispelled later, when it becomes clear that there is a second part of artificial divination, carefully distinguished from the first and based on conjecture.[24] Artificial divination consists in part of conjecture, in part of long observation (Div. 2. 26) 'The genera of divination

---

[21] De plac. Hipp. et Plat. 130. 33; 204. 31; 224. 7 De Lacy.
[22] Ibid. 130. 24; 154. 5; 176. 14; 200. 22; 218. 29; 226. 30.
[23] On the similar views of the Pyrrhonists see D.L. 9. 94.
[24] Div. 1. 34 seems to make the same distinction, though rather less clearly.

which are revealed by conjecture or noted on the basis of outcomes [*eventa*], as I have already said, are called artificial, not natural' (*Div.* 1. 72).

The conjectural division of artificial divination is so called because it relies on conjectural argument, argument which makes use of evidence for a conclusion which falls short of a conclusive case for it.[25] The principal motive for supplementing the method of long observation seems to have been the need to cover unusual cases that do not fall under the experience-based theorems established by that method. Its most important application is to portents and prodigies. They require the diviner to go beyond the relatively mechanical application of generalizations based on long observation and form a conjecture; this involves interpretation, providing an argument for assigning a particular meaning to unusual occurrences like the appearance of sweat on statues or the gnawing of shields by mice (*Div.* 1. 97, 99).

As in other fields, the plausibility, likelihood, or reasonableness attaching to conjectural conclusions can be represented in a favourable light, as providing the best available reasons for the conclusion in question, or unfavourably, as mere plausibility or apparent reasonableness. Exploiting the pejorative implications of 'conjecture', Cicero argues, like the Empiricists, that plausible divinatory conjectures for different and conflicting interpretations of the same event can be constructed on the basis of the same evidence, just as they can in forensic oratory (*Div.* 2. 55). He means to imply that the credibility of an interpretative conjecture in divination has little to do with the force of the evidence and a great deal to do with the cleverness and persuasive skill of the diviner who proposes it, and he proceeds to mock some of Quintus' examples. If the spectacle of mice gnawing on shields is supposed to prefigure defeat in battle, Cicero asks, should he fear a rise in the price of vegetables if he observes mice chewing on his copy of Epicurus' book on pleasure, or for the health of the state if they are seen at work on Plato's *Republic* (*Div.* 2. 59)?[26]

---

[25] Conjectural divination is taken up at *Div.* 1. 72 ff. and criticized at *Div.* 2. 55 ff.

[26] Chrysippus is credited with an argument that there are no such things as portents (*Div.* 2. 61). But it seems that he is objecting not so much to the view that there are unusual occurrences that provide a basis for divinatory conjecture, but to portents conceived of as violations of what is possible in nature, as contrary to or out of step with fate. For there is a Stoicized conception of the portent as an event of a type which occurs very infrequently but is nevertheless the result of fated causal

Let us now briefly consider the last variety of evidence exploited by divination, the kind on which natural divination is based. In contrast to artificial divination, it is supposed to be directly accessible even to those who do not command the technical, artistic resources of the professional diviner. The messages with which natural divination is concerned can come in the form of dreams, the pronouncements of those in a frenzy, or certain kinds of oracles. These differ from the lightning bolts, fissured livers, and stellar configurations studied by long observation, as well as the sweating statues and hungry mice that occupy conjectural divination, by directly representing the events they forecast. Someone carried away by a divine afflatus predicts that an event will occur more or less by saying that it will, a dream either by allowing a god to appear and tell the dreamer that it will or by depicting its occurrence. The ability to understand what one is being told or to recognize what one is being shown corresponds to the simple capacity to grasp the phenomena as such that was contrasted with the technical, instruction-dependent ability to see them as signs in Sextus Empiricus' examination of the indicative sign (cf. *M.* 8. 203).[27]

We now have in hand all the materials necessary to support the claim that the Stoics were not tied to a distinction precisely analogous to that between indicative and commemorative signs. The Stoic account of the sign preserved in Sextus Empiricus is an example of their characteristic tendency to provide technically precise reconstructions of crucial notions (cf. *PH* 2. 104; *M.* 8. 396). I wish to suggest that the notion of sign made precise by their semiotic theory was comprehensive enough to embrace the varieties of evidence captured by the references to signs in the account of divination. And the distinction between indicative and commemorative

---

processes, albeit hidden ones. Such, for instance, is the birth of a colt from a mule (*Div.* 2. 49).

[27] Of course the apparently straightforward distinction between artificial and natural divination appears much less secure under examination. Oracles, e.g. the pronouncements of the Pythia at Delphi, would seem to be just the sort of thing that require skilful interpretation if they are to make any sense at all. And it may be with this problem in mind that Quintus at one point treats the act of interpretation itself as the result of divine inspiration (*Div.* 1. 35). Dreams also often seem to require interpretation (*Div.* 1. 58; 2. 129, 144, 147). Cicero charges that divination by dreams is not a matter of nature at all, but of conjecture (*Div.* 2. 147). He considers and rejects a view of divination by dreams as the observation of correlations between dreams and events of certain types (*Div.* 2. 146). And he knows of arguments that all the methods of natural divination ought to be reclassified as artificial (*Div.* 1. 116).

signs is not exhaustive of the notion of the sign they needed to explicate.[28]

None the less, a common thread runs through these heterogeneous kinds of evidence. The relation between the evidence and that for which it is evidence can be formulated as a conditional only if an account of the conditional weaker than connection is in force. Connective conditionals exploit necessary connections. The connection between antecedent and consequent they express obtains necessarily, independently of other necessary relations or contingent matters of fact. To grasp the truth expressed by such a conditional is to understand that the antecedent excludes the falsity of the consequent by itself. None of the three kinds of evidence made use of by divination is like this. Viewed as the antecedent of a conditional, a divinatory sign does not by itself exclude the falsity of the consequent, which is excluded, if it is, by conditions which are not captured in the antecedent.

This in turn has a further epistemologically significant consequence. While a connective conditional is in principle self-certifying—accessible to reason apart from experience—the recognition of the evidential relation between the antecedent and consequent of a merely Philonian conditional depends on a second relation between the conditional and the background evidence that supports it. Co-observational sign-conditionals are based on the constant conjunctions recorded by the method of long observation, and this method does not acquaint us with the real underlying causes that require the outcome described in the consequent. None the less, even though we are not in a position to state what necessitates and explains the regularities we have observed, they are facts about the world on which inferential projections can be based. Dreams and prophetic utterances also do not necessitate and explain the outcome to which they point, but they can be relied upon when and because they come from a divine source. The element of conjecture in conjectural divination is in the transition from a range of considerations to an interpretation of the sign's meaning; that

---

[28] The *De divinatione* tends to restrict the expression 'sign' or 'mark' (*signum* or *nota*) to matters that are the concern of artificial divination by long observation (*Div.* 1. 25, 34, 127, 130; 2. 26). But events whose divinatory significance must be discovered by conjecture are also sometimes referred to as signs (1. 74, 75; 2. 53). It is difficult to find episodes of natural divination called signs, however (perhaps 1. 127).

interpretation then takes the form of a Philonian conditional linking the sign with the event it forecasts.

5. Sign-inference and Demonstration

We must now attempt to discover what the relation between the Stoics' theory of sign-inference and their conception of demonstrative inference is. Demonstrative theory is not the same thing as syllogistic theory. Aristotelian syllogistic and its Stoic counterpart are both concerned with the characterization of formally valid arguments, and the demonstrative theory of both schools imposes further conditions on syllogistically valid arguments.[29] In the context of Stoic philosophy the features that distinguish demonstrative arguments from merely valid arguments are very different from those required by Aristotle, however. According to the Stoics, a valid argument must satisfy two further conditions to qualify as a demonstration: (1) it must be true, i.e. have true premises and consequently a true conclusion; and (2) its conclusion must be somehow revealed by its premises. Requirement (2) is interpreted in several conflicting ways in the different accounts of demonstration preserved by Sextus, however. This variety reflects a dispute about the nature of the evidential support at issue in demonstration. I shall argue that this dispute helps to explain what the motive might have been for the autonomous theory of signs we have been examining.

Let us begin with the simplest and most straightforward, though not the first mentioned, account of demonstration preserved by Sextus, and the only one explicitly ascribed to the Stoics (Account I) (*M.* 8. 411–24).[30] According to Account I, a demonstration is a true, valid argument which has a non-evident conclusion revealed by the premisses—where true arguments are those valid arguments which have true premises and, therefore, a true conclusion. The notion of revelation to which it appeals is a very simple one: the conclusion cannot be as evident as the premises, for if it were, it would not be revealed by them but by itself. A conclusion is revealed

---

[29] There are certain complexities in Stoic logic having to do with non-syllogistically valid arguments that can be ignored here.

[30] With the following treatment of the subject compare J. Brunschwig, 'Proof Defined', in Barnes *et al.* (eds.), *Doubt and Dogmatism*, 125–60; J. Barnes, 'Proof Destroyed', ibid. 161–81.

by a set of premises if it follows from them and is non-evident.[31] And this seems to be the view behind Stoic characterizations of demonstration outside Sextus Empiricus.[32] Within his treatment of the subject, it seems to be equivalent to the final requirement in one of the briefer characterizations of demonstration as a true and valid argument that establishes a non-evident conclusion (is παραστατικὸς ἀδήλου) (*M*. 8. 314).

According to a second account (Account II) expounded by Sextus in the immediately preceding passage, however, an argument meeting all of these requirements is not yet a demonstration (*M*. 8. 302 ff.). As in Account I, the requirement that the argument lead to a non-evident conclusion follows the requirements that it be valid and true.[33] But according to Account II there are two ways of leading validly to a non-evident conclusion, only one of which qualifies an argument as a demonstration (*M*. 8. 310). The premisses can lead to a non-evident conclusion merely progressively (ἐφοδευτικῶς) or in a manner at once progressive and revelatory (ἐφοδευτικῶς καὶ ἐκκαλυπτικῶς). Here, in Account II, it is only arguments satisfying all these requirements including the last that are styled demonstrations. Before trying to explain the issue behind this more restrictive conception of revelation, I want to call attention to certain structural peculiarities of this account that are also found in yet another account (Account III) (*PH* 2. 135 ff.). The introduction of the distinction between two ways of reaching

---

[31] 'For having a non-evident conclusion ... [the demonstrative argument] reveals this through the premisses' (*M*. 8. 423).

[32] Demonstration is 'a transition from the more to the less well apprehended' (D.L. 7. 45); 'ratio quae ex rebus perceptis ad id quod non percipiebatur adducit' (Cicero, *Luc*. 26; cf. *Div*. 2. 103); 'Everyone would agree that demonstration is an argument transmitting trust [πίστις] from what is agreed to matters that are contested' (Clement, *Stromata*, 8. 3. 5, cf. 8. 3. 7).

[33] J. Brunschwig has drawn attention to important differences between the first exposition of demonstration in this passage (*M*. 8. 302–9) and the recapitulation at *M*. 8. 310, notably the requirement that a demonstration be true. In the recapitulation it is clearly treated as a distinct requirement; in the first exposition, though perhaps alluded to, it is not clearly separated, and arguments with a non-evident conclusion are treated as a subdivision of valid rather than true arguments (*M*. 8. 305). I am not completely convinced by Brunschwig's arguments that this difference cannot be accounted for without supposing that two distinct accounts of demonstration have been conflated here ('Proof Defined', 144–5). At the same time, I am not sure that he is not right, in which case a still more complicated account than that offered here would be necessary. Anyone who studies Sextus' discussion of demonstration will agree with Brunschwig that this is a text 'the genesis of which was evidently complicated in the extreme' ('Proof Defined', 149).

a non-evident conclusion breaks with the previous pattern of definition by division. Prior to this stage, the exposition proceeded by
partitioning the proximate genus of arguments into those that meet
the next restriction and those that do not. The class of arguments
satisfying the restriction then becomes the proximate genus for the
next division. Arguments are merely progressive which satisfy the
requirement to lead to a non-evident conclusion, but not the next
and final requirement, doing so in a fully revelatory manner. The
qualification 'progressive' just restates the fact that they take us
from the premises to a previously unknown conclusion. But this
is the first time the arguments left behind by the next refinement
in the definition receive a new designation.

   Another surprising feature of the final stage of Account II is the
use of the inference from sweat to the existence of invisible pores
twice, first to illustrate arriving at a non-evident conclusion, then
to do so in a manner at once progressive and revelatory. This has
the odd consequence that when an example of an argument satisfying only the requirement to arrive at a non-evident conclusion is
given (*M.* 8. 308), it represents a step back from the level of fully
demonstrative argument reached with the example of intelligible
pores. This is a departure from the procedure followed thus far of
illustrating each stage in the definition with an example that does
not satisfy the next stage. When these arguments were cited twice,
the first time was to illustrate the requirement just introduced, the
second to help illustrate the requirement defining the next stage by
failing to satisfy it.

   I should like to suggest that these structural peculiarities are best
regarded as the result of a later attempt to revise an account of
demonstration essentially equivalent to Account I. This suggestion receives some support from Account III, which adds to the
peculiarities it shares with Account II a few of its own. In apparent agreement with Account I, it calls arguments leading to
non-evident conclusions demonstrative ($\dot{\alpha}\pi o\delta\epsilon\iota\kappa\tau\iota\kappa o\iota$). But it then
immediately goes on to draw the distinction between merely pro-
gressive and progressive and revelatory argument, apparently after
the item the exposition is intended to define, demonstration, has
been reached. What is more, at each previous stage Sextus' practice
had been to define the new characteristic and then employ its name
in the characterization of the next characteristic. So, for instance,
starting with the genus argument, we learn that some arguments

are concludent, some non-concludent (*PH* 2. 140). An argument is concludent when the conditional formed by taking the conjunction of the premises as the antecedent and the conclusion as the consequent is sound: 'Some concludent arguments are true, some are not. Arguments are true whenever [in addition to meeting the concludency requirement] the consequent and the antecedent of the corresponding conditional are both true.' The demonstrative stage is introduced in the same way: 'Some true arguments are demonstrative, some not. True arguments are demonstrative when they lead to a non-evident conclusion by means of pre-evident premisses' (*PH* 2. 140). But when the time comes to distinguish merely progressive from progressive and revelatory arguments, the exposition breaks with precedent and does not distinguish two types of demonstrative argument, but reverts to a descriptive phrase to characterize the proximate genus of the division: 'Some arguments leading to a non-evident conclusion lead us in a manner that is merely progressive and some in a way that is at once progressive and revelatory' (*PH* 2. 141). Apart from minor verbal variations, it is identical to the corresponding section of Account II, in which the appellation 'demonstrative' is not applied in the course of the exposition but is withheld until the summary, where it is reserved for arguments that satisfy all the requirements set out in the exposition, including the last and most restrictive (*M*. 8. 307–8).

A further problem with Account III is the confusion in the summary with which it concludes.[34] There is a καί ('and') in the summary of Account III omitted in one manuscript but found in the others: 'A demonstration ought to be (1) an argument, (2) true, (3) have a non-evident conclusion [and (4)?] be revealed [*sic*] by the power of the premisses' (*PH* 2. 143). The variation in the manuscripts seems to point to an uncertainty on the part of the copyists about the relation between the summary and the exposition of Account III. The καί makes it absolutely clear, albeit clumsily, that there is a fourth requirement on demonstrative argument distinct from (3). This brings Account III into line with Account II, but at the cost of a conflict with the preceding exposition, in which (3) is treated as a sufficient qualification for demonstration and (4), apparently, as the defining characteristic of a type of demonstration.[35] Without the καί, the account is ambiguous. It is possible to view

---

[34] Attention is drawn to this problem by J. Brunschwig, 'Proof Defined', 154–5.
[35] On this point I agree with Brunschwig, ('Proof Defined', 152), and disagree

revelation of the conclusion as a requirement over and above having a non-evident conclusion or as just another way of stating the non-evidence requirement. The first reading is open to the objections stated, for it brings the summary into conflict with the exposition by allowing only arguments that satisfy the last and most stringent requirement to count as demonstrations. The second brings the summary into line with exposition, but at the cost of giving 'revelation' a different meaning in each.

One solution would be to bracket the whole phrase '[καὶ] ἐκκαλυπτόμενον ὑπὸ τῆς δυνάμεως τῶν λημμάτων as an interpolation.[36] If Account III were a unified whole, this would be the best way out of the difficulties presented by its summary. But another solution is possible if, as I have already suggested, and shall now argue, II and III are not the independent, unified accounts of demonstration they pretend to be, but rather revised versions of accounts very much like I. If this is right, point (4) need not be an interpolation due to a later hand; it could well be part of a correct summary of what Sextus, or his source, intended to express in the immediately preceding exposition of Account III. The source of the difficulty would then be the conflict between the older account, which makes up the first part of the exposition to (3), where it reaches demonstrative arguments, and the newer, more restrictive, account, which has been grafted onto it without sufficient care. By contrast, Account II has been reworked so that it avoids identifying arguments satisfying only its penultimate requirement as demonstrative.

Were the last distinction made in Account III an organic part of the concept of demonstration being expounded, the expression 'demonstrative' would either have been withheld until the end of the exposition and applied only then to arguments at once progressive and revelatory, as in Account II, or, if it had been properly applied earlier, reapplied when the time came to distinguish *types* of demonstrative argument, not replaced with a descriptive periphrasis. To be sure, it is not necessary to draw the same conclusions about both Account II and Account III. It could be maintained that Account III is the result of grafting the last distinction onto an account of demonstration like that of Account I while maintaining

with Barnes, who holds that the demonstrative arguments reached at stage (3) of the exposition are not yet demonstrations ('Proof Destroyed', 178 n. 2).

[36] Proposed by Brunschwig, 'Proof Defined', 155 with n. 51.

that Account II is an independent and organic account of demonstration. It could even be that Account III was clumsily altered
to make it agree with Account II. I have preferred to treat them
together because the manner in which the distinction between progressive and revelatory modes of argument is introduced represents
such a sharp break with the pattern of division in both accounts.

The two accounts could have been revised in something like the
following way. We start with an account or accounts of demonstration like I and like II and III except that it or they terminate with
the requirement for a non-evident conclusion (3)—for the sake of
simplicity let us suppose that there was one account with one author.
The example used to illustrate the last requirement is the famous
proof of the existence of intelligible pores. The example is highly
satisfactory to certain revisionists, who agree that all the conditions
specified in the account are necessary, but they notice that if those
conditions are also regarded as sufficient, as was in fact intended by
the author of the definition, arguments which, unlike this example,
they do not recognize as demonstrations will be so classified. They
then decide to revise the existing account by supplementing it with
a further requirement imposed on demonstrative argument. In the
course of revising the standard account, they change as little as
possible. The proof of the existence of intelligible pores is retained
as an example in its old place, even though it now illustrates more
than is necessary. If the account being revised equates revelation
with leading to a non-evident conclusion, as Account I does, the
revisionists may have viewed themselves as clarifying the old unrevised account by drawing out the latent meaning of 'revelation'. But
in supplementing the existing accounts, they do not proceed as the
original author had. Instead of partitioning the class of arguments
produced by the previous division into those that satisfy the next
requirement and those that do not, they adopt an adverbial mode of
expression (ἐφοδευτικῶς, ἐκκαλυπτικῶς) and distinguish two *ways* of
meeting the requirement to lead to a non-evident conclusion. The
prominence this gives to the penultimate requirement is a trace of
the final and definitive status that it enjoyed in the older unrevised
account.

Having used the example of intelligible pores to illustrate the non-
evidence requirement, the authors of the revised account need an
example that satisfies this requirement in the minimally progressive
manner the older account failed to distinguish with a stage of its

own. To understand the motives for the revision we need to discover
how this example fails to do what a genuinely revelatory argument
is supposed to do:

[Arguments leading to a non-evident conclusion] only progressively are,
for example, those that seem to depend on faith and memory [οἱ ἐκ πίστεως
καὶ μνήμης ἠρτῆσθαι δοκοῦντες]. For example, an argument of this sort:

   If some god has said to you that this man will be wealthy, then this man
      will be wealthy.
   But this god (I indicate Zeus for example) has said that this man will be
      wealthy.
   Therefore this man will be wealthy.

We assent to the conclusion not so much on account of the necessity of the
premisses as trusting [πιστεύοντες] in the declaration of the god.

   Arguments leading to a conclusion in a manner both progressive and
revelatory are such as the following. [*The example of the proof of intelligible
pores is set out again.*] (*PH* 2. 141–2; cf. *M*. 8. 308–9)

What is the basis for this new distinction? In Account I the
requirement that the conclusion be revealed by the premisses was
simply a requirement that the apprehension of the conclusion come
about through the prior acceptance of the premisses; it was intended
to exclude cases in which the conclusion, though implied by the
premisses, could be grasped by itself independently of argument.
In the revised accounts this does not amount to revelation. Instead
of the requirement imposed by Account I that the conclusion be
revealed by the premisses (ἐκκαλύπτεσθαι ὑπὸ τῶν λημμάτων) (*M*. 8.
422), there is a new requirement that the conclusion be revealed
by the power or nature (δύναμις or φύσις) of the premisses (*M*. 8.
309, 310; *PH* 2. 143). This is presumably another way of making
the point that, in the example of the merely progressive argument,
it is not the necessity of the premisses but, for example, faith in
the declaration of a god that is responsible for establishing the
conclusion.

On the face of it, this seems wrong. The examples of merely progressive and fully revelatory argument share the same logical form;
the premisses of one necessitate its conclusion only if the premisses
of the other necessitate its conclusion. Yet the new, stricter revelation requirement seems merely to restate the requirement that
the argument be concludent. Something more must be at issue,
however, since merely progressive arguments have already been

certified as concludent.[37] The view behind the new requirement
has not been well expressed. It is not so much the relation between
premisses and conclusion, formally the same in both types of argument, as the character of the premisses which is at issue. What we
have learnt of Stoic divination should help us to see in what way
merely progressive arguments are supposed to be deficient. The
example—the declaration of Zeus that this man will be wealthy—is
recognizable as an example of natural divination, which is fairly
represented here as dependent on faith in the pronouncements of
the gods. It stands in sharp contrast to the rational insight into the
real nature of things that enables us to make out necessary relations
between different states of affairs in nature of the kind illustrated
by the inference to the existence of intelligible pores. As we have
seen, the signs employed in natural divination and the events they
predict stand in a relation strong enough to support only Philonian
conditionals.

The revised accounts of demonstration, then, appear to impose
the additional requirement that the hypothetical premisses of a
demonstration be grounded in the nature of the matters at issue,
in relations that will, when conditional formulation is called for,
be formulable as connective conditionals. This is clear from the
way the example of a fully revelatory argument is handled: it is
represented as turning on a necessary connection grounded in our
preconceptions (*PH* 2. 142; cf. *M.* 8. 309).[38] The revisionists, then,
hold that the hypothetical premisses of a demonstration, properly so
called, must be grounded in natural and necessary relations stronger
than the co-ordination sufficient for Philonian conditionals.

Why this requirement was imposed in terms of revelation remains
unclear, however. One motive has already been suggested: the wish
to represent this revision as a way of understanding the traditional
requirement that the premisses of a demonstration reveal its conclusion. To be revelatory in this new and stricter sense, however,
an argument must do more than add to our stock of knowledge by
effecting a syllogistically valid transition from true premisses to a
true non-evident conclusion. It must also make clear how the truth
asserted in the conclusion is required by the nature of the matters at
issue in the premisses. To grasp it will then be to understand why,
if the world is as the non-hypothetical premisses of the demonstra-

[37] Cf. ibid. 136–7.
[38] Cf. ibid. 153 n. 48, crediting G. Striker with this insight.

tion state it is—a fact typically established by observation—it can only be because it is also as the conclusion of the demonstration states it is. Thus the conclusion deduced in this way can explain, or be an essential part of the explanation, why the state of affairs that furnished the demonstration with its point of departure obtains. Inferences dependent at any stage on merely truth-functional hypothetical premisses cannot do this because a grasp of these premisses, though it may entitle us to draw a conclusion, fails to capture why states of the world that do not include the truth asserted in the conclusion are necessarily excluded by the truth of the non-hypothetical premisses and therefore fails to explain why the state of affairs described by the non-hypothetical premiss could not have obtained just as well without the conclusion being true.

Talk of explanation and understanding cannot help reminding us of Aristotle's view of demonstration. The philosophers who used the strict conception of revelation in their attempts to define demonstration seem to have been engaged in the same delicate business of trying to specify the conditions over and above validity and the truth of the premisses that an argument must satisfy if it is to serve the explanatory task they assign to demonstration. As in Aristotelian demonstration, logically valid argument is to capture relations that go beyond formal logical validity, for the understanding produced by the grasp of a demonstration is not simply the understanding of why the conclusion follows from the premisses given the rules of formal logic. The demonstration, for example, that there are intelligible pores not only justifies the conclusion that this is so, but also shows why the world can only be as observation shows it is *because* there are intelligible pores, which explain, or are an essential component of the explanation, why sweat appears on the skin. Of course, it is not explanation in quite the Aristotelian sense. Very roughly speaking, demonstration of this kind proceeds to rather than from the causes. It reveals rather than embodying or exhibiting an explanation in the Aristotelian manner. But this seems to have been what the revisionists were driving at with their insistence on a stricter sense of revelation.

Analogues of some of Aristotle's other requirements for the premisses of a demonstration find a place in this conception of demonstration as well.[39] A demonstration cannot be from premisses that need to be demonstrated, except that in the present case, this

---

[39] Cf. Barnes, 'Proof Destroyed', esp. 176 ff.

does not require that they be self-explanatory in the manner of Aristotelian first principles, but only that their truth not stand in need of justification itself. There must then be premisses that can be grasped without demonstration. Perception is one source of such knowledge, and it can secure certain non-hypothetical premisses directly. Non-truth-functional hypothetical premisses such as the connective conditional are, as we have seen, in principle self-certifying. To grasp a connective conditional as such is to understand thereby both why and that the consequent is required by the antecedent alone. Reference to a direct intellectual grasp of such conceptually imposed necessities, parallel to the direct grasp of perceptual truths by perception, is attested in Sextus Empiricus.⁴⁰ But it is especially prominent in Galen, according to whom human beings are equipped with two natural criteria, perception and intellect (*De plac. Hipp. et Plat.* 542 De Lacy; cf. *De opt. doctr.* ii. 89–90 *SM*).⁴¹ He calls directly evident matters 'axioms'. Axioms directly evident to the senses are truths like 'the sun is bright' (*De simp. med. temp. ac fac.* xi. 461 K). But in general he seems to think that the term is more appropriately applied to matters directly evident to the mind (*Institutio logica*, 4. 16 Kalbfleisch; cf. 39. 18 ff.; 40. 3 ff.; *De meth. med.* x. 36. 14 ff. K). The natural criterion of the intellect depends on the grasp of consequence and conflict that plays such a large part in the rationalist conception of inference.⁴² And this grasp affords a direct insight into truths of the kind captured by connective conditionals.

But merely Philonian conditionals are not like this; each of them must be accepted on the strength of considerations that it does not capture. And these considerations cannot be evidence that could support a demonstrative argument; if they were, it would be possible to frame a demonstrative argument without Philonian conditionals. According to proponents of the revised conception

⁴⁰ τὰ αὐτόθεν κατ' αἴσθησιν ἢ διάνοιαν προσπίπτοντα (*M.* 7. 25; cf. 8. 141, 362).

⁴¹ For further discussion and more references, cf. I. von Müller, 'Über Galens Werk vom wissenschaftlichen Beweis', *Abhandlungen der k. Bayer. Akademie der Wissenschaften*, 20/2 (1895), 405–78 at 430 ff. On Galen's own views see now J. Barnes, 'Galen on Logic and Therapy', in F. Kudlien and R. J. Durling (eds.), *Galen's Method of Healing* (Leiden: Brill, 1991), 50–102; J. Hankinson, 'Galen on the Foundations of Science', in J. A. López Férez (ed.), *Galeno: Obra, pensamiento e influencia* (Madrid: Universidad Nacional de Educación a Distancia, 1991), 15–29; G. E. R. Lloyd, 'The Theories and Practices of Demonstration in Galen', in M. Frede and G. Striker (eds.), *Rationality in Greek Thought* (Oxford: Oxford University Press, 1996), 255–77.   ⁴² Cf. Frede, *Die stoische Logik*, 80.

of demonstration, arguments including such conditionals always
rely upon undemonstrated assumptions that are neither demon-
strable nor directly grasped without the need for argument. This
also means they cannot be explanatory in the manner required. And
it may be an outlook of this kind that is behind the view that the
conclusion of a merely progressive argument does not follow from
the nature or power of the premises.

The revised conception of demonstration brings the outlook behind indicative signification to mind. And the example of intelligible pores is a syllogistic reconstruction of what Sextus elsewhere
treats as an indicative sign-inference (cf. *M.* 8. 146). The example of
a merely progressive argument with which it is contrasted cannot,
however, be connected with commemorative signification in the
same way. Nevertheless, though drawn from the field of natural divination, the example may have been intended to illustrate a broader
type of argument embracing those dependent on co-observation as
well. Arguments of this type are briefly characterized—'such, for
example, as those dependent on faith and memory'. This seems
to be a catch-all for those bases of hypothetical inference too weak
to permit the formulation of connective conditionals (or other hypothetical premises grounded in consequence or conflict). I have
taken the cogency of the example to depend solely on faith in divine
veracity, rather than a combination of faith and memory.[43] And it
is possible that the reference to memory is meant to pick out inferences grounded in co-observation. Memory is, of course, referred
to in the name of commemorative signification, and in other characterizations of empirical reasoning (cf. e.g. S.E. *M.* 8. 274).[44] And
reference to the dependence of co-observational inference on memory is also well attested in Cicero's discussion of divination (*Div.*
1. 12, 127; 2. 146). If this is right, there is a considerable overlap between merely progressive arguments and the sign-inferences
discussed in connection with divination and the other arts. And it
is clear that an account of signs embracing types of evidence too
weak to permit the formulation of fully revelatory arguments would
help classify evidence rendered non-demonstrative by the stringent
standards imposed in the revised accounts of demonstration. It is

---

[43] Cf., however, Brunschwig, 'Proof Defined', 142–3, who takes both grounds to
be involved in the argument.

[44] Cf. Galen, *De sect. ingred.* iii. 2. 5–9; 3. 12; 7. 6 *SM*; *Subfig. emp.* 50. 29–51. 11
Deichgräber.

also plain that the Stoic sign defined with reference to the Philonian conditional is such an account. It may be, then, that this conception of the sign and the notion of merely progressive argument are different and perhaps even complementary ways of handling the same problem.

To evaluate this suggestion about the relation between Stoic conceptions of sign-inference and demonstration we need to look more closely at certain developments that might explain the evolution and revision of the Stoic conception of demonstration. This in turn will enable us to make a conjecture about the history of the sign in relation to other developments in the Stoic framework. If we take Chrysippus' views as our starting-point, there are two developments that need to be explained. Chrysippus distinguished carefully between merely truth-functional hypothetical syllogisms and those grounded in consequence and conflict. And he insisted that the underlying relation between the atomic propositions out of which the hypothetical premiss is composed be reflected in its surface form. Undoubtedly, some legislation of usage was involved; relations which might in ordinary language be expressed as conditionals were to be formulated as negated conjunctions if they did not satisfy the connective criterion (cf. Cicero, *Fat.* 15). But relations that could not have been formulated as conditionals if the connective criterion had been in force are formulated as conditionals in the merely progressive arguments of Accounts II and III. And the reliance on a weaker than connective account of the conditional implicit in the discussion of merely progressive argument is made explicit in the Stoic definition of the sign. The first development in need of explanation, then, is the move away from the negated conjunction as the standard mode of formulating weaker, merely truth-functional, hypothetical connections and the revival of non-connective conditionals.

The second development is in views about the range of inferences to be classified as demonstrative. Although Chrysippus distinguished very carefully between stronger and weaker hypothetical propositions, he did not exclude the latter from demonstrative argument. According to Galen's report, he considered the third indemonstrable to be particularly useful in the kind of demonstrations made use of in everyday reasoning, including those employed in the law courts (*Institutio logica*, 33. 3–5 Kalbfleisch). This generous conception of demonstration is compatible with Account I.[45]

The dearth of evidence bearing on these issues from the late Hellenistic and imperial periods makes it hard to trace these developments with precision or to arrive at conclusions that are more than conjectural. None the less, there are indications of a change in the intellectual climate behind the developments in need of explanation. As is well known, there was a tendency in the Stoa, as well as in the broader philosophical world now profoundly influenced by it, towards a greater sympathy with the ancients, Plato and Aristotle. In the Stoa, Posidonius is the most famous example. In his case this revival of sympathy was accompanied by the increased openness to aetiology to which Strabo objected. This more generous estimation of the power of human reason to penetrate the nature of things makes a more stringent view of what is to qualify as a demonstration natural. According to such a view, only arguments which somehow express this insight deserve to be called demonstrations. Galen reflects this tendency when he rejects Chrysippus' third indemonstrable as useless for demonstration (*Institutio logica*, 32. 17–21; 34. 18–19 Kalbfleisch). His principal ground—the uselessness of the merely truth-functional relation Chrysippus permits it to express—is not compatible with a move to a non-connective account of the conditional, however. It would then have called for the repudiation of the first two indemonstrables as well. But he also argues for a different interpretation of the negated conjunction on grounds which are neutral as far as a final decision about the admissibility of merely truth-functional hypothetical premises into demonstrative arguments is concerned. He suggests that a syllogism verbally identical to Chrysippus' third indemonstrable will be acceptable if its negated conjunction expresses a relation of partial

---

[45] For somewhat different reasons, Brunschwig also believes that this account belongs to Chrysippus ('Proof Defined', 158–60). But while Brunschwig views it as the culmination of the efforts to define demonstration to which the other definitions preserved by Sextus attest, I prefer to see the other definitions as later efforts for which this definition furnished a point of departure. Ebert, who divides the testimony somewhat differently, would push the origin of the discussion back still further. He credits a conception of proof roughly corresponding to my Account I, which does not distinguish between two ways of revealing a non-evident conclusion, to the Dialectical school. The distinction between two forms of revelation characteristic of my Accounts II and III is, on his view, a mistake of Zeno's maintained by Cleanthes. Matters were first set right again, he believes, by Chrysippus, to whom he attributes the definition of demonstration at D.L. 7. 45. See *Dialektiker*, 219 ff. with the summary at 299–302.

conflict or contrariety between its conjuncts (*Institutio logica*, 33. 14–18 Kalbfleisch), and he believes that this relation is what is customarily expressed by the negated conjunction in the Greek language (*Institutio logica*, 10. 9–13 Kalbfleisch).

The argument from ordinary usage could, then, have pre-empted the negated conjunction for a purpose different from the one assigned to it by Chrysippus. And there is some evidence that the negated conjunction had already been called on to express a non-truth-functional relation. Cicero transmits a list of seven indemonstrables, the canonical five and a further two with negated conjunctions as premises (*Top*. 55–7).[46] The sixth is identical with the third indemonstrable. The seventh appears to be invalid: 'It is not the case that *P* and *Q*; not *P*; therefore *Q*.' But a possible way of understanding the augmented list that avoids the need to postulate a mistake or a textual confusion has been suggested.[47] On this view, the two new indemonstrables are grounded in a paradisjunctive proposition.[48] A paradisjunctive proposition is true if and only if (1) the disjuncts cannot all be true, i.e. in Galen's terms stand in a relation of partial conflict, and (2) one of them is true. Understood in this way, even the seventh indemonstrable of the augmented list will be valid, and the sixth is no longer redundant. Though it shares its surface form with the third indemonstrable, the two differ in underlying logical form.

We can add to these reasons for abandoning the orthodox Chrysippean interpretation of the negated conjunction a consideration that may have counted against his view of the conditional. After relating Chrysippus' suggestion that the Chaldeans reformulate their theorems as negated conjunctions, Cicero objects on the ground that this would call for a massive revision of ordinary usage, e.g. in medicine and geometry (*Fat*. 15). What we have been able to gather of Chrysippus' views of medicine seems to support Cicero, though geometry is another matter. Thus there may have been a view that

---

[46] The augmented list is also found in Martianus Capella 4. 415–20, on which cf. Galen, *Einführung in die Logik: Kritisch-exegetischer Kommentar mit deutscher Übersetzung*, trans. J. Mau (Berlin: Akademie-Verlag, 1960), 42–3.

[47] By Frede, *Die stoische Logik*, 161–6. This is, of course, only one way of putting the pieces of the puzzle together. For another, and on the whole subject of the indemonstrables after Chrysippus, see now K. Ierodiakonou, 'The Stoic Indemonstrables in the Later Tradition', in K. Döring and T. Ebert (eds.), *Dialektiker und Stoiker: Zur Logik der Stoa und ihrer Vorläufer* (Stuttgart: Steiner, 1993), 187–200.

[48] On paradisjunctives cf. Frede, *Die stoische Logik*, 98–100.

Chrysippus' understanding of the conditional was in too much conflict with ordinary language. As we have seen, Galen shows that this
kind of complaint was made. We are now in a position to sketch
in a little more detail a conjecture about the development of the
more stringent, revised understanding of demonstration embodied
in Accounts II and III:

(1) The negated conjunction is used to express a stricter than
truth-functional form of implication as suggested.

(2) A view linking demonstration more closely to rational insight
into the nature of things arises in opposition to Chrysippus' more
generous conception; Galen is a late representative of this tendency.

(3) The particular view we are concerned with, however, develops
in a context where interest persists in a wide range of inferences
in which the evidence does not make possible genuinely demonstrative reasoning as judged by the new stricter standards. That
is, an interest in many or all of the arguments Chrysippus called
demonstrations continues, but the correspondingly generous attitude towards the use of the term 'demonstration' has disappeared.

(4) But with the negated conjunction taken for another purpose,
it becomes necessary to fall back on a Philonian conception of
the conditional if the weaker hypothetical relations on which non-
demonstrative arguments depend are to be formulated as the premisses of arguments. Of course, a conditional true according to the
Philonian account may also satisfy stricter standards that entitle it
to figure as the premiss of a demonstration.

The distinction between merely progressive and fully revelatory
arguments, then, is a crude attempt to respond to the need which
now arises for a way to separate arguments based on conditionals
embodying a rational insight into the nature of things from those
based on the merely truth-functional conditionals that are the basis
of merely progressive argument.

6. The Purpose of the Stoic Theory

I have already suggested that the Stoic account of signs preserved
by Sextus Empiricus served the same end, and we have seen how
the appeal to the Philonian criterion makes that account suitable
for that purpose. I want now to show that, in view of their need
to distinguish a class of inferences grounded in non-connective,

merely truth-functional, hypothetical propositions, the most natural way for the Stoics to handle this requirement was with a theory of signs. The principal ground for this conclusion is the tradition of using the term 'sign' to contrast forms of evidence, and the corresponding inferences, which are in one way or another inferior, with their superior counterparts. In Study I above we saw how Aristotle contrasted sign-inference with demonstration, and then, within the class of signs marked off in this way, distinguished between signs and tokens, again assigning the inferior part to signs. And we also touched briefly on the rhetorical tradition after Aristotle, which made a number of similar distinctions with the same pair of terms.

But contrasts of this kind were not confined to rhetoric. Galen was familiar with several:

> It is necessary to discover the twofold nature of the matters from which physicians prognosticate and orators demonstrate and persuade. One division of matters taken as the premisses of demonstrations, whether epistemic or persuasive, is necessary and involves inferences where one of the terms from which the premiss is composed follows the other always. In the other division it does not follow always or necessarily but for the most part only. According to another principle of division, one division is dependent on empirical observation [τήρησις ἐμπειρική], while the other depends on rational consequence [λογικὴ ἀκολουθία], i.e. indication. These are the underlying substantive differences, but all have not made use of the names for them in the same way. Those who proceed more suitably (I pass over the others) think it fit to use the term 'token' [τεκμήριον] of the evidence that always signifies correctly and 'sign' [σημεῖον] of the other kind according to the first principle of division. In the case of the second principle of division, the sign is from observation, the token from indication. (*In Hipp. prog.* v/9/2. 373. 1–14 CMG)[49]

The two principles of division are quite different. The first is recognizable as a version of the updated Aristotelian conception we have already encountered in the rhetorical tradition. The second, also approved by Galen, aligns the distinction between the sign and the token with the distinction between commemorative and indicative signs, so that it is no longer the relative frequency with which the sign (or token) is followed by the signified, but the nature of the relation between them that is the basis of the distinction between sign and token.[50] They agree in using 'token' to designate the su-

---

[49] Cf. *In Hipp. de acut. morb. vict.* v/9/1. 118. 1 CMG.

[50] In this way agreeing with the pseudo-Galenic *De optima secta*, which confines

perior, and 'sign' the inferior, types of evidence they distinguish.
They are both, then, representatives of the low conception of signs.

It is clear, then, what a Stoic distinction between signs and tokens would have been like. It would have turned on the distinction
between the merely truth-functional relation between the sign and
signified and the genuinely connective relation between the token
and that of which it is a token. It would have had a strong affinity with Galen's second distinction, but differed from it by not
confining the sign to relations grasped on the basis of empirical
observation, which is only one, albeit the most prominent, of several modes of epistemic access to such relations. But did the Stoics
recognize a distinction between signs and tokens in this way? In
Galen's report of Chrysippus' view on the location of the ruling
part of the soul, it will be recalled, Chrysippus claimed that the
matter escapes us because there are no tokens from which to syllogize a conclusion. It is possible that the term 'token' is being used
without a technical distinction in mind. But it is also possible that
it is being used in the technical sense that the Stoics would most
likely have given it. The question that concerned Chrysippus is
not susceptible to resolution by direct inspection, nor is it the kind
of issue on which the observation of empirical regularities is able
to throw light. The point Chrysippus could be making by using
the expression 'token' is that we in particular lack the only kind
of evidence that promises to be of help in this situation, namely
evidence that warrants the formulation of a genuinely connective
conditional with the right kind of non-evident consequent. As we
have seen, Chrysippus places a great deal of weight on the distinction between connective and non-connective conditionals, but is
very generous in the application of the expression 'demonstration'.
A distinction between signs and tokens would have given him a
way of distinguishing evidence of different kinds without mention
of the hypothetical propositions in virtue of which the evidence is
evidence.

The need for such a distinction would have been more urgent
after the adoption, if it occurred, of a Philonian account of the conditional described above. For the difference in the relations between
the component propositions of the two types of hypothetical proposition would no longer have been marked by their external form in

the term 'sign' to commemorative signs (i. 108. 8; 109. 13; 126. 12; 127. 11; 149.
8 K).

the way characteristic of Stoic logic. Yet, as the evidence furnished by Sextus' different accounts of demonstration shows, the distinction between strong and weak hypothetical propositions continued to be regarded as of the utmost importance. A distinction between signs and tokens along the lines sketched above again recommends itself. A token would be a piece of evidence which, taken together with the appropriate conditional, gives rise to a genuine demonstration according to the revised conception of demonstration, while a sign does not.

Because the Stoic account of the sign transmitted by Sextus cites the Philonian conditional, we know it is non-Chrysippean, and I have tried to suggest that it makes the most sense when viewed in connection with developments after Chrysippus.[51] We know that it formulates the most generic conditions for being evidence at all. And we have seen how the notion of the species so called homonymously with the genus was used by the Stoics. Within the genus sign there are potentially several species characterized by more restrictive differentia. A set of premises the conjunction of which satisfies the conditionalization requirement can qualify as a set of demonstrative premises (or the premises of a progressive argument). An atomic proposition which is the antecedent of a conditional satisfying connective strictures can qualify as a token—if tokens are recognized. And when taken together with this conditional it can be incorporated in a demonstration. The species of the sign so called homonymously with the genus, then, would be made up of atomic propositions related to what they signify only by non-connective conditionals, with the result that incorporation into demonstrations satisfying the revised standards of Accounts II and III is impossible. If this is right, the Stoic conception of the sign does double duty. But in its customary use of pieces of evidence which are no more than signs, it will cover the evidence of the kinds that concern divination and the empirical arts. This agrees well with the view of signs in the Stoic treatment of divination as well as the presumably empirical examples used by Sextus to illustrate the Stoic theory.[52]

---

[51] T. Ebert has recently argued that the theory belongs to an earlier, pre-Chrysippean period in the Stoa's history and that it was taken over in large part from the Dialectical school, whose most prominent members were Diodorus Cronus and his student Philo. I examine the evidence for this view in the appendix to this study.

[52] There is no mention of signs homonymously so called with the genus in Stoic contexts, but there is evidence that such a distinction was current. It will be recalled that Aristotle termed those signs that do not qualify as tokens 'anonymous'. And in

The Stoic conception of the sign, then, moves in a direction opposite to that cited by Sextus when he claims that the more specialized and refined, as opposed to the broader and more common, use of the term 'sign' applies to the kind of evidence which meets the strictest and most stringent standards, the indicative sign (*M*. 8. 143). Instead, according to the Stoics, talk of signs in the strictest sense is most appropriate in connection with evidence that satisfies only weaker and less stringent standards. The Stoics were best known for the severity of their views about virtue and knowledge, requiring of their ideal, the wise man, unerring certainty in all his judgements. And this presumably contributed to the tendency to assume that they must have looked with favour on the indicative sign because of its promise of unassailable, rationally warranted certainty. But the very precision with which the Stoics characterized the kind of rational insight on which inferences of the indicative type depend, involving as it does an understanding of *why* things must be as we infer them to be, suggested that the conditions necessary for it are very rarely satisfied even by the wise man. He must instead rely to a very large extent on weaker inferential relations of the kind exemplified by empirically ascertained relations of co-occurrence and sequence. Thus the notion of signification of which, as Sextus notes, the Stoics give the most exact account applies to the kind of low or common inference to which, in its very different way, the commemorative account of signification was meant to apply.

APPENDIX

The Evidence for a Dialectical
Origin of the Stoic Theory of Signs

The existence of a Dialectical school distinct from the Megarian school is controversial. The case in favour is made by D. Sedley,[53] doubts have been raised by K. Döring.[54] I am not concerned here with this wider controversy,

---

a later anonymous commentary they are said to be homonymously so called with the genus (*In rhet*. 3. 26; 4. 19–26 Rabe).

[53] 'Diodorus Cronus and Hellenistic Philosophy', *Proceedings of the Cambridge Philological Society*, 203 (1977), 74–120.

[54] 'Gab es eine dialektische Schule?', *Phronesis*, 34 (1989), 293–310.

but only with T. Ebert's contention that the Stoic theory of the sign had its origin in the Dialectical school.

The principal piece of evidence for this thesis is a passage in chapter 9 of the pseudo-Galenic *Historia philosopha*, where, as we have already had occasion to observe, a definition of the sign essentially the same as that in Sextus is preserved, but commemorative and indicative signs are represented as species of the genus sign determined by this definition. This passage makes no mention of the Stoics; according to it, it is the dialecticians who define the sign as 'a proposition antecedent in a sound conditional and revelatory of the consequent' (*DG* 605. 10–11). By itself, this decides nothing. As Ebert notes, the διαλεκτικός need mean nothing more than a practitioner of dialectic or, as we should say, a 'logician'.[55] Used in this way, it can refer to members of different philosophical schools. Ebert cites Cicero's use of the term as a case in point (cf. *Luc.* 143; D.L. 1. 17). I am not sure he is right to suppose that matters are all that different in Sextus, but that does not matter for present purposes. As Ebert acknowledges, his arguments require that the *Historia philosopha* be familiar with the Dialectical school under this designation.

But he believes this is established by an earlier passage in chapter 4 of the same work. The chapter is concerned to explain how philosophical schools receive their names. The author tells us, for example, that the Peripatetic school is so called from an activity, that the Stoic and Academic schools are so called from places, and so on. To be sure, everything that a partisan of the Dialectical school could wish for is found in the text that appears in Kühn, which provides not one but, as it seems, two explanations for the name of a Dialectical school, though the first is notably more mysterious than the second: ἥδε δι' ἔνστασιν, ὡς Κυνική, διαλεκτική. ἡ δ' ἀπὸ μέρους τῆς φιλοσοφίας ὃ μάλιστ' ἐπετήδευσαν, ὡς διαλεκτική. ἡ δὲ ἀπὸ τόπου, ὡς Στωϊκή . . . (xix. 230). Ebert rightly chooses not to rest too much weight on the second explanation, as the second occurrence of διαλεκτική and the sentence to which it belongs are not to be found in the critical text published by Diels in his *Doxographi Graeci* of 1879, who also brackets the first and only occurrence of διαλεκτική as an interpolation (602. 5–7). Still, Ebert remarks that it is unclear whether Kühn derives the extra material in his version from manuscript evidence or whether it is rather a matter of conjecture.[56]

This question can be answered, however, and in a way that throws light on both the significance of the first occurrence of διαλεκτική here and the reference to dialecticians in the discussion of signs in chapter 9. Though our passage is not discussed by Diels, the first part of the solution to the problem it presents is already implicit in the conclusions he drew in his

---

[55] *Dialektiker*, 26.
[56] Ibid. 67 n. 4; id., 'The Origin of the Stoic Theory of Signs in Sextus Empiricus', *Oxford Studies in Ancient Philosophy*, 5 (1987), 83–126 at 113 with n. 42.

inaugural dissertation, *De Galeni historia philosopha* (Bonn, 1870) (=*Diss.*) and restated in improved form in the Prolegomena to his *Doxographi Graeci* (=*Prol.*). C. Wachsmuth made an important further contribution in his review of Diels's dissertation (*Gött. gel. Anz.* (1871: 18), 698–712). Though he accepted Diels's conclusions, Wachsmuth drew attention to pieces of evidence that Diels had overlooked, which he was then able to use when he returned to the subject in the *Doxographi Graeci* (Wachsmuth, esp. 701–2; cf. Diels, *Prol.* 238).

Roughly speaking, the story is as follows. The Florentine manuscript designated A by Diels was the sole basis for the *editio princeps*, which appeared as part of an edition of Aristotle's works, the Aldine of 1497. This edition was in turn the basis of further editions of 1525, also in Venice, and of 1538 in Basel, in which a small amount of progress correcting the worst errors of the first edition was made, none of it based on the manuscripts (cf. *Prol.* 238–9). Like A, the *editio princeps*, and Diels's own text, they contain only the first occurrence of διαλεκτική, though naturally without Diels's brackets. The second explanation makes its first appearance in the Latin translation of Iulianus Martianus Rota, which appeared in 1540 or possibly as early as 1528 (cf. Wachsmuth, 701–2). Though he seems to have deserved high marks for Latinity and learning, Rota was not a faithful translator (*Diss.* 6–7; *Prol.* 239–41; Wachsmuth, 699, 707). Among other things, he altered the order of the chapters and filled gaps with passages drawn from Plutarch or with inventions of his own. Thus he renders the passage with which we are concerned: 'De cognominibus philosophiae . . . partim ab adversando, ut cynica [partim ab aliqua eius portione, cui prae ceteris operam dederint, ut] dialectica.' The brackets are mine and enclose the new matter introduced by Rota. Note also that the second explanation, Rota's invention, replaces rather than, as in Kühn, supplementing the first explanation.

That much of Rota's translation is invented was recognized by Andreas Lacuna in 1543 (*Diss.* 24–5; *Prol.* 239; Wachsmuth, 708). But his was a voice in the wilderness that had no influence on the subsequent history of the work. When Charterius put together his edition of 1679, he used both the Greek text of the Basel edition of 1538 and Rota, supplying Greek for Rota's Latin when he found none in his text (*Diss.* 9; *Prol.* 240). He produced the curious double explanation found in Kühn's edition of 1830 by preserving διαλεκτική in its original place and adding Greek to correspond to Rota's invented Latin explanation. Kühn often did little more, and in the *Historia philosopha* did nothing more, than transcribe Charterius (*Diss.* 7; *Prol.* 241 with n. 2; Wachsmuth, 700).[57]

---

[57] Cf. I. Müller's judgement of Kühn in his edition of *De placitis Hippocratis et Platonis* (Leipzig: Teubner, 1874), 60–1, 69. Diels and Müller were judging Kühn by the standards of 19th-cent. textual scholarship. Without disputing their factual

In some places where he followed the authority of Rota, Charterius italicized the Latin (*Diss.* 9; *Prol.* 241). This feature is faithfully preserved in Kühn's edition, though in our passage only the first clause of the sentence corresponding to Rota's invention is italicized: 'Partim a pugnaci contentione, ut Cynica et dialectica. *Partim a parte aliqua philosophiae*, cui prae ceteris operam dederint, ut dialectica. Partim a locis . . .'

The Latin translation of 1341 by Niccolò da Reggio (N), based on a manuscript not identical with A or B, omits all mention of a Dialectical school. (It can be found in part II of the second impression of the *Opera Galieni* that appeared in Venice in 1502 under the care of Hieronymus Surianus, pp. 574–80.) In the second Florentine manuscript used by Diels (B) διαλεκτική is not found after Κυνική; instead, we find the patently absurd ἡ δ' ἀπὸ χώρας ὡς ἡ διαλεκτική ἡ δὲ ἀπὸ τόπου ὡς ἡ Στωϊκή. Thus if this passage is to support the claim that the *Historia philosopha* was familiar with a Dialectical school, it will have to do so on the strength of the reading in A: ἡδὲ δι' ἔνστασιν, ὡς Κυνική, διαλεκτική.

But A is not easy to make sense of here, as we can see if we ask why Rota was moved to supply a new explanation for διαλεκτική and Diels to treat it as an interpolation. The passage tells us that the Cynical school is so called δι' ἔνστασιν, and as it seems, the Dialectical school as well (though we should need to restore a καί or a καὶ ἡ here to bring this out properly). I suspect that the sense of ἔνστασις most familiar to readers of philosophical texts is that of 'objection'. Niccolò da Reggio renders δι' ἔνστασιν as 'ab instanciis' (i.e. 'instantiis'), presumably using the plural to indicate that the practice or custom of objecting is somehow responsible for the Cynics' name. LSJ also recognizes a sense meaning 'opposition'. But it is not clear whether the passages they cite would support the sense of habitual opposition or a persistent tendency to oppose implied by Rota's 'ab adversando' or Charterius' 'a pugnaci contentione'. Stephanus offers 'pugnax contentio instantis adversario, h.e., ἀνταγώνισμα', though without any citations. But in any case, even if the term can mean this, this is not the traditional account of why the Cynics were called 'dog-like'. In some ways it might seem to suit a Dialectical school better, though not as an explanation for its name. It would rather explain why an ἐνστατικὴ αἵρεσις was so called. Rota's invention does a far better job of explaining Διαλεκτική.

There is, however, another sense of ἔνστασις, the second entry in LSJ, often though not always in the phrase ἔνστασις βίου, meaning 'way of life'. It is especially well attested in connection with the Cynics, because their

conclusions, V. Nutton passes a somewhat kinder judgement on Kühn and his edition in *Karl Gottlob Kühn and his Edition of the Works of Galen: A Bibliography and Introduction Compiled by Vivian Nutton* (Oxford: Oxford Microform publications, 1976), 7–8.

school was characterized to an unusual extent by its way of life rather than, say, a common body of doctrines (D.L. 6. 103; Jul. Imp. *Orationes*, vi. 201ᵃ Hertlein).[58] But it is also found in Stoic authors like Epictetus and the Church Fathers.[59] The way of life for which the Cynics were notorious handily explains why the school is so called, and is indeed a traditional explanation for the Cynics' name.[60] To be sure, it is not impossible to imagine a similar explanation for the name of a Dialectical school, which would take its name from their constant practice of argument. But it seems far more likely that we are dealing with a gloss introduced by a scribe who, like Rota, Charterius, and Niccolò da Reggio, had trouble understanding δι' ἔνστασιν and intended it as an alternative for Κυνική. Apparently there is no dearth of interpolations in the manuscripts and the archetype, many of them quite foolish (*Prol.* 234, 241).

If this is right, reference to a Dialectical school disappears from chapter 4. We get a better sense of how the author understands διαλεκτικός, I suggest, from chapter 1, where Socrates is credited with giving philosophy its tripartite form by adding ethics and dialectic to physics, which had been the sole concern of his predecessors (597. 1–598. 2, esp. 597. 15–16) and chapter 2, where the author tells us that, in view of his intention to provide an introduction for beginners, he will omit the subtleties and refined embellishments of the dialecticians (598. 10–11 *DG*). Here dialecticians are almost certainly simply logicians. Compare the attitude evinced in Cicero's remarks about the 'totum tortuosum genus disputandi' (*Luc.* 98) or the 'subtile vel spinosum potius disserendi genus' (*Fin.* 3. 3), and Diogenes Laertius' remark about τῶν λόγων τέρθεια characteristic of the philosophers called dialecticians for this reason (1. 17). Chapter 9, on the sign, is in fact the first of a short sequence of chapters concerning logical matters: syllogisms (ch. 10), definition (ch. 11), the criterion (ch. 12),

---

[58] On the ancient debate about whether Cynicism should be viewed as a philosophy see M.-O. Goulet-Cazé, 'Le Cynisme est-il une philosophie?', in M. Dixsaut (ed.), *Contre Platon*, i. *Le Platonisme dévoilé* (Paris: Vrin, 1993), 273–313. Goulet-Cazé recognizes that the reference to an ἔνστασις in ch. 4 of the *De historia philosopha* has to do with this question (218 n. 19).

[59] The 18th-cent. Dutch scholar Tiberius Hemsterhuis provides a history of this sense with numerous citations. See Θωμᾶ τοῦ μαγίστρου κατ' ἀλφάβητον ὀνομάτων Ἀττικῶν ἐκλογαί *ex dispositione Nicolai Blancardi*, ed. J. S. Bernard (Leipzig: Hartmann, 1833), 296–7.

[60] Simplicius distinguishes seven principles on the basis of which philosophical schools received their names (*In cat.* 3. 30–4. 9 Kalbfleisch). Cf. Simplicius, *Commentaire sur les Catégories*, ed. I. Hadot *et al.*, i (Leiden: Brill, 1990), 48–62. The last of these is 'in accordance with their way of life', and it is in this way, Simplicius maintains, that the Cynics received their name (4. 6–7). This view is well attested among other Neoplatonic commentators. Cf. Philoponus, *In cat.* 2. 24–9 Busse; Ammonius, *In cat.* 2. 2–8 Busse; Olympiodorus, *In cat.* 3. 20–30 Busse; Elias, *In cat.* 111. 1–32 Busse. I am grateful to M. Bonazzi for drawing my attention to this material.

truth (ch. 13), and division (ch. 14). If we accept Diels's conclusions about the order of the chapters that he prints as chapters 15–19, but which are found after chapter 35 in the manuscripts, this sequence concludes with demonstration in chapter 15 (cf. *Prol.* 243). In none of them are any schools named or differences in doctrine mentioned. And if this is the right order, the author then makes a transition to natural philosophy in chapter 16, after noting that he has touched on matters relating to the logical part of philosophy only very briefly (συντομώτατα) here, having discussed them in more detail in another work (608. 4–7). In other words, it seems as if the dialecticians' account of the sign in chapter 9 belongs to a very concise survey of the logical *part* of philosophy, which part the author has already called *dialectic*.

Ebert's further arguments presuppose that the definition of the sign and the distinction between commemorative and indicative signification discussed in chapter 9 of the *Historia philosopha* belong together and that the original source of the theory to which they belong must be sought either in the Stoa or the Dialectical school.[61] But the burden of my argument in this study is that the distinction and the definition do not form a unity and that, if we must look for the origin of the distinction outside the Stoa, the most likely place is not the Dialectical school but in medicine. If this is right, it is possible to agree with Ebert that the distinction between commemorative and indicative signs is not Stoic without agreeing that it must be Dialectical or that its source and that of the definition of the sign must be sought in the same place.

[61] *Dialektiker*, 67 ff. Ebert also argues that the Περὶ σημασιῶν of Philo referred to in a book-title of Chrysippus, Πρὸς τὸ περὶ σημασιῶν Φίλωνος (D.L. 7. 191), should be interpreted as 'about signs' rather than, as the more usual view holds, having something to do with meaning ('The Origins', 108–12; *Dialektiker*, 60–5). But without the support of the *Historia philosopha*, this seems less plausible. Though the alternative interpretation is also speculative, in view of the fact that Chrysippus is known to have disagreed with Philo's teacher, Diodorus, about word-meaning, there is much to be said for it. Cf. K. Döring, *Die Megariker: Kommentierte Sammlung der Testimonien* (Amsterdam: B. R. Grüner, 1972), 138–9; P. Hadot, 'Liste commentée des œuvres de Chrysippe (D.L. VII 189–202)', in R. Goulet (ed.), *Dictionnaire des philosophes antiques*, ii (Paris: CNRS Éditions: 1994), 336–56 at 341.

STUDY IV

Epicurean Sign-inference in Philodemus

As we have seen, the framework Sextus Empiricus used to classify the epistemological positions that he examines divides objects of knowledge into two classes: knowledge of evident matters is treated by the philosophers in their theories of the criterion, while the transition (μετάβασις) from the evident by means of which non-evident matters are apprehended is discussed under the head of signs and demonstrations (σημεῖα, ἀποδείξεις) (*M.* 7. 24–6, 396; 8. 140, 319; *PH* 2. 96). It is not hard to see how badly suited this framework is to the more ancient philosophers whom Sextus credits with theories of the criterion, e.g. Parmenides or Heraclitus (*M.* 7. 111 ff., 126 ff.). If the argument of the previous studies is correct, it also led Sextus, or the tradition on which he relied, to misunderstand the Stoics by erroneously imputing to them a high-conception sign-inference, in this way obscuring the real character and purpose of their theory of signs. The philosophers whom the framework appears to suit best are Epicurus and his followers. Indeed, there is reason to suppose that Epicurus played a large, perhaps the largest, part in giving currency to some of its most important terms and notions.[1] None the less, his account of the means by which knowledge is extended to embrace non-evident truths presents surprising difficulties. There is no dearth of testimony that Epicurus believed such knowledge has its origin in knowledge of evident matters; and he often makes this point with the aid of the vocabulary of 'signs'

---

[1] On πρόληψις cf. D. Sedley, 'Epicurus On Nature Book XXVIII', *Cronache ercolanesi*, 3 (1973), 5–83 at 14–16; on ἐνάργεια cf. F. H. Sandbach, 'Ennoia and Prolepsis in the Stoic Theory of Knowledge', in A. A. Long (ed.), *Problems in Stoicism* (London: Athlone, 1971), 22–37 at 33; on κριτήριον cf. G. Striker, 'Κριτήριον τῆς ἀληθείας', *Nachrichten der Akademie der Wissenschaften in Göttingen*, phil.-hist. Kl. 2 (1974), 47–110 at 58–9; trans. in ead., *Essays in Hellenistic Epistemology and Ethics* (Cambridge: Cambridge University Press, 1996), 22–76 at 28–9.

and 'demonstrations' familiar to us from Sextus Empiricus (*Ep. Hdt.* 38, 39; *Ep. Pyth.* 87, 97, 104; cf. D.L. 10. 32; Lucretius, 1. 423–5, 693–4; 4. 482 ff.). Rather, the difficulty is to discover a consistent and satisfying interpretation of all that he has to say about the matter.

1. Epicurus

Epicurus' use of analogy in his theorizing about the non-evident sets him apart from the other figures we have studied. To put matters crudely, an item or process in our experience is taken as a model for a non-evident one, which is then conceived as, *mutatis mutandis*, like its evident model. When a philosopher uses analogy as Epicurus does, it is fair to ask whether he makes or observes a distinction between the use of analogy to suggest a hypothesis and its use to prove it true.[2] This way of putting the question unsurprisingly implies that the idea of proof by analogy, unlike its use to suggest hypotheses, is to be viewed with suspicion. Even if we put the difficulties concealed by the qualification *mutatis mutandis* aside, and, as later Epicureans did, treat arguments by analogy as a species of inference on a level with what we would call inductive inference, the well-known difficulty of justifying such inferences remains. What entitles us to put an inference from an observed regularity to the conclusion, however qualified, that this regularity obtains universally beside an unexceptionably valid deductive argument and view the conclusion as following in the same way from the premises put forward in its support? But if we cannot do this, what is the nature of the support, if any, lent to the conclusion of an inductive argument by its premises?

It might at first seem that concerns about Epicurus' use of analogy are misplaced, however. The most prominent method of proof on display in the *Letter to Herodotus*, where Epicurus expounds the basic tenets of his physics, seems not to be analogical at all. Instead, Epicurus typically proves a non-evident thesis by establishing that its contradictory has an implication shown to be false by observation.[3] Thus there is no such thing as creation *ex nihilo*, because,

---

[2] The question is so put by R. Robinson, *Plato's Earlier Dialectic*, 2nd edn. (Oxford: Oxford University Press, 1953), 205.

[3] D. J. Furley, 'Knowledge of Atoms and Void in Epicureanism', in J. P. Anton

if there were, anything could come to be anywhere or at any time without any seeds, which is evidently not the case (38; cf. Lucretius, 1. 159 ff.). In the same way, the existence of void is demonstrated by showing that, if there were no void, and thus no place for objects to move, motion would be impossible, as it evidently is not (*Ep. Hdt.* 40; cf. Lucretius, 1. 334 ff.).

On the other hand, Epicurus' most conspicuous use of analogy is in connection with unexplained natural phenomena for which he offers multiple explanations. To understand his approach to these matters, it is essential to see that he speaks of 'phenomena' in two ways: as we do, of natural phenomena in need of explanation because their causes are hidden from us, but also of the phenomena in our experience, which are the basis or point of departure for inferences about non-evident matters. Epicurus did not subscribe to the strict form of empiricism which denies that we ever see the causes of an event at work because, it insists, we observe only *that* events occur and in what sequence and never *why*. When he recommends that we seek causal explanations for meteorological— and indeed all non-evident—matters by observing in how many ways like matters in our experience come about, it is clear that he takes observation to be perfectly capable, so far as it goes, of seeing causes bring about their effects (*Ep. Hdt.* 80). Only in this way is he able to make the processes whose explanation is evident serve as a model for the analogous explanation of natural phenomena with non-evident causes. The term 'experience' is not very common in Epicurus or his followers. But if we call what is grasped without inference, and furnishes the basis for it, experience, it is plain that Epicurus had an exceptionally rich conception of experience. This is not to be confused with his view of what we might call the ultimate basis of experience: the element of sensory experience which, he insists, somehow cannot fail to be true and is to be sharply distinguished from the additions of opinion, which can. To ensure that the ultimate basis of experience is true, he is forced to conceive it in very impoverished terms indeed.

This could suggest that Epicurus' view is that the phenomena in our experience give rise to knowledge of the non-evident by performing two distinct functions. They first suggest analogous

and G. L. Kustas (eds.), *Essays in Ancient Greek Philosophy* (Albany: SUNY Press, 1971), 607–19, repr. in id., *Cosmic Problems* (Cambridge: Cambridge University Press, 1989), 161–71.

explanations for the natural phenomena under investigation by providing observable models for them. But the phenomena, though not necessarily the same phenomena, must then be used to refute theories about the non-evident by contradicting implications of theirs and, less often, to confirm a theory by contradicting an implication of its contradictory. The existence of a plausible analogy based on some points of resemblance would not, on this view, establish that the analogy obtains *in toto*. It remains a conjecture until confirmed by the phenomena acting in their second capacity, to which any similarity between them and non-evident matters is irrelevant. In the *Letter to Pythocles* multiple explanations modelled on the phenomena in our experience are proposed for meteorological phenomena such as the waxing and waning of the moon, the varying lengths of night and day, thunder and lightning, and the like (cf. Lucretius, 5. 534 ff.). And it could seem that analogy is being used in an unexceptionable way in these cases to suggest aetiological hypotheses that can be neither decisively confirmed nor falsified by the evidence at our disposal. The burden of Epicurus' complaint against those who reject multiple explanations would then be that it is irrational to prefer one to the others arbitrarily, and since, on his view, the purpose of natural philosophy is to free us from superstitious fear of the gods, unnecessary as well (cf. *Ep. Pyth.* 87). To this end, all we need to know is that the phenomenon in question can be explained naturally, not which natural explanation is correct.

Closer examination shows that this cannot be entirely right, however. The explanations discovered by the 'multiple method' or the 'possible method', as Epicurus calls it (*Ep. Pyth.* 87, 97), are more than epistemically possible, i.e. possible for all we know or all we can say. Rather, Epicurus seems to have regarded all the explanations compatible with the phenomena as objectively possible. Indeed, he seems to have held that they are realized either at some time in connection with some occurrences of the natural phenomenon in question in our world or in some world in the infinite universe (cf. Lucretius, 5. 526–33). The method that makes multiple explanations available to us, then, does more than discover hypotheses about how natural phenomena may be caused for all we know; it provides causally sufficient explanations for them, which obtain either in another world or at some time in ours.

This goes some way towards explaining the part assigned to contestation (ἀντιμαρτύρησις) and non-contestation (οὐκ ἀντιμαρτύρησις) as tests of truth in Epicureanism. These are mentioned together with attestation (ἐπιμαρτύρησις) and non-attestation (οὐκ ἐπιμαρτύρησις) by Epicurus himself, and they occupy the central place in Sextus Empiricus' account of Epicurean epistemology, with, however, a curious change of emphasis to which we shall have to return (*Ep. Hdt.* 51; cf. D.L. 10. 34; S.E. *M.* 7. 203 ff.). Falsity arises when an opinion is not attested or is contested, truth when it is attested or not contested. Attestation and non-attestation apply to opinions about evident matters. The opinion, for example, that that is Plato over there awaits attestation. It can legitimately be accepted as true if upon closer inspection it is confirmed, and rejected as false if it is not. For their part, contestation and non-contestation concern non-evident matters. The use of contestation to eliminate false opinions presents no problems. A thesis is contested when it is seen to have an observable consequence that the phenomena show to be false, i.e. one that is not attested by them. But it has always been much harder to understand how Epicurus could have supposed that the mere absence of contestation can establish the truth of an opinion. Inevitably it often happens that several incompatible theories about the non-evident causation of a natural phenomenon are uncontested (cf. Lucretius, 6. 703 ff.). In the light of Epicurus' views about multiple explanation, however, it seems that what is shown to be true by non-contestation is not that a particular episode of a phenomenon or its occurrence in this world is caused in this particular way, let alone that every episode is so caused, but that the uncontested opinion is, unlike e.g. superstitious appeals to divine agency, a genuine explanation: the natural phenomenon in question can, in a very robust sense, occur as this explanation maintains it does; indeed, episodes of it are somewhere or at some time so caused.

If non-contestation secures truth conceived in this way, the strong claims that Epicurus makes on its behalf become easier to understand. His innovation was to construe theories first put forward in the spirit of universal explanation—as applicable at all times and in all places to a natural phenomenon in need of explanation—so that they apply only to some episodes of it or its occurrence in some worlds, when a plurality of theories are not contested by the phenomena. But if the explanatory power of a theory can be relativized to worlds or occasions in this way, why should not its contestation be made relative in the same way, so that it shows only that the theory does not apply on this occasion or in this world, not that it could not apply anywhere or ever? Imagine for a moment that one could somehow directly observe the circumstances in which a meteorological phenomenon arises, in this way determining which explanation does obtain, and thereby which others do not. The explanations not obtaining should be no less possible for being seen not to apply in this case. An experience of this kind, then, would be more like the non-attestation of an opinion than its contestation, which makes it clear that contestation differs from non-attestation not only because it concerns non-evident matters, but in the way in which it shows opinions about them to be false. It is an instrument of aetiology applied to *theories*, which aim to discover how things must or can be by nature, as opposed to the contingent matters of fact that are candidates for attestation or non-attestation. Contestation shows that the contested theory *could* not be true.[4] Neither direct inspection of the kind just imagined nor the failure of an observable implication of the theory in question to obtain 'as it happens' will do this. There must be some feature of the case that prevents us from reinterpreting the theory so that it applies only some of the time, perhaps that it is contested by phenomena that cannot fail to obtain themselves. It seems to be in this way, for example, that the hypothesis that there is no void is contested by the phenomenon of motion, without which no cosmos can come to be or exist.

A full discussion of Epicurus' account of non-contestation is outside our present scope, but it should already be clear that the modest tone that Epicurus adopts in his pronouncements about aetiology by multiple explanation is misleading. Behind his cautious strictures to be satisfied with multiple explanations when the limits placed on human knowledge do not permit greater accuracy is a conception of the space enclosed by those limits that is quite remarkable for its optimism (cf. *Ep. Hdt.* 80; *Ep. Pyth.* 87, 94, 95, 98). According to Epicurus, not merely are only theories that are uncontested by the phenomena true, all of them are, in that they can and sometimes do explain natural phenomena. The phenomena are, then, a control on theories about the non-evident. For present purposes it is most significant that theories earn the imprimatur of the phenomena by being compatible with them, with the result

---

[4] A point that is lost if one opposes contestation and attestation, as Sextus Empiricus sometimes does (cf. *M.* 8. 324).

that the straightforward inference to *the* correct theoretical conclusion about a non-evident subject-matter plays a far smaller part in Epicurus' epistemology than one would have expected. To be sure, Epicurus does in effect infer the basic tenets of his natural philosophy from the phenomena; they are proved true because their contradictories are contested by the phenomena. But even in these cases Epicurus speaks of their unique agreement with the phenomena (μοναχὴ τοῖς φαινομένοις συμφωνία), which suggests that he regards such proofs as a special case of the more common multiple explanation (*Ep. Pyth.* 86).

Outside of Philodemus, we first hear of a relation of consequence or implication (ἀκολουθία) in the account of Epicurean epistemology preserved by Sextus. But this is the account of non-contestation in which the puzzling shift of focus already mentioned occurs; in it, attention is directed away from the cases so prominent in Epicurus' own use of non-contestation, where several competing theories are not contested by the phenomena, to those in which, beyond having no observable implications contested by the phenomena, the opinions at issue have contradictories which are (*M.* 7. 213). Here the non-contestation that *P* has effectively become the contestation that not-*P*.[5] This is, to be sure, equivalent to the inference that *P*, but this conception of non-contestation is probably of later Epicurean inspiration.[6] If we choose to speak of inference in connection with Epicurus' own use of non-contestation, then, we must do so circumspectly. For the most part, the phenomena against which a theoretical opinion is checked do not license the conclusion that the natural phenomenon at issue is caused in *this* way without qualification. If you will, talk of inference conceals an ambiguity which our expectations make it hard for us to notice. For we tend to assume that this episode of a natural phenomenon is caused by these conditions only if the relation between them exemplifies a universal law-like relation between natural phenomena of this, and causal conditions of that, type. But according to Epicurus, we are typically entitled to conclude only that a natural phenomenon is caused in a certain way among others. If we call these 'aetiological inferences', one of the most distinctive features of Epicurean epistemology will be the large part that aetiological inferences play at the expense of inferences from the phenomena in our experience to their necessary causal conditions, which tell us how things in fact are at

⁵ Cf. Striker, 'Κριτήριον', 75–6.   ⁶ Cf. Heintz, *Studien*, 103 ff.

the same time that they exemplify the universal law-like relations with which, in common with many of Epicurus' predecessors and contemporaries, we are more comfortable.

It should now be clear that the opposition between the use of analogy to suggest hypotheses about how things might be and its use in inferences establishing how they are is not well suited to Epicurus' method. Because there is not a single cause but many, analogies could fail to establish *the* non-evident cause of a natural phenomenon without on that account being relegated to the supporting part of suggesting hypotheses in need of additional confirmation. To discover what part they do play, we need to ask whether and how they contribute to establishing that a non-evident opinion agrees or conflicts with the phenomena. Does a theory that represents the non-evident causal conditions which give rise to a natural phenomenon as similar or analogous to processes observed taking place in our experience *eo ipso* agree with the phenomena? Does the rejection of such a theory or the postulation of one which represents non-evident matters as behaving in a way that has no analogue in our experience bring one into conflict with the phenomena? If so, it would seem that analogy is able to establish by itself the objective possibility of an opinion regarding the non-evident, which is equivalent in Epicurus' view to establishing that the natural phenomenon in question is caused in this way among others. In the case of some natural phenomena, where only one theory is suitably analogous to the phenomena, it may even suffice to establish the universal and unqualified truth of that theory.

The clearest indications that Epicurus considered analogy equal to these tasks are furnished by passages in the *Letter to Pythocles* that call attention to the multiple explanations for meteorological phenomena suggested by the phenomena in our experience and warn against arbitrarily preferring one to the others. Epicurus observes, for example, that the waxing and waning of the moon could come about in all of the ways in which we see similar processes occurring in our experience (94). The same is true of the way in which the moon gets its light; it may be the source of its own light or receive it from the sun, just as some things in our experience have their own light while others receive it from another source (95). The impression left by these passages that the phenomena imply the possibility of their non-evident analogues is strengthened when Epicurus goes on to suggest that the rejection of other possible theories implicit in the adoption of one as the sole explanation for the natural phenomena in question constitutes a repudiation of the phenomena in our experience—a failure, if you will, to see them as the signs they are (97). Most striking of all is the way in which, after a survey of competing explanations for the variation in the lengths of night and day over the course of the year suggested by analogous occurrences in our experience, he amplifies his insistence that it is necessary to speak of meteorological matters in a manner consonant (συμφώνως) with the phenomena with the further remark that those who adopt only one of the possible explanations are in conflict (μάχονται) with the phenomena (98).

Here, similarity to the phenomena appears to come very close to agreement with them, and Epicurus seems to regard the repudiation of any of the theories that agree with the phenomena in this way not only as a rash presumption of knowledge which it is not possible for human beings to possess—though he does say this as well—but as in conflict with the phenomena, which, as it seems, imply the possibility of their non-evident analogues.[7] To say that natural phenomena cannot come about in other than one way flies in the face of the evidence afforded by similar phenomena in our experience, which *shows* that they can. What is more, much of Epicurus' talk of 'signs' and 'signification' can be interpreted as concerned with analogical projections of this kind. In the middle of his discussion of the aetiology of lightning, Epicurus observes that one will be able to grasp the ways in which it can come about by adhering to the phenomena and being able to grasp what is similar to them (102). A short while thereafter, in the discussion of thunder, he insists that one's explanations will be uncontaminated by myth if in drawing conclusions (σημειῶται) about the non-evident one follows the phenomena as one should (104). If we connect these passages as it seems we should, it appears that Epicurus takes signs, or at any rate some of them, to be similar to what they signify and to discharge their function as signs of the non-evident precisely by being similar to the items they signify.

It might still be argued that the contribution of the phenomena in our experience is confined to *suggesting* explanations for natural phenomena. Because of Epicurus' distinctive conviction that

---

[7] Cf. *Ep. Pyth.* 90, where it appears that it is not the view that worlds originate in a vortex of some kind that Epicurus means to reject as in conflict with the phenomena, but the view that they arise of necessity only in this way.

compatibility with the phenomena is not only a necessary but also a sufficient condition for the truth of a theory, there would be a stronger presumption in favour of the theories suggested by analogy than if absence of contestation were regarded as establishing only that a theory is possible for all we know; analogy would still belong to the preliminary stage of an enquiry that is able to achieve definite results only after the hypotheses it brings to light have been tested for implications incompatible with the phenomena, where this is not simply a matter of being unlike them. Epicurus does sometimes write in a way which suggests or is consistent with this view of the matter (e.g. *Ep. Pyth.* 92, 93, 98–9). It may be the view that best describes much of his practice; perhaps it is the position he should have taken. But he need not have seen things in this way himself. It was open to him to regard the discovery that a theory has implications contradicted by the phenomena as showing not that analogy is an unreliable guide to the conditions prevailing in the non-evident realm, but rather that the argument at issue was based on a faulty analogy or a specious likeness. To this way of thinking, the search for such implications acts as a check on the misuse of analogy, but there can be no conflict between its results and those of a properly constructed analogy.

At all events, Epicurus' successors inherited many arguments in which the fact that items of a certain kind have a certain feature or behave in a certain way in our experience is put forward as a ground for the conclusion that relevantly similar items have a similar feature or behave in a similar way outside our experience. On a number of occasions, in cases of what he calls unique agreement, Epicurus even argues for a universally applicable account of a natural phenomenon by means of analogy. The opinion that the sun is about as large as it appears, for instance, is established by an appeal to the behaviour of signal fires in our experience (*Ep. Pyth.* 91). The nature of the minimal theoretical magnitudes is established by a comparison with that of *minima visibilia* (*Ep. Hdt.* 58). Even the argument for the existence of void, the paradigm of an unexceptionably non-analogical argument, presents an appearance in Epicurus very different from the one that it presents in Sextus Empiricus (*Ep. Hdt.* 39–40; *M.* 7. 213–14). In Epicurus' version it is only a step on the way to the conclusion which it is his principal aim to establish: namely, that the universe is made up, at bottom, of bodies and void and nothing else. And his way of stating the conclusion—that apart

from these nothing can be conceived either apprehensively ($\pi\epsilon\rho\iota$-
$\lambda\eta\pi\tau\hat{\omega}s$) or analogously to the things apprehended—might suggest
that it rests on the projection beyond our experience of conditions
shown to obtain in our experience, broadly construed, by a combination of observation and inference.

Epicurus' failure to say anything very definite about the standing
of such projections is that much less surprising in view of his and
his followers' well-known scorn for logic.[8] It may not be necessary
to study logic to pose the kind of questions that we have put to Epicurus, but it surely helps to bring them into focus. It is one thing
to speak, as Epicurus does, of broadly logical notions of agreement
($\sigma\upsilon\mu\phi\omega\nu\acute{\iota}a$) and conflict ($\mu\acute{a}\chi\eta$), or to use, apparently without mentioning, that of consequence ($\acute{a}\kappa o\lambda o\upsilon\theta\acute{\iota}a$), but quite another to make
them an object of study in their own right. Both the Stoics and
the Aristotelians attempted, albeit in very different ways, to give a
rigorous account of what it is for a conclusion to follow validly from
the premises of an argument, and the Stoic account crucially relied
on an analysis of relations of consequence and conflict between the
propositional components of complex propositions.

Some ancient authorities, and the scholars who have followed
their lead, conclude that since the Epicureans had much to say
about epistemological matters, which are the concern of logic according to the broader, ancient conception of the discipline, they
did in effect recognize a logical, along with an ethical and a natural, part of philosophy.[9] This is fair enough so far as it goes, but
it risks obscuring the effect that a concern with more narrowly
logical issues—what we call logic, and what the Stoics and other
philosophers of the Hellenistic period called dialectic—is likely to
have on a philosopher's treatment of epistemological issues. As we
have seen, both the Aristotelians and the Stoics make their logic
serve broadly epistemological purposes in their accounts of proof
or demonstration ($\acute{a}\pi\acute{o}\delta\epsilon\iota\xi\iota s$). The Stoics agreed with Aristotle that
a demonstration is an argument by grasping which one comes to
know. Their accounts of valid argument are of course very different,
and the conditions, apart from constituting a valid argument, that
they require the premises and conclusion of a demonstration to
satisfy also differ in a way that reflects their different conceptions
of the knowledge to which it gives rise. But however great the dif-

---

[8] Cf. H. Usener (ed.), *Epicurea* (Leipzig: Teubner, 1887), frr. 243, 257.
[9] Cf. ibid., fr. 242.

ferences between these two accounts, they crucially agree that to come to know by means of a demonstration, one must grasp the purely logical relation of consequence that obtains between its premisses and conclusion.

2. Philodemus and his Sources

In a philosophical climate in which such purely logical matters had become the object of study in their own right, questions about the legitimacy of inferences that project what is true in our experience beyond our experience, either without qualification or analogically, were bound to stand out more prominently. Later Epicureans were unable to avoid them, and they are aired in the *De signis* of Philodemus, an Epicurean of the first century BC, which is the only substantial testimony about the extensive Epicurean discussion of the subject after Epicurus to have survived.[10] Though potentially a very rich source, this work presents special difficulties because of the way in which it has come down to us. What we have is the remains of a single papyrus roll, part of the library buried in Herculaneum by the eruption of Mount Vesuvius in AD 79 and uncovered in the eighteenth century. The concluding thirty-eight columns have survived, along with eight fragments from the earlier part of the roll. Edited texts were published by T. Gomperz in the nineteenth century,[11] and more recently by P. H. and E. A. De Lacy.[12] Though in comparatively good condition, this is a papyrological text heavily dependent on restoration involving varying

---

[10] The subscription at the end of the papyrus which names Philodemus as the author and gives the title presents difficulties. Some letters cannot be read at all; others are hard to make out. It was read as Περὶ σημείων καὶ σημειώσεων by T. Gomperz (see following note). Περὶ φαντασιῶν καὶ σημειώσεων was defended by R. Philippson, 'Zur Wiederherstellung von Philodems sogennante Schrift Περὶ Σημείων καὶ Σημειώσεων', *Rheinisches Museum*, 64 (1909), 1–38 at 3. On the basis of a recent examination of the papyrus, D. Delattre has confirmed Περὶ σημείων καὶ σημειώσεων as the best reading. He also discovered a gamma beneath the title that had not been noticed before, which would make the part of a roll that we have the end of the third book of Philodemus' *De signis*. Cf. 'En relisant les subscriptiones des PHerc. 1065 et 1427', *Zeitschrift für Papyrologie und Epigraphik*, 109 (1995), 39–41.

[11] T. Gomperz (ed.), *Herkulanische Studien*, i. *Philodem über Induktionschlüsse* (Leipzig: Teubner, 1865).

[12] Philodemus, *On Methods of Inference*, ed. P. H. and E. A. De Lacy, 2nd edn. (Naples: Bibliopolis, 1978).

degrees of conjecture, from the nearly certain to the highly speculative.[13]

The surviving part recounts a controversy over sign-inference between the Epicureans and a group of unnamed opponents. It is divided into four sections, which recount the views of either two or three Epicurean authorities.[14] The first, already under way at the point where the surviving part of the papyrus begins, commences with a catalogue of the opponents' arguments against the Epicurean position, (1a. 1–v. 36 (chs. 1–7));[15] they are answered in sequence in columns xi. 26–xix. 4 (chs. 17–26). The account of both objections and replies is due to Philodemus' teacher, Zeno of Sidon, and this is Philodemus' own report of those views as they were related to him by Zeno (xix. 4–9; (ch. 27)). Placed oddly in between this pair of objections and replies is another set of objections and replies, presumably also due to Zeno. The second section contains another report of Zeno's views due to Philodemus' fellow student Bromius (xix. 9–xxvii. 28 (chs. 27–43)). The third relates the views of Demetrius of Laconia, another Epicurean teacher and a younger contemporary of Zeno (xxviii. 13–xxix. 16 (ch. 45)). The last begins after a short lacuna by describing the manner in which an unnamed 'he' handles the issues under discussion (xxix. 20–xxxviii. 22 (chs. 46–59)). It has sometimes been viewed as a report of how Demetrius treated the subject in oral, as opposed to written, discussion, but the identification of the source as Demetrius has also been vigorously contested.[16] The four sections differ in their handling of the same issues in

---

[13] On the character of the Herculaneum papyri and the special difficulties they present see R. Janko, 'Philodemus Resartus: Progress in Reconstructing the Philosophical Papyri of Herculaneum', *Proceedings of the Boston Area Colloquium in Ancient Philosophy*, 7 (1991), 271–305.

[14] Cf. R. Philippson, 'Philodemos', *RE* xix (1938), 2444–82 at 2451.

[15] The chapter-numbers are the De Lacys'.

[16] The view that the speaker is Demetrius is defended by Philippson, 'Philodemos', 2451, who cites the διαλεγόμενος of xxix. 24; he defends this view, and a restoration which lends support to it, at greater length in 'Zur Wiederherstellung', 33, 37–8. (Originally he had supposed that the fourth section was also due to Zeno; see id., *De Philodemi libro*, 5.) It is opposed by Sedley, 'On Signs', 240 n. 3, who is followed on this point by J. Barnes, 'Epicurean Signs', in J. Annas and R. H. Grimm (eds.), *Oxford Studies in Ancient Philosophy*, suppl. vol. (Oxford: Oxford University Press, 1988), 91–134 at 93 n. 9; for earlier arguments against Demetrius' authorship see Natorp, *Forschungen*, 239 n. 1; A. Schmekel, *Die Philosophie der mittleren Stoa in ihrem geschichtlichen Zusammenhange dargestellt* (Berlin: Weidmann, 1892), 340.

tone and emphasis, and perhaps in doctrine as well. Philodemus does not attempt a critical synthesis in the surviving portion, and what we have could fairly be regarded as a notebook or a source-book.[17]

Our understanding of the debate he recounts would be greatly improved if we could say with confidence who the Epicureans' opponents were. Although the suggestion of Gomperz, that Zeno's opponent is Posidonius, has not met with favour, the scholarly consensus is that they are Stoics.[18] But the evidence is not so strong that alternatives can be confidently excluded. Recent proponents of the view that the opponents are Stoics have tended to express a degree of dissatisfaction with their own case, and it has also been suggested that the opponents included Academics.[19] There is one piece of circumstantial evidence: one opponent is named 'Dionysius' (VII. 5–6; XI. 13–14), and the most likely candidate among bearers of the name known to us is the Stoic Dionysius of Cyrene.[20] But the case ultimately depends on how well the views and arguments of the opponents in the *De signis* can be made to square with known Stoic views, and the difficulties in the way of this conclusion are not negligible.

None the less, I shall not defend a new conclusion about the identity of the opponents. I do, however, want to air the difficulties that face the standard view more fully in order to discover precisely what further conclusions it commits us to. In particular, I shall argue that the identification of the opponents as Stoics can be maintained only if allowance is made for the distorting effect on their position of the Epicurean perspective from which it is being

---

[17] Cf. Barnes, 'Epicurean Signs', 92; *On Methods of Inference*, ed. De Lacy and De Lacy, 156.

[18] Gomperz, *Herkulanische Studien*, 13; F. Bahnsch, *Des Epicureers Philodemus Schrift Περὶ σημείων καὶ σημειώσεων: Eine Darlegung ihres Gedankengehalts* (Lyck: Wiebe, 1879), 5; Philippson, *De Philodemi libro*, 5 *et passim*; *On Methods of Inference*, ed. De Lacy and De Lacy, 156, 214 ff.; Sedley, 'On Signs', 240–1; Barnes, 'Epicurean Signs', 93–4. Natorp, *Forschungen*, 239, is sympathetic to the view that the opponents belong to the school of Posidonius.

[19] Cf. E. Asmis, *Epicurus' Scientific Method* (Ithaca, NY: Cornell University Press, 1984), 198; ead., 'Epicurean Semiotics', in G. Manetti (ed.), *Knowledge through Signs: Ancient Semiotic Theories and Practices* (Turnhout: Brepols, 1995), 155–85.

[20] Cf. Philippson, *De Philodemi libro*, 4; Natorp, *Forschungen*, 239; *On Methods of Inference*, ed. De Lacy and De Lacy, 98 n. 28, 159 n. 5; Sedley, 'On Signs', 241, Barnes, 'Epicurean Signs', 93 with n. 12; J. L. Stocks, 'Epicurean Induction', *Mind*, NS 34 (1925), 185–203, repr. in id., *The Limits of Purpose and Other Essays* (London: Benn, 1932), 266–93; on Dionysius himself see Schmekel, *Die Philosophie* 298–303.

viewed. In other words, I want to suggest, the opponents can be regarded as Stoics only if the Epicureans have misunderstood their position. But this misunderstanding is worth exploring in some detail, because it is motivated by deeper disagreements that promise to throw light on the issues at the heart of the ancient debate about the nature and purpose of inference from the evident to the non-evident.

3. Similarity vs. Elimination

Let us then postpone identifying the opponents as Stoics, and restrict ourselves to what can be said about them on the basis of the *De signis*. The controversy is between proponents of two methods of sign-inference. The Epicureans advocate the method of similarity, their opponents the method of elimination (ἀνασκευή).[21] Roughly speaking, the first prescribes how to project features that items of a certain type have been observed to have in our experience onto items of the same or a similar type lying outside our experience. It embraces what have traditionally been considered inductive inferences from a finite sample of a kind to a conclusion about its whole population—e.g. that from the fact that all human beings in our experience are mortal to the conclusion that all human beings, wherever they may be, are mortal—as well as others which we should call analogical—e.g. inferences from the behaviour of macroscopic bodies to that of atoms, or from that of bodies on earth to those in the heavens. As we have seen, the latter are especially important in Epicurean natural philosophy. But the method is the same in each case: similarity in another respect is projected via one, already acknowledged, relation of similarity. A preliminary characterization of the competing method of elimination advocated by the opponents is much harder to produce; indeed, as we shall see, it is surprisingly hard to say what that method is.

But the principal issue in dispute is clear. The opponents argue that only their method produces cogent inferences which necessitate their conclusions, and they attempt to establish that the method of similarity cannot give rise to inferences with the required cogency. Their arguments directly against the method of

[21] This is the translation favoured by Sedley, 'On Signs'; Barnes, 'Epicurean Signs', prefers 'rebuttal'. For reasons shortly to be explained, the De Lacys' choice of 'contraposition' will not do.

similarity, and the responses they elicited from the Epicureans, are by far the most straightforward and easily understood parts of the controversy. The opponents propose inferences with the same form as similarity inferences whose conclusions the Epicureans accept but which differ by reaching conclusions unacceptable to the Epicureans. If the opponents are right, then the method will mistakenly project features belonging to items in our experience onto items outside of our experience to which they do not belong. It will, for example, require us to conclude that atoms are coloured and perishable, because all objects in our experience are (XVII. 11 (ch. 24)). What is more, it will lead us to exclude (i.e. project the absence of) genuine possibilities because they are not attested in our experience. The opponents appeal to a very diverse set of unique phenomena to support this contention—the magnet is the only stone that draws metal, the square of four the only figure with a perimeter equal to its area—all of which would have been excluded had our experience been more limited (cf. I. 19 ff. (ch. 3); IX. 35–8 (ch. 14); XI. 9 ff. (ch. 16); XIV. 33 (ch. 20); XV. 13 (ch. 21)).

The Epicureans respond that the similarity method does not in fact license these inferences, a contention that they attempt to support by a more detailed specification of the method, showing how, when well and carefully applied, it excludes faulty inferences of these kinds. The question that remains is, of course, whether any amount of refinement in the method can guarantee that it will not sanction any faulty inferences. I want to put consideration of this part of the debate aside for the moment, however, in order to concentrate attention on the more difficult part of the argument set in train by the opponents' claim that only the method of elimination can give rise to legitimate sign-inferences; for it is in this part of the controversy that issues about the basic character and purpose of sign-inference are most fully aired. But clarity about the difference between the two methods is made harder to achieve by apparent variations in the Epicureans' own attitude towards elimination. There are passages which suggest each of the following three views.

(1) The method of elimination is coequal with, and independent of, the method of similarity. There are thus two methods of sign-inference, and the opponents' mistake is only to deprive us needlessly of a perfectly sound method and the inferences it sanctions. This view is suggested by the fullest discussion of the difference

between the two methods (XI. 26 ff. (ch. 17)), and by the contrasts
several times made between them (XIV. 2 ff. (ch. 19); XXVIII. 17–25
(ch. 45); XXXVII. 30–8 (ch. 58)).

(2) The method of elimination, though perfectly sound, is wholly
dependent on that of similarity. The similarity method pervades
that of elimination, and the latter is secured by the former (VII.
10–12 (ch. 10)). In consequence, the method of elimination has
no independent power to produce sound inferences without the
support of the similarity method (VIII. 21 ff. (ch. 13); cf. XVII. 8 ff.
(ch. 24)). If successful, this argument would show that the opponents' position is even weaker, for by rejecting similarity, they have
deprived themselves of the power to make any sign-inferences at all.

(3) The method of similarity is the *sole* method of sign-inference
(XXX. 37–XXXI. 1 (ch. 47)). If successful, this argument would be
still more destructive of the opponents' position.

The passages that point to (1) and (2) can be reconciled. Everything that Philodemus says that is suggestive of independence is
compatible with the claim that the method of elimination is ultimately dependent on the method of similarity. The apparent differences are to be explained by the dialectical contexts of the different passages. In some passages Zeno grants that the opponents'
method does capture some valid sign-inferences; his aim in them is
to show that even so, and with issues about the ultimate standing of
elimination put aside, elimination fails to capture a range of sign-
inferences that are captured by similarity. And since the bulk of the
passages pointing to both (1) and (2) come from the part of the *De
signis* whose source is Zeno, an interpretation that shows them to
be in harmony is to be preferred. But the passage on which (3) is
based cannot be so easily reconciled with the material cited in (1)
and (2), and it has been the object of much scholarly concern.[22] It
could be that a substantive disagreement is involved; the passage
denying that there is any method of sign-inference apart from similarity occurs in the fourth section of the *De signis*, and could thus
represent a disagreement with Zeno.[23]

A few lines after insisting that similarity is the only method of

---

[22] Cf. Bahnsch, *Des Epicureers Philodemus*, 21–2; *On Methods of Inference*, ed. De
Lacy and De Lacy, 122 n. 96; Schmekel, *Die Philosophie*, 340.
[23] Cf. Barnes, 'Epicurean Signs', 101–2, who defends an interpretation along these
lines.

sign-inference, however, Philodemus' source in the fourth section explains himself in this way:

> Those who say that the method by elimination depends on sign-inference by similarity, even if they say virtually the same thing that we do, by leaving the suspicion in their teaching that there are *two* methods of sign-inference intertwined with each other . . . [*there is a short lacuna in which they are presumably said to go wrong in some way*]. (XXXI. 8–17 (ch. 48))

What is more, he seems happy to speak of signs in connection with inferences by elimination (XXXI. 36–XXXII. 6 (ch. 49); XXXV. 31–2 (ch. 53); XXXVI. 21–4 (ch. 55)).[24] And he distinguishes two relations of consequence obtaining between the phenomena and non-evident matters, similarity and another that supports elimination, and appears to fault the opponents, just as Zeno had, for recognizing only the second (XXXVII. 1–XXXVIII. 8 (chs. 57–8)). It appears, then, that it is neither the soundness of the inferences by elimination admitted by Zeno, nor the application of the eliminative account to them, to which the source of this part of the *De signis* objects. Rather, he seems to want to reject any account of the relation between elimination and similarity which accords the standing of a method of sign-inference to the use of elimination. What his objections do show is that he cannot be Zeno. Indeed, it seems to be precisely Zeno's approach to which he objects, for as we have seen, it does give the impression that there are two methods of sign-inference by its talk of dependence. The explanation of why the source for this section wanted to reserve the status of a method of sign-inference for similarity in this way will have to wait until more clarity is achieved about the issues in dispute between the Epicureans and the partisans of elimination.

The difference between the two methods receives the most detailed attention at XI. 26–XII. 35 (ch. 17).[25] To understand this passage, it is essential first to remove a possible source of confusion. ἀνασκευή, which I have rendered as 'elimination', is translated throughout by the De Lacys as 'contraposition'.[26] But this passage, in which the clearest reference to the principle of contraposition is made, shows that this cannot be right, because in it Zeno answers

[24] Cf. Philippson, 'Zur Wiederherstellung', 37.

[25] Where Zeno answers the first two of the opponents' arguments; they are not preserved in the surviving part of the papyrus roll, which begins with the third argument.

[26] Who follow Bahnsch, *Des Epicureers Philodemus*, 8, on this point.

an argument of the opponents, who have striven to link elimination
with contraposition, by trying to show that elimination, though a
sufficient condition for contraposition, is not a necessary one; the
inconceivability to which the method of similarity gives rise is also
sufficient:

> For granted that 'If the first, then the second' is true whenever 'If not the
> second, not the first either' is true, it does not therefore follow that only the
> elimination method is cogent. For 'If not the second, not the first either'
> comes out true sometimes inasmuch as, when the second is hypothetically
> eliminated, by its very elimination the first is eliminated too—as in 'If
> there is motion, there is void', since, when the second is hypothetically
> eliminated, by its mere elimination motion will be eliminated too, so that
> such a case fits the elimination type—but sometimes not in this way but
> because of the very inconceivability of the first being, or being of this kind,
> but the second not being, or not being of this kind . . . (XI. 32–XII. 19
> (ch. 17))[27]

The part played by contraposition in the dispute, then, is that of a
minimum necessary condition accepted by both parties for a true
conditional.[28]

What is more, closer inspection reveals that something more than
bare contraposition is at issue. The requirement that a conditional
contrapose is met by conditionals which satisfy only the Philonian
account, according to which a conditional is true as long as it does
not begin with a true antecedent and conclude with a false consequent, a demand notoriously satisfied by conditionals such as 'If it
is day, then I am talking' (cf. S.E. *PH* 2. 110). Rather, Zeno seems
to have taken the relevant requirement to amount to the *impossibility* that the first obtain if the second does not (cf. XIV. 15–17
(ch. 19)). And he grants that both elimination and inconceivability
are sufficient conditions for this more restrictive requirement; the
opponents go wrong, he maintains, by supposing that only elimination is. It might seem that this more restrictive requirement
in terms of impossibility already specifies necessary and sufficient
conditions for a strict form of implication, however. Why, then, is it
treated here only as a necessary condition for a satisfactory account
of the conditional corresponding to a sign-inference? But perhaps
this is a misleading way of putting the question. The Epicureans'

---

[27] Cf. Sedley, 'On Signs', 245; Barnes, 'Epicurean Signs', 99. The translation is
that of Long and Sedley, *The Hellenistic Philosophers*, i, § 18 F. 1–4.
[28] Cf. ἀντιστρόφως XXXIII. 6 (ch. 50).

motives for participating in the debate were largely epistemologi-cal. They were less interested in the truth conditions of conditional propositions than in how it is we come to know that the implications exploited in inferences to conclusions about non-evident matters are true. Their demand, then, was for a perspicuous account of what it is about these implications by grasping which we come at the same time to see that those conditions are fulfilled.

In any case, it was agreed by the Epicureans and their opponents that these implications must satisfy the strengthened requirement that it is impossible for the first to obtain if the second does not; the issue in dispute was rather whether elimination was the only account of the conditional satisfying this requirement also able to perform the required epistemological task. This Zeno denies. In the passage cited above he allows that those conditionals in which, by the bare elimination of the first, the second is co-eliminated as well, are true by elimination; but he immediately goes on to insist that they do not exhaust the valid sign-inferences because others are true, roughly speaking, when it is not conceivable that the first obtain and the second fail to, a condition to which the method of similarity gives rise. The contrast is drawn in essentially the same terms several times elsewhere in the *De signis*, and inference by elimination is illustrated, as it is here, by that from motion to void (XIV. 11–23 (ch. 19); XXVIII. 16–25 (ch. 45); XXXVII. 7–17 (ch. 57); XXXVII. 34–XXXVIII. 8 (ch. 58)).

The identification of the Epicureans' opponents as Stoics de-pends on whether a link between the doctrine of elimination and known Stoic views can be established. The term ἀνασκευή has no special claim to be a Stoic one.[29] Indeed, it is better attested in Epicurean contexts, notably in Sextus Empiricus' account of Epi-curean epistemology (*M*. 7. 214).[30] It is, however, brought into relation with συνάρτησις ('connection') in the pseudo-Galenic trea-tise *De optima secta* (i. 116. 17 ff. K).[31] And as we have already

[29] It is not, so far as we know, a technical term in Stoic logic, as is optimistically suggested by the De Lacys (*On Methods of Inference*, 95 n. 19) and J.-P. Dumont, 'Confirmation et disconfirmation', in Barnes *et al.* (eds.), *Science and Speculation*, 273–303 at 288.

[30] Asmis, *Epicurus' Scientific Method*, 198–201, defends the view that it is an Epicurean concept on the strength of its use there.

[31] Cited by the De Lacys (*On Methods of Inference*, 95 n. 19) and Sedley, 'On Signs', 245–6. I think it is just as likely that the connection it reports between συνάρτησις and ἀνασκευή was made by a non-Stoic familiar with the Stoic view as that it was made by a Stoic. The practice of making such connections is not

noted, there are good reasons to suppose that the connective account of the conditional was advocated by Chrysippus and that, though the nature of the incompatibility referred to is not specified in the definition, it is logical rather than empirical.

Such an account appears well suited to the conditionals under discussion in the *De signis*. The way in which the opponents use elimination to construct alternative formulations of the Epicurean inferences would seem to support the identification of ἀνασκευή with συνάρτησις, understood in this way as a conceptually authorized necessary connection (IV. 10 ff. (ch. 6); XXXIV. 36 ff. (ch. 52)).[32] For in the reformulation that the opponents offer of the Epicureans' inference to the mortality of human beings wherever they may be, this conclusion is made to follow from premises in which the mortality belonging to human beings in our experience is taken to belong to them in so far as they are or *qua* human beings. And that the Epicureans took themselves to be engaged in a debate about the conditional is shown by the remark, in the fourth section of the *De signis*, that inconceivability, not elimination, is the best way of judging (κρίσις) the conditional, for which they use the technical term employed in Stoic logic, συνημμένον (XXXIII. 1 ff. (ch. 50)).[33]

But if elimination is to be identified with the Stoics' connective account of the conditional, and inconceivability is an Epicurean alternative, it becomes quite difficult to say what the difference between them is:

Elimination (συνάρτησις): $P{\rightarrow}Q$ iff not-Q is incompatible with P.

Inconceivability (ἀδιανοησία): $P{\rightarrow}Q$ iff (P&not-Q) is inconceivable.

To be sure, one could try to make something of the apparently more subjective and psychological character of the Epicurean cri-

unknown among medical writers. Galen, *De meth. med.* x. 126. 10–127. 3 K=fr. 45 Deichgräber, connects the indication of the medical Rationalists and 'emphasis', the fourth and apparently most stringent criterion of the conditional listed by Sextus Empiricus after συνάρτησις at *PH* 2. 110–12. But it may be enough that the two terms were brought into connection in this way, for the Epicureans could have used 'elimination' to characterize the Stoics' view, even if it was not the term the Stoics would have preferred themselves.

[32] Cf. Sedley, 'On Signs', 247.
[33] The term κρίσις is also used of the rival accounts of the conditional by Sextus Empiricus (*M.* 8. 245).

terion, inconceivability. But 'inconceivability' may well describe a perfectly objective relation between concepts.[34] And even if the Epicureans are open to criticism on this score, the charge of psychologism raises comparatively subtle issues; one does not expect rival 'psychological' and 'logical' conceptions to capture a strikingly different range of conditionals; rather, they should give different accounts of a more or less agreed sample of true conditionals. The *De signis*, however, presupposes both that they differ in their extensions and that the underlying difference because of which they do is too obvious to need any but the briefest explanation.

What is more, closer inspection suggests a more complicated relation between elimination and inconceivability than is implied by the contrast drawn in the passage at XI. 32 ff. (ch. 17) that we have already examined, where both are said to satisfy the test of contraposition. It is clear from this passage and others that the division between the two is meant to exhaust valid sign-inferences, but it is less clear that it is meant to be exclusive as well, despite the evidence which seems to link inconceivability solely with similarity (cf. XIV. 14–28 (ch. 19)). Although the Epicurean sources of the *De signis* may have disagreed among themselves about whether elimination inferences like that from motion to void are properly termed 'sign-inferences', none denied that they were valid inferences. The question naturally arises whether inconceivability applies to the conditionals exploited in them as well as those in similarity inferences. The method of similarity itself makes it clear that motion without void is impossible (cf. VIII. 28–32 (ch. 13)); it would be surprising if it were not also inconceivable. And in the fourth section of the *De signis* inconceivability is said to apply in inferences of both kinds, albeit in a passage whose train of thought is hard to follow (XXXVII. 24–XXXVIII. 8 (ch. 58)).[35]

---

[34] Cf. Barnes, 'Epicurean Signs', 125–6.

[35] The De Lacys begin a new chapter (58), at XXXVII. 24, and they take the distinction made there between the inferential transition to perceptible matters ($\alpha i \sigma \theta \eta \tau \acute{a}$) and that to those grasped by reason ($\tau \grave{a} \; \lambda \acute{o} \gamma \psi \; \theta \epsilon \omega \rho \eta \tau \acute{a}$) to introduce a new train of thought. Philodemus immediately proceeds: 'in spite of this difference, they disregard the distinctive features of each form of inference' (trans. De Lacys); and he goes on to distinguish, in a now familiar way, between similarity and elimination inferences, illustrated by inferences from motion to void and from the mortality of human beings in our experience to those outside it respectively. But the difference at issue must be between two relations of consequence, rather than between the perceptible and imperceptible items about which inferences are drawn. That distinction cuts across the division between similarity and elimination inferences;

It is plain that the opponents stand accused of ignoring the difference between two ways in which the second proposition can
follow the first in a conditional by assuming that there is only one:
namely, elimination. The difference is illustrated by the now familiar inferences from motion to void and from the mortality of
human beings in our experience to the mortality of human beings
everywhere. The passage concludes with the remark that the inconceivability is the same in both cases. This comes as a surprise after
the pains taken by the Epicureans to distinguish the two forms of
inference. But the view that the inconceivability is the same in both
cases could have been held by an Epicurean who regarded elimination and similarity as two distinct methods, both of which give rise
to inferences satisfying the inconceivability requirement. Although
the connections exploited by the corresponding conditionals are of
a different kind, it would, then, be equally inconceivable that the
second fail to obtain when the first does in both cases. And even
if the claim is a mistake of the opponents to which the Epicureans
object,[36] the Epicureans' objection would seem to be to the opponents' suggestion that the inconceivability was indistinguishable,
not to the view that it applies in both cases.

Perhaps, then, implications true by elimination should be re-

inference to conclusions about both types of item is possible by both methods. Indeed, on closer inspection, it is clear that the distinction with which the chapter
begins is between types of items about which similarity inferences, not inferences
quite generally, are drawn. For the transition from perceptibles to perceptibles is
said to arise in accordance with complete indistinguishability (ἀπαραλλαξία), while
the matters grasped by reason, to which the second kind of transition is made, are
characterized as analogous to the phenomena (cf. XIX. 25–9 (ch. 30)).

   This problem can be solved by taking XXXVII. 24 ff. more closely with the immediately preceding argument in the De Lacys' ch. 57 (cf. Sedley, 'On Signs', 261
n. 54; Natorp, *Forschungen*, 244, n. 2). At issue in that chapter is a distinction,
ignored by the opponents, between two kinds of consequence (ἀκολουθία); one, it
seems, supports elimination inferences, while the other is based on similarity. Consequence of the second kind is illustrated by an inference concerning the behaviour
of atoms, partially interrupted by a lacuna. And the distinction between inference
to perceptible and to theoretical entities that Philodemus immediately proceeds to
make is a parenthetical elaboration which is part of the account of similarity inference. The difference referred to at XXXVII. 29–30 is not this difference; rather,
reference to a difference here marks a resumption of the main topic, the difference
between two kinds of consequence. The train of thought would, then, be from the
opponents' failure to grasp the difference between the two forms of consequence to
a corresponding failure to understand the difference between two ways in which the
second proposition of a conditional follows the first.

   [36] Cf. Sedley, 'On Signs', 260 n. 53.

garded as a special case of inconceivability.[37] And this appears to
be confirmed by the claim, earlier in the same part of the *De signis*, that inconceivability, not elimination, is the best criterion of
the conditional (XXXII. 31–XXXIII. 9 (ch. 50)). For the Epicurean
complaint here seems to be that their opponents have conflated
one of two types of true conditional with the test of the truth of all
conditionals with the result that they reject conditionals not satisfying the elimination account, thereby needlessly forgoing the many
inferences based on implications true in virtue of similarity. The
criterion of inconceivability is best, then, because it captures all and
only the true conditionals, not merely a proper subset of them.[38]

The problem of how to understand the contrast between inconceivability and elimination, on the assumption that the latter is
equivalent to the Stoic criterion of the conditional, connection, still
remains, however. If elimination is connection, when the opponents
reject the Epicurean inference from the mortality of human beings
in our experience to the conclusion that human beings, wherever
they may be, are mortal, they mean to deny that the negation of
this conclusion is incompatible with the evidence from which it is
said to follow. The truth expressed in the observational claim does
not, on their view, exclude the possibility that things may be different elsewhere; or if it does, it is owing to an implicit reliance on
a premiss which goes beyond the experience from which the Epicureans claim to be making their inference: namely, that the human
beings in our experience are mortal *qua* and in so far as they are
human. But if this is so, they are hardly likely to have conceded
that it is nevertheless inconceivable that this conclusion fail to obtain if the evidence is true. Surely, they would have held that it is
conceivable. On the other hand, it is hard to see why, if elimination is connection, the Epicureans did not contest their opponents'
claim that the implications exploited by similarity inferences do

---

[37] If so, the instinct that led Philippson, *De Philodemi libro*, 41–2 with n. 7, to
treat elimination as a species of inconceivability was sound, though he went too far
when he made the difference between the two a matter of probability.

[38] The remark with which the passage concludes—that the opponents do not
lock down the inferences captured by elimination by any other means than inconceivability (XXXIII. 7–9)—could be taken to make the point made in several other
passages: namely, that elimination depends ultimately on the method of similarity
for the hypothetical connections that it exploits (cf. Sedley, 'On Signs', 260); but I
am inclined to think that it means that the conditionals to which elimination applies
are, like those produced by similarity, which is not mentioned here, true when, and
because, they satisfy the inconceivability criterion (cf. XV. 37 (ch. 21)).

not satisfy the elimination test together with the claim that it is conceivable that the evidence be such and the conclusion still not obtain.

The passage about inconceivability just examined affords some help by exposing a gap between the different claims that the Epicureans and their opponents were willing to make on behalf of elimination, behind which there may be a corresponding gap between the Epicureans' conception of elimination and that of their opponents (XXXII. 31–XXXIII. 9 (ch. 50)). It is clear from this passage that the opponents took themselves to be giving an account of the conditional satisfied by all and only true conditional propositions. The Epicureans, on the other hand, demote it to an account applying to some true conditionals, on a level with the method of similarity; each captures a distinct set of true conditionals, but what makes the conditionals to which they apply all true in the last analysis is that they satisfy the test of inconceivability. As we have seen, the Epicureans believe their opponents go wrong by taking a sufficient condition for being a true conditional to be necessary as well. In view of the difficulties that we have had distinguishing the Epicurean criterion of inconceivability from elimination, when it is understood as connection, it is worth considering the possibility that elimination, as it is understood by the Epicureans in *De signis*, is a relation narrower than the one the Stoics intended to capture with συνάρτησις.

There is evidence suggesting that it might be in a passage discussing contraposition that we have already discussed. After explaining that elimination applies when, by the elimination of the second, the first is co-eliminated as well, Zeno immediately goes on to characterize similarity and the inconceivability to which it gives rise in these terms:

> . . . but sometimes not in this way [by elimination] but because of the very inconceivability of the first being, or being of this kind, but the second not being, or not being of this kind: for instance, 'If Plato is a man, Socrates is a man too'. For given that this is true, 'If Socrates is not a man, Plato is not a man either' comes out true as well, not because by the elimination of Socrates Plato is co-eliminated, but because it is impossible to conceive of Socrates not being a man but Plato being a man. And that belongs to the similarity method. (XII. 14–30 (ch. 17))[39]

---

[39] The translation is that of Long and Sedley, *The Hellenistic Philosophers*, i, §

If elimination is equivalent to Stoic connection, it is hard to see anything more than a logical blunder here. When a conditional is composed of two existential propositions, it is easy enough to switch from speaking of the elimination of the items whose existence is asserted to talk of the negation of the propositions in which their existence is asserted.[40] But the logical form of the similarity implication cited as an example by Zeno does not permit such a straightforward translation into the idiom of item elimination. As he rightly notes, to say that if Plato is a man, it is inconceivable that Socrates not be a man, is not to say that Plato or his existence is in any way dependent on Socrates or his. But a proponent of connection would never maintain that it is. Rather, he would take the conditional at issue as equivalent to something like the following:[41]

If (Plato exists and he is a man), *then* not-(Socrates exists and he is not a man).

This conditional will satisfy the elimination account, understood as συνάρτησις, if and only if the contradictory of its consequent, i.e. 'Socrates exists and he is not a man', is incompatible with the antecedent, which seems very much like something the Epicureans should want to maintain. For what it is worth, the verb συναρτᾶσθαι is used both of connections of similarity between evident and non-evident matters (XXXIII. 28 (ch. 51)) and of narrowly eliminative relations recognized as such by the Epicureans (XXXV. 5 (ch. 53)).

Perhaps more significant is Zeno's answer to the opponents' argument from unique cases. One of their examples is the square of four, which alone has a perimeter equal to its area (1. 30–2 (ch. 3)). Zeno maintains that this distinctive characteristic, far from posing a problem for the method of similarity, is, on the contrary, discovered by experience. Anyone who takes away this variation among squares

---

18 F. 4–5, and it takes up immediately where the quotation above leaves off (cf. n. 27).

[40] Cf. Sedley, 'On Signs', 243. The De Lacys' awkward rendering 'the denial of Socrates', 'the denial of Plato', brings out the difficulty; one expects a that-clause to be denied, rather than an object. Dumont, 'Confirmation', 288, takes the passage to be about the co-elimination of 'the attribution of "man" to Plato' by the elimination of its application to Socrates, but there is nothing corresponding to 'the attribution of man' in the text. The assumption that relations between propositional items and their truth values is at issue is natural enough, but is it right?

[41] No special weight is to be placed precisely on this way of analysing the conditional. What is essential is that the conditional proposed by Zeno be seen to be of something like this order of logical complexity.

of four is in conflict with the phenomena (xv. 19–25 (ch. 21)).[42]
It would be ridiculous, he continues, for someone making sign-
inference from what is manifest to be in conflict ([μά|χε]σθαι) with
what is manifest. Thus Philodemus is willing to use the language
of 'taking away' and 'incompatibility' in connection with a similarity inference, and he immediately goes on to connect the inference described in these terms with inconceivability (xv. 26–xvi. 1
(ch. 21)).[43]

To be sure, it may be that incompatibility and inconceivability
could have been distinguished so that someone might consistently
maintain that it is inconceivable that the consequent does not necessarily obtain when the antecedent does, while denying that the
contradictory of the consequent of this conditional is incompatible
with its antecedent. But such a distinction would have been a subtle
one, requiring some explanation. As things stand, it is hard to see
why an Epicurean who held that it is inconceivable that the first
obtain while the second does not would not also want to maintain
that the contradictory of the consequent is incompatible with the
antecedent. There is, in other words, no obvious reason why a commitment to similarity could not be combined with an acceptance
of the connective account of the conditional. A proponent of the
connective account who wished to reject similarity implications, on
the other hand, would not, as Zeno implies, do so on the ground
that, for example, the elimination of Socrates leaves the existence
of Plato unaffected, but rather because, on his view, the contradictory of the consequent of the more complicated conditional cited
above is compatible with its antecedent. In sum, there is a question
why, despite the fact that there is room for argument on this point,
the debate is not about whether similarity implications satisfy the
elimination account, but rather whether their failure to do so, which
Zeno takes to be obvious, prevents them from giving rise to sound
inferences.

We should, then, take seriously the suggestion that, at least to the
Epicurean way of thinking, a narrower relation than that envisaged
by the connective account of the Stoics is at issue, a relation in some
way parallel to that of similarity and, like it, capable of support-

[42] αὐτοὶ γὰρ οἱ τετρά|[γωνοι ἀριθμοὶ] πάντες ἐκ πείρας | [βεβασανισμένοι] ταύτην
αὐ|τὴ[ν τὴν διαφο]ρὰν ἐν αὐτοῖς | ὑπά[ρχο]υσα[ν π]αρέδειξαν, ὥσ|τε τὸν ἀν[αιροῦν]τ᾽
αὐτὴν μά|χεσθαι τοῖς ἐνα[ρ]γ[έ]σι.

[43] Cf. Epicurus' own talk of conflict with the phenomena at *Ep. Pyth.* 98, discussed
above.

ing *some* of the conditionals satisfying the test of inconceivability. And we should also keep it in mind that there is a difference to which the Epicureans are unlikely to have attended as much as they should between the question concerning the conditions that must be satisfied by a pair of propositions, P and Q, if they are to be the antecedent and consequent of a true conditional and the question how one comes to grasp 'If P, then Q' as true. If, as I have already suggested, it was the latter question which most interested the Epicureans, then the relation in question should, like similarity, help answer this more epistemologically oriented question. It should be a relation that it is within the power of human beings to grasp, and by grasping which, one at the same time comes to see that the conditions that must be satisfied by a true conditional are fulfilled by 'If P, then Q'.[44] But what might that narrower relation be? The almost universal tendency has been to conclude, or consider the possibility, that elimination applies to causal-explanatory relations, roughly speaking between outcomes and their causally necessary conditions.[45] The inference from motion to void cited throughout the *De signis* satisfies this description.[46] And just such a causal connection seems to be at issue in a passage already cited from the fourth part of the *De signis*, where two forms of consequence (ἀκολουθία) are contrasted:

And because some unperceived things follow on appearances in such a way as to have a unique connection with them, since all appearances are products of elements or things made of elements or are conjoined with

[44] The first-person plural in Philodemus' account of the test of the true conditional may not be without significance (XXXIII. 1–7 (ch. 50)): 'the best test of the true conditional and the proper sign [is] when *we* are not able to conceive that the first obtains and the second does not and conversely'.

[45] Bahnsch, *Des Epicureers Philodemus*, 9–10; Philippson, *De Philodemi libro*, 39, 42; Barnes, 'Epicurean Signs', 100; Asmis, *Epicurus' Scientific Method*, 201; Sedley, 'On Signs', 261.

[46] If the opponents are Stoics, they cannot have accepted the inference, for they held that there is no void space within the cosmos and that motion nevertheless takes place within it. Curiously, the inference is cited in other contexts which show familiarity with Stoic logic, though whether this is evidence for the existence of a logically minded group of Epicureans, as is argued by J. Mau, 'Über die Zuweisung zweier Epikur-Fragmente', *Philologus*, 99 (1955), 93–111, can be disputed. (There are traces of Epicurean interest in proof theory; cf. S.E. *M*. 8. 337.) In the *De signis* at least, the example seems to be accepted for the sake of argument as one to which the elimination account would apply were it a valid inference in the first place. That is, the Stoics, if the opponents were Stoics, could have allowed the inference to enter the argument because the Epicurean account of why it goes through would, if true, have qualified it as an elimination inference (cf. *Ep. Hdt*. 40).

them in some other way—and for that reason it is judged that they are eliminated if the elements are not posited—our opponents formulate after this pattern the consequence of the unseen on the seen; but since there is consequence in another way, as when there is a similarity or analogy with similar or analogous things . . . (xxxvii. 1–12 (ch. 57))[47]

But the suggestion that elimination is at bottom a causal relation is confronted with a difficulty from the start. It is clear that the opponents took the elimination account to apply to the inferences, discussed several times in the *De signis*, from '*qua*' or 'in so far as' premisses (iv. 11 (ch. 6); xxxv. 3–4 (ch. 52)). And many of these inferences, e.g. that from the mortality of human beings in our experience in so far as they are human beings to the conclusion that human beings everywhere are mortal, do not immediately fit the causal-explanatory pattern exemplified by the inference from motion to void.

Matters are made more difficult by the way the Epicureans tend to evade those of the opponents' arguments that point to a broader conception of elimination which is closer to the connective account of the conditional. For in the case of the proposed inferences from *qua* premisses, the Epicureans treat elimination as the means by which the truth of the premisses is to be grasped, rather than regarding it as an account of the truth of the conditional exploited in the inference whose antecedent is the *qua* premiss. Thus, for example, the Epicureans represent elimination as their opponents' preferred test of the truth of the proposition 'Human beings are mortal *qua* and in so far as they are human beings' rather than of the conditional whose antecedent this is and whose consequent is 'Human beings everywhere are mortal' (iv. 11–13 (ch. 6); xxix. 4–12 (ch. 45)).[48]

Thus their response, that the point of departure proposed by the opponents, 'Human beings are mortal *qua* and in so far as they are human beings', cannot be *confirmed* or *established* by elimination (however much it may satisfy the eliminative account), but must itself be the conclusion of an inference by similarity (xvi. 31–xvii. 11 (ch. 24)), though potentially a fair epistemological point, fails to confront the logical point of their opponents if they are defending a connective account of the conditional which requires something like a *qua* premiss as an antecedent. At best, then, the extension

---

[47] The De Lacys' trans., slightly altered.
[48] xxxv. 3–4 (ch. 52) is neutral, but compatible with this view.

of the concept of elimination agreed upon for the sake of much of the argument satisfies the description 'causal-explanatory', but it cannot be what the opponents *meant* by elimination, or how the Epicureans—to the extent that they allowed that it applied some-how to the *qua* inferences or statements—understood it, even if they saw causal-explanatory relations as its sole semiotically interesting application.

But if the narrower relation for which we are looking cannot be a causal-explanatory one in this way, the stress on causal connec-tions in the *De signis* may, none the less, have put us on the right track. I should like to suggest that, at least in the context of the *De signis*, elimination is best understood as a relation between items that are in the first instance non-propositional, of which that be-tween outcomes and their necessary causal conditions is only the most conspicuous and semiotically useful example. Such a relation between two items holds precisely when, by the elimination of the second, the first is co-eliminated, just as it is put in the *De signis*. It holds between an outcome and its causally necessary conditions, to be sure, but also between an object and each of its essential properties and between pairs of necessarily co-instantiated proper-ties. Such an account of elimination would apply to relations of the kind exemplified by that obtaining between motion and void (on the Epicurean view) as well as those expressed in *qua* propositions. As required, it conspicuously fails to hold of similarity relations. And in many cases at least, it can be seen to obtain by a kind of thought experiment which brings to light the inconceivability which is the essential mark of the true conditional according to the Epicureans. What is more, this understanding of elimination also exhibits some affinities with philosophical applications of elimina-tion outside Philodemus and Epicureanism, especially when the term ἀναιρεῖν, also used by Philodemus, is allowed to capture the same notion (cf. XII. 7–12). Elimination was applied by Aristotle, and in the Pyrrhonian tradition, as a test of conceptual dependence, mutual in the case of relatives like father–son or double–half, uni-directional in that of items related as posterior to prior like human being–mammal.[49]

---

[49] Cf. Sedley, 'On Signs', 246–7 with nn. 22, 23; Barnes, 'Epicurean Signs', 131, additional note c. There is of course nothing about the terms ἀνασκευάζειν and ἀναιρεῖν or the basic idea of 'taking away' which they express that makes them inapplicable to the negation of propositions, and ἀναιρεῖν is used by Galen in just

But viewed in this way, elimination cannot be identified with the Stoics' connective account of the conditional. For connection is a logical relation between the component propositions of a conditional that is meant to obtain *whenever* the second follows the first. It was presumably intended to capture relations between outcomes and their causally necessary conditions, when properly formulated as conditionals, but it was not confined to them or the broader class of eliminations just described. The causal relation between non-propositional items to which elimination applies supports a logical relation of consequence between propositions, viz. connection, that also obtains in cases where relations of the kind which elimination captures are absent. For example, a relation of consequence obtains between the conjunction of the premises of a valid argument and its conclusion. But if elimination cannot be identified with connection, then either the Epicureans' opponents are not Stoics who adhere to this view or the view of elimination with which they are saddled is a distortion of their real position.

In view of the circumstantial evidence pointing to the Stoa, the second possibility merits serious consideration.[50] And I should like to suggest that an explanation along these lines is a plausible solution to some of the difficulties presented by the *De signis*. For the mistake it imputes to the Epicureans is not an unnatural one: to see a disagreement about the nature of consequence, when the real disagreement between them and the Stoics, if it is they, was over

this way in his account of the relation of deficient consequence (or contrariety) between two propositions (*Inst. log.* 10. 9 Kalbfleisch), and by Aristotle throughout the *Topics*.

[50] That it is possible to take principles of Stoic logic intended to govern propositions as applying to subpropositional items instead is proved by the frequency with which it has been done. As an example of the first indemonstrable—'If the first, then the second. But the first. Therefore the second'—ps.-Ammonius gives: 'If man, then animal. But the first. Therefore, the second' (*In an. pr.* 68. 25 Wallies; I owe the example to Mates, *Stoic Logic*, 2 n. 4). Also worth considering in this connection are the totally hypothetical syllogisms, on which see I. M. Bochenski, *La Logique de Théophraste* (Collectanea Friburgensia, NS 32; Freiburg, 1947), 111–16, esp. 114. It is also telling that Natorp, *Forschungen*, 241, with this passage of Philodemus in view, takes the Stoics to require: 'ist A, so ist auch B, denn wäre nicht B, so würde A nicht sein; oder, die A als A (sofern sie A sind) sind B, also sind alle A B'; elsewhere he takes elimination to be the test of a 'beständige Verknüpfung im Dasein' (246). Clearly relations between subpropositional items rather than propositions is at issue. Though this is a mistaken reading of Stoic views on the conditional, it is, I should like to suggest, the right way to understand elimination in the *De signis*.

which inferences belong to the concept's extension.[51] As we noted earlier, on this view, the Epicureans might have done better to contest the opponents' claim that similarity inferences do not satisfy the elimination requirement. For it would not obviously have been out of place for an Epicurean to argue that careful study of the phenomena, in the course of which, as they put it, not a trace or spark of opposition presents itself, shows that all claims about matters outside our experience representing them as dissimilar in certain respects are excluded because in conflict with our experience. Indeed, as we have already observed, they do sometimes speak this way (XV. 19–25 (ch. 21)).[52]

Such a mistake would have been that much easier, as the examples agreed upon for the sake of argument by both parties, such as the inference from motion to void, as the Epicureans understood it, satisfied a description in terms of elimination. Their mistake, then, would have been to pass illegitimately from the fact that the conditional premises of the inferences admitted by the Stoic opponents (if only for the sake of argument) were, in Epicurean terms, true by elimination to the conclusion that to be true by elimination in this way is what it is to be a true conditional according to the Stoics.[53] It may also have been a mistake to which the Epicureans were predisposed, because for reasons of their own they had already distinguished between inferences grounded in similarity and those based on causal connections. Thus, in his exposition of atomic theory Lucretius directs his readers' attention to the motion of dust motes visible in the rays of the sun, which affords an unusual example of a piece of evidence exemplifying both semiotic relations. It is, he tells us, an image and simulacrum from which we may infer (*conicere*) the behaviour of the invisible atoms, which are also in perpetual motion; but, he immediately goes on to add, this phenomenon is still more worthy of attention, for the visible motion of the dust motes signifies the hidden motion of the atoms because it

---

[51] This would explain Demetrius' identification of the opponents' failure to understand the relation between elimination and similarity as their most significant and pervasive error (XXVIII. 15 (ch. 45)), for he seems to be chiding them for taking the Epicureans' inferences as failed attempts to produce elimination inferences when, as he sees it, they obviously do not satisfy the elimination requirement, but are perfectly good inferences all the same because they do satisfy the similarity account (XXVIII. 15–25 (ch. 45)).

[52] Cf. n. 42 above.

[53] Cf. Natorp, *Forschungen*, 246, who seems to have done just this.

is—to paraphrase freely—the necessary causal precondition of that motion (2. 112–41).[54]

I shall therefore treat the opponents as Stoics from now on. If this is right, the Epicurean argument against elimination is wide of the mark. Their cause was not advanced by their attempt to distinguish kinds of conditionals. Their real task was to vindicate the claim of a class of implications to be true. But the kind they make up is not a logician's kind, distinguished by an interesting logical feature; as we have seen, all the difficulties raised against similarity implications from the point of view of the connective account of the conditional could equally well be raised from that of inconceivability. The disagreement between the Epicureans and their opponents was less about the essential character of the relation of consequence than about when and where it obtains. Let us now examine the rest of the Epicureans' case in the light of these conclusions.

4. Similarity as the Ultimate Basis of Signification

The Epicureans resort several times to the charge that the opponents' arguments are self-refuting. Thus the source of the fourth section of *De signis* maintains that when the opponents argue on the basis of the unique phenomena already experienced that items outside our experience may differ from those within it, they employ the method of similarity themselves, and thus effect a reversal of their own position (περικατωτροπή) (XXIX. 24–XXX. 15 (ch. 46)). Zeno too lodges this complaint against the opponents (XI. 9–26 (ch. 16)), and he objects to their argument that the sun is not, as Epicurus maintains, about as large as it seems because, like other rapidly moving objects, it can appear very slowly from behind an obstacle only if it is very large, on the grounds that it employs the method of similarity (X. 20–6 (ch. 15)). In a similar way, the Pyrrhonists' arguments against sign-inference and demonstrations were said by their opponents to be instances of sign-inference and demonstration, and thus to undermine themselves (S.E. *M.* 8. 278, 281–2, 480–1). But as their response showed, this kind of argument is a treacherous weapon. For the opponents may reply, as the Pyrrhon-

---

[54] 'hoc etiam magis haec animum te advertere par est | corpora quae in solis radiis turbare videntur, | quod tales turbae motus quoque materiai | significant clandestinos caecosque subesse' (2. 125–8).

ists often did, that, on the assumption that the method of similarity is sound, which they have adopted only for the sake of argument, it follows that it is unsound, so that the charge of self-refutation can be levelled with more justice against the method of similarity itself.[55]

More promising is the argument that specific inferences to which the opponents *are* committed depend on similarity. Philodemus maintains that the opponents' own arguments that human beings are receptive to wounds, illness, old age, and death, and that there are no Pans and Centaurs, employ the method of similarity (XXXI. 23–36 (ch. 48)). But the Epicureans concentrated on a less anecdotal, more systematic, argument in the same spirit. As we have already observed, they repeatedly charge that their opponents' preferred method, elimination, is wholly dependent on the method of similarity, so that attacks on the latter threaten to demolish the former as well. The point is especially clear in the part of the *De signis* due to Zeno. According to him, the method of similarity pervades that of elimination, which is, he maintains, confirmed or secured by similarity (VII. 8–11 (ch. 10)). He returns to this point in the next column, where he explains in some detail how the inference from motion to void, which he accepts as a genuine instance of sign-inference by elimination, ultimately derives its cogency from the method of similarity (VIII. 21–IX. 9 (ch. 13)). It exploits a necessary connection between motion and void, so that the first is impossible without the second. But, according to Zeno, we come to grasp this connection by seeing that there is space in all cases of motion in our experience. As a result of our assessment (*epilogismos*) of these cases, we take it that all moving objects move in similar conditions, and we infer (σημειούμεθα) that motion is impossible without void.[56] In other words, the necessary connection between motion and void exploited by the elimination inference from the existence of motion to that of void is itself the conclusion of a sign-inference by similarity from the behaviour of moving objects in our experience to that of moving objects in any place and of any size.

[55] The Epicureans may not have grasped the dialectical character of their opponents' argument. Cf. *On Methods of Inference*, ed. De Lacy and De Lacy, 103 n. 40.

[56] On *epilogismos* in Epicurus and Philodemus see M. Schofield, 'Epilogismos: An Appraisal', in M. Frede and G. Striker (eds.), *Rationality in Greek Thought* (Oxford: Oxford University Press, 1996), 221–37. Schofield proposes 'assessment' as the best translation. Cf. also Sedley, 'Epicurus on Nature', 27–34, esp. 31.

The source of the fourth section holds a similar view (XXXV. 35–XXXVI. 7 (ch. 53)), but, as we have seen, he disagrees with Zeno about the implications which the priority of the similarity method holds for the standing of elimination; at least some of the time he appears to withhold the status of a sign-inference from elimination inferences altogether (XXX. 37–XXXI. 1 (ch. 47)). We should now be in a better position to understand why. The first thing to notice is how similar elimination inferences and so-called *qua* truths are on the Epicurean view. Zeno maintains that *qua* truths, e.g. that human beings are mortal in so far as they are human, are established through the method of similarity, not by elimination (XVII. 3–11 (ch. 24)). The point is made in considerably more detail in the fourth section, whose source immediately goes on to apply it to elimination inferences as well (XXXV. 4 ff. (ch. 53)). The transition from *qua* relations to eliminative signs is somewhat obscure, but the train of thought seems to be this. First, the source argues that *qua* relations are established by the method of similarity. For example, as a result of surveying many and various human beings, who, though they vary in other respects, show no variation in respect of mortality, we come to see that humanity is inseparable from mortality in such a way that human beings are mortal in so far as they are and *qua* human beings. He then observes that a distinctive feature of these relations 'is not so in the case of things apprehended only through the elimination of the sign' (XXXV. 29–31 (ch. 53)) (trans. De Lacy). But he immediately goes on to say that, even in these cases, the relation exploited in the inference is secured by the method of similarity, giving as examples the connection between motion and void and that between smoke and fire.

What is obscure is the distinctive feature said here to belong to *qua* relations but not to sign-inferences by elimination. Clearly the difference is not that the first rests on similarity, while the second does not; according to this passage, they both do. What is more, semiotic relations like that between motion and void are not distinguished from *qua* relations by the fact that *elimination* applies only to them. The passage is a response to the opponents' charge that the Epicureans' inferences are valid only if from a *qua* premiss, and that such inferences make use of the method of elimination (XXXV. 1–4 (ch. 52); cf. IV. 5–10 (ch. 6)). The Epicureans' answer does not deny that elimination applies to *qua* premisses, but, rather, insists that such premisses are secured by a prior application of the method of similarity, a feature that they share with relations of the kind exemplified by that between motion and void. What is secured by the method of elimination, if anything, is that void exists; but the relation between motion and void that supports this inference is secured by the method of similarity no less than *qua* relations are. *Qua* relations differ from those exploited by elimination inferences, it seems, by belonging to one of the four types, discussed in the immediately preceding section, to which the expressions '*qua*' and 'in so far as' are applied (XXXIII. 33 ff. (ch. 52)).[57] On the other hand, the feature that sets relations like those between motion and void and smoke and fire apart from *qua* relations is that they support sign-inferences.[58] *Qua* relations do not support sign-inferences; rather, they are the conclusions of such inferences.[59]

Similarity, then, gives rise to sign-inferences that secure necessary connections, some of which, like that between motion and void, can in turn support further inferences by elimination. The sharp distinction between similarity and elimination inferences on which the Epicureans insist, and the priority they grant to the former, are natural in the light of this conclusion. This probably explains why the source of the fourth section objects to his colleagues', particularly Zeno's, way of characterizing elimination as dependent on similarity, on the grounds that it suggests that there are two methods of equal standing interwoven with each other, even if, in so doing, they say virtually the same thing as he does (XXXI. 8–16 (ch. 48)). But how is his seeming willingness to speak of signs in connection with elimination to be reconciled with the apparently stronger claim, made a few lines earlier, that there is no correct method of sign-inference besides that of similarity (XXX. 37–8 (ch. 47))?

I offer the following speculative suggestion. The Epicureans embrace a conception of sign-inference according to which it is the means by which conclusions with theoretical significance are inferred from the starting-points afforded by observation. That

[57] Cf. Barnes, 'Epicurean Signs', 120–3, for a full discussion of the varieties of *qua* truth distinguished in this passage.

[58] The Epicureans' claim to make sign-inferences in accordance with each of the four varieties of *qua* statement probably means, then, that the conclusions of the sign-inferences will belong to each of the four types (XXXIV. 27–9 (ch. 52)).

[59] On this point I agree with A. A. Long, 'Reply to Jonathan Barnes, "Epicurean Signs"', in J. Annas and R. H. Grimm (eds.), *Oxford Studies in Ancient Philosophy*, suppl. vol. (Oxford: Oxford University Press, 1988), 140–3, who rejects Barnes's view ('Epicurean Signs', 120–1) that the Epicureans 'agree with their opponents that valid sign inferences must sometimes rest on *qua* truths'.

human beings are mortal *qua* human, that they are mortal wherever they may be, or that motion is impossible without void, are
all conclusions of the required type. Some of them will involve
truths about items lying outside the reach of direct observation,
so-called theoretical entities; others will be about observable items,
but about them *qua* of a certain nature. In either case, to grasp such
a truth is to grasp a truth that goes beyond what is given in experience, although it must ultimately be derived from experience. To
the Epicurean way of thinking, the method of similarity is alone
capable of inferring theoretical conclusions of this kind from the
starting-points afforded by observation, such as that human beings
in our experience are mortal, or that objects move in our experience
only when there is space into which they may move.

   If the function of a method of sign-inference is to effect semiotic transitions of this kind, elimination inferences will not qualify.
It may appear that the inference from motion to void belongs beside that from the mortality of human beings in our experience
to the mortality of human beings wherever they may be. But on
the Epicurean view, the existence of void does not follow from the
phenomenon of motion alone, but from that phenomenon taken together with the fact that motion is impossible without void; whereas
the mortality of human beings always and everywhere does follow
by similarity from the phenomena alone, without any further assumptions which need themselves to be inferred, as does the extra
assumption on which the first inference depends. That void is implied by motion, then, belongs beside the *conclusion* that human
beings wherever they may be are mortal rather than the inference
by which this conclusion is inferred.[60]

   Perhaps this is part of the point of fragment 1, where Philodemus seems to say that the composition or construction (σύνθεσις) of
sign-inferences does not come about by elimination, but is grasped
through the sense impressions (φαντασίαι) that lend themselves to
this purpose (1–6).[61] At all events, it appears to be the point of the

---

   [60] But why is the Epicurean method of similarity not itself dependent on just such
an assumption: viz., as the opponents suggest, that matters outside our experience
are similar to those within it (II. 25 ff. (ch. 5))? The account of how experience gives
rise to inconceivability is the Epicureans' answer.

   [61] Cf. Philippson, *De Philodemi libro*, 33, on whose restorations the text printed
by the De Lacys depends (ibid. 7; 'Zur Wiederherstellung', 12). 'That lend them-
selves to this purpose' is my guess at the meaning of φαν | [τασιῶν] τῶν τὰς χρείας
ἀποδι | [δουσῶν.

passage near the beginning of the fourth section where the term 'composition' also occurs in the explanation of the source's refusal to countenance any method of sign-inference apart from similarity:

But our opponents, in attempting to discredit the method of sign-inference according to similarity, render all non-evident matters unsignified. For there is no correct method of sign-inference other than this. But although [εἰ καἰ] the leading signs [τὰ προηγούμενα τῶν σημείων] are sometimes dissimilar and sometimes even opposite, of necessity they receive the composition [σύνθεσις] that proceeds in accordance with the method of similarity if they are going to demonstrate, as we established in the earlier account. (XXX. 33–XXXI. 8 (ch. 47))

The passage is a cryptic one, but I should like to suggest that it makes the most sense if viewed as concerned with the method of composing or constructing sign-inferences. In it the Epicurean claim that similarity is the sole method of signification is, as it seems, supported, by the further claim that, even in conditions that suggest otherwise, the composition of the sign-inference is in accordance with similarity. Every sign-inference, then, is put together in accordance with the method of similarity.

But is every genuine sign-inference in turn a similarity inference? It all depends on the circumstances which suggest that similarity is not the only method of signification. The principal difficulty is the reference to 'leading signs'. It is usually assumed that the term is being used in a technical sense, but that sense has long puzzled interpreters.[62] It occurs in three other passages in the fourth section (XXXII. 2 (ch. 49); XXXVI. 19 (ch. 55), 33–4 (ch. 56)).[63] In the second of these Philodemus' source warns against the danger of ignoring the variety of leading signs; for, he continues, had the opponents paid proper attention to it, 'they would never have judged it right to make use only of those signs which are eliminated if the non-evident fails to obtain' (XXXVI. 17–24 (ch. 55)). Are the signs they are led to neglect in this way those linked to the matters they signify by similarity? If they are, leading signs should embrace examples of both the elimination and the similarity types. The impression that they do is strengthened by the first of the three passages:

They disregard the fact that we do not say that all things are signified by

---

[62] Cf. *On Methods of Inference*, ed. De Lacy and De Lacy, 121 n. 95; Sedley, 'On Signs', 262 n. 55.

[63] I assume that προηγούμενον and προηγητικόν are synonymous, but perhaps this is not so (cf. *On Methods of Inference*, ed. De Lacy and De Lacy, 123 n. 98).

similarity when the leading is taken as a sign, but some only. Thus they ask in cases of elimination what sort of similarity we have, as though they will not be asked in the case of similars how elimination applies, and even more in the case of opposites. (XXXI. 36–XXXII. 8 (ch. 49))[64]

Surprisingly, this passage appears to put sign-inferences by similarity alongside those that proceed by elimination. The opponents are pictured as pointing to sign-inferences by elimination, and asking the Epicureans to identify an element of similarity in them. Presumably these are inferences that the Epicureans accept, such as that from motion to void and that from smoke to fire. The Epicurean response is to observe that the opponents could be asked with equal justice to explain how elimination applies in cases of sign-inference by similarity.[65]

The circumstances suggesting that similarity is not the sole method of signification mentioned in the preceding column seem, then, to be precisely those adduced by the opponents here: namely, that some leading signs are not linked to the matters they signify by a relation of similarity, but are dissimilar or even opposite to them. Motion is not similar to void, smoke is not similar to fire. (The lack of examples makes it hard to cite a sign which is the opposite of the matter it signifies.) According to the source of the fourth section, the proper Epicurean response is that even in these cases the *composition* of the sign-inference is by the method of similarity. These should be cases in which the relation on which the inference depends, though it satisfies the elimination account, is secured by the method of similarity. If this is right, then the source of the fourth section allows talk of 'signs' in connection with elimination inferences. What he denies is that there is a *method* that makes possible the composition of sign-inference apart from simi-

---

[64] As Sedley notes ('On Signs', 262 n. 55), a translation with a different emphasis is possible: 'They overlook the fact that we do not say that all sign-inferences by similarity are made by apprehending the *antecedent* [προηγούμενον] sign, but only some.' But this suggestion is motivated by the conviction that the fourth section does not countenance eliminative signs, against which I have already argued. What is more, the rendering I have adopted seems to fit the immediately following lines better. I do not know, however, what to make of the reference to opposites, or whether it is to be connected with the reference to opposites in the preceding column (XXXI. 3 (ch. 47)).

[65] Presumably, the inferences they have in mind are or should be accepted by their opponents; in the next column, in an argument already mentioned, the Epicureans point to similarity inferences to which, they claim, the opponents are committed (XXXI. 26–35 (ch. 48)).

larity; his complaint against his colleagues is that they suggest that there are two *methods* of sign-inference with their talk of dependence.[66]

Such a position is perfectly consonant with the Epicurean view that, though it applies to some inferences, elimination does not by itself give rise to, or secure, inferences. Suppose we grant the source of the fourth section the notion of a complete or autonomous sign-inference. An inference of this kind must win new knowledge by inferring a conclusion from grounds which are known independently of inference. Similarity inferences satisfy the requirement by starting from the phenomena which are grasped non-inferentially by direct observation. Elimination inferences do not, because they fail to put their conclusions into an inferential relation with the evidence directly given in the phenomenon, but instead make assumptions which themselves need to be established by sign-inference; when they are supplemented so that the eliminative relations they exploit are shown to follow from the phenomena, the complete inference produced in this way is by similarity. According to the Epicureans, the opponents' mistake is to suppose that elimination provides direct epistemic access to eliminative inferences when it only characterizes a relation exploited in those inferences that we can come to grasp only by means of similarity (cf. XVII. 3–8 (ch. 24).[67]

---

[66] I am inclined to agree with Philippson, 'Zur Wiederherstellung', 38, and disagree partially with Sedley, 'On Signs', 262 n. 55, that the emphasis is on 'method' rather than 'sign-inference' here, but the matter is a complicated one. The term 'sign' is used several times in connection with elimination inferences, in a way that makes it hard to view them merely as quotations of the opponents, and the verb form σημειοῦσθαι seems to me to be used of elimination inferences at XXXI. 38 (ch. 49). But the term 'sign-inference', or a sense of it, may be restricted to similarity inferences. Such an assumption might help to explain the otherwise puzzling argument at XXXVI. 24 ff. (ch. 56). There Philodemus' source accuses the opponents of going astray by failing to take account of the fact that the expression 'sign' is used sometimes of the phenomenon with reference to which the sign-inference is composed, and sometimes of the sign-inference itself. Struck by the difference between leading signs (actually leading ἐναργήματα) and the non-evident matters they signify, the opponents mistakenly do away with the method of similarity by confounding the two, i.e. presumably the two senses of 'sign', the sign proper, which is unlike the signified, and the sign-inference, which in the last analysis is by the method of similarity. If this is right, even though motion is a sign of void, the transition from motion to void must in the last analysis be viewed as part of a sign-inference by similarity.

[67] If this is right, Demetrius is the odd man out when he remarks (XXIX. 4 ff. (ch. 45)): 'it is an error not to have perceived that the description "insofar as this thing is of this description" . . . is not in all cases captured through elimination but many are captured also through similarity, as for example, that the man who has been beheaded, insofar as he has been beheaded, since his head does not grow again,

5. Epicurean Sign-inference

Although the Epicurean position promises to infer all the conclusions that Epicurean natural philosophy requires from the evidence afforded by experience alone without the aid of a special
faculty of reason, which is the distinctive mark of the rationalism
that we investigated in Study II above, it will hardly qualify as a
form of empiricism either. None the less, the distinctive character
of the Epicureans' position in the *De signis* emerges most clearly
from a comparison with the empiricism that we also investigated in
Study II.

Readers of Philodemus have often been struck by the affinities between the Epicurean views he defends and the position of the medical Empiricists.[68] Thus, like the Empiricists, Philodemus speaks
frequently of *epilogismos*; he distinguishes between one's own experience (πεῖρα) and the testimony of others (ἱστορία), just as they
did between autopsy and history (XVI. 35–7 (ch. 24); cf. e.g. Galen,
De sect. ingred. iii. 3. 19–20 *SM*); and the transition according to
similarity of which the Epicureans speak at least sounds very much
like the transition to the similar, the method by which the medical Empiricists generate suggestions about how to treat new cases
unlike those of which they have had past experience.[69] Most sig-
nificantly, once we have realized that the paradigmatic Epicurean
sign-inference is not from motion to void, but rather from the
co-occurrence of motion and space in our experience (VIII. 33–5
(ch. 13); XXXV. 35 (ch. 53)), it becomes clear that the Epicureans
and Empiricists share a conception of sign-inference that assigns
the crucial part to the projection of observed regularities. In view of
these affinities, it is regrettable that Philodemus' promise to discuss
the views of some physicians about inference by similarity is not
fulfilled in any of his surviving works (XXXVIII. 25 ff. (ch. 60)).

Yet Sextus Empiricus treats Epicurus as a partisan of indicative
signification (*M*. 8. 177), and the inference from motion to void and

---

dies . . .' (trans. De Lacys); for this seems to indicate that some *are* captured by
elimination (cf. Sedley, 'On Signs', 240 n. 3).

[68] Cf. Philippson, *De Philodemi libro*, 44 ff., who goes so far as to hold that Zeno
of Sidon was directly influenced by the Empiricists (56); P. H. and E. A. De Lacy,
'Supplementary Essay III: The Sources of Epicurean Empiricism', in *On Methods
of Inference*, 165–82 at 165 ff.; Frede, 'An Empiricist View of Knowledge', 241–2.

[69] Cf. Philippson, *De Philodemi libro*, 56; Natorp, *Forschungen*, 239 n. 2.

many other Epicurean inferences like it appear to be paradigms of the kind of reasoning rejected by the Empiricists as instances of empty rationalist speculation (cf. Galen, *De sect. ingred.* iii. 9. 6–7; 10. 5–10 *SM*). The extent to which the two schools part ways is especially clear in a passage where Philodemus treats the relation between motion and void and that between smoke and fire as alike secured by the method of similarity (xxxv. 4–xxxvi. 8 (ch. 53)). The latter is of course a favourite example of the commemorative sign (cf. S.E. *PH* 2. 100; *M.* 8. 152); the former would be regarded by a medical Empiricist as an indicative sign. In Epicurean terms, the Empiricists confine sign-inference to conclusions about matters that are indistinguishable from those furnishing it with its point of departure, while the Epicureans themselves also permit inferences to conclusions about matters analogous to the phenomena, which they describe as grasped by reason, precisely the description under which they are declared inaccessible to human knowledge by the Empiricists (xxxvii. 24 ff. (ch. 58)).[70]

What is more, although the Epicureans insist that some—indeed the most basic and essential—sign-inferences are not by elimination, and further, that even the eliminative inferences they accept are secured by similarity inferences, they agree that relations of elimination when grasped are grasped as necessary (cf. viii. 30–ix. 2 (ch. 13); xii. 27 (ch. 17)). In other words, the Epicureans seem to deny only that there is a non-inferential grasp of necessary relations of the eliminative types; but their method infers truths that are necessary and to some of which they are willing to apply '*qua*' and 'in so far as' in precisely the same way as their opponents. Nor, as we have seen, do the Epicureans show any trace of the Empiricists' reluctance to speak of the natures of things (xv. 11 (ch. 20); xviii. 1 (ch. 25); xxiv. 8 (ch. 39); xxvii. 24 (ch. 43); xxxiii. 17 (ch. 51)). All of these features of the Epicureans' view suggest an affinity with the Rationalists.

The Epicureans of the *De signis* seem, then, to have combined features of rationalism and empiricism that were regarded by their adherents as irreconcilable. Setting out from starting-points that at least at first appear like those from which Empiricists proceed, the Epicureans infer all the necessary, potentially explanatory, relations a Rationalist could wish from a basis that he and his Empiricist counterpart agree is inadequate. What is more, the distinction

[70] Cf. n. 35.

between inferences from one evident item to another and those from evident to the non-evident, though recognized by the Epicureans, has nothing like the importance for them that it had in the debate between Rationalists and Empiricists (XXXVII. 24 ff. (ch. 58)).[71] In Sextus Empiricus a different kind of signifying relation is made responsible for revealing each of the two kinds of item inferred by signs, naturally and temporarily non-evident matters. Both the kind of item revealed and the kind of relation between it and the sign by which it is inferred enter into the characterization of indicative and commemorative signification (*PH* 2. 99; *M*. 8. 156). But nothing—certainly not the distinction between elimination and similarity—corresponds to this distinction among relations of signification in the Epicurean positions. Inferences to one kind of item depend on much the same kind of grounds and insights into the nature of things as inferences to the other, so that the inference from smoke to fire can rub shoulders with that from motion to void.

  This divergence between Empiricism and Epicureanism is in part due to their different conceptions of experience. An austere conception of experience according to which it is confined to the grasp of facts *that* and cannot reveal the cause because of which was common to medical Rationalism and Empiricism and essential to the characterization of their differences. Experience taken in this way is what the Rationalists denied was adequate to the constitution of the medical art and the Empiricists maintained was sufficient to this end. As we have already noted, Epicurus' conception of experience was much more generous than this. And the Epicureans of the *De signis* seem to share the generous conception of the founder. Their reply to the opponents' argument that the method of similarity licenses inferences to conclusions which the Epicureans reject, e.g. that atoms have colour or are perishable, is a case in point (v. 1 ff. (ch. 7)). For they insist that it is not *qua* body that observable bodies have these features; observable bodies, they maintain, are perishable in so far as they participate in a *nature* opposed to the corporeal: namely, void. And the way in which talk of a thing's nature and its possession of features *qua* thing of a certain kind seems to be entering into the characterization of the point of departure for inference would have been viewed with suspicion by Empiricists and Rationalists alike.

  The Epicureans' account of how the properties that can legiti-

  [71] Cf. n. 35.

mately be projected become salient in the course of the right kind of assessment or taking stock of the phenomena, for which their preferred term is *epilogismos*, was meant to lay concerns of this kind to rest. It is not that we read off the relevant features at a single glance, so to speak. It takes a great deal of experience and close attention to the phenomena. But the Epicureans' generous conception of experience values extensive experience for reasons different from those for which it is valued by more austere conceptions. Adherents of an austere conception may suppose that repeated experience that, for example, an item of a certain kind has a certain feature justifies increased confidence that other items of the same kind have the same feature by adding to our inductive evidence for it, or that it tends to increase our confidence without justifying it, or that it somehow prepares the way for reason to grasp the underlying causes that explain why items of this kind have this feature. But they cannot concede that it does what the Epicureans maintain it does, viz. somehow make it inconceivable that items of this kind could lack this feature, and in this way lay the basis for an inference to the conclusion that all such items everywhere and at all times have this feature. There is no place in the Empiricists' empiricism for the kind of reflection upon the phenomena which allows the Epicureans to discriminate between observed features which can be projected beyond experience and those which cannot.

It is nevertheless telling that, when the Empiricists do recognize a form of reasoning—a kind which they insist is common to all humankind and confined to the phenomena and which does not satisfy the standards imposed on reason by the Rationalists or count as reason as it is understood in the debate with Rationalism—they use the term *epilogismos*, which the Epicureans apply to the assessment of the phenomena that prepares the way for inference beyond the evident. Allowing for differences between the two schools in their use of the term, it is nevertheless fair to say that, for the Empiricists, close attention to the phenomena—however much aid it may give us in forming reliable expectations about what is to come, discovering what has gone before, and intervening to bring about the results we desire—never puts us in a position to go beyond them, whereas for the Epicureans it does.[72] It is of course precisely on this point

---

[72] The Empiricists build a concern with the phenomena into their definition of *epilogismos*, the Epicureans do not and hence speak of *epilogismos* of the phenomena (ὁ τῶν φαινομένων ἐπιλογισμός) in connection with sign-inference (XXII. 37–8 (ch. 38);

that the opponents fasten when they press their Epicurean opponents to clarify where experience leaves off and inference begins. In effect, while they accuse the Epicureans of illegitimately reading into experience what is not there, the Epicureans accuse them of illegitimately helping themselves to non-evident principles without deriving them from experience or, rather, acknowledging that that is what they have done.

Both charges may have merit depending on what further assumptions are accepted by the parties to the debate. The Epicureans in particular are vulnerable to a challenge that resembles the dilemma we saw the Empiricists using against the Rationalists above (Study II, section 4). The notion of a complete or autonomous sign-inference that I used to interpret the Epicurean position firmly declines any assistance that might be afforded by a direct grasp of relations of elimination, preferring instead to infer such relations from the phenomena. By appealing to the phenomena in this way, the Epicureans aim to find a firm and indisputable basis for knowledge. Yet it is plain that the Epicureans require a certain amount of assessment or taking stock in order to discover what is given in the phenomena as a point of departure for sign-inference. Here it will be natural to press the Epicureans to explain why the problem that the appeal to the phenomena was meant to solve does not arise all over again. Will this assessment of the phenomena take the form of reasoning or inference? If so, will it require undisputed starting-points at a still more fundamental level? If so, will these starting-points suffice by themselves to support the necessary conclusions or must reasoning about them be guided by other principles? If further principles are required, what is their provenance?

Undoubtedly the Epicureans will want to resist this line of argument, but the point is clear. The idea that there are phenomena beyond dispute is most plausible when a thin notion of the phenomena and a correspondingly impoverished conception of experience are in force. But it is no longer plausible that the phenomena conceived in this way can afford a basis for inference or for the required inferences. As we saw, the method of similarity applied to what might at first seem to be phenomena licenses too many sign-inferences and to the wrong conclusions. If a richer conception of

XXIV. 3–5 (ch. 39); XXVII. 23 (ch. 43); cf. VIII. 35 (ch. 13); XIII. 32 (ch. 18); XVII. 33–4 (ch. 25); XXIII. 5 (ch. 38)). See Schofield, 'Epilogismos', 232–3, 236.

experience that permits a more discriminating understanding of the phenomena is adopted, it becomes easier to suppose that inferences to the required conclusions are possible, but at the cost of opening the way for disagreement about what is given in the phenomena as opposed to belonging to a theory which must itself be inferred from the phenomena or be authorized in some other way.

How faithful to Epicurus are the Epicurean positions defended in the *De signis*? The question has elicited strikingly different answers: both that the Epicureans of the *De signis* are to be credited with little or no originality and that Zeno was the inventor of an Epicurean logic.[73] The later Epicureans' commitment to broadly analogical modes of inference was not an innovation. Their defence of the claim that relations of similarity support conditionals was new to be sure, but it merely served to make explicit the inferential use that Epicurus and his followers had already been making of similarity. The distinction between inference by elimination and by similarity may have had some basis in Epicurus' own teaching, but the later Epicureans seem to have turned to it with a new insistence (cf. Lucretius, 2. 112–41). Their contention that all inferences to the non-evident were at bottom grounded in inferences by similarity was very likely new; their elaborate defence of it certainly was.

The later Epicureans' most notable departure from Epicurus is not to be looked for in any of these developments, however, but rather in the range of similarity-based inferences they were willing to contemplate. The multiple explanations so prominent in Epicurus' own use of analogy as a mode of inference are conspicuous by their absence in Philodemus, and it seems that this is not only a difference of emphasis, to be explained by accidents in the transmission of the Epicureans' writings. Indeed, taken together with the account of non-contestation in Sextus Empiricus, which makes it no longer applicable to the multiple explanations which were its *raison d'être* in Epicurus, their absence in the *De signis* suggests that later Epicureans gave up or de-emphasized this most distinctive feature of Epicurus' own position. In fact, in Sextus' account of Epicurean epistemology inference by similarity has also disappeared along with multiple explanation, though whether

---

[73] Bahnsch, *Des Epicureers Philodemus*, 5, 37–8, holds the first view, Philippson, *De Philodemi libro*, 31–2 *et passim*, the second; the latter's views about the uniqueness of Zeno are effectively criticized by Schmekel, *Die Philosophie*, 338–9.

its absence is due to further developments in Epicurean epistemology or merely reflects the interests of Sextus or his sources is
hard to say.

Were the Epicureans whose views are preserved by Philodemus
trying, if only unconsciously, to render the views of their master
more respectable? If so, by whose lights were they to be made respectable? In view of the probable identity of the opponents, the
first answer to suggest itself is the Stoics'. Certainly it is from
the opponents that the pressure to make inferences by similarity
logically respectable came. It is their standards of sound inferential
practice that the Epicureans accepted when they attempted to show
that similarity can give rise to true conditionals. But although, as
we have seen, there was room in Stoicism for disagreement about
this, many Stoics seem to have placed considerably less confidence
in the powers of inference to solve aetiological problems in natural philosophy than did the Epicureans. And it is telling that the
example of the elimination method most frequently cited by the
opponents, 'If there is motion, then there is void', was specifically
rejected by Stoic natural philosophy.[74] Instead, it seems to have
played the part of an inference already prominent in Epicureanism
to which the elimination account would have applied if the relation which the Epicureans believed obtains between motion and
void actually did. And it appears that the opponents were more
concerned to show the Epicureans what their—the Epicureans'—
position should be, given their attachment to certain inferences,
than to compel the Epicureans to accept their—the opponents'—
own inferences. The defence of the method of similarity, which
connects the Epicureans to Epicurus—though not to the prodi-
gality of the multiple method—and through him to Presocratic
natural philosophy shows how willing they were to defend un-
orthodox positions in the face of strong pressure to conform. We
have seen under just how much strain the commitment to analogy as a mode of inference was put in the new climate of logical sophistication in which the Epicureans were compelled to
defend it.

This brings us back to the difficulty which we noted at the beginning of this study. Though it must be indebted to the leading Hellenistic schools of philosophy, the framework which divides epis-

[74] Cf. n. 46.

temic labour between directly given evidence and the demonstrations and sign-inferences by which knowledge of the non-evident is won accommodates the epistemological positions of those schools very imperfectly. We saw how it left Epicurus' distinctive reliance on multiple explanations out of account, and we have seen how misleading and one-sided a picture it gives of Stoic epistemology. But if this framework led Sextus to misrepresent some of the positions he examines, the evidence of Philodemus shows that it was not simply a doxographical construction, which enjoyed no support among practising philosophers. Though not the position of any single one of the formative Hellenistic philosophers, the framework exerted a real and gradually increasing influence, which may have been unrealistically amplified in Sextus' report, but was not invented by him or his sources.

Conclusion

PHILIPPSON compared ancient testimony about signs to the River Alpheus, which disappears from view to flow underground for part of its course.[1] Much of the subject's history is invisible to us and can only be conjectured. Were it not for the accident that preserved part of Philodemus' *De signis*, for example, we would not know about the later Epicureans' views or even that sign-inference had been an especially important concern of theirs. Sextus' single mention of Epicurus and his followers as adherents of the view that the sign is a sensible is so plainly meant as a doxographical counterweight to the Stoic view that the sign is a *lekton* and, therefore, intelligible that we might have been forgiven for thinking that there was little to Epicurean sign theory had we had no other evidence (*M.* 8. 177). Philippson's point is well taken, then. Only a few traces of a much more extensive discussion have come down to us. But to the extent that his simile suggests that ancient thought about sign-inference was like a single stream, however winding and subterranean, it may mislead. As we have seen, the failure of Sextus or his sources to take the full range of issues that were discussed under the head of sign-inference into account exacerbated the problem already presented to interpreters by the shortage of testimony. The framework he used to organize his examination of dogmatic epistemology presupposes what I earlier dubbed a high conception of sign-inference, which suits only some of the positions he considers. It fits the Epicurean view, which he ignores, for example, but does not apply to the Stoic theory, which is his prize exhibit.

In Study II I argued that Sextus' or his sources' confusion was due to a conception of dogmatism that he is elsewhere at pains to repudiate. To this way of thinking, to be dogmatic is to purport to go beyond evident matters and pronounce about the non-evident, according to a conception of evident and non-evident to which Pyrrhonism is not committed. This view became entangled with the framework dividing epistemic labour between the criterion on

[1] *De Philodemi libro*, 57.

the one hand and sign-inference and demonstration on the other, so that signs—apart from the commemorative sign, which Sextus regards as a special exception peculiar to Pyrrhonism and medical Empiricism—are all taken to serve *this* dogmatic purpose. But, as we saw, if the Stoic theory of signs is dogmatic, it is for reasons other than these. The conception of dogmatism that is responsible for the mistaken classification of the Stoic theory is more at home in medical Empiricism than Pyrrhonism, indeed the form of medical Empiricism from which Sextus was most eager to distinguish Pyrrhonism. And it seems to have been taken over with the distinction between commemorative and indicative signification from the debate between medical Empiricists and Rationalists, where I argued that this distinction had its origin.

But even the indicative signs championed by the Rationalists are not perfectly accommodated by Sextus' framework. It is possible to view indicative sign-inferences as applications of a theory or as the means by which the theory is established. Conceived in the first way, they often seem to hold much more promise than when viewed in the second way, and it is likely that indicative signification was originally tied much more closely to the first conception. But if Sextus can be faulted for failing to leave room for a Rationalist theory to be confirmed in any other way than by inference from the evident, we have seen that at least some Rationalists appeared to make indicative signs do double duty as the ground for and the application of their theories. The question how the non-evident contents of a theory can be inferred from directly given evidence was a theme of the debate between medical Rationalists and Empiricists, and this debate was the germ from which Sextus' case against indicative signification grew after the Pyrrhonian technique of cultivating arguments of every degree of quality and relevance was applied to it.

But different as they are, the conceptions of sign-inference that have emerged in the course of the investigation can be put into some relation to each other. It is possible to see them as the results of different answers to questions that were at a basic level common to the figures and schools which we have been studying. Two themes that emerged early in the enquiry will help give us the fresh perspective we need to make out the element of unity in the subject and to view the differences and similarities between the contributions to the ancient debates about sign-inference in their true proportion.

These are the idea of furnishing evidence for a conclusion and the tendency to assign the inferior part to sign-inference in contrast to inferences which are in one way or another superior.

Let us begin with Aristotle. The clarity he brought to certain essential distinctions will make it easier to formulate the important questions. The definition of the syllogism provides a clear account of valid argument (not all valid arguments to be sure, but those that can be of service in arguing for something—that is the point of requiring that something other than the premises follow of necessity from them). The theory of the categorical syllogism provides a rigorous formal specification of the conditions an argument must satisfy to be a syllogism. When he wants to distinguish kinds of argument suited to different purposes, Aristotle imposes further conditions beyond those specified in his syllogistic theory. In the case of the invalid second- and third-figure sign-inferences and, perhaps, a certain kind of argument from for-the-most-part premisses, he relaxes the requirement that the argument be valid. The theory set out in the *Posterior Analytics* is an attempt to describe the conditions that a syllogism must satisfy if it is to be, in Aristotle's pregnant phrase, a demonstration of the *because* rather than merely of the *that*, by embodying the scientific explanation of its demonstrandum. We detected a tendency in Aristotle to contrast demonstrations satisfying these requirements with syllogisms from signs. Though these must satisfy analogues of the requirements that a demonstration proceed from premises that are better known than and prior to the conclusion, they are syllogisms of the *that*. When we have grasped the premises of this kind of syllogism as facts *that*, we are entitled to add its conclusion to our stock of facts *that*: that is, the function of signs is to furnish evidence for a conclusion.

But though Aristotle assigns the epistemic functions of scientific explanation and inference from evidence to the syllogism, it is not on his view the means by which knowledge of the first principles is won. How it is we come to know the starting-points of demonstration according to Aristotle is a notoriously difficult question. The grasp of first principles by intuition is the culmination of a process that begins with perception, but it is plain that it is not an inferential one. First principles are not justified by observation, or if they are, it is not by knowing that they are that we stand in the cognitive relation to them that is grasping them as first principles. To grasp them in this way is not to see that they follow from, or are in some other way confirmed by, the evidence afforded by observation. As a result, signs furnished by observation play a negligible part in Aristotle's official method of science, with its focus on the grasp of first principles by intuition and explanation by demonstration from them. And when signs of a very heterogeneous character are put forward in support of a theory in Aristotle's scientific works, it cannot be that the first principles of the theory are to be grasped as such on the strength of the evidence provided by signs, however helpful it may be to see that these principles are supported by evidence in this way. Instead, signs receive special attention in the discussion of rhetoric and kindred forms of argument, where contingent particular facts *that* are what matters.

Of the views that we have investigated, the various Epicurean positions—along perhaps with a strand of thought in medical Rationalism—stand in starkest contrast to this part of Aristotle's position. The Epicureans do seem to have believed that the principles of natural philosophy can be inferred from the evidence afforded by observation. They were aided in reaching this conclusion by their use of analogy as a mode of inference. But as we have seen, their attachment to analogy did not stand alone and could not have been added to the positions of their rivals; it is inseparable from a more generous conception of experience than Aristotle's austere conception. There are no doubt many degrees of austerity, and the task of drawing the line between experience and the something more involved in knowledge and understanding is surprisingly difficult, as we can see from Aristotle's attempt to do so at the beginning of the *Metaphysics* (A 1, $981^{a}1$ ff.). But the essential mark of an austere conception is the restriction on which Aristotle insists there, limiting experience to the *that* ($981^{a}29$). This has the consequence that any explanation that attempts to specify the causes because of which, i.e. strictly speaking any explanation at all, must go beyond experience.

As we have seen, this restriction forms no part of Epicurus' conception of experience. So far as it goes, experience can show causes at work. When the search for explanations makes it necessary to go beyond experience, it seems to be because of a different kind of limit on, or incompleteness to, experience. Some things are too small or too far away to observe. We can, for example, observe motes of dust in motion, but we cannot see the minute bodies imparting motion to them. We are so situated in relation to many heavenly phenomena that we observe effects whose causes are beyond the reach of direct observation. It is this way of conceiving experience that makes inference by analogy possible. Since we observe not merely that things are a certain a way, but, with the aid of *epilogismos*, the features in virtue of which they can or must be so, i.e. what is permitted and required by their natures, we are entitled to project what we know of items in our experience onto items which are similar in respect of the relevant features outside of it. This richer conception of experience not only makes inference by analogy possible, it is also essential if it is to serve the aetiological purposes to which it is put in Epicureanism and not merely generate ever more remote explananda. When Lucretius describes Epicurus' mind venturing beyond the flaming ramparts of the world and wandering through the infinite universe to bring back news of what can and cannot be, it is perhaps more than just the inspired praise of a true believer; it is as if Epicurus had been to places where no one else had been and seen things that no one else had seen (1. 72–7). It is also likely that the metaphors in earlier views of inference in which the Epicurean approach had its roots were much more alive for their authors than they are for us, e.g. Anaxagoras' claim that the phenomena are the vision of the non-evident, or Hippocratic talk of the vision of the intellect.

This conception of inference and the understanding of evidence that complements it explain a feature of Epicurean views that sets them apart from some of the other approaches that we have studied. An interest in marking off and defining a kind of argument that explains its conclusion by deducing it from first principles seems to have been distinctive of Aristotle, and it was certainly not shared by Epicurus. The Epicureans did not have this motive for distinguishing between demonstrations and sign-inferences or drawing an equivalent distinction in other terms, but neither did they have reasons to make some of the other distinctions between kinds of inference that we have found being made in other schools. On the Epicurean view, although we draw inferences about different kinds of things in natural philosophy and in ordinary life, the method we use is the same in both: inferences in each have their roots in experience and involve a grasp of necessities in the same way. On the basis of observed correlations it becomes inconceivable not only that smoke might occur without fire, but also that minute invisible bodies might move apart from the analogue of visible space, void.

We may make some inferences with aetiological ends in view and some merely in order to gain factual knowledge. Some inferences may disclose more fundamental causes while others leave deeper questions unanswered. But these differences do not correspond to a difference between types or methods of sign-inference. Thus there is no basis for a distinction between sign-inferences which are confined to furnishing evidence for a conclusion because grounded in, for example, merely empirical relations and those which can also serve aetiological purposes because they are based on necessary relations of consequence and exclusion authorized by the underlying nature of things—i.e. no basis for a distinction like that between commemorative and indicative signs or a distinction between sign-inference and demonstration of the kind to which some Stoic accounts of demonstration seem to point.

The medical Empiricists did have a reason to distinguish between kinds of sign-inference, however. We saw in Study II that they were probably the first to use the terms 'commemoration' and 'indication' to mark such a distinction. And in Study IV it became clear that the affinities between medical Empiricism and Epicureanism, especially the way in which they make observation of correlations between events or properties the basis for sign-inference, should not obscure the very considerable differences between them. The Empiricists share an austere conception of experience with their Rationalist opponents. Theirs is, like Aristotle's and Galen's and unlike that of Asclepiades of Bithynia, a generous version of the austere conception, which concedes a considerable measure of autonomy and practical effectiveness to experience, but insists that the necessary relations of consequence and exclusion required by the nature of things are forever beyond the reach of experience and to be grasped, if at all, by a special faculty of reason. As a result, the Empiricists also agree that inferences extending knowledge beyond what is given in experience can be made only by grasping such relations with the aid of such a faculty. They do not dissent from the Rationalist conception of indicative sign-inference, but question only whether the conditions necessary for it can be met.

When we turned to Stoic views in Study III, we saw not only that the relation between their account of signs and the distinction between commemorative and indicative signs was not what Sextus took it to be, but also that the actual relation between their views and the distinction is rather complicated. The Stoic definition of the sign captures the minimum notion of what it is to be evidence for a conclusion, or rather conclusive evidence—an important qualification. It was therefore especially well suited to capture sign-inferences grounded in empirical correlations, but at the same time it left room for imposing more stringent standards if the need was felt for a subclass of inferences grounded in a necessary relation stricter than correlation. We saw that the connective criterion of the true conditional could be brought into relation with both natural philosophy and epistemology in the way required to put together an analogue of the indicative sign. When one matter is of such a *nature* as to require another, there will be an appropriately related conditional, 'If the first, then the second', the contradictory of whose consequent is incompatible with its antecedent; and this incompatibility will in principle be such that it can be grasped by reason independently of experience. When the antecedent is more evident than the consequent, so that one can come to know that the consequent is true through first grasping that the antecedent is, we have something very much like an indicative sign.

As we noted, there is evidence that at least some Rationalist physicians drew on Stoic theory and vocabulary in their own positions. But as we also saw, the version of the Stoic view that enjoyed the imprimatur of Chrysippus, was much less optimistic about how often we are in a position to grasp natural relations of consequence than many Rationalists, and thus inclined to see many fewer occasions for inferences based on them. The definition of demonstration preserved by Sextus whose Stoic credentials are the strongest and which was probably endorsed by Chrysippus does not restrict demonstration to inferences analogous to indicative sign-inferences. The only requirement imposed on a demonstration apart from being valid and having true premises is that the premises reveal the conclusion, where this is understood in the same way as it was in the definition of the sign. The minimal notion of furnishing evidence for a conclusion is still in force. If there is a difference, it is that the definition of the sign says what it is to be a *piece* of evidence, while the definition of demonstration says what it is to be an *argument* that furnishes evidence. This conception of demonstration, I suggested, complements what we know of Chrysippus' hesitant attitude towards aetiology and his disinclination to make it dependent on demonstration. Yet as we discovered, the two other definitions of demonstration transmitted by Sextus, which I argued should be viewed as later attempts to alter the first, try to connect demonstration more closely with aetiology. And I suggested that impulses like this may also have inspired a distinction between sign-inference and demonstration according to which inferences that qualify as sign-inferences but do not satisfy the requirements now imposed on demonstration are treated as sign-inferences narrowly so called and assigned the function of merely furnishing evidence for a conclusion.

But though these versions of the Stoic account bring demonstration closer to Aristotle's conception by assigning it an explanatory function, it is not the explanatory function that Aristotle reserves for demonstration. Inferences like that from the failure of the planets to twinkle to their nearness, which satisfy the requirements of the modified Stoic account by delivering a conclusion about the underlying nature of things are, as we have seen, still not demonstrations by Aristotle's lights. This is because an Aristotelian demonstration is less concerned to disclose new truths than to bring about understanding by exhibiting the explanatory relation that obtains between the explanans captured by the premises and the explanandum stated in the conclusion. A Stoic demonstration of this kind, on the other hand, resolves a matter previously unclear or in doubt by an inference from truths already grasped. It is still a sign-inference in a way in which Aristotelian demonstrations are not. If it serves an explanatory purpose, it is not directly by presenting an explanation in the Aristotelian manner, but rather by uncovering necessary conditions for a natural phenomenon that belong to its explanation. It contributes to explanation by deducing a conclusion that answers, or is part of the answer to, a request for explanation. If you will, a demonstration of this kind is an inference to the best explanation, with the difference that it is not because the conclusion best explains the evidence that we are justified in inferring it, but rather because it is inferred in the right way that it is *the* explanation.

In the introduction to this enquiry I attributed to Aristotle the path-breaking recognition that an argument may lack deductive validity without relinquishing all claim to influence rational minds. Arguments that make their conclusions likely or probable are, in his terms, reputable and may sometimes, depending on the circumstances, deserve to influence our judgement. But I also claimed that after Aristotle this was a path largely not taken. Like most such judgements, this one needs qualification, and I shall conclude by suggesting very roughly how one might go about adding the necessary qualifications; to do more would be the task of another enquiry. As always when investigating the philosophy of the Hellenistic period, we confront the problem presented by the dearth of primary sources and the gaps in the secondary reports that have reached us. Arguments from silence are especially dangerous here, and the possibility that others set out on and even travelled further down the path broken by Aristotle cannot be ruled out. But the evidence we have seems to indicate that there was little concern with probable reasoning where we would most expect to find it, while the interest we do find is often in unexpected quarters and based on approaches that are in important ways different from Aristotle's.

If, for example, we follow the tradition inaugurated by Cicero and render the Greek term πιθανός (plausible, persuasive) as *probabilis*, it appears that the Academic philosopher Carneades developed a theory of probability. To do this, or rather to translate either πιθανός or *probabilis* as 'probable', can, as is well known, be misleading. In this case, however, as long as due caution is observed, the risks are fewer. For Carneades' theory explains how different degrees of confidence in a belief can be warranted and how, if what is at stake matters enough, we can increase the degree of confidence that is warranted. But Carneades' theory is not about signs, at least what is usually meant by signs. The probable impression with which it is concerned is intended as an alternative to the cognitive impression, the self-evident perceptual impressions that are assigned the place of fundamental importance in Stoic epistemology.[2] The burden of Carneades' argument is that using the evidence of the senses is not a matter of grasping self-evident impressions, but rather of appreciating the complicated relations among impressions and between impressions and the conditions in which they are formed in virtue of which they add to or detract from each other's plausibility. It is not a theory about the use of these impressions as signs or evidence from which a conclusion about matters that are not themselves within reach of observation is to be inferred. A view about how signs can lend probability to a conclusion could draw on some of the same considerations and would complement the account of probable impressions that we do have, but whether Carneades or

[2] I have discussed Carneades' arguments and their context in 'Academic Probabilism and Stoic Epistemology', *Classical Quarterly*, NS 44 (1994), 85–113.

other Academics had much to say about this subject is not clear from the evidence.

The Stoics too used a term that Cicero renders as *probabilis*, namely εὔλογος, which is usually translated as 'reasonable' (*Luc.* 100). It is most prominent in Stoic ethics, where an appropriate action is defined as one having a reasonable defence (D.L. 7. 107; Cicero, *Fin.* 3. 58). We also find a definition of the reasonable proposition and an intriguing contrast between the cognitive impression and the reasonable (D.L. 7. 75, 177). A reasonable defence of an action will presumably take into account both an agent's moral responsibilities and what the likely consequences of the actions open to the agent are in the light of the available evidence. That this factual dimension figured in Stoic accounts is clear from a favourite example of theirs: that it is reasonable to expect a safe journey by boat if, for example, the sea is calm, the distance not too great, and so on (cf. Cicero, *Luc.* 100; Philodemus, *De signis* VII. 32–7; Epictetus 2. 5. 10–11). Unfortunately, if the Stoics had more to say about how evidence can make a view reasonable, it has not come down to us. It is plain, however, that if they did explore this issue, it was not under the head of 'signs'. For Aristotle tokens, which furnish conclusive evidence, are one kind of sign among others. In his writings Aristotle sometimes calls signs 'strong' or 'sufficient', and these usages are easy to document in other Greek authors as well, which is just as we would expect, since they reflect the ordinary idea that evidence comes in different strengths. But to judge by the Stoic definition, a sign which is not sufficient to establish the conclusion, is not a sign at all. Chrysippus' books on πιθανὰ συνημμένα (*pithanos* conditionals) are most likely a red herring (D.L. 7. 190).[3] The conditional 'If someone bore something, she is its mother' is given as an example of a *pithanos* proposition, and it is pointed out that a hen that has borne an egg is not its mother (D.L. 7. 75). The point seems to be that this conditional is only superficially plausible and not a real conditional. The fact that if someone bore something this is a good albeit not conclusive reason to suppose that she is its mother goes unremarked here. Of course, it may have been remarked somewhere else. One would like to know more about the element of conjecture in conjectural divination and other spheres of activity. If it is sometimes permitted to accept that one thing is the sign of another on the basis of conjecture—perhaps to accept

---

[3] Cf. J. Barnes, '*Πιθανὰ συνημμένα*', *Elenchos*, 6 (1985), 453–67.

it as reasonable—an analogue of the Epicureans' complaint against the eliminative relations exploited in their opponents' inferences becomes tempting. Surely that X is a sign of Y is itself accepted on the strength of an inference from evidence, i.e. a sign-inference. And it is at least as important to understand this sign-inference as the other. What we seem to miss by comparison with Aristotle is an integration of probable, reputable, or reasonable argument, call it what you will, in a broader understanding of argument. Of course this may be owing to the state of our evidence, so I can only report the suspicion that the issue did not receive the kind of attention from the Stoics that it had from Aristotle.

It is to the medical Empiricists that we must look for an unambiguously receptive attitude towards reasoning on the basis of probable evidence. Their approach is, to be sure, different from Aristotle's in a way that reflects their exclusive reliance on empirical correlations as a basis for inference. Roughly speaking, they held that when we observe one of a pair of correlated items we expect the other with a level of confidence proportionate to the observed relative frequency of their correlation, and they distinguished four levels of frequency: always, for the most part, half the time, and rarely (Galen, *Subfig. emp.* 45. 25–30; 58. 15 ff. Deichgräber; cf. *On Medical Experience*, 95, 112 Walzer; [Galen], *Def. med.* xix. 354. 12 ff. K =fr. 58 Deichgräber). They used this view in their polemic against the Rationalists to argue that they were in a position to do justice to the stochastic character of the medical art in a way their opponents were not.[4] If the theorems of the art are themselves stochastic, they maintain, it is only to be expected that some well- and properly made prognoses turn out false and that some correctly chosen therapies are ineffective (cf. [Galen], *De opt. sect.* i. 114 K). On the other hand, the insights into the underlying nature of things claimed for reason by the Rationalists did not, the Empiricists maintained, leave room for any degree of confidence less than certainty, so that every failed therapy and untrue prognosis must show that the Rationalist physician who prescribed the therapy or made the prognosis lacked the knowledge to which he laid claim.

The most striking feature of the Empiricists' approach was the

---

[4] I have discussed this debate in 'Failure and Expertise in the Ancient Conception of an Art', in T. Horowitz and A. I. Janis (eds.), *Scientific Failure* (Lanham, Md.: Rowman and Littlefield, 1994), 81–108.

way it broke the stranglehold of the for-the-most-part, which is elsewhere so prominent in ancient thought. Its weakness by comparison with Aristotle's account may have been in the way it handled the task of combining pieces of non-conclusive evidence or resolving conflicts between them. For if Aristotle's account did not distinguish degrees of evidential support in the way the Empiricists' did, it revealed a sensitivity to the ways in which evidence can combine to make a case stronger and how considerations whose credentials are the same prior to being confronted with each other can, when pitted against each other in argument, be seen to offer better or worse support for opposed conclusions. The Empiricists' commitment to confirming all theorems by experience, on the other hand, would in principle have required them to draw conclusions in situations where pieces of evidence interact, so to speak—either by tending to increase the likelihood of a common conclusion or because one tends to undermine the other—only on the basis of vast amounts of past experience of these interactions.

Bibliography

Ancient Works

ALEXANDER OF APHRODISIAS, *In Aristotelis Analyticorum priorum librum I commentarium*, ed. M. Wallies (CAG II.1; Berlin: Reimer, 1883).
—— *In Aristotelis Topicorum libros octo commentaria*, ed. M. Wallies (CAG II.2; Berlin: Reimer, 1891).
—— *Quaestiones, De fato, et De mixtione*, ed. I. Bruns (CAG suppl. II.1; Berlin: Reimer, 1892).

AMMONIUS, *In Aristotelis Analyticorum priorum librum I commentarium*, ed. M. Wallies (CAG IV.6; Berlin: Reimer, 1899).

ANON., *The Medical Writings of Anonymus Londiniensis*, ed. and trans., W. H. S. Jones (Cambridge: Cambridge University Press, 1947).

ANON. and STEPHANUS, *In Artem rhetoricam commmentaria*, ed. H. Rabe (Berlin: Reimer, 1896).

ARISTOTLE, *The Complete Works of Aristotle*, ed. J. Barnes (2 vols.; Oxford: Oxford University Press, 1984).
—— *The Works of Aristotle*, ed. W. D. Ross (12 vols.; Oxford: Oxford University Press, 1928–52).
—— *Ars rhetorica*, ed. L. Spengel (Leipzig: Teubner, 1847).
—— *Ars rhetorica*, ed. R. Kassel (Berlin: De Gruyter, 1976).
—— *De insomniis, De divinatione per somnum*, trans. P. J. van der Eijk (Berlin: Akademie-Verlag, 1994).
—— *Organon Graece*, ed. T. Waitz (2 vols.; Leipzig: Hahn, 1844–6).
—— *Posterior Analytics*, trans. J. Barnes, 2nd edn. (Oxford: Oxford University Press, 1994).
—— *Prior and Posterior Analytics*, ed. W. D. Ross (London: Oxford University Press, 1949).
—— *Les Réfutations sophistiques*, trans. L.-A. Dorion (Paris: Vrin, 1995).
—— *Topica et sophistici elenchi*, ed. W. D. Ross (London: Oxford University Press, 1958).
—— *Topiques I–IV*, ed. J. Brunschwig (Paris: Les Belles Lettres, 1967).

CICERO, *Academicorum reliquiae cum Lucullo*, ed. O. Plasberg (Leipzig: Teubner, 1922; repr. Stuttgart, 1980).
—— *De divinatione*, ed. A. S. Pease (Darmstadt: Wissenschaftliche Buchgesellschaft, 1977); repr. of *University of Illinois Studies in Language and Literature*, 6 (1920), 161–500, and 8 (1923), 153–474.

CICERO, *De divinatione, De fato, Timaeus*, ed. W. Ax (Leipzig: Teubner, 1933; repr. Stuttgart, 1980).

—— *De natura deorum*, ed. W. Ax (Leipzig: Teubner, 1933; repr. Stuttgart, 1980).

CLEMENT OF ALEXANDRIA, *Stromata I–VIII*, ed. O. Stählin, rev. L. Früchtel and U. Treu (2 vols.; GCS; Berlin: Akademie-Verlag, 1963–85).

DIOGENES LAERTIUS, *Vitae philosophorum*, ed. M. Marcovich (Stuttgart and Leipzig: Teubner, 1999).

GALEN, *Opera Quae Exstant*, ed. K. G. Kühn (20 vols.; Leipzig: Cnobloch, 1821–33; repr. Hildesheim: Olms, 1965).

—— *Scripta Minora*, ed. G. Helmreich, J. Marquardt, and I. Mueller (3 vols.; Leipzig: Teubner, 1884–93).

—— *De placitis Hippocratis et Platonis*, ed. I. Müller (Leipzig: Teubner, 1874).

—— *De placitis Hippocratis et Platonis*, ed. and trans. P. de Lacy (3 vols.; CMG v/4/1, 2; Berlin: Akademie-Verlag, 1978–85).

—— *In Hippocratis prognosticum*, ed. I Heeg (CMG IX/2; Berlin: Akademie-Verlag, 1915).

—— *Institutio logica*, ed. K. Kalbfleisch (Leipzig: Teubner, 1896).

—— *Einführung in die Logik: Kritisch-exegetischer Kommentar mit deutscher Übersetzung*, trans. J. Mau (Berlin: Akademie-Verlag, 1960).

—— *Institutio logica*, trans. J. S. Kieffer (Baltimore: Johns Hopkins University Press, 1964).

—— *Three Treatises on the Nature of Science*, ed. and trans. M. Frede, trans. R. Walzer (Indianapolis: Hackett, 1985).

PHILODEMUS, *Herkulanische Studien*, i. *Philodem über Induktionschlüsse*, ed. T. Gomperz (Leipzig: Teubner, 1865).

—— *On Methods of Inference*, ed. P. H. and E. A. De Lacy, 2nd edn. (Naples: Bibliopolis, 1978).

SEXTUS EMPIRICUS, *Opera*, ed. H. Mutschmann and J. Mau (3 vols.; Leipzig: Teubner, 1914–58); vol. iv, *Indices*, ed. K. Janaceck (1962).

SIMPLICIUS, *Commentaire sur les Catégories: Traduction commentée sous la direction d'Ilsetraut Hadot*, i (Leiden: Brill, 1990).

Suidae Lexicon, ed. A. Adler (5 vols.; Leipzig: Teubner, 1929–38).

THEOPHRASTUS, *Die logischen Fragmente des Theophrast*, ed. A. Graeser (De Gruyter: Berlin, 1973).

Collections of Testimonies

ARNIM, H. VON (ed.), *Stoicorum Veterum Fragmenta* (3 vols.; Leipzig: Teubner, 1903–5); vol. iv, *Indices* (1924).

DEICHGRÄBER, K. (ed.), *Die griechische Empirikerschule: Sammlung der Fragmente und Darstellung der Lehre*, 2nd edn. (Berlin: Weidmann, 1965).

DIELS, H. (ed.), *Doxographi Graeci* (Berlin: De Gruyter, 1879).
—— and KRANZ, W. (eds.), *Die Fragmente der Vorsokratiker*, 6th edn. (3 vols.; Berlin: Weidmann, 1951–2).
DÖRING, K., *Die Megariker: Kommentierte Sammlung der Testimonien* (Amsterdam: B. R. Grüner, 1972).
HÜLSER, K. (ed.), *Die Fragmente zur Dialektik der Stoiker* (4 vols.; Stuttgart: Frommann-Holzboog, 1987–8).
LONG, A. A., and SEDLEY, D. (eds.), *The Hellenistic Philosophers* (2 vols.; Cambridge: Cambridge University Press, 1987).
NAUCK, A. (ed.), *Tragicorum Graecorum Fragmenta*, 2nd edn. (Leipzig: Teubner, 1926).
RADERMACHER, L. (ed.), *Artium Scriptores: Reste der voraristotelischen Rhetorik* (Sitzungsberichte der philosophisch-historischen Klasse der Österreichischen Akademie der Wissenschaften, 227/3; 1951).
STADEN, H. VON, *Herophilus: The Art of Medicine in Early Alexandria* (Cambridge: Cambridge University Press, 1989).
USENER, H. (ed.), *Epicurea* (Leipzig: Teubner, 1887).

Modern Works

ALLEN, J., 'Academic Probabilism and Stoic Epistemology', *Classical Quarterly*, NS 44 (1994), 85–113.
—— 'The Development of Aristotle's Logic: Part of an Account in Outline', *Proceedings of the Boston Area Colloquium in Ancient Philosophy*, 11 (1995), 177–205.
—— 'Epicurean Inferences: The Evidence of Philodemus' De signis', in J. Gentzler (ed.), *Method in Ancient Philosophy* (Oxford: Oxford University Press, 1998), 306–49.
—— 'Failure and Expertise in the Ancient Conception of an Art', in T. Horowitz and A. I. Janis (eds.), *Scientific Failure* (Lanham, Md.: Rowman and Littlefield, 1994), 81–108.
—— 'Pyrrhonism and Medical Empiricism: Sextus Empiricus on Evidence and Inference', in W. Haase (ed.), *Aufstieg und Niedergang der römischen Welt*, II. 37. 1 (Berlin: De Gruyter, 1993), 646–90.
ASMIS, E., 'Epicurean Semiotics', in G. Manetti (ed.), *Knowledge through Signs: Ancient Semiotic Theories and Practices* (Turnhout: Brepols, 1995), 155–85.
—— *Epicurus' Scientific Method* (Ithaca, NY: Cornell University Press, 1984).
BAHNSCH, F., *Des Epicureers Philodemus Schrift Περὶ σημείων καὶ σημειώσεων: Eine Darlegung ihres Gedankengehalts* (Lyck: Wiebe, 1879).
BARNES, J., 'Epicurean Signs', in J. Annas and R. H. Grimm (eds.), *Oxford Studies in Ancient Philosophy*, suppl. vol. (Oxford: Oxford University Press, 1988), 91–134.

258   Bibliography

BARNES, J., 'Galen on Logic and Therapy', in F. Kudlien and R. J. Durling (eds.), *Galen's Method of Healing* (Leiden: Brill, 1991), 50–102.

—— 'Πιθανὰ συνημμένα', *Elenchos*, 6 (1985), 453–67.

—— *The Presocratic Philosophers*, 2nd edn. (London: Routledge, 1982).

—— 'Proof and the Syllogism', in Berti (ed.), *Aristotle on Science*, 17–59.

—— 'Proof Destroyed', in Barnes *et al.* (eds.), *Doubt and Dogmatism*, 161–81.

—— 'Rhetoric and Poetics', in id. (ed.), *The Cambridge Companion to Aristotle* (Cambridge: Cambridge University Press, 1995), 259–85.

—— BURNYEAT, M., and SCHOFIELD, M. (eds.), *Doubt and Dogmatism: Studies in Hellenistic Epistemology* (Oxford: Oxford University Press, 1980).

—— BRUNSCHWIG, J., BURNYEAT, M., and SCHOFIELD, M. (eds.), *Science and Speculation: Studies in Hellenistic Theory and Practice* (Cambridge and Paris: Cambridge University Press and Éditions de la Maison des Sciences de l'Homme, 1982).

BARWICK, K., 'Die Gliederung der rhetorischen Τέχνη und die horazische Epistula ad Pisones', *Hermes*, 57 (1922), 1–62.

—— 'Die "Rhetorik ad Alexandrum" und Anaximenes, Alkidamas, Isokrates, Aristoteles und die Theodekteia', *Philologus*, 110 (1966), 212–45.

BERTI, E. (ed.), *Aristotle on Science: The Posterior Analytics* (Padua: Antenore, 1981).

BOBZIEN, S., 'Chrysippus' Theory of Causes', in K. Ierodiakonou (ed.), *Topics in Stoic Philosophy* (Oxford: Oxford University Press, 1998), 196–242.

—— *Determinism and Freedom in Stoic Philosophy* (Oxford: Oxford University Press, 1998).

BOCHENSKI, I. M., *La Logique de Théophraste* (Collectanea Friburgensia, NS 32; Freiburg, 1947).

BONITZ, H., *Index Aristotelicus*, vol. v of *Aristotelis Opera*, ed. I. Bekker (Berlin: Reimer, 1870; repr. Darmstadt: Wissenschaftliche Buchgesellschaft, 1960).

BROCHARD, V., *Les Sceptiques grecs*, 2nd edn. (Paris: Vrin, 1887).

BRUNSCHWIG, J., 'La formule ὅσον ἐπὶ τῷ λόγῳ chez Sextus Empiricus', in A.-J. Voelke (ed.), *Le Scepticisme antique* (Cahiers de la *Revue de théologie et de philosophie*, 15; Geneva, 1990), 107–21; repr. in id., *Études sur les philosophies hellénistiques: Épicurisme, stoïcisme, scepticisme* (Paris: Presses Universitaires de France, 1995), 321–42; trans. in id., *Papers in Hellenistic Philosophy* (Cambridge: Cambridge University Press, 1994), 244–58.

—— 'L'Organon: Tradition grecque', in R. Goulet (ed.), *Dictionnaire des philosophes antiques*, i (Paris: CNRS, 1989), 485–502.

—— 'Proof Defined', in Barnes *et al.* (eds.), *Doubt and Dogmatism*, 125–60.

—— 'Sur le système des "prédicables" dans les Topiques d'Aristote', in *Energeia: Études aristotéliciennes offertes à Mgr. Antonio Jannone* (Paris: Vrin, 1986), 145–57.

BURKERT, W., 'Στοιχεῖον: Eine semasiologische Studie', *Philologus*, 103 (1959), 167–97.

BURNYEAT, M. F., 'Enthymeme: Aristotle on the Logic of Persuasion', in Furley and Nehamas (eds.), *Essays on Aristotle's Rhetoric*, 3–55.

—— 'The Origins of Non-deductive Inference', in Barnes *et al.* (eds.), *Science and Speculation*, 193–238.

—— and FREDE, M. (eds.), *The Original Sceptics: A Controversy* (Indianapolis: Hackett, 1997).

CAIZZI, F. DECLEVA, 'Aenesidemus and the Academy', *Classical Quarterly*, NS 42 (1992), 176–89.

CHIESA, C., 'Sextus Sémiologue: Le problème des signes commémoratifs', in A.-J. Voelke (ed.), *Le Scepticisme antique* (Cahiers de la *Revue de théologie et de philosophie*, 15; Geneva, 1990), 151–66.

COOPER, J., 'Ethical-political Theory in Aristotle's Rhetoric', in Furley and Nehamas (eds.), *Essays on Aristotle's Rhetoric*, 193–210.

DELATTRE, D., 'En relisant les subscriptiones des PHerc. 1065 et 1427', *Zeitschrift für Papyrologie und Epigraphik*, 109 (1995), 39–41.

DETEL, W., 'Αἴσθησις und Λογισμός: Zwei Probleme der epikureischen Methodologie', *Archiv für Geschichte der Philosophie*, 57 (1975), 21–35.

DILLER, H., '"Οψις ἀδήλων τὰ φαινόμενα', *Hermes*, 67 (1932), 14–42.

DÖRING, K., 'Gab es eine dialektische Schule?', *Phronesis*, 34 (1989), 293–310.

DUMONT, J.-P., 'Confirmation et disconfirmation', in Barnes *et al.* (eds.), *Science and Speculation*, 273–303.

EBERT, T., *Dialektiker und frühe Stoiker bei Sextus Empiricus: Untersuchungen zur Entstehung der Aussagenlogik* (Göttingen: Vandenhoeck and Ruprecht, 1991).

—— 'The Origin of the Stoic Theory of Signs in Sextus Empiricus', *Oxford Studies in Ancient Philosophy*, 5 (1987), 83–126.

EDELSTEIN, L., 'Methodiker', in *RE* suppl. vi (1935), 358–73; trans. in id., *Ancient Medicine*, ed. O. and C. Temkin (Baltimore: Johns Hopkins University Press, 1967), 173–91.

EIJK, P. J. VAN DER, 'Diocles and the Hippocratic Writings on the Method of Diaetetics and the Limits of Causal Explanation', in R. Wittern and P. Pellegrin (eds.), *Hippokratische Medizin und antike Philosophie* (Hildesheim: Olms, 1996), 229–57.

FREDE, D., 'The Stoic Notion of Causality', unpublished paper delivered at the Colloquium in Classical Philosophy, Princeton University, Dec. 1975.

FREDE, M., 'The Empiricist Attitude towards Reason and Theory', in

R. J. Hankinson (ed.), *Method, Metaphysics and Medicine: Studies in the Philosophy of Ancient Science* (Edmonton: Academic Printing and Publishing, 1988), 79–97.

—— 'The Empiricists', in id., *Essays in Ancient Philosophy*, 234–60.

—— 'An Empiricist View of Knowledge: Memorism', in S. Everson (ed.), *Epistemology* (Cambridge: Cambridge University Press, 1990), 225–50.

—— *Essays in Ancient Philosophy* (Oxford: Oxford University Press, 1987).

—— 'The Method of the So-called Methodical School of Medicine', in Barnes *et al.* (eds.), *Science and Speculation*, 1–23; repr. in id., *Essays in Ancient Philosophy*, 261–78.

—— 'The Original Notion of Cause', in Barnes *et al.* (eds.), *Doubt and Dogmatism*, 217–49.

—— 'Des Skeptikers Meinungen', *Neue Hefte für Philosophie*, 15–16 (1979), 102–29; trans. in id., *Essays in Ancient Philosophy*, 179–200.

—— *Die stoische Logik* (Göttingen: Vandenhoeck and Ruprecht, 1974).

FRITZ, K. VON, *Die ἐπαγωγή bei Aristoteles* (Sitzungsberichte der bayerischen Akademie der Wissenschaften, phil.-hist. Klasse, 5; 1964).

FURLEY, D. J., 'Knowledge of Atoms and Void in Epicureanism' in J. P. Anton and G. L. Kustas (eds.), *Essays in Ancient Greek Philosophy* (Albany: SUNY Press, 1971), 607–19; repr. in id., *Cosmic Problems* (Cambridge: Cambridge University Press, 1989), 161–71.

—— and NEHAMAS, A. (eds.), *Essays on Aristotle's Rhetoric* (Princeton: Princeton University Press, 1994).

GLIDDEN, D., 'Skeptic Semiotics', *Phronesis*, 28 (1983), 213–55.

GOEDECKEMEYER, A., *Die Geschichte des griechischen Skeptizismus* (Leipzig: Dieterich, 1905; repr. Aalen: Scientia Verlag, 1968).

GOMPERZ, T., 'Beiträge zur Kritik und Erklärung griechischer Schriftsteller, III', *Sitzungsberichte Wien*, 83 (1876), 3–37; repr. in id., *Hellenika* (2 vols.; Leipzig: Veit, 1912), i. 236–74.

GOULET-CAZÉ, M.-O., 'Le Cynisme est-il une philosophie?', in M. Dixsaut (ed.), *Contre Platon*, i. *Le Platonisme dévoilé* (Paris: Vrin, 1993), 273–313.

GRICE, H. P., 'Meaning', *Phil. Rev.* 67 (1957), 377–88; repr. in id., *Studies in the Ways of Words* (Cambridge, Mass.: Harvard University Press, 1989), 213–23.

—— 'Meaning Revisited', in N. V. Smith (ed.), *Mutual Knowledge* (London: Academic Press, 1982), 223–50; repr. in id., *Studies in the Ways of Words* (Cambridge, Mass.: Harvard University Press, 1989), 283–303.

HADOT, P., 'Liste commentée des œuvres de Chrysippe (D.L. VII 189–202)', in R. Goulet (ed.), *Dictionnaire des philosophes antiques*, ii (Paris: CNRS Éditions: 1994), 336–56.

HANKINSON, R. J., 'Galen on the Foundations of Science', in J. A. López Férez (ed.), *Galeno: Obra, pensamiento e influencia* (Madrid: Universidad Nacional de Educación a Distancia, 1991), 15–29.

HEINTZ. W., *Studien zu Sextus Empiricus* (Halle: Niemeyer, 1932).

IERODIAKONOU, K., 'The Stoic Indemonstrables in the Later Tradition', in K. Döring and T. Ebert (eds.), *Dialektiker und Stoiker: Zur Logik der Stoa und ihrer Vorläufer* (Stuttgart: Steiner, 1993), 187–200.

JACKSON, B. D., 'The Theory of Signs in St. Augustine's *De Doctrina Christiana*', in Markus (ed.), *Augustine*, 92–147.

JAEGER, W., *Diokles von Karystos: Die griechische Medizin und die Schule des Aristoteles* (Berlin: Weidmann, 1938).

JANKO, R., 'Philodemus Resartus: Progress in Reconstructing the Philosophical Papyri of Herculaneum', *Proceedings of the Boston Area Colloquium in Ancient Philosophy*, 7 (1991), 271–305.

JUDSON, L., 'Chance and "Always or for the Most Part" in Aristotle', in id. (ed.), *Aristotle's* Physics*: A Collection of Essays* (Oxford: Oxford University Press, 1991), 73–99.

KANTELHARDT, A., *De Aristotelis rhetoricis* (Göttingen: Dieterich, 1911); photographically reproduced in Stark (ed.), *Rhetorika* [page-references are to the original page-numbers, not to the additional continuous pagination of the reprint].

KASSEL, R., *Der Text der aristotelischen Rhetorik: Prolegomena zu einer kritischen Ausgabe* (Berlin: De Gruyter, 1971).

KNEALE, W., and KNEALE, M., *The Development of Logic* (Oxford: Oxford University Press, 1962).

KUDLIEN, F., 'Herophilos und der Beginn des medizinischen Skepsis', *Gesnerus*, 21 (1964), 1–13.

LLOYD, G. E. R., *Polarity and Analogy: Two Types of Argumentation in Early Greek Thought* (Cambridge: Cambridge University Press, 1966).

—— *Science, Folklore and Ideology: Studies in the Life Sciences in Ancient Greece* (Cambridge: Cambridge University Press, 1983).

—— 'The Theories and Practices of Demonstration in Aristotle', *Proceedings of the Boston Area Colloquium in Ancient Philosophy*, 6 (1990), 371–401; repr. in id., *Aristotelian Explorations* (Cambridge: Cambridge University Press, 1996), 7–37.

—— 'Theories and Practices of Demonstration in Galen', in M. Frede and G. Striker (eds.), *Rationality in Greek Thought* (Oxford: Oxford University Pres, 1996), 255–77.

LONG, A. A., 'Reply to Jonathan Barnes, "Epicurean Signs"', in J. Annas and R. H. Grimm (eds.), *Oxford Studies in Ancient Philosophy*, suppl. vol. (Oxford: Oxford University Press, 1988), 140–3.

MAIER, H., *Die Syllogistik des Aristoteles* (2 pts. in 3 vols.; Tübingen: Laupp, 1896–1900).

MANSFELD, J., 'Aenesidemus and the Academics', in L. Ayres (ed.), *The Passionate Intellect: Essays on the Transformation of Classical Traditions*

Presented to Professor I. G. Kidd (New Brunswick, NJ: Transaction Publishers, 1995), 235–48.

MARKUS, R. A. (ed.), *Augustine: A Collection of Critical Essays* (Garden City, NY: Doubleday, 1972).

—— 'St. Augustine on Signs', in id. (ed.), *Augustine*, 61–91.

MARX, F., 'Aristoteles' Rhetorik', *Berichte über die Verhandlungen der kgl. sächsischen Gesellschaft der Wissenschaften zu Leipzig*, phil.-hist. Classe, 52 (1900), 241–328; photographically reproduced in Stark (ed.), *Rhetorika* [page-references are to the original page-numbers, not to the additional continuous pagination of the reprint].

MATES, B., *Stoic Logic* (Berkeley: University of California Press, 1953).

MAU, J., 'Über die Zuweisung zweier Epikur-Fragmente', *Philologus*, 99 (1955), 93–111.

MIGNUCCI, M., '"Ὡς ἐπὶ τὸ πολύ" et nécessaire dans la conception aris- totélicienne de la science', in Berti (ed.), *Aristotle on Science*, 173–203.

MORRISON, D., 'Philoponus and Simplicius on Tekmeriodic Proof', in E. Kessler *et al.* (eds.), *Method and Order in Renaissance Philosophy of Nature: The Aristotle Commentary Tradition* (Aldershot: Ashgate, 1997), 1–22.

MUELLER, I., 'Introduction to Stoic Logic', in J. M. Rist (ed.), *The Stoics* (Berkeley: University of California Press, 1978), 1–26.

MÜLLER, I. VON, 'Über die dem Galen zugeschriebene Abhandlung Περὶ τῆς ἀρίστης αἱρέσεως', *Sitzungsberichte der philosophisch-philologischen Klasse der K. Bayer. Akademie der Wissenschaften* (1898), 53–162.

—— 'Über Galens Werk vom wissenschaftlichen Beweis', *Abhandlungen der K. Bayer. Akademie der Wissenschaften*, 20/2 (1895), 405–78.

NATORP, P., *Forschungen zur Geschichte des Erkenntnisproblems im Altertum* (Berlin: Wilhelm Hertz, 1884).

NUTTON, V., *Karl Gottlob Kühn and his Edition of the Works of Galen: A Bibliography and Introduction Compiled by Vivian Nutton* (Oxford: Oxford Microform publications, 1976).

PATZIG, G., 'Erkenntnisgründe, Realgründe und Erklärungen (zu *Anal. Post. A* 13)', in Berti (ed.), *Aristotle on Science*, 141–56; repr. in id., *Gesammelte Schriften* (3 vols.; Göttingen: Wallstein, 1993–6), iii. 125– 40.

PHILIPPSON, R., *De Philodemi libro, qui est Περὶ σημείων καὶ σημειώσεων et Epicureorum doctrina logica* (Berlin: Berliner Buchdruckerei Actien- Gesellschaft, 1881).

—— 'Philodemos', *RE* xix (1938), 2444–82.

—— review of W. Heintz, *Studien zu Sextus Empiricus*, in *Berliner philo- logische Wochenschrift*, 53 (3 July 1933), 594–8.

—— 'Zur Wiederherstellung von Philodems sog. Schrift Περὶ Σημείων καὶ Σημειώσεων', *Rheinisches Museum*, 64 (1909), 1–38.

PRIMAVESI, O., *Die aristotelische Topik: Ein Interpretationsmodell und seine Erprobung am Beispiel von Topik B* (Munich: Beck, 1996).

RAPHAEL, S., 'Rhetoric, Dialectic and Syllogistic Argument: Aristotle's Position in "Rhetoric" I–II', *Phronesis*, 19 (1974), 153–67.

RIETH, O., *Grundbegriffe der stoischen Ethik* (Berlin: Weidmann, 1933).

ROBINSON, R., *Plato's Earlier Dialectic*, 2nd edn. (Oxford: Oxford University Press, 1953).

ROSS, W. D., *Aristotle*, 5th edn. (London: Methuen, 1949).

RYAN, E. E., *Aristotle's Theory of Rhetorical Argumentation* (Montreal: Les Éditions Bellarmin, 1984).

SANDBACH, F. H., 'Ennoia and Prolepsis in the Stoic Theory of Knowledge', in A. A. Long (ed.), *Problems in Stoicism* (London: Athlone, 1971), 22–37.

SCHMEKEL, A., *Die Philosophie der mittleren Stoa in ihrem geschichtlichen Zusammenhange dargestellt* (Berlin: Weidmann, 1892).

—— *Die positive Philosophie* (Berlin: Weidmann, 1938).

SCHOFIELD, M., 'Cicero for and against Divination', *Journal of Roman Studies*, 76 (1986), 47–65.

—— 'Epilogismos: An Appraisal', in M. Frede and G. Striker (eds.), *Rationality in Greek Thought* (Oxford: Oxford University Press, 1996), 221–37.

SEDLEY, D., 'Diodorus Cronus and Hellenistic Philosophy', *Proceedings of the Cambridge Philological Society*, 203 (1977), 74–120.

—— 'Epicurus On Nature Book XXVIII', *Cronache ercolanesi*, 3 (1973), 5–83.

—— 'The Negated Conjunction in Stoicism', *Elenchos*, 5 (1984), 312–16.

—— 'On Signs', in Barnes *et al.* (eds.), *Science and Speculation*, 239–72.

SLOMKOWSKI, P., *Aristotle's* Topics (Leiden: Brill, 1997).

SOLMSEN, F., *Die Entwicklung der aristotelischen Logik und Rhetorik* (Neue philologische Untersuchungen, 4; Berlin: Weidmann, 1929).

SPRUTE, J., 'Aristotle and the Legitimacy of Rhetoric', in Furley and Nehamas (eds.), *Essays on Aristotle's* Rhetoric, 117–28.

—— *Die Enthymemtheorie der aristotelischen Rhetorik* (Göttingen: Vandenhoeck and Ruprecht, 1982).

STADEN, H. VON, 'Experiment and Experience in Hellenistic Medicine', *Bulletin of the Institute of Classical Studies*, 22 (1975), 178–99.

—— 'Hairesis and Heresy: The Case of the Haireseis Iatrikai', in B. F. Meyers and E. Sanders (eds.), *Jewish and Christian Self Definition*, iii (London: SCM Press, 1982), 76–100.

—— 'Jaeger's "Skandalon der historischen Vernunft": Diocles, Aristotle and Theophrastus', in W. M. Calder (ed.), *Werner Jaeger Reconsidered* (Athens, Ga.: Scholars Press, 1992), 227–65.

STARK, R. (ed.), *Rhetorika: Schriften zur aristotelischen und hellenistischen Rhetorik* (Hildesheim: Georg Olms, 1968).

STOCKS, J. L., 'Epicurean Induction', *Mind*, NS 34 (1925), 185–203; repr. in id., *The Limits of Purpose and Other Essays* (London: Benn, 1932), 266–93.

STOPPER, M. R., 'Schizzi pirroniani', *Phronesis*, 28 (1983), 265–97.

STRIKER, G., 'Aristotle and the Uses of Logic', in J. Gentzler (ed.), *Method in Ancient Philosophy* (Oxford: Oxford University Press, 1998), 209–26.

—— 'Κριτήριον τῆς ἀληθείας', *Nachrichten der Akademie der Wissenschaften in Göttingen*, phil.-hist. Kl. 2 (1974), 47–110; trans. in ead., *Essays in Hellenistic Epistemology and Ethics* (Cambridge: Cambridge University Press, 1996), 22–76.

—— 'Notwendigkeit mit Lücken: Aristoteles über die Kontingenz der Naturvorgänge', *Neue Hefte für Philosophie*, 24–5 (1985), 146–64.

TECUŞAN, M. (ed.), *The Fragments of the Methodists* (2 vols.; Studies in Ancient Medicine, 24; Leiden: Brill, forthcoming).

THUROT, C., *Études sur Aristote: Politique, Dialectique, Rhétorique* (Paris: Durand, 1860).

VAHLEN, J., *Beiträge zu Aristoteles' Poetik* (Leipzig: Teubner, 1914).

—— 'Zur Kritik aristotelischer Schriften (Poetik und Rhetorik)', *Sitzungsberichte der Wiener Akademie*, 38 (1861), 59–148; repr. in id., *Gesammelte philologische Schriften* (2 vols.; Leipzig: Teubner, 1911), i. 13–105.

VALLANCE, J. T., *The Lost Theory of Asclepiades of Bithynia* (Oxford: Oxford University Press, 1990).

VERBEKE, G., 'La philosophie du signe chez les Stoïciens', in J. Brunschwig (ed.), *Les Stoïciens et leur logique* (Paris: Vrin, 1978), 401–24.

WEIDEMANN, H., 'Aristotle on Inference from Signs (*Rhetoric* I 2, 1357[b]1–25)', *Phronesis*, 34 (1989), 343–51.

WERSDÖRFER, H., *Die Φιλοσοφία des Isokrates im Spiegel ihrer Terminologie: Untersuchungen zur frühattischen Rhetorik und Stillehre* (Kl.-Philol. Stud. 13; Leipzig, 1940).

WÖRNER, M., *Das Ethische in der Rhetorik des Aristoteles* (Munich: Karl Alber, 1990).

Index Locorum

Aeschylus
  PV 484: 45
Alcmaeon
  B1: 3
Alexander of Aphrodisias
  De anima, 115. 6 ff.: 156
  In an. pr. 21. 25: 150
  In Top. 8. 16: 150
    214. 12 ff.: 52 n. 71
Ammonius
  In cat. 2. 2–8: 192 n. 60
[Ammonius]
  In an. pr. 68. 25: 224 n. 50
Anaxagoras
  B 9: 11
  B 12: 11
  B 13: 11
  B 21a: 2
Andocides
  3. 2: 1 n. 1
Anonymous
  In rhet. (Rabe) 3. 26: 187–8 n. 52
    4. 19–26: 187–8 n. 52
Anonymous (Segueranius: *Rhet. Graec.* Spengel–Hammer)
  i. 379. 12–17: 35–6 n. 37
Antiphon (Blass)
  fr. 72: 1 n. 1
Aristophanes
  Nub. 369: 3
Aristotle
  An. post. 1. 1, 71^{a}8–9: 38
    1. 2, 71^{b}9–16: 73
    1. 2, 71^{b}18: 73
    1. 2, 71^{b}20–2: 73
    1. 2, 71^{b}21–2: 76
    1. 4, 73^{a}21–3: 73
    1. 6, 74^{b}5–12: 73, 74 n. 95
    1. 6, 75^{a}20–2: 75 n. 97
    1. 6, 75^{a}31–4: 75
    1. 6, 75^{a}33–4: 73
    1. 6, 75^{a}33: 75 n. 98
    1. 7, 75^{b}1: 74
    1. 13, 78^{a}27–9: 75
    1. 13, 78^{a}36–^{b}3: 76

  1. 13, 78^{b}12: 75
  1. 21, 82^{b}35: 19 n. 8
  1. 30, 87^{b}19–27: 74
  1. 30, 87^{b}22 ff.: 31
  2. 2, 90^{a}6–7: 7
  2. 8, 93^{a}36 ff.: 77
  2. 8, 93^{a}36–7: 76
  2. 12, 96^{a}8–19: 31, 74
  2. 16, 98^{b}19 ff.: 75, 76
  2. 17, 99^{a}1–3: 77
  2. 17, 99^{a}3: 73
An. pr. 1. 1, 24^{b}18–20: 21
  1. 8, 29^{b}29 ff.: 31
  1. 13, 32^{b}5–22: 74
  1. 23, 41^{b}1–3: 21
  1. 24, 69^{a}14–15: 38
  1. 27, 43^{b}33: 31
  1. 28, 44^{b}7–8: 21
  1. 32, 47^{a}2 ff.: 69
  1. 32, 47^{a}13–18: 24
  1. 32, 47^{a}16–17: 25
  2. 23, 68^{b}9–14: 72
  2. 23, 68^{b}9–13: 13, 21
  2. 24, 69^{a}1 ff.: 39
  2. 24, 69^{a}15–16: 39
  2. 24, 69^{a}16: 39
  2. 27, 70^{a}4–5: 23
  2. 27, 70^{a}4: 23
  2. 27, 70^{a}7–9: 23
  2. 27, 70^{a}7: 29 n. 26
  2. 27, 70^{a}9–11: 13, 23, 55
  2. 27, 70^{b}4–5: 23
  2. 27, 70^{b}7 ff.: 13
  2. 27, 70^{b}32 ff.: 72
De divinatione per somnum, 1, 462^{b}26 ff.: 77 n. 102
De gen. et corr. 6, 333^{b}24: 19 n. 9
EE 1. 6, 1216^{b}26–8: 2
EN 1. 3, 1094^{b}12–27: 18
  2. 2, 1104^{a}1 ff.: 18
  2. 2, 1104^{a}13–14: 2
  6. 3, 1139^{b}31–2: 73
  10. 9, 1180^{b}16–23: 94
Metaph. A 1, 981^{a}1 ff.: 245
  A 1, 981^{a}5–12: 94

Aristotle, *Metaph.* (*cont.*):
A 1, 981^a29: 245
Γ 2, $1004^b22\text{-}5$: 16
$\varDelta$ 3, 1014^a26 ff.: 45
E 1, 1025^b13: 19 n. 9
Z 4, 1029^b13: 19 n. 8
Po. 16, 1454^b20 ff.: 2
Rhet. 1. 1, 1354^a1 ff: 15
  1. 1, $1354^a1\text{-}11$: 14
  1. 1, 1354^a11 ff.: 20
  1. 1, $1354^a13\text{-}18$: 82
  1. 1, 1354^a14: 81
  1. 1, 1354^b16 ff.: 20
  1. 1, $1354^b16\text{-}22$: 82
  1. 1, 1355^a3 ff.: 82
  1. 1, $1355^a3\text{-}14$: 82
  1. 1, $1355^a7\text{-}8$: 82
  1. 1, $1355^a10\text{-}15$: 19
  1. 1, 1355^a20 ff.: 17 n. 5
  1. 1, 1355^a24: 80
  1. 1, $1355^a29\text{-}35$: 16
  1. 1, $1355^a29\text{-}33$: 17, 70 n. 92
  1. 1, $1355^b10\text{-}12$: 93
  1. 1, $1355^b15\text{-}17$: 16
  1. 1, $1355^b17\text{-}21$: 16
  1. 2, $1355^b26\text{-}35$: 15
  1. 2, 1355^b26: 16
  1. 3, $1355^b28\text{-}32$: 16
  1. 2, 1355^b35 ff.: 20, 82
  1. 2, $1356^a25\text{-}6$: 18, 22 n. 14
  1. 2, $1356^a32\text{-}4$: 15
  1. 2, 1356^b4: 17
  1. 2, $1356^b15\text{-}17$: 32, 68
  1. 2, 1357^a1 ff.: 30
  1. 2, $1357^a1\text{-}7$: 18
  1. 2, $1357^a3\text{-}4$: 80
  1. 2, $1357^a5\text{-}7$: 30
  1. 2, $1357^a13\text{-}15$: 18, 19
  1. 2, 1357^a13: 40
  1. 2, 1357^a14: 19 n. 8
  1. 2, 1357^a16: 19
  1. 2, $1357^a22\text{-}1358^a2$: 21: 63
  1. 2, $1357^a22\text{-}33$: 30, 34, 36 n. 38
  1. 2, 1357^a22: 30 n. 29
  1. 2, $1357^a27\text{-}32$: 30-1
  1. 2, $1357^a31\text{-}2$: 24
  1. 2, $1357^a32\text{-}3$: 23, 55
  1. 2, $1357^a34\text{-}{}^b1$: 23
  1. 2, 1357^a34: 23
  1. 2, $1357^b4\text{-}5$: 28
  1. 2, $1357^b5\text{-}6$: 30
  1. 2, 1357^b9: 28
  1. 2, 1357^b14: 30

  1. 2, $1357^b21\text{-}2$: 28
  1. 2, 1357^b22: 30
  1. 2, $1357^b23\text{-}7$: 18
  1. 2, $1357^b25\text{-}6$: 19 n. 8
  1. 2, 1357^b26: 19, 40
  1. 2, 1357^b28: 38
  1. 2, 1357^b29: 39
  1. 2, $1358^a2\text{-}33$: 47
  1. 2, 1358^a14 ff.: 43
  1. 2, $1358^a22\text{-}6$: 15
  1. 2, $1358^a23\text{-}6$: 18
  1. 2, 1358^a27: 45
  1. 2, $1358^a31\text{-}2$: 45
  1. 3, 1358^a36 ff.: 18
  1. 3, 1358^b20 ff.: 85
  1. 3, 1358^b29: 42
  1. 3, 1359^a6: 22 n. 14, 29 n. 25
  1. 3, $1359^a7\text{-}8$: 28
  1. 4, 1359^a30 ff.: 18
  1. 4, $1359^a30\text{-}9$: 19 n. 8
  1. 4, 1359^b9 ff.: 22 n. 14
  1. 4, $1359^b11\text{-}16$: 22 n. 14
  1. 4, $1359^b12\text{-}16$: 15, 18
  1. 4, $1359^b18\text{-}33$: 19 n. 8
  1. 9, $1366^a23\text{-}8$: 85
  1. 9, $1367^b24\text{-}6$: 36 n. 39, 41 n. 44
  1. 9, 1368^a26 ff.: 48 n. 64
  1. 12, 1372^a6 ff.: 50-1 n. 68
  1. 12, 1372^a35: 50-1 n. 68
  2. 1, 1377^b18: 85
  2. 1, 1378^a16: 85
  2. 2, $1379^b16\text{-}19$: 42 n. 45
  2. 2, 1379^b36: 42 n. 45
  2. 3, 1380^a15: 42
  2. 4, 1381^a7: 42 n. 45
  2. 5, 1382^a30: 42 n. 45
  2. 6, $1383^b31\text{-}4$: 42 n. 45
  2. 7, 1385^b7: 42 n. 45
  2. 8, 1386^b2: 42 n. 45
  2. 18, $1391^b23\text{-}6$: 85
  2. 19, $1392^b14\text{-}{}^a8$: 58
  2. 20, 1393^a27 ff.: 39
  2. 21, $1394^a23\text{-}7$: 18
  2. 21, $1394^a24\text{-}7$: 19 n. 8
  2. 22, $1395^b24\text{-}6$: 19
  2. 22, $1396^a33\text{-}{}^b1$: 19 n. 9
  2. 22, $1396^b21\text{-}2$: 45
  2. 22, 1396^b21: 47 n. 62
  2. 22, 1396^b22: 44
  2. 22, $1396^b28\text{-}1397^a1$: 47 n. 61, 47 n. 62
  2. 22, $1396^b33\text{-}1397^a1$: 44

2. 22, 1397^a3–4: 17, 55
2. 22, 1397^a4: 28
2. 23, 1397^a7–19: 50
2. 23, 1397^a20–3: 50
2. 23, 1397^a23–$^b11$: 50, 53
2. 23, 1397^a29: 52
2. 23, 1397^b12 ff.: 43
2. 23, 1397^b27–1398^a3: 50
2. 23, 1398^a3 ff.: 51
2. 23, 1399^a9–17: 50–1 n. 68
2. 23, 1399^a16: 51 n. 69
2. 23, 1399^a28 ff.: 51
2. 23, 1399^b13 ff.: 51
2. 23, 1399^b19–30: 41
2. 23, 1399^b30 ff.: 50–1 n. 68
2. 23, 1400^a4: 51 n. 69
2. 23, 1400^b2: 52 n. 71
2. 23, 1400^b4: 28
2. 23, 1400^b15: 45, 47
2. 23, 1400^b16: 51 n. 69, 52
2. 24, 1400^b34–7: 17, 55
2. 24, 1401^a12: 52
2. 24, 1401^a24–$^b3$: 54
2. 24, 1401^a33: 52
2. 24, 1401^b2: 57
2. 24, 1401^b3–9: 57
2. 24, 1401^b8: 52
2. 24, 1401^b9 ff.: 28
2. 24, 1401^b9: 28, 55
2. 24, 1401^b20 ff.: 57
2. 24, 1401^b24: 36
2. 24, 1401^b29: 57
2. 24, 1401^b34: 57
2. 24, 1402^a2–29: 58
2. 24, 1402^a2–8: 17
2. 24, 1402^a2–5: 40
2. 24, 1402^a7 ff.: 59
2. 24, 1402^a13–16: 60
2. 24, 1402^a15: 57
2. 24, 1402^a16: 58
2. 24, 1402^a17–23: 59
2. 24, 1402^a17: 51 n. 69
2. 24, 1402^a22–4: 58
2. 24, 1402^a22–3: 60
2. 24, 1402^a26–7: 62
2. 25, 1402^b2–3: 62 n. 82
2, 25, 1402^b12–1403^a16: 62
2, 25, 1402^b12–14: 55
2. 25, 1402^b13–1403^a16: 21
2. 25, 1402^b13: 29
2. 25, 1402^b14: 28
2. 25, 1402^b15: 23
2. 25, 1402^b17–18: 39

2. 25, 1402^b20–1403^a3: 63
2. 25, 1402^b22–8: 62–3 n. 82
2. 25, 1402^b24–35: 63
2. 25, 1402^b26: 63 n. 83
2. 25, 1402^b30–4: 63
2. 25, 1402^b35–1403^a1: 63, 66
2, 25, 1403^a2–5: 26, 40
2. 25, 1403^a5–6: 63
2. 25, 1403^a5: 39, 63
2. 25, 1403^a6–10: 64–6, 78–9
2, 25, 1403^a11: 30
2. 25, 1403^a13–16: 26
2. 26, 1403^a17–33: 48
2. 26, 1403^a18–19: 42, 44
3. 1, 1403^b13–15: 45, 47 n. 62
3. 2, 1404^b33: 42
3. 19, 1419^b27: 44
SE 1, 165^a17–19: 48
1, 165^a17–18: 53
1, 165^a23: 44
1, 165^a25: 16 n. 4
1, 165^a28–37: 56
1, 165^a31: 16
1, 165^a34–7: 48
2, 165^b3–4: 16
4, 165^b23–4: 48
4, 165^b23: 44
4, 166^a22–3: 48 n. 63
4, 166^a33: 48 n. 63
4, 166^b1: 48 n. 63
4, 166^b10: 48 n. 63
4, 166^b20–2: 48
4, 166^b20: 48 n. 63
4, 166^b22–3: 48 n. 63, 58
5, 166^b28: 48 n. 63
5, 166^b32–3: 52
5, 166^b34–6: 58
5, 166^b37 ff.: 52
5, 166^b37–167^a20: 58
5, 166^b37: 48 n. 63
5, 167^a1: 58 n. 77
5, 167^a7 ff.: 52 n. 71, 58
5, 167^a7–14: 58
5, 167^a21: 48 n. 63
5, 167^a36; 48 n. 63
5, 167^b1 ff.: 57
5, 167^b1: 48 n. 63, 57
5, 167^b8–12: 57
5, 167^b8–11: 28
5, 167^b8: 36
5, 167^b10–11: 36
5, 167^b21: 48 n. 63
5, 167^b37: 48 n. 63

Aristotle, *SE* (*cont.*):
  6, 168^{b}1 ff.: 58
  6, 168^{b}11 ff.: 52
  6, 168^{b}11–12: 59
  6, 168^{b}14–16: 58
  6, 169^{a}18: 44
  7, 169^{a}22: 57
  7, 169^{a}37: 57
  7, 169^{b}2: 57
  7, 169^{b}11: 57
  9, 170^{a}36–8: 16 n. 4, 70 n. 92
  9, 170^{b}8–11: 16 n. 4, 70 n. 92
  11, 172^{b}5–8: 16 n. 4, 70 n. 92
  11, 172^{b}5: 44
  12, 172^{b}25: 49
  12, 172^{b}31: 45
  15, 174^{a}18: 45
  15, 174^{a}21: 45
  16. 175^{a}5 ff.: 70
  16, 175^{a}5–16: 17 n. 5
  16, 175^{a}17–19: 17, 70 n. 92
  20, 177^{b}31: 49
  24, 179^{b}17 ff.: 49
  25, 180^{a}23 ff.: 52, 58
  25, 180^{a}28–9: 58
  25, 180^{a}34 ff.: 61 n. 81
  25, 180^{b}8 ff.: 58
  34, 183^{b}1: 70 n. 92
  Top. 1. 1, 100^{a}1 ff.: 16
    1. 1, 100^{a}25–7: 21
    1. 1, 100^{a}27–8: 73
    1. 2, 101^{a}25 ff.: 17 n. 5
    1. 3, 101^{b}5–10: 93
    1. 6, 102^{b}27–35: 50 n. 67
    1. 6, 102^{b}35 ff.: 50 n. 67
    1. 12, 105^{a}13–14: 38
    1. 18, 108^{a}26–37: 17, 70 n. 92
    2. 2, 110^{a}10–13: 49
    2. 11, 115^{b}11 ff.: 52
    3. 6, 119^{a}38 ff.: 43 n. 48
    8. 2, 157^{a}34–7: 65 n. 89
    8. 8, 160^{b}1–5: 65 n. 89
    8. 10, 161^{a}1–2: 62 n. 82
    8. 10, 161^{a}14: 62
    8. 14, 163^{b}9–16: 17
    8. 14, 163^{b}20: 4 n. 51
[Aristotle]
  Rhet. ad Alex. 12, 1430^{b}34–5: 26 n. 19
Augustine
  De civitate Dei, 5. 1: 161 n. 18
  De dialectica, ch. 5: 4
  De doctrina Christiana, 2. 1. 1: 3–4

    2. 1. 2: 4
    2. 2. 3: 4
Celsus
  De medicina, proem. 27–9: 166
  28: 96
  39: 96
Cicero
  De legibus, 1. 45: 95 n. 10, 156 n. 9
  Div. 1. 11: 162
    1. 12: 162, 163, 164, 166, 180
    1. 16: 163
    1. 25: 169 n. 28
    1. 29: 163
    1. 34: 162, 166 n. 24, 169 n. 28
    1. 35: 163, 168 n. 27
    1. 36: 164 n. 19
    1. 58: 168 n. 27
    1. 72 ff.: 167 n. 25
    1. 72: 162, 164, 167
    1. 74: 169 n. 28
    1. 75: 169 n. 28
    1. 82: 162, 165
    1. 86: 163
    1. 97: 167
    1. 99: 167
    1. 109: 163, 164
    1. 116: 168 n. 27
    1. 118: 162, 165
    1. 127: 163, 164, 169 n. 28, 180
    1. 130: 169 n. 28
    2. 8: 162
    2. 26–7: 162
    2. 26: 166, 169 n. 28
    2. 35: 165
    2. 49: 167–8 n. 26
    2. 53: 169 n. 28
    2. 55 ff.: 167 n. 25
    2. 55: 167
    2. 59: 167
    2. 61: 167–8 n. 26
    2. 100: 162
    2. 103: 148, 171 n. 32
    2. 129: 168 n. 27
    2. 130: 162, 165
    2. 144: 168 n. 27
    2. 146: 168 n. 27, 180
    2. 147: 168 n. 27
  Fat. 12 ff.: 152
    15–16: 161
    15: 181, 183
    41: 156 n. 11, 157
    43–4: 157

44: 157
Fin. 3. 3: 192
    3. 58: 251
Luc. 17: 1
    22: 95 n. 11
    26: 101, 148, 171 n. 32
    32: 103
    41–53: 102
    83–6: 102
    98: 192
    100: 251
    105: 103
    110: 103, 106 n. 18
    122: 106 n. 18
    143: 151 n. 4, 189
ND 2. 166–7: 162
Part. orat. 39–40: 36
Top. 55–7: 183
    59: 157
[Cicero]
    Rhet. ad Heren. 2. 11: 36
Clement
    Stromata, 6. 2: 1 n. 2
    8. 3. 5: 171 n. 32
    8. 3. 7: : 171 n. 32

Democritus
    B 167: 11
Demosthenes
    25. 76: 44 n. 51
Diogenes of Apollonia
    B 4: 3
Diogenes Laertius
    1. 17: 189
    6. 103: 192
    7. 45: 148, 182 n. 45
    7. 71: 150–1 n. 3
    7. 72: 157 n. 12
    7. 73: 152
    7. 74: 150–1 n. 3, 157 n. 12
    7. 75: 251
    7. 78: 149
    7. 107: 251
    7. 177: 251
    7. 190: 251
    7. 191: 193 n. 61
    9. 94: 166 n. 23
    9. 96: 118, 125
    9. 103: 100
    9. 115: 89
    10. 32: 195
    10. 34: 198

Elias
    In cat. 111. 1–32: 192 n. 60
Empedocles
    B 84: 10
    B 100: 10
Epictetus
    2. 5. 10–11: 251
Epicurus
    Ep. Hdt. 37–8: 7
    38: 195, 196
    39–40: 203
    39: 195
    40: 196, 221 n. 46
    51: 198
    58: 203
    80: 196, 199
    Ep. Pyth. 86: 200
    87: 195, 197, 199
    90: 202 n. 7
    91: 203
    92: 203
    93: 203
    94: 199, 201
    95: 199, 201
    97: 195, 197, 202
    98–9: 203
    98: 199, 202
    102: 202
    104: 195, 202

Galen
    De aliment. facult. (vi Kühn), 455.
        5: 96
    De causis continentibus (Deichgrä-
        ber), 141. 1–3: 91
    De comp. medic. sec. gen. (xiii Kühn),
        366. 5 ff.: 112 n. 21
    De dign. puls. (viii Kühn), 780.
        14 ff.: 145
    De locis affectis (viii Kühn), 14. 7 ff.:
        93
    De meth. med. (x Kühn), 36. 14: 179
        126. 10 ff.: 133, 154
        163. 14 ff.: 110
    De opt. doctr. (ii *SM*), 89–90: 179
    De ord. lib. prop. (ii *SM*), 82. 3–10:
        131 n. 33
    De plac. Hipp. et Plat. (De Lacy),
        110. 20–112. 2: 165
        114. 1 ff.: 165
        130. 24: 166 n. 22
        130. 33: 166 n. 21
        152. 23–7: 164

Galen, *De plac. Hipp. et Plat.* (De
  Lacy) (*cont.*):
   154. 5: 166 n. 22
   170. 23–7: 164
   176. 14: 166 n. 22
   192. 3–7: 165
   200. 22: 166 n. 22
   204. 31: 166 n. 21
   218. 29: 166 n. 22
   220. 5–9: 164
   224. 7: 166 n. 21
   226. 30: 166 n. 22
   542: 179
De sanitate tuenda (iv/2 CMG), 161:
  93
De sect. ingred. (iii *SM*), 2. 5–9: 180
  n. 44
   3. 12: 180 n. 44
   3. 19–20: 234
   7. 1 ff.: 91
   7. 6: 180 n. 44
   9. 4–6: 94
   9. 6–7: 96, 235
   9. 9–13: 92
   9. 13–19: 92
   9. 21–2: 94
   10: 92
   10. 5–10: 235
   10. 8–9: 166
   10. 9: 96
   10. 23–4: 110, 112
   11: 96
   11. 8: 112 n. 21
   11. 9–10: 112
   11. 10–12: 109
   11. 16–19: 95 n. 10
   12. 22 ff.: 98
   14: 97 n. 15
In Hipp. de acut. morb. vict. (CMG
  v/9/1), 118. 1: 35–6 n. 37, 185
  n. 49
In Hippocr. de med. officina (xviiiB
  Kühn), 649: 95 n. 11, 156 n. 9
In Hipp. prog. (CMG v/9/2), 373.
  1–14: 35–6 n. 37, 185
Institutio logica (Kalbfleisch), 4. 16:
  179
   10. 9–13: 183
   24. 14–16: 154
   32. 17–21: 182
   33. 3–5: 182
   33. 7: 155
   33. 14–18: 183

   34. 18–19: 182
   39. 18 ff.: 179
   40. 3 ff.: 179
On Medical Experience (Walzer),
  85 ff.: 92
   88: 92
   91–2: 135
   95: 252
   98–9: 133
   98: 92
   100: 95 n. 10
   102: 95 n. 10
   103: 95 n. 10, 96
   104–5: 95 n. 10
   107: 95 n. 10
   111: 95 n. 10
   112: 252
   132–3: 95 n. 10
   133–5: 96, 98, 112 n. 21
   133: 112 n. 21
   135: 95 n. 10
   136: 95 n. 10
   137: 95 n. 10
   139: 95 n. 10
   140: 112 n. 21
   141: 95 n. 10
   153–4: 92
   153: 95 n. 10
Subfig. emp. (Deichgräber), 43. 11–
  14: 92
   44. 10: 155
   45. 25–30: 252
   50. 29–51. 11: 180 n. 44
   58. 15 ff.: 252
   62. 24–31: 95 n. 10, 112 n. 21
   63. 20–6: 155
   64. 7: 155
   64. 31: 96
   67. 32–5: 98
   68. 5: 98
   68. 25 ff.: 113
   70. 14 ff.: 113
   87. 7: 92, 95
   87. 12 ff.: 113
   88. 19–24: 92
   88. 25: 92
   89. 12–15: 95
[Galen]
  Def. med. (xix Kühn), 354. 12 ff.:
   252
   394. 8–12: 109
   396. 12–14: 110
  De optima secta (i Kühn), 108. 8:

185–6 n. 40
109. 13: 185–6 n. 40
110. 14–16: 134
114: 252
116–17: 154
116. 17 ff.: 213
119. 12 ff.: 136
119. 17 ff.: 136
120. 2–121. 9: 136
120. 3–5: 136
121. 16–18: 136
122. 11–124. 8: 134
123. 17–18: 135
124. 1–2: 135
126. 12: 185–6 n. 40
127. 11: 185–6 n. 40
133. 16: 135
133. 19–134. 8: 135
134. 10–11: 135
149. 8: 185–6 n. 40
159. 1–2: 136
162. 12–13: 136
187. 17: 137
188. 7–8: 137
189. 7: 137
Historia philosopha (Diels), 597. 1–
  598. 2: 192
598. 10–11: 192
602. 5–7: 189
605. 9–18: 108
605. 10–19: 117
605. 10–11: 189
605. 11: 150–1 n. 3
608. 4–7: 193
Introductio seu Medicus (xiv Kühn),
  683. 11 ff.: 96 n. 13
Gorgias
  Hel. 13: 3

Herodotus
  1. 57: 2 n. 2
  2. 43: 2 n. 2
  2. 58: 2 n. 2
  2. 104: 2 n. 2
  2. 33: 2
  3. 38: 2 n. 2
  7. 238: 2 n. 2
  9. 100: 2 n. 2
[Hippocrates]
  Vict. 1. 11–12: 2
  VM 1. 3: 97
    22: 2

Homer
  Iliad, 10. 218–54: 41
Hyperides (Blass)
  fr. 195: 1 n. 1

Isocrates
  10. 11: 47
  13. 16: 46 n. 57, 47
  15. 183: 47
  Ep. 6. 8: 47

Lucretius
  1. 72–7: 246
  1. 159 ff.: 196
  1. 334 ff.: 196
  1. 423–5: 195
  1. 693–4: 195
  2. 112–41: 226, 239
  2. 125–8: 226 n. 54
  4. 482 ff.: 195
  5. 526–33: 197
  5. 534 ff.: 197
  6. 703 ff.: 198

Martianus Capella
  4. 415–20: 183 n. 46

Olympiodorus
  In cat. 3. 20–30: 192 n. 60

Philodemus
  De signis (De Lacy), Ia. 1–v. 36: 206
  I. 19 ff.: 209
  I. 30–2: 219
  II. 25 ff.: 230 n. 60
  IV. 5–10: 228
  IV. 10 ff.: 214
  IV. 11–13: 222
  IV. 11: 222
  v. 1 ff.: 236
  VII. 5–6: 207
  VII. 8–11: 227
  VII. 10–12: 210
  VII. 32–7: 251
  VIII. 21 ff.: 210
  VIII. 21–IX. 9: 227
  VIII. 28–32: 215
  VIII. 30–IX. 2: 235
  VIII. 33–5: 234
  VIII. 35: 237–8 n. 72
  IX. 4: 7
  IX. 35–8: 209
  X. 20–6: 226

Philodemus, *De signis* (De Lacy)
   (*cont.*):
    XI. 9 ff.: 209
    XI. 9–26: 226
    XI. 13–14: 207
    XI. 26 ff.: 210
    XI. 26–XIX. 4: 206
    XI. 26–XII. 35: 211
    XI. 32 ff.: 215
    XI. 32–XII. 19: 212
    XII. 7–12: 223
    XII. 14–30: 218
    XII. 27: 235
    XIII. 32: 237–8 n. 72
    XIV. 2 ff.: 210
    XIV. 11–23: 213
    XIV. 14–28: 215
    XIV. 15–17: 212
    XIV. 33: 209
    XV. 11: 235
    XV. 13: 209
    XV. 19–25: 220, 225
    XV. 26–XVI. 1: 220
    XV. 37: 217 n. 38
    XVI. 31–XVII. 11: 222
    XVI. 35–7: 234
    XVII. 3–11: 228
    XVII. 3–8: 233
    XVII. 8 ff.: 210
    XVII. 11: 209
    XVII. 33–4: 237–8 n. 72
    XVIII. 1: 235
    XIX. 4–9: 206
    XIX. 9–XXVII. 28: 206
    XIX. 25–9: 215–16 n. 35
    XXII. 37–8: 237–8 n. 72
    XXIII. 5: 237–8 n. 72
    XXIV. 3–5: 237–8 n. 72
    XXIV. 8: 235
    XXVII. 23: 237–8 n. 72
    XXVII. 24: 235
    XXVIII. 13–XXIX. 16: 206
    XXVIII. 15–25: 225 n. 51
    XXVIII. 15: 225 n. 51
    XXVIII. 16–25: 213
    XXVIII. 17–25: 210
    XXIX. 4 ff.: 233 n. 67
    XXIX. 4–12: 222
    XXIX. 20–XXXVIII. 22: 206
    XXIX. 24–XXX. 15: 226
    XXX. 33–XXXI. 8: 231
    XXX. 37–XXXI. 1: 210, 228
    XXX. 37–8: 229

    XXXI. 6: 7
    XXXI. 8–17: 211
    XXXI. 8–16: 229
    XXXI. 23–36: 227
    XXXI. 26–35: 232 n. 65
    XXXI. 36–XXXII. 8: 232
    XXXI. 36–XXXII. 6: 211
    XXXI. 38: 233 n. 66
    XXXII. 2: 231
    XXXII. 31–XXXIII. 9: 217
    XXXIII. 1 ff.: 214
    XXXIII. 1–7: 221 n. 44
    XXXIII. 6: 212 n. 28
    XXXIII. 7–9: 217 n. 38
    XXXIII. 17: 235
    XXXIII. 28: 219
    XXXIII. 33 ff.: 229
    XXXIV. 27–9: 229 n. 58
    XXXIV. 36 ff.: 214
    XXXV. 1–4: 228
    XXXV. 3–4: 222
    XXXV. 4–XXXVI. 8: 235
    XXXV. 4 ff.: 228
    XXXV. 5: 219
    XXXV. 29–31: 228
    XXXV. 31–2: 211
    XXXV. 35–XXXVI. 7: 228
    XXXV. 35: 234
    XXXVI. 17–24: 231
    XXXVI. 19: 231
    XXXVI. 21–4: 211
    XXXVI. 24 ff.: 233 n. 66
    XXXVI. 33–4: 231
    XXXVII. 1–XXXVIII. 8: 211
    XXXVII. 1–12: 222
    XXXVII. 7–17: 213
    XXXVII. 24 ff.: 215–16 n. 35, 235, 236
    XXXVII. 24–XXXVIII. 8: 215
    XXXVII. 29–30: 215–16 n. 35
    XXXVII. 30–8: 210
    XXXVII. 34–XXXVIII. 8: 213
    XXXVIII. 25 ff.: 234
    fr. 1. 1–6: 230
Philoponus
  In an post. 97. 20 ff.: 75 n. 98
    170. 27 ff.: 75 n. 98
  In cat. 2. 24–9: 192 n. 60
Photius
  Bibliotheca, 212, 170^{a}12 ff.: 118
Plato
  Grg. 453 D ff.: 16
    458 E ff.: 15

465 A: 93
501 A: 93
Phd. 92 C–D: 7
Phdr. 267 A: 59 n. 79
270 B: 93
273 B–C: 59 n. 79, 61 n. 80
Sph. 246 B: 123
Tht. 162 E: 7
163 B–C: 130 n. 32
185 B: 144
Ti. 40 E: 7
70 C–D: 165 n. 20
91 A: 165 n. 20
Plotinus
2. 3. 1: 161 n. 18
3. 1. 5: 161 n. 18
Plutarch
De Stoic. repugn. 1056 B: 157
1047 C: 165
[Plutarch]
Vit. Hom. 212: 162
Porphyry
De abstinentia, 3. 3: 128 n. 31

Quintilian
5. 9. 3: 35 n. 37
5. 9. 8: 35 n. 37
5. 9. 9–10: 36

scholium in Hermogenem, *Inventio*
(*Rhet. Graec.* Walz), v. 407–8:
35–6 n. 37
Sextus Empiricus
M. 1. 309–10: 151 n. 4
5. 1 ff.: 161 n. 18
7. 22: 107
7. 24–6: 87, 194
7. 25: 7, 148, 179 n. 40
7. 111 ff.: 194
7. 126 ff.: 194
7. 135: 102
7. 140: 2
7. 145: 114
7. 203 ff.: 198
7. 213–14: 203
7. 213: 200
7. 214: 213
7. 241: 126
7. 327 ff.: 98
7. 357: 102
7. 358: 100
7. 364–8: 98
7. 394–61: 148

7. 394: 7
7. 396: 87, 194
7. 402 ff.: 102
8. 4 ff.: 126
8. 4: 123, 126
8. 6: 102
8. 10: 124
8. 12: 127
8. 53–4: 98
8. 112: 151 n. 4
8. 140: 7, 87, 107, 148, 149, 194
8. 141–299: 87, 108
8. 141–2: 99, 114
8. 141: 179 n. 40
8. 143: 188
8. 145–8: 108
8. 145: 109
8. 146: 95, 180
8. 151: 109
8. 152–4: 109
8. 152: 235
8. 154: 109, 131
8. 156: 104, 107, 109, 115, 236
8. 157: 116
8. 158: 140
8. 177: 234, 242
8. 178: 101 n. 16
8. 180: 149
8. 183 ff.: 126
8. 184: 102
8. 187 ff.: 126
8. 187–8: 126
8. 189: 126
8. 193: 5, 128
8. 200–1: 5
8. 203: 168
8. 206: 137
8. 207: 126
8. 215 ff.: 129
8. 215–38: 129
8. 240–1: 130
8. 244 ff.: 126
8. 245: 116, 150, 151, 158, 214 n.
33
8. 249: 150–1 n. 3
8. 251: 117
8. 254–5: 116, 159
8. 257 ff.: 124
8. 265: 117, 151
8. 266–8: 159
8. 266: 159 n. 15
8. 274: 130, 134, 180
8. 275: 156 n. 9

Sextus Empiricus, *M.* (*cont.*):
  8. 277: 149
  8. 278: 226
  8. 280: 132, 135
  8. 281–2: 226
  8. 288: 155
  8. 289: 149
  8. 291: 106, 133, 134
  8. 299: 149
  8. 300 ff.: 148
  8. 302 ff.: 171
  8. 302–9: 171 n. 33
  8. 305: 171 n. 33
  8. 306: 95
  8. 307–8: 173
  8. 308–9: 176
  8. 308: 172
  8. 309: 95, 176, 177
  8. 310: 171, 176
  8. 314: 171
  8. 319: 87, 148, 194
  8. 322–5: 99
  8. 324: 199 n. 4
  8. 336: 101 n. 16
  8. 337: 221 n. 46
  8. 354–5: 102
  8. 357–60: 98
  8. 362: 100, 179 n. 40
  8. 364–6: 98
  8. 393: 7
  8. 396: 98, 99, 103, 120, 122, 168
  8. 411–24: 170
  8. 415 ff.: 149
  8. 416: 152
  8. 422: 176
  8. 423: 171 n. 31
  8. 428: 151 n. 4
  8. 443: 150
  8. 451: 159
  8. 480–1: 226
  11. 165: 103
PH 1. 9: 100
  1. 12: 102
  1. 13: 99, 100, 103–4 n. 17
  1. 21–4: 144
  1. 21–2: 100
  1. 21: 140
  1. 28–9: 102
  1. 193: 100
  1. 198: 100
  1. 227: 104
  1. 236–41: 90
  1. 236: 97

  1. 237: 144
  1. 238: 142
  1. 239: 141
  1. 240: 142
  2. 13: 107
  2. 43–4: 98
  2. 95–6: 99, 107, 114
  2. 96: 7, 87, 148, 194
  2. 97–133: 87, 108
  2. 97–8: 108
  2. 97: 114
  2. 98: 95, 109, 114
  2. 99: 109, 236
  2. 100–1: 109
  2. 100: 235
  2. 101: 116, 117, 118, 119, 120, 130
  2. 102: 104, 115, 140
  2. 104 ff.: 158
  2. 104–5: 159
  2. 104: 115, 116, 119, 120, 122,
    144, 150, 159, 162, 168
  2. 106: 150–1 n. 3
  2. 109: 117
  2. 110–12: 117, 151, 155, 158,
    213–14 n. 31
  2. 110: 212
  2. 111: 152
  2. 116: 159
  2. 118 ff.: 117
  2. 118: 117, 122
  2. 131: 149
  2. 134 ff.: 148
  2. 134: 149
  2. 135 ff.: 149, 171
  2. 140: 95, 173
  2. 141–2: 176
  2. 141: 173
  2. 142: 95, 177
  2. 143: 173, 176
  2. 167: 150
  3. 6: 101 n. 16
  3. 65: 102
  3. 151 ff.: 144
Simplicius
  In cat. 3. 30–4. 9: 192 n. 60
    4. 6–7: 192 n. 60
Sophocles
  OT 916: 1 n. 2
Strabo
  2. 3. 8: 164
Suda (Adler)
  i. 294. 18 ff.: 75 n. 98
  iv. 351: 88 n. 1

Themistius
   In an. post. 6. 25: 75 n. 98
    17. 22–7: 75 n. 98
    28. 16–29: 75 n. 98
    37. 8–11: 75 n. 98

Theophrastus (Graeser)
   fr. 38: 43 n. 48
Thucydides
   1. 10: 2
   1. 20–1: 2

General Index

Academics 102, 103, 189, 207, 250–1
Aenesidemus 89–90, 117–18, 129–30,
  131, 133, 138–9
analogismos 112–13
analogy 10–12, 196–8, 201–4, 205,
  208, 215–16 n. 35, 222, 235,
  239, 245–6
Anaxagoras 2, 10–11
art 14, 15, 17–18, 19 n. 8, 20, 42, 44–
  6, 49, 51, 81–2, 92–4, 105, 113,
  131–7, 161–5, 187, 236, 252
Asclepiades of Bithynia 91–2, 94, 126,
  143, 247
astrology 152–3, 160, 161
attestation and non-attestation 198–9
Augustine 3–4, 161 n. 18

Bromius 206

Callippus 51 n. 96
Carneades 250
causes, Stoic views of 155–8, 159, 161,
  163–4, 167–8 n. 26, 169, 178
  see also under explanation
Chrysippus 150, 152–3, 156, 160–1,
  164–6, 181–4, 186–7, 193 n. 61,
  214, 248, 251
conditionals 12, 116–17, 149, 150–4,
  157–8, 158–60, 169–70, 177,
  179–81, 182, 183, 184, 186–7,
  189, 212–23, 224–6, 239, 240,
  248, 251
  see also elimination; inconceivability
conjecture 166–9, 197, 251–2
conjunctions, negated 153, 158, 160,
  181–4
consequence (ἀκολουθία) 152–5, 185,
  198, 200, 204–5, 211, 215–16 n.
  35, 221–2, 224, 226
  and exclusion (μάχη) 95, 112, 157,
  179–81, 204, 223–4 n. 49, 247
contestation and non-contestation
  197–200, 239
Corax and Tisias 51 n. 69, 59, 60–1

criteria 87–8, 100, 119, 140, 144, 148,
  179, 192, 194, 242–3
Cynics 189, 191–2

deception:
  in dialectic 16–17, 61, 70–1
  in rhetoric 16–17, 62
  see also under topos
Demetrius of Laconia 206
Democritus 2 n. 6, 10–11, 102, 123
demonstration, 6–7
  Aristotelian 6, 15, 33, 33–4 n. 35,
    72–8, 170, 178–9, 204–5, 244,
    245, 246, 248–9
  Stoic 6, 87, 147–50, 160, 165, 170–
    84, 186–7, 204–5, 248–9
  see also under signs
development in Aristotle 14–15, 20–2,
  29, 40, 55, 58, 68, 79–86
dialectic:
  Aristotelian 13, 19 n. 8, 42–4, 60–1,
    65 n. 89, 66–7, 70–1; *see also
    under* rhetoric
  Stoic: *see* logic, Stoic
Dialectical school 107 n. 19, 182 n.
  45, 187 n. 51, 188–93
Diocles of Carystus 96–7
Diodorus Cronus 151–2, 187 n. 51
Diogenes of Apollonia 3
Dionysius of Cyrene 207
divination 77 n. 102, 160–4, 165, 166–
  70, 177, 180, 187, 251
  see also astrology

εἶδος 45–8, 49, 81, 84–5
εἰκός: *see* likelihood
Eleatics 102
elimination, method of 208–26, 227–
  33, 235, 236, 238, 239, 240
Empedocles 10
Empiricism, medical 5–6, 9, 88–9, 89–
  93, 95–101, 105–8, 109, 110–14,
  115 n. 30, 118, 123, 128, 130,
  132–5, 137, 139, 144–6, 154–5,

163–4, 166, 168, 234–8, 243,
  247, 252–3
see also under Pyrrhonian scepticism
empiricism, Stoic 161–6, 180, 185–8
ἔνδοξος: *see* reputable
enthymemes 13, 17, 18–20, 23, 45–6,
  48
  and the categorical syllogism 13,
    23–4, 26, 32, 67–8, 70–2
  omission of premises in 19–20, 24–
    6
  reputable character of 8, 14–15, 18,
    20, 23, 29–30, 34–8, 42, 54–5,
    57, 62, 67, 68, 70–2, 80
  see also under likelihood; signs
Epicurus 7, 88, 195–204, 239–41, 242,
  246
epilogismos:
  in Epicureanism 227, 234, 237, 246
  in medical Empiricism 112–13, 141,
    237–8
Erasistratus 126
ethos: *see* πίστις
evidence:
  for a conclusion 1–2, 3–6, 8, 11, 13–
    14, 25, 35 n. 37, 40, 61–2, 67,
    71–3, 75–8, 87–9, 98, 100–1,
    107, 110–12, 117, 129, 130,
    134, 138, 148–9, 150–1 n. 3,
    164–9, 170, 179–80, 184–8, 197,
    202, 217–18, 225, 233, 237,
    243–53
  =self-evidence 1, 87, 97–100, 101–2,
    105–7, 109, 111, 114, 121, 124–
    5, 141, 143–4, 146, 147–8, 159,
    170, 173, 179, 194, 195–6, 198,
    208, 219, 236–7, 241, 242, 248,
    250; *see also* non-evidence
example: *see* paradigm
explanation 3, 10, 154, 235–7, 248
  and causes 156–7, 159, 163, 169,
    221–3
  and demonstration 15, 73–6, 77–8,
    178–80, 244–6, 248–9
  multiple 196–9, 200–2, 239–41

fallacy: *see under* topos
for-the-most-part 30–5, 40, 63–4, 74,
  244

Gorgias 3

Heraclides of Tarentum 90, 113

Heraclitus 194
Herodotus 2, 11
Herophilus 96–7, 126
Hippocratic medicine 96–7
  analogy, use of, in 11
  signs in 2
history (discipline) 2
history (source of knowledge) 92, 113,
  133, 164–5, 234

inconceivability 212–21, 223, 226, 230
  n. 60, 237
indication (of therapies) 136, 142
  see also under signs
induction 5, 12, 195, 208, 237
  in Aristotle 14, 19–20, 35 n. 36, 38–
    40, 56, 65 n. 89, 70
intelligibles: *see under* sensibles
invalid argument: *see* deception; enthymemes; *and under* signs
invention, topoi as method of 69–70
Isocrates 45–7, 51

lekta 117, 124, 242
likelihood 166
  enthymemes from 14, 23–5, 26, 30,
    31–2, 33–5, 37, 40, 55, 58–66,
    78–9
logic:
  Aristotelian 6–7, 52, 170, 204
  Epicurus' attitude towards 204
  Stoic 6–7, 117, 124, 204–5, 213–14;
    see also *lekta*
  see also conditionals; consequence;
    demonstration; syllogism
λογικός 19 n. 8
Lysias 51

medicine: *see* Empiricism; Hippocratic
  medicine; Methodism; Rationalism
memory 5, 110, 134, 142, 176, 180
Menodotus 113, 141
Methodism 90–1, 97 n. 15, 141–3, 145
multiple explanation: *see under* explanation

necessity 30–5, 37, 65, 74, 78–9, 157
  see also consequence; syllogism
non-evidence 94–5, 97–102, 103, 105,
  107, 121, 124–5
  varieties of 108–9, 114, 125, 127,
    236

objection 23, 26, 40, 53, 62 n. 82, 63–7, 78–9
oratory: *see* rhetoric

Pamphilus 51 n. 69
paradigm, argument by 14, 19, 20, 24, 35 n. 36, 38–40, 55, 62–7, 71, 78–9
Parmenides 194
pathos: *see* πίστις
phenomena 2, 87, 100, 102, 105, 126, 129–30, 168, 196–203, 209, 211, 220, 226, 230, 233, 235, 237, 238, 246
  natural 196–203, 245–6, 249
  Pyrrhonian attitude towards 100–1, 105–6, 112, 114, 141–4
Philinus of Cos 96
Philo the dialectician 151–4, 158–60, 169–70, 177, 179, 181, 184, 186–7, 193 n. 61, 212
physiognomonics 13, 72
πίστις 20, 81–3, 84–5
Plato:
  on art 93
  on demonstration 7
  on rhetoric 15–16
Posidonius 164, 182, 207
predicables, 42, 50 n. 67
Presocratic philosophy:
  signs in 2–3, 7
  use of analogy by 10–11
probability 39, 73, 249–53
  see also likelihood
Ptolemy of Cyrene 90
Pyrrhonian scepticism 102, 143–5, 223, 226–7, 242
  and medical Empiricism 89–91, 97–106, 108, 113, 139–42, 144–6, 243
  and signs 8–9, 89, 114–15, 118, 122, 125, 226–7

qua propositions 222–3, 228–30, 235–6

Rationalism, medical 9, 91–7, 101, 107–8, 109, 112, 114, 123, 132–9, 147, 154–5, 235–8, 243, 247–8, 252
  see also under reason
reason:
  Rationalist conception of 91–7, 100, 106, 110–13, 134–6, 141–3, 155,

237, 247–8, 252
  Pyrrhonian attitude towards 103–5, 122, 140, 142
refutation 62–7, 78–9
  see also objection
reputable (ἔνδοξος): *see under* enthymeme
rhetoric 1, 185, 245
  adversarial character of 16, 17–18, 29, 34, 67
  deception in 17–18
  genres of 18, 85
  relation to dialectic 15–18, 20, 22 n. 14, 38, 51, 56–7, 58–9, 60–1, 70
  see also under enthymemes; signs

self-evidence: *see* evidence
sensibles 125–9, 134, 137
  and intelligibles 120, 123–5, 242
signs:
  commemorative 9, 88–9, 107–8, 109–12, 114–21, 123, 128, 133, 139–42, 147, 154, 158, 168, 180, 185, 188, 189, 193, 226, 236, 243, 247
  and demonstrations 6–7, 185, 194–5, 241, 246
    in Aristotle 15, 72–8, 185, 244–5
    in Stoicism 87, 147–50, 160, 170, 184–7, 247–9
  enthymemes from 23–31, 34–5, 36, 38, 40–2, 50, 52, 54–8, 62–3, 67–8, 70–1, 79–80, 83–4
  high and low conceptions of 6–7, 9, 148, 186, 188, 194
  indicative 9, 88–9, 107–8, 109–10, 114–22, 124–5, 127–8, 130–2, 134, 136–8, 139, 141, 144–5, 147, 154, 158, 160, 162, 168, 180, 185, 188, 189, 193, 226, 234–6, 243, 247
  natural and given 4–5
  nature of 3–4
  in rhetoric 1, 13–15
  Stoic theory of 4–5, 9–10, 88–9, 115–22, 124–6, 139, 144, 146, 147–50, 154–5, 158–61, 162, 164, 168, 181, 184–8, 189, 193, 194, 243, 247–8, 251
  and tokens, 1, 2, 8, 14 n. 2, 27–8, 30, 37, 72, 185–7
  in tragedy 1–2
  see also elimination; similarity

similarity, method of 208–11, 215–21,
226–33, 235, 239–40
sophistic 16, 70–1
see also under topos
Stoics 101
opponents in Philodemus 207–8,
213, 224–6, 240
see also conditionals; divination; *and
under* causes; demonstration;
signs
στοιχεῖον (element) 44–5, 47
syllogism:
categorical 13, 21, 24, 26–7 n. 20,
27 n. 21, 27 n. 22, 36–9, 56,
67–72, 80, 170, 244
definition of 21, 24, 30, 32, 56, 68
see also enthymemes; topos

τεκμήριον: *see* token
Theodas 113, 141
Theodorus 51 n. 69
Thucydides 2
Tisias: *see* Corax and Tisias
token 164
see also under signs
topos 17, 40–1, 81, 84–5
examples of 50–1, 53
of fallacious argument 52–4, 57–9,
70
nature of 42–4, 47–9, 51, 53
see also invention
transition to the similar (in Empirical
medicine) 113, 234

Zeno of Sidon 206, 211, 213, 228, 239